T0355552

CONTEMPORARY JEWISH WRITING IN EUROPE

Jewish Literature and Culture
Series Editor, Alvin H. Rosenfeld

CONTEMPORARY JEWISH WRITING IN EUROPE

A GUIDE

EDITED BY
VIVIAN LISKA
AND
THOMAS NOLDEN

INDIANA UNIVERSITY PRESS
Bloomington and Indianapolis

This book is a publication of

Indiana University Press
601 North Morton Street
Bloomington, IN 47404-3797 USA

http://iupress.indiana.edu

Telephone orders 800-842-6796
Fax orders 812-855-7931
Orders by e-mail iuporder@indiana.edu

© 2008 by Indiana University Press
All rights reserved

No part of this book may be reproduced or utilized in any form or by any means, electronic or mechanical, including photocopying and recording, or by any information storage and retrieval system, without permission in writing from the publisher. The Association of American University Presses' Resolution on Permissions constitutes the only exception to this prohibition.

The paper used in this publication meets the minimum requirements of American National Standard for Information Sciences—Permanence of Paper for Printed Library Materials, ANSI Z39.48-1984.

Manufactured in the United States of America

Library of Congress Cataloging-in-Publication Data

Liska, Vivian, date
Contemporary Jewish writing in Europe : a guide / edited by Vivian Liska
and Thomas Nolden.
p. cm. — (Jewish Literature and Culture)
Includes bibliographical references and index.
ISBN-13: 978-0-253-34875-3 (cloth : alk. paper) 1. Jewish literature—Europe—History and criticism. 2. European literature—Jewish authors—History and criticism. 3. Jewish literature—20th century—History and criticism. 4. Jewish authors—Europe—Biography. 5. Jews—Europe—Intellectual life. 6. Judaism and literature—Europe.
I. Nolden, Thomas. II. Title.
PN842.L57 2008
809'.88924—dc22

2007022547

1 2 3 4 5   13 12 11 10 09 08

In memory of my father, Michael Liska (1915–2003)
—V. L.

In memory of my brother, Matthias Nolden (1952–1956)
—T. N.

CONTENTS

∾

Foreword

Modern Jewish literature is rich, varied, complex, and endlessly interesting, but in conceptual terms it is also notoriously elusive and resistant to precise definition. Attempts to explain it biographically, thematically, linguistically, and otherwise can be intellectually engaging, but to date no one has succeeded in developing a unified or comprehensive theory of Jewish writing. The same holds true for efforts to achieve clarity concerning the nature of Jewish music, Jewish art, Jewish humor—indeed, Jewish identity itself in the post-Enlightenment period. Religiously observant Jews may feel little or no ambiguity about such matters, but others are challenged and, at times, even befuddled by them. Asked to state what defined him as a Jew, Albert Einstein, who was distant from Judaism although not from a meaningful sense of connection to the Jewish people, is reported to have remarked that he might not be able to put a persuasive answer into words but could play it eloquently on the violin. The anecdote rings true, even as it is bound to leave unsatisfied those who yearn for greater conceptual precision.

Within the literary realm, questions about who is a Jewish author and what the constituent features of Jewish writing might be date back at least as far as the period of emancipation and, by and large, remain unresolved to this day. Far from deterring constructive thinking about Jewish creativity, however, the open-endedness of the questions have been a prod to scholars and critics to engage in serious reflection on the Jewish literary imagination and the compelling body of writings it has produced. The present survey of contemporary Jewish writing in Europe is an example of such thinking at its most probing. Before commenting further on what this volume hopes to achieve, a short look backward in time might be instructive.

Now largely forgotten, Joseph Leftwich's *Yisröel: The First Jewish Omnibus* (1933) was popular in its own day and helped to draw significant attention to the development of a transnational Jewish literature. Leftwich's anthology, one of the earliest of its kind, gathered together writings by some seventy-five Jewish authors from a dozen different countries who wrote in a variety of European languages in addition to Yiddish and Hebrew. Presenting a rich sampling, Leftwich's collection confirmed the existence of Jewish literary production on an international scale and aptly illustrated Israel Zangwill's belief that the "literature of Israel in its widest sense comprises the contributions made by Jews to the thesaurus of the world." Leftwich himself admitted that although he was unable to locate any unity within the corpus of writings he had assembled, he nevertheless succeeded in demonstrating that Jewish writers were active in many different lands, were writing in several tongues, and were producing an engaging body of literature about a people that "we and the world call Jews."

Yisröel appeared shortly after Hitler's rise to power in Germany, clearly demonstrating considerable creative vitality on the part of Jewish authors. However, within a dozen years of the book's appearance, a number of contributors whose works were represented in its pages were to meet a terrible fate. Among the German writers, Lion Feuchtwanger, Franz Werfel, Arnold Zweig, Max Brod, and others went into exile in the United States, England, and Palestine. Ernst Toller and Stefan Zweig committed suicide. The French Jewish writer Benjamin Crémieux was seized and shot by the Germans. Isaac Babel was murdered in Stalin's prisons, as were other Russian Jewish writers shortly thereafter. With its cultural heartlands overrun and largely destroyed, European Jewish literature, like the Jewish population itself, had been brutally decimated, with its future in serious doubt.

Against this background, the literature highlighted in *Contemporary Jewish Writing in Europe* is astonishing. In countries where the Jewish population today represents no more than a tiny percentage of what it had been in the prewar period, Jewish writing not only exists but is flourishing. Its definitional contours and connecting links may remain as uncertain as those that Leftwich encountered when he selected the stories for his anthology, but however one defines it, a new literature by and about a people that "we and the world call Jews" has been steadily developing in Europe and demonstrates, beyond any doubt, the resiliency of the Jewish creative imagination in our own day.

This book maps the progress of Jewish literature during the past few decades in Austria, Germany, the Netherlands, Scandinavia, Great Britain, France, Italy, Hungary, Poland, and Russia. As the volume editors point out, "Europe is both a space and a concept." Jewish authors residing in Europe have been influenced by and are active participants in an intense, ongoing debate about the Continent's past and evolving sense of what its future might be. Because European history and identity are intimately bound up with Jewish history and identity, this debate inevitably involves the Jews in a central way and has stimulated Jewish writers to think continually and creatively about who they are and how they find themselves positioned within a changing Europe. Their responses to these issues are as varied as the writers themselves, all of whom possess multiple affiliations and many-sided identities. As this book demonstrates, the literary yield despite such challenges has been considerable.

In addition to offering valuable surveys of contemporary Jewish literature and clarifying readings of some of its more prominent texts, the contributors enable readers to understand the emergence of this body of work against the backdrop of critical developments that have taken place on the Continent during the past few years. These include: the student-led social and political protests of 1968; the end of the Communist era in the former Soviet-dominated states of Eastern Europe; the repercussions of the ongoing Arab-Israeli conflict within Europe; the arrival of new immigrant groups from Muslim lands and the challenges they bring with them to "the idea of Europe"; the sometimes unwelcome but widespread Americanization of European culture; and the introduction and impact of new global technologies. The influence of these and other developments is shaping a Europe that is new and, in some ways, unsure about its future course. For Jews living on the Continent, as well as for a great many others, the trauma of the Holocaust and the legacy of pain and loss it carries with it are always lurking in the background. Even if today's Jewish writers do not bear the wounds of this catastrophic event as part of their personal experience, it is in most cases a permanent part of their consciousness. For many the legacy left behind by the tyrannies of Soviet rule is also a major factor in how they conceive of Europe and their own place within it.

Given these pressures from both the present and the past, it is not surprising that contemporary European Jewish writers favor certain genres—autobiography, memoir, bildungsroman, family saga—that are particularly amenable to historical reflection, or that the themes appearing prominently in their works often focus on experiences of rupture, displacement, persecution, loss, and recovery. In interesting ways, these efforts at recovery give rise to the exploration of old and new Jewish identities mostly in cultural and political rather than religious terms. Since some of today's European Jewish writers were raised in the Sephardic communities of North Africa and South America, a preoccupation with the challenges of exile and the need to adjust to life on a new continent also is apparent in several of the works surveyed in this book.

The preceding by no means exhausts the attractions of contemporary European Jewish writing, which has a comic as well as a serious side; an occasional religious dimension as well as a preponderantly secular or worldly one; a strongly felt, if often ambivalent, fascination with Israel; as well as a complex absorption in diasporic existence, to name just a few aspects. This literature, in sum, is as varied in its thematic foci as it is in the languages it employs and does not speak in anything remotely like a common authorial voice. For all their differences, many of the authors whose works are analyzed in this book share certain cultural affinities as well as historical memories. It is interesting to see them grouped together and to reflect on how they link up with or diverge from earlier traditions of Jewish writing to create something new. However these matters evolve over time, it is already clear that an impressive corpus of literature has been emerging in Europe over the past few decades, attesting to a vital resurgence in postwar European Jewish culture. By providing readers with a detailed overview of this fascinating but hitherto uncharted territory, this book adds immeasurably to our knowledge of a crucial dimension of contemporary Jewish creativity.

ALVIN H. ROSENFELD

Acknowledgments

This volume has been in the making for quite some time and has relied on the enthusiasm and patience of many colleagues and friends. We owe great thanks to Alvin H. Rosenfeld for the judicious advice he shared with us most graciously during each phase of this book's conception, and to Geoffrey H. Hartman for the inspiration he offered to this project.

Our colleagues Sergio Parussa, Alla Epsteyn, and John Neubauer generously provided responses to individual queries and requests. Our research assistants in Belgium (Luc Acke, Anke Brouwers, and Katrien Vloeberghs) and the United States (Emily Coit, Joshua Miller, and Sharon Rosenfeld) ably guided the manuscript through to its final version. Their work was supported by grants from our respective academic home institutions: the University of Antwerp and its Institute of Jewish Studies, and Wellesley College.

Last, but not least, we would like to thank our spouses and children: Sandy, Lucie, and Anna Nolden; and Charles, Nathalie, Jacques, Tamara, and Daphne Morsel. Their counsel, companionship, and perspective we acknowledge with deep gratitude.

INTRODUCTION

THOMAS NOLDEN & VIVIAN LISKA

The revitalization of Jewish culture is one of the most remarkable developments in recent European history. The trauma and losses caused by the Shoah had a devastating effect on European Jewry and still touch the Jewish communities to their core. And yet, a quarter century after the end of World War II, Jewish culture in France, Germany, Austria, Italy, England, the Netherlands, Hungary, and even Poland started to gain strength again and has been developing intriguing facets ever since.

Since 1980 an ever-growing number of Jewish writers born during or after World War II have entered the public sphere, demonstrating the liveliness, productivity, and diversity of contemporary Jewish culture. In their works they present unique responses to general societal developments and fundamental ideological changes brought about by the student protests of 1968, the complex events in the Near East, the collapse of Communist regimes, and by global migration. These authors address the often hostile attitudes of the gentile societies in which they live, as well as the changes in the demographic structure of Jewish communities both at the local level—where many members of the survivor generation have passed away—and at the global level—where the center of Jewish life has moved from Eastern Europe to Israel, the United States, and parts of Western Europe.

While there are numerous anthologies of contemporary American Jewish literature, as well as university-level courses and research projects, its European counterpart has thus far remained a largely unexplored area of critical scholarship. Critics who have analyzed the complex literary production of Jewish writers in Europe have done so from an exclusively national angle.

Points of Departure

This volume presents a map that permits readers to gain an understanding of the commonalities as well as the differences that characterize the literary productions of Jewish writers across European national borders. It surveys how writers of fiction in different countries have explored a variety of possible relationships to the traditions of Judaism as well as to the cultural, literary, and historical contexts of the countries of which they are citizens. Unlike the literature created by the survivors, the literature contained in this volume originates not in the immediate experience of the Nazi genocide but rather in the secondary trauma of growing up within families shattered by the Shoah. In the words of the American critic Geoffrey H. Hartman: "The eyewitness generation expressed a return of memory despite trauma; this 'second' generation expresses the trauma of memory turning in the void, and is all the more sensitive, therefore, to whatever tries to fill the gap" (2000, 18).

Focusing our attention on the writings of these generations of authors, we were intrigued to learn how the "second" and "third" generations of Jewish writers and their aesthetics have been shaped by the legacy of the victims and by the testimonies of the survivors, how they have been addressing and probing what has been called the "limits of representation" resulting from the notion that the Shoah ruptured and destroyed the very ability of language to articulate the suffering experienced in the concentration camps. The Dutch critic Elrud Ibsch has emphasized how younger authors "free themselves from . . . the generic restrictions" that shape the accounts of the witnesses to "claim their own way" and "to choose" their own genre, poetic program, and language. And yet they too will have to "explore their own limits of representation" (2000, 6). These writers cannot ignore the hiatus that sets the world of their ancestors apart from their own; their art cannot simply build a "bridge of memory" between today and yesterday.

Thus, many of the paradigms that literary criticism has used to interpret the documents of the witnesses and the stories of the survivors may provide little help in understanding the work of their successors. Their aesthetic point of departure is no longer predicated on T. W. Adorno's famous—and frequently misunderstood—admonition with regard to "Writing Poetry after Auschwitz," but rather is based on the very challenge of "Writing after 'The Death Fugue'": The literary production of the younger, second and third generations of Jewish writers is not defined solely by the historical events per se but also by their predecessors' responses to the crisis of representation, by their attempts to deal with the wounds which the Shoah—and for many also the terror of the Soviet regime—inflicted on the history of Jewish writing.

However, even this characterization does not adequately do justice to contemporary Jewish literature in Europe because it fails to account for the situation in which, for example, many of the currently exiled Sephardic writers of Maghrebi descent found themselves when they began to write in French or Spanish. The cultural and societal shifts brought about by decolonization comprise another important *point fixe* that has characterized contemporary Jewish writing both in France—which, after Russia, possesses the largest Jewish community in Europe—and in Spain, whose small Jewish population has nevertheless produced a highly interesting literature. Reina Roffé, who was born in Argentina and currently lives in Spain, begins one of her stories with this sentence: "During the bitterest days of my European exile, I turn to the photo album where I keep, along with more recent memories, a few images from my childhood . . ." (1999, 14). Here the notions of exile and diasporic existence are introduced to contemporary European Jewish writing not just as a *point de détail* but as decisive impulses behind a large segment of this writing, emphasized by authors whose origins are not in Europe but rather in Latin America or North Africa.

Here, too, the reader is confronted with the emergence of a generation of writers for whom the exodus—for example, from the Maghreb—is not the defining moment of their own but rather of their parents' biographies. Like the writing of their East European–born peers, which is not shaped by personal memory of Jewish life before the genocide or of the sufferings resulting from persecution, the works of many younger Sephardic writers living in France or Spain are conceived from sites of displacement, from a cultural, national, historical, and linguistic distance to the *haras* or *mellahs* (the Jewish ghettos of North Africa) in which their parents grew up as observant Jews.

New Beginnings

Barbara Honigmann, who left her native East Berlin to settle in France and who thus is writing from the experience of manifold displacement herself, uses a phrase that resembles Geoffrey H. Hartman's earlier formulation. She calls her generation's relationship toward Judaism a "re-conquering of our Judaism out of a void" (1994, 25). This phrase is noteworthy for a variety of reasons. Using the first-person plural, Honigmann rightly conceives of her own return to Judaism as a collective phenomenon which set in during the seventies and early eighties all over Europe. The political imperative of the era of student revolts had been to put the cause of internationalism above ethnic (not to mention Zionist) concerns, leading many young Jews in western Europe to ignore the little they knew about their roots. The initial wave of politicization in the late sixties and seventies had left little space for the exploration of ethnic, religious, regional, and cultural differences. Marxist doctrines aimed to persuade Jews in both the western and eastern parts of Europe that any affiliation other than solidarity with the working class was tantamount to false consciousness, a remnant of bourgeois ideology. In the West many of the Jews who had come of age in the communes and on the barricades would not reconnect to their ethnic and cultural heritage until after the student rebellion had reached its ideological climax, opening up discourses beyond the realm of class politics.

Although the dynamics of societal discourse and identity politics in Eastern Europe had undoubtedly taken a different path since the end of World War II, the stories related by Jews growing up in this part of the Diaspora are not at all incompatible with the experiences of their peers in Western Europe. Communist governments were interested in portraying Communists as the foremost victims of fascism and downplayed the persecution of the Jews, who often found themselves singled out as undesirable citizens. Many of them had envisioned these Communist countries to be safe havens in which, according to Marxist ideology, ethnic and religious differences would no longer give rise to prejudice and persecution—an illusion that was often dispelled by anti-Semitic campaigns.

Communist administrations disregarded the pain suffered by their Jewish populations during the era of Nazi persecution by folding their particular experience into a general notion of victimhood, which featured Communists as the "real" targets of Nazi wrath. Either subscribing to the ideal that Marxist universalism was to supersede ethnic particularity or fearing state-sponsored forms of anti-Semitism, Eastern Jewry largely became "invisible" Jews. Censorship succeeded in making Jewish writers' work "illegible," cutting those writers off from their readers and forcing them to emigrate or to find presses willing to publish their work abroad.

With the unraveling of the ideological master narratives and the dissolution of the borders between East and West, many Jews began to shed their apprehensions concerning their heritage and to wonder about the course Judaism had taken in the United States, where a multitude of voices had created different strands of Jewish identities and communities and had started to contribute to the public discourse. What earlier had been denounced as a category of the accidental and the subjective was now embraced as a particularity worth exploring. Identity politics began to surpass ideological politics and questions arose regarding how to assert, define, and act out this newly regained identity.

The call for such a reassessment and reassertion was most prominently issued by the French essayist Alain Finkielkraut, who in his seminal essay "Le juif imaginaire" (The Imaginary Jew, 1980) summoned his peers to shed obsolete matrixes of self-understanding and to search instead for notions of Jewishness that would adequately reflect their own historical situation as members of the "générations d'après." The subsequent paths taken by the peers of Roffé, Honigmann, and Finkielkraut all over Europe show that this reinvention was a matter of conscious choice and creative work—indeed, an act of conquest fought against the Nazis' attempt to annihilate the Jewish people and its traditions, against a long history of acculturation, and against a conception of the political that proved incompatible with the self-assertive notion of the particular, the ethnic, and the religious. Scholars, intellectuals, and, last but certainly not least, artists and writers have long taken up Finkielkraut's polemic challenge to reinvent themselves as imaginative Jews.

Conceiving the European Diaspora

While this transformation was certainly not confined to the Europe "after the fires," to quote Peter Demetz's famous formulation, it is important to complement the critical attention paid to Jewish writing in present-day Israel and the United States with a preliminary survey in order to assess the degree to which one can talk about Jewish writing as a constitutive element of contemporary European culture and to what extent one can conceive of a distinct European notion of Jewish letters differentiated from the cultural production of the United States as the "other" Jewish Diaspora.

While there can be no doubt that the concept of the "void" aptly describes the situation out of which this cultural movement developed, one has to acknowledge that this development did not occur "in a void" but rather in the historically overdetermined political and cultural space represented by postwar Europe. It is significant that Europe, which is currently reshaping its contours and redefining its political and cultural profile, is grappling with renewed waves of anti-Semitism. These developments bring into focus the Jewish heritage, which so prominently participated in shaping the European tradition. They reveal frightening continuities as well as promising breaks with the past through diverse manifestations of heightened vigilance. Indeed, Europe is charged with a past that has defined contemporary Jewish identity in a most crucial manner. And yet contemporary Europe also must be seen as a framework that offers the possibility of renegotiating the relationship between Jewish and non-Jewish cultures and providing the space for unique modes of articulation and enunciative positions.

The juxtaposition of poems by two Jewish Hungarian authors illustrates this ambiguity quite clearly. Whereas Ottó Orbán opens one of his poems on the following pessimistic note:

Europe
I have always backed off from the word (2003, 210)

Ágnes Gergely can optimistically proclaim:

Europe, I love you.
Without having had to be modeled on you.
Nor in space, nor in time do you make demands
Above my strength. This parchment is finite.
Definitive. I am European. (2003, 200)

From an American point of view—and particularly in relation to Jewish history—Europe is often seen as a more or less homogeneous entity, an "old world" in which persecution and destruction predominated and in which the present is still darkened by the shadow of recent history that is fairly evenly spread out over the entire continent. However, the comparative approach adopted in this volume can open up perspectives that reveal how each contemporary national Jewish literature is colored by its respective national emplacement, culture, history, and literary tradition. The diversity of this literature is the result of obvious differences between the various historical, cultural, and social conditions in the respective European countries, as well as less predictable relational factors such as long-established or recent affinities between the Jewish communities and the local culture.

We have in mind several phenomena occurring simultaneously when we say that the notion of Europe is overdetermined. Europe is both a space and a concept, and the contours of each of these categories are the subject of intense debate. We have included an essay on Russian Jewish literature because we believe that the literary historian is well advised to follow the historiographical paradigm most recently articulated by Tony Judt in his seminal study *Postwar: A History of Europe Since 1945:* "The history of the two halves of post-war Europe cannot be told in isolation from one another" (2005, 5). The same, we believe, holds true for a history of the European Jewish Diaspora of letters: a discussion of the course Jewish writing has been taking in Western and Eastern Europe yields mutually enlightening insights into the interplay between ideology and literature.

Another editorial decision concerning the countries represented in this volume was based less on any intellectual argument than on what we perceive to be a dearth of literary density. There are no entries addressing Jewish writing in countries like Belgium (although it has a comparatively large Jewish population), the Czech Republic, Spain, Switzerland, or Rumania (although it comprises the Bukowina, a cultural landscape which gave birth to writers like Paul Celan and Rose Ausländer). Unfortunately, this leaves important writers like Philippe Blasband (Belgium), Ivan Klima (Czech Republic), Reina Roffé (Spain), Daniel Ganzfried (Switzerland), Danilo Kiš (Yugoslavia), and Norman Manea (Rumania) homeless, as it were. Since we are striving to position the works of contemporary Jewish writers within the context of those of their peers, in such cases we feel justified in referring our readers to such other sources of information as *Jewish Writers of the Twentieth Century* (2003), edited by Sorrel Kerbel, and the *Encyclopedia of Modern Jewish Culture* (2005), edited by Glenda Abramson, both of which are most valuable resources.

Mention of the latter points to yet another intricacy any literary historian of Europe's Jewish Diaspora is forced to acknowledge: Born in Rumania in 1936, Norman Manea was deported as a five-year-old to a labor camp in the Ukraine, from which he returned to his home at the end of the war. Some forty years later, Manea—now a writer highly critical of the party—received permission to leave his country, then ruled by dictator Nicolae Ceaușescu, in order to settle in New York, where he has been writing some of his most important pieces of fiction in the Rumanian language. Meanwhile, Rumanian media has labeled him a "cosmopolitan," an "extra-territorial" figure—terms traditionally reserved by the dictionary of anti-Semitism for Jews unwelcome in their homeland.

Similar trajectories led the Polish-born writer Ewa Kuryluk and numerous others to various destinations within and outside Europe, including the Prague-born Maxim Biller, who, in his German-language collection of stories, incorporates a tale written in the Czech language. His sister, Elena Lappin, was born in Moscow, grew up in Prague, and wrote her first novel while living in London. The German writer Gila Lustiger, who writes in German, settled in France, where she lives with Parisian author Emmanuel Moses (who, in his novels, reminisces about his childhood spent in Israel). Hungarian György Dalos spent almost two decades in Austria before establishing a pied-à-terre in Berlin. Returning from a long journalistic assignment in Bonn, French writer Luc Rosenzweig went on to direct the European cultural TV channel ARTE. Miro Silvera was born in the Syrian city of Aleppo and settled in Italy. Ilan Stavans was born in Mexico to an East European Jewish family and lived in Spain before settling in the United States. Dutch writer Carl Friedman lives in Belgium. East Berlin–born writer and painter Barbara Honigmann joined her family in Strasbourg, who belong to the Orthodox community surrounding the yeshiva of Rav Abitol. The Rumanian-born poet Zsófia Balla resides in Budapest. The Swedish writer Göran Rosenberg spent his formative years in Israel (like the Munich-based writer Rafael Seligman, the Scottish writer Simon Louvish, and the Irish writer Ronit Lentin, to name but a few). The Polish-born writer Jackie Jakubowski emigrated to Sweden. Reina Roffé, as was previously mentioned, emigrated from fascist Argentina to Spain. Ljudmila Ulitskaya travels back and forth between her native Russia and the United

States. Philippe Blasband was born in Teheran and now lives in Brussels. Daniel Dencik grew up within a Swedish Jewish family in Copenhagen and speaks both Danish and Swedish fluently. Peter Stephan Jungk grew up in the United States and Salzburg, Austria, lived in Israel, and currently resides in Paris.

Indeed, the dynamics of these multiple trajectories reveal that Jewish writing is a truly transnational phenomenon reflecting the extraterritorial situation of many Jewish writers. As such, the history of Jewish writing on the European continent eventually will need to be told in a manner in which the European Diaspora at large rather than individual European nation-states provides the foundational methodological framework. Our volume is but a stepping-stone toward such a history and, as such, necessarily takes into account what the notion of transnationality entails, namely, that Jewish writers participate in different cultural and national contexts simultaneously, among which the one that encapsulates their mother tongue must not be neglected. The fact that the relationship between ethnic origin, national background, ideological affiliation, and linguistic attachment can take on vastly different configurations must not discourage us from critically re-creating the national contexts and literary traditions from which these individuals have emerged as writers.

In this spirit, we have not eliminated multiple discussions of individual writers who, like Clive Sinclair, are mentioned in several essays because we do not perceive the need to attribute their work to a single national context. To do justice to the transnational dynamics of Jewish writing, we encouraged our contributors to include the work of writers who left their native countries to settle and write in Israel or in other countries, often holding on to their native tongues as the preferred medium of their writing. And yet there are Polish-born Jewish authors living in the United States or in Israel writing in Yiddish as well as Polish, Finnish Jewish authors who write in Swedish, and so forth. Thus, the excitement created by Jewish writing in present-day Europe undoubtedly is fueled by the energy it derives from recovering notions of the Jewish experience as well as from reappropriating notions of Jewish literary traditions. This literature simultaneously excites as a literature that appropriates, if not creates, present-day Europe at large as the prismatic setting of its cultural origin and the perlocutionary forum of its literary accomplishments.

Common (Narrative) Grounds

Many contemporary authors whose works are discussed in this volume share similar backgrounds, to which they have responded in similar ways. Displacement and persecution often have punctuated their families' past, which in an overwhelming number of cases was communicated to them only in bits and pieces. "Postmemory," a term coined by literary critic Marianne Hirsch, acknowledges how much second- and third-generation writing is instigated by the need to re-create a picture of the past from sources and documents that need to be collected, assembled, verified, and comprehended. To be sure, the endeavor of "writing against silence" is shared by the children of the survivors of the Shoah as well as the children of refugees leaving the Maghreb during the wars of independence. Likewise, the children of Sephardic immigrants from North Africa have made it their task to give voice to their parents' and grandparents' predicament of displacement, which had left the older generation in a state of "mutisme," incapable of articulating their feelings of loss and pain.

Jewish writers across Europe have turned to the genre of the family saga to illustrate the vicissitudes of the modern Jewish experience at large by rendering multigenerational tableaux featuring ancestors enjoying emancipation or struggling to achieve it, tempted by secularization, pressured into assimilation, displaced by pogroms, haunted by persecution, or blinded by ideologies. The Jewish imperative to remember is undoubtedly a driving concern of this kind of writing, which, however, not only strives to complete the annals of Jewish history but also seeks to complement what Europe's collective memory so often tried to ignore.

The notion of *zakhor,* the Jewish command to remember, is also at work when writers present intimate portraits of individual forebears whose stories are set against the larger backdrop of European history. Often evoking the kaddish in secular form, such writings pay homage to those individuals who, in one way or another, embody for the authors essential features of Jewish existence.

The vignettes of the life of a survivor offered by Dutch writer Carl Friedman in her internationally acclaimed *Tralievader* (Nightfather, 1991) emphasize the many difficulties involved in the encounter between father and daughter. Conversely, the title of Pierre Pachet's biography of his father, *Autobiographie de mon père* (Autobiography of my father, 1987), indicates the author's desire to create a mirror in which the offspring can distinguish the contours of their own Jewishness.

The various forms of historical fiction likewise provide complex links between the past and present Jewish experience to ascertain notions of a tradition that fell victim to the factual power of history. In this respect, Jewish writer Michelene Wandor, based in England, has created in the figure of a Jewish female minstrel a fictional ancestor crisscrossing the borders of Inquisition-ridden Europe and confounding male expectations of female faithfulness. Parallels and differences between the Inquisition and the Shoah are also explored and fictionalized in registers ranging from the dramatic to the burlesque in Robert Menasse's novel *Vertreibung aus der Hölle* (Expulsion from Hell, 2001). In most cases, however, historical fiction tends toward the factual rather than the imaginative, a trajectory which certainly characterizes the path taken by Polish Jewish writer Hanna Krall, whose first book, *Sublokatorka* (*The Subtenant,* 1985), subscribed to the aesthetics of the avant-garde, while most of her later work makes use of documentary forms proper. Occasionally writers model their historical fiction on forms pertaining to Jewish historiography, like Alain Gluckstein's allusion to the genre of the *yizker bikher,* the memorial books authored by survivors of Polish Jewish communities to preserve the memory of Jewish life before the Shoah.

The aliyah narrative, conversely, shifts the reader's attention not toward the past of the Diaspora but into the present of the Jewish homeland, which is often juxtaposed with the countries authors have left behind in order to live temporarily or settle permanently in Israel. Encounters with Orthodox Judaism as well as with the political realities within Israel and the latter's conflicts with its neighbors are usually in the foreground of such narratives.

Scanning certain segments of a country's population, the society novel customarily pitches the Jewish protagonist against his or her surroundings to assess how a nation actually measures up to self-proclaimed standards of tolerance toward the Other.

The memoir proper and its fictional counterpart, the bildungsroman, undoubtedly are the most prominent genres in contemporary Jewish writing in Europe. There is little need to keep both genres apart since the most representative writers in each category have quite consciously conflated their contours by appropriating generic features: Ruth Klüger's autobiography *Still Alive: A Holocaust Girlhood Remembered* incorporates samples from the young writer's early poetry into the main text, whereas Georges Perec's *W, ou le souvenir d'enfance* (*W, or The Memory of Childhood,* 1975) synoptically offers up the author's sparse recollections of his childhood by means of a fictional narrative retrieved from memory.

The bildungsroman is the preferred genre in terms of laying bare the psychological tribulations accompanying a protagonist's quest to ascertain his or her Jewish identity. This genre's enormous popularity reflects the degree to which present-day European Jewry's identity—rather than forms of practice—has become "the primary way of being ethnic" where ethnicity has taken on a purely "expressive" function (Gans 1979, 9). In this regard, the narrative focus on the individual offers an ample perspective onto what Jewishness for many authors entails. It allows them to articulate the intricacies of the interplay between the private and the political, the personal and the public, Jewish and non-Jewish experiences, tensions that are often played out in the arena of sexual encounters between Jewish and non-Jewish characters.

An intriguing subgenre of the bildungsroman is the picaro narrative, which Israeli literary critic Sidra DeKoven Ezrahi sees resurfacing in contemporary Jewish letters: "Performing in Italian, in German, and in French, these artists resurrect a cultural Jewish attitude, that of the story as a meliorative version of history, and a set of characters, shlemiels in varying degrees of incredulity and heroic self-reinvention, in a European theatre empty of Jews" (2001, 294).

Any discussion of genres dear to Jewish European writers must also mention such subgenres as the detective novel, in which the figure of the culprit and of the seeker of truth are often presented along ethnic lines. In pursuit of the bad guy, the detective discovers the anti-Semite holding a high public office (as, e.g., in Clément Weill Raynal's *Le tombeau de Rachi* [Rachi's tomb, 1997]) or is suspected to be among the clergy (as in Eliette Abécassis's *Qumran* [*Qumran Mystery*, 1996]). At times, however, the lines become blurred, as in Leon de Winter's *SuperTex* (1991) or Doron Rabinovici's *Suche nach M. (The Search for M, 2000)*. The fact that writers nowadays employ a genre traditionally associated with escapist entertainment to address deadly serious subject matter (genocide or revisionism) shows the distance the younger generation of Jewish writers has put between themselves and the aesthetic concerns expressed by their predecessors. This return of the comical in contemporary Jewish discourse has been examined by critic Sander L. Gilman, doyen of the study of contemporary Jewish literature, in his essay "Is Life Beautiful? Can the Shoah Be Funny? Some Thoughts on Recent and Older Films."

A look at the enunciative gestures prevalent in contemporary Jewish writing in Europe suggests that, beyond the distinctive character of an individual author's voice and the impact of specific national traditions and contexts, there is a core of aesthetic strategies and narrative attitudes shared, by and large, by these authors. The reason for this may be explained by what Gilles Deleuze and Félix Guattari have identified as the third characteristic of minor literature: "In it everything takes on a collective value. Indeed, precisely because talent isn't abundant in a minor literature, there are no possibilities for an individuated enunciation that would belong to this or that 'master' and that could be separated from a collective enunciation" (1986, 17).

Whereas the testimony of the survivor as well as the literature grounded in the experience of persecution eschewed the tone of accusation and angry indictment of the persecutors, the writing by second- and third-generation Jews has given ample expression to a "J'accuse" aimed at vindicating the victims and condemning the tormenters. Commemorating a dark past or scrutinizing present difficulties, contemporary European Jewish literature exhibits a self-confident resilience and resistance despite overwhelming odds, coupled with a confidence in the future.

Curiously, a similar vivacity in tone—but certainly not in content—is occasionally directed at Jews themselves when self-assertive young Jewish characters castigate in older Jews what to their minds smacks of self-denial or Jewish self-hatred. This gesture of "épater le juif" pervades the narratives of Maxim Biller, André Spire, and Alexandr Melikhov, among others, echoing the distinctively male-centered, combative narrative gestures characteristic of early works by American Jewish novelists like Philip Roth and Saul Bellow.

At the opposite end of the spectrum, we find contemporary voices that address representatives of the past with reverence and surround now lost traditions with nostalgic longing. There is, to be sure, no shortage of writers capable of avoiding the perils of a sentimental attitude, which distinguishes good literature from folkloric kitsch. Self-referential checks and meta-reflections permit their narratives to re-create scenes from the former centers of Jewish life and narrative modes associated with, for example, the oral traditions of the shtetl or the *hara* and the *mellah.*

To be sure, these observations regarding the common narrative ground of Jewish writing in present-day Europe have to be considered in light of the immense diversity of literary expression and representation this literature has generated within individual national contexts shaped by powerful ideological, cultural, and literary traditions. Russian Jewish writing is heavily impacted by the literary achievements of nineteenth-century Russian realism. In several of his poems the Austrian writer Robert Schindel creates a sophisticated dialogue with Paul Celan. Katia Rubinstein's *Mémoire illettrée d'une fillette d'Afrique du Nord à l'époque coloniale* (Illiterate memoir of a North African girl in colonial times, 1979) reflects a unique *métissage* of the Parisian feminist autobiography and the Judeo-Spanish oral narratives of Tunisia's Jewish ghetto. The omnipresence of the motif of betrayal in Ivan Klima's novels has been viewed as a response to the experiences of Kafka's protagonists. Echoes of German Jewish romantic women writers can be heard in the works of their present-day successors. Reina Roffé is not only a biographer of her compatriot Juan Rulfo but also a practitioner of magic realism in her own fictional work.

Differences, Parallels, Resemblances

The essays collected in this volume measure the impact of such national traditions, circumstances, and contexts and thus invite an assessment of the differences in degree, intensity, and mode of interaction between Jewish culture and its non-Jewish local counterparts. Our intention to do justice to this diversity explains the differences in approach that distinguish the various essays. While each respects the empirical givens characterizing a specific national context, the mode of presentation of the different Jewish national literatures necessarily varies according to the material at hand and the perspective adopted by each contributor. For example, some essays are more systematic in their presentation of individual writers, whereas others emphasize close readings of central texts.

Despite such differences, we sincerely believe that the factual knowledge and interpretative expertise displayed in these national case studies will provide a stimulating initial look at contemporary Jewish writing in Europe. Ultimately we are interested in inspiring additional dialogues across individual literary and cultural fields of study. Widening the coordinates of our inquiry will enable us to map recent European Jewish writing not merely as individual segments of diverse national literatures but, more comprehensively and succinctly, as a representative sampling of Jewish writing in the Diaspora. As such, this inquiry transcends the concerns arising out of particular national contexts and draws expressly from its experience outside the promised land and from a point beyond personal memory in order to establish a connection to the traditions of Judaism as well as to the past and present of the Jewish people.

Not long ago Bryan Cheyette and Laura Marcus issued the call for what they referred to as the "transgressive" move to "build bridges across supposedly different histories of diaspora" (1998, 2). Whereas literary criticism has often failed to appreciate the transnational trajectory of Jewish culture and writing and has instead attempted to categorize—often with the best of intentions— Jewish writers as "contributors" to the national literatures of which they most certainly are a part, studies in culture and theory have tended to err in the opposite direction and have troped the "Jew" as the "nomadic other." Not only have "writing and Jew(daism) become metonyms of one another" (Shapiro 1994, 183), but the "Jew" has recently been promoted from being Europe's persecuted Other to the "implicit model of European identity" (Delamarre 1979, 96). As literary critics we may be able to correct and complement such hyperbolic constructions by presenting close readings of the texts that Jewish authors throughout Europe have produced as artists of hybrid affiliations and complex identities. Thus, we are ultimately less interested in more closely defining the "nature" of the Jewish writer than in discovering more broadly the cultural productivity and "imaginary plentitude" (Hall 1990, 236) of the European Diaspora of Jewish letters.

Although the volume editors requested that contributors maintain a balance between general survey and critical analysis, identify in their surveys all representative texts and authors, and include (if applicable) references to authors living outside their country of origin as long as they are still writing in their native language, nevertheless the individual contributions to this volume necessarily differ somewhat in format. After all, differences in the literature being surveyed necessitate a variety of methodological approaches to reflect, for example, that some literatures already have received more critical attention than others and thus can be presented more effectively with selections of close readings of individual works and references to further readings. Other Jewish literatures still await this kind of attention and thus require a broad overview of existing authors and works.

Thus, the contributor discussing Jewish writing in Scandinavian countries is faced with challenges and constraints foreign to one dealing exclusively with

Austria or Germany. Eva Ekselius, in her pioneering contribution on Jewish writing in Scandinavia, surveys the works of Jewish writers in Sweden, Norway, Denmark, and Finland. Her essay, which maps a surprisingly rich scene of Jewish letters, is unprecedented in its scope yet must sacrifice a level of interpretation normally reserved for discussion of smaller bodies of work. Jewish writing in contemporary Austria and Germany has been the subject of many recent studies, affording the contributors the opportunity to emphasize nuances heretofore neglected.

Many of the contributors have in their own work explored various ways of addressing the complexities that arise in any geographical demarcation along the lines of cultural, linguistic, and national spheres. Christoph Miething, who for many years has been working within the broad conceptual framework of *Romania Judaica,* has noted, "recent theorems of 'alterity' can only avoid falling victim to the perils of relativism, particularism, and dogmatism as long as they don't betray the cosmopolitan tradition of modern Jewish thought" (1998, viii). In his present essay Miething discusses contemporary Jewish authors in Italy as heirs of a tradition in which "*italianità* and *ebraicità* are felt to be complementary components of a single identity."

In his work on Hungarian Jewish life and letters, Péter Varga has stressed the fact that the very location of the historic Hungary between "two different centers of political power structures, of societal institutions, and of conceptions of historical progress" (1997, 83) immensely complicates the typologies of Jewish life in a space that previously was situated at yet another border, namely, the one separating Jews from the East and those from the West. As he demonstrates in his essay, this typology becomes even more intriguing once we realize that several representatives of contemporary Hungarian Jewish letters have written large portions of their oeuvre while living in Germany.

Concentrating on Jewish writers living in the port city of Odessa, Rainer Grübel has cleared a methodological path through various critical attempts to conceptualize the complex relationship between cultural production and geographical coordinates by reading space as "context," thereby introducing a "term common to all the disciplines" that must be consulted in the study of minority voices, and emphasizing that the category of space must not be read materialistically as a "purely empirical entity" (2000, 433). In their present essay Grübel and co-author Vladimir Novikov stress that Jewish writing in present-day Russia positions itself quite self-consciously "at Europe's periphery" as well as "in the space between Jewish tradition and dominant Russian culture. The negotiation of this de-centric positioning primarily entails a distancing from the highly centralized structure of Soviet and Russian culture."

Monika Adamczyk-Garbowska and Antony Polonsky have used the metaphor of the "landscape after a battle" (2001, xli) to analyze how the literary imagination of postwar Polish Jewish authors has dealt with the devastating impact of a nation's attitude toward its Jewish population in the spaces formerly inhabited by this minority. Adamczyk-Garbowska thus discusses how Jewish life in Poland appears as a *lieu de mémoire* within a field of coordinates that features the United States and Israel as important contemporary spaces of the Polish Jewish existence.

Vivian Liska explores contemporary Austrian Jewish literature in terms of its handling of the specifically Austrian National Socialist past, the present relationship between Jews and non-Jews, and the Austrian Jewish literary and cultural heritage. Although this literature deals with Jewish topics, its authors reject a closed and unified concept of Jewish identity and similarly turn their backs on the previous generation of Jewish writers, such as Paul Celan. Liska embeds these attitudes in a specifically Austrian context and shows, through close readings of individual passages by three major contemporary Austrian Jewish writers, how the literary expression of this attitude results in a "poetics of everyday life" that is both radically postmodern and—albeit in unexpected ways—part and parcel of an Austrian Jewish tradition.

In his essay on contemporary German Jewish literature, Stephan Braese analyzes the shift in attitude among Jews since the early postwar years. He shows how the generation to which most contemporary authors belong rejects the sense of shame about living in Germany that predominated among the survivors who established themselves in the country of the perpetrators. This generation also rejects the lip service paid to universalism that still determined the Jewish identity of the "second generation." Instead, the most recent literature by German Jews is both more confrontational regarding the German past and more conscious and proud of its Jewish identity. In his discussion of five major authors living and writing in Germany today, Braese explores the rich diversity in attitudes to the tensions between a desire to deal with specifically Jewish issues and the aspiration to transcend the narrow boundaries of a particularist minority literature.

In his essay on Jewish writing in contemporary France, Thomas Nolden compares the various ways in which Sephardic writers from the Maghreb relate to France primarily as a former colonial power, whereas their French-born Ashkenazi co-religionists experience the country primarily as a society that came to terms with its collaborationist past quite late.

As Bryan Cheyette proposes in his survey of Jewish writing in Great Britain, even when the relationship between Jews and the host nation is not troubled by a history of government-sponsored anti-Semitism, Jewish authors find themselves involved in the work of "radical interrogation and reworking of the prevalent myths."

Elrud Ibsch demonstrates that in the Netherlands a young generation of Jewish authors has been publishing works entirely unconcerned with the traditions of Jewish writing in their country. As Ibsch argues persuasively, one of the reasons for this postmodern attitude can be found in the fact that previously Jewish writers never considered themselves "minority writers" and thus enjoyed a status free from the pressures of cultural assimilation or of self-justification.

It is important to stress that readers seeking simple, if not definitive, answers to the definitional question "Who is a Jewish author?" will be disappointed. The volume editors have refrained from suggesting to their contributors a working definition that would go beyond the criterion of an author's self-designation as a Jew. Most contributors concentrated their readings on the works of authors who, in addition to considering themselves Jewish writers, are concerned with Jewish experiences in their fiction. Admittedly, such decisions on the part of the volume editors and the contributors may fall short of the ideal of comprehensiveness—something readers might expect of a guidebook to Jewish writing in contemporary Europe. And yet, to our way of thinking this ideal, which admittedly is hard to attain, is a virtue only if it is not marred by the vice of prescriptive—and thus restrictive—definitions. Similarly, the crucial questions "What constitutes Jewish writing?" or "What defines Jewish literature?" shape each individual essay without, however, leading to a unified theory of such a literature. Dieter Lamping once suggested that Ludwig Wittgenstein's idea of "family resemblances" may be a promising way of conceptualizing the connections that link the authors and their works discussed in this volume. The notion of "family" here suggests an ethnic core that at the same time is somewhat softened by the notion of "resemblance." After all, not all members of the same family resemble each other. And even members of different families often display striking similarities.

The volume editors have resisted the temptation to partake in intriguing theoretical discussions growing out of the reading of texts by contemporary Jewish writers. The intentions of this volume are rather modest, namely, to serve as a research tool that ideally will enable the reader to gain a better understanding of an existing literature based on an acquaintance with as large a segment of this literature as possible. Some of the most suggestive theorems concerning Jewish writing have been based on rather slim textual evidence and would benefit from a reading of the works by authors who have often gone unnoticed.

Striking a balance between close readings of individual texts and general surveys of larger movements and underlying themes, the essays in this volume portray Jewish authors throughout Europe as writers and intellectuals of multiple affiliations and hybrid identities who, in their own languages and stylistic manners, have all accepted anew the old challenge that arose with the Babylonian exile, namely, "to sing our songs in a foreign land" (Hartman 1985, 205).

NOTE

Unless otherwise stated, all translations of primary texts in this volume are by the individual contributors. Each essay's "Works Cited" section is followed by a list of texts available in English by the authors mentioned in the individual essays.

WORKS CITED

Abramson, Glenda, ed. 2005. *Encyclopedia of Modern Jewish Culture.* London: Routledge.

Adamczyk-Garbowska, Monika, and Antony Polonsky. 2001. Introduction to *Jewish Writing in the Post-War World: Poland,* ed. Monika Adamczyk-Garbowska and Antony Polonsky, x–xlix. Lincoln: University of Nebraska Press.

Cheyette, Bryan, and Laura Marcus. 1998. "Introduction: Some Methodological Anxieties." In *Modernity, Culture and "the Jew,"* ed. Bryan Cheyette and Laura Marcus, 1–20. Stanford, Calif.: Stanford University Press.

DeKoven Ezrahi, Sidra. 2001. "After Such Knowledge, What Laughter?" *Yale Journal of Criticism* 14 (1): 287–313.

Delamarre, Alexandre J.-L. 1979. "Méditation sur la modernité." *Esprit* 29: 80–96.

Deleuze, Gilles, and Félix Guattari. 1986. *Kafka: Toward a Minor Literature.* Trans. Dana Polan. Minneapolis: University of Minnesota Press.

Finkielkraut, Alain. 1980. *Le juif imaginaire.* Paris: Seuil.

Friedman, Carl. 1991. *Tralievader.* Amsterdam: Van Oorschot.

Gans, Herbert. 1979. "Symbolic Ethnicity: The Future of Ethnic Groups and Cultures in America." *Ethnic and Racial Studies* 2: 1–20.

Gergely, Ágnes. 2003. "Imago 9—The Parchment," trans. Nathaniel Tarn. In *Contemporary Jewish Writing in Hungary,* ed. Susan R. Suleiman and Éva Forgács, 199–200. Lincoln: University of Nebraska Press.

Gilman, Sander L. 2000. "Is Life Beautiful? Can the Shoah Be Funny? Some Thoughts on Recent and Older Films." *Critical Inquiry* 26: 279–308.

Grübel, Rainer. 2000. "Ein literarischer Messias aus Odessa: Isaak Babels Kontrafakturen des Chassidismus und der odessitische Kontext jüdisch-russischer Kultur." In *Jüdische Autoren Ostmitteleuropas im 20. Jahrhundert,* ed. Hans Henning Hahn and Jens Stüben, 429–81. Frankfurt am Main: BKGE.

Hall, Stuart. 1990. "Cultural Identity and Diaspora." In *Identity, Community, Culture, Difference,* ed. J. Rutherford, 222–37. London: Lawrence and Wishart.

Hartman, Geoffrey H. 1985. "On the Jewish Imagination." *Prooftexts* 5: 201–20.

———. 2000. "Introduction: Darkness Visible." In *Holocaust Remembrance: The Shapes of Memory,* ed. Geoffrey H. Hartman, 1–22. Oxford: Blackwell.

Hirsch, Marianne. 1997. *Family Frames: Photography, Narrative, and Postmemory.* Cambridge, Mass.: Harvard University Press.

Honigmann, Barbara. 1994. "Damals, dann und danach." *Literaturmagazin* 34: 19–32.

Ibsch, Elrud. 2000. Foreword to *The Conscience of Humankind: Literature and Traumatic Experiences.* Vol. 3 of *Proceedings of the 15th Congress of the International Comparative Literature Association,* ed. Elrud Ibsch, 5–7. Amsterdam: Rodopi.

Judt, Tony. 2005. *Postwar: A History of Europe Since 1945.* New York: Penguin.

Kerbel, Sorrel, ed. 2003. *Jewish Writers of the Twentieth Century.* New York: Fitzroy Dearborn.

Klüger, Ruth. 2001. *Still Alive: A Holocaust Girlhood Remembered.* New York: Feminist Press, CUNY.

Lappin, Elena, ed. 1994. *Jewish Voices, German Words: Growing Up Jewish in Postwar Germany and Austria.* North Haven, Conn.: Catbird.

Menasse, Robert. 2001. *Vertreibung aus der Hölle.* Frankfurt am Main: Suhrkamp.

Miething, Christoph. 1998. Introduction to *Judentum und Moderne in Frankreich und Italien,* ed. Christoph Miething, vii–xi. Tübingen: Niemeyer.

Orbán, Ottó. 2003. "Europe." Trans. Edwin Morgan. In *Contemporary Jewish Writing in Hungary,* ed. Susan R. Suleiman and Éva Forgács, 210. Lincoln: University of Nebraska Press.

Pachet, Pierre. 1987. *Autobiographie de mon père.* Paris: Belin.

Perec, Georges. 1975. *W, ou le souvenir d'enfance.* Paris: Denoël.

Rabinovici, Doron. 1997. *Suche nach M.* Frankfurt am Main: Suhrkamp.

Roffé, Reina. 1999. "Exotic Birds." In *Voices of the Diaspora: Jewish Women Writing in Contemporary Europe,* ed. Thomas Nolden and Frances Malino, 15–20. Evanston, Ill.: Northwestern University Press.

Rubinstein, Katia. 1979. *Mémoire illettrée d'une fillette d'Afrique du Nord à l'époque coloniale.* Paris: Stock.

Shapiro, Susan. 1994. "Écriture judaïque: Where Are the Jews in Western Discourse?" In *Displacements: Cultural Identities in Question,* ed. Angelika Bammer, 182–201. Bloomington: Indiana University Press.

Varga, Péter. 1997. "Varianten jüdischer Selbstwahrnehmung in Ungarn." In *Jüdische Selbstwahrnehmung: La prise de conscience de l'identité juive,* ed. Hans Otto Horch and Charlotte Wardi, 83–101. Tübingen: Niemeyer.

Weill Raynal, Clément. 1997. *Le tombeau de Rachi.* Paris: Le Cerf.

de Winter, Leon. 1991. *SuperTex.* Amsterdam: De Bezige Bij.

TEXTS AVAILABLE IN ENGLISH

Finkielkraut, Alain. 1980. *The Imaginary Jew.* Trans. Kevin O'Neill and David Suchoff. Lincoln: University of Nebraska Press.

Friedman, Carl. 1995. *Nightfather.* Trans. Arnold and Erica Pomerans. New York: Persea.

Ganzfried, Daniel. 2002. "The Sender" (excerpts). Trans. Rafaël Newman. In *Contemporary Jewish Writing in Switzerland,* ed. Rafaël Newman, 1–25. Lincoln: University of Nebraska Press.

Kiš, Danilo. 1994. *Garden, Ashes.* Trans. William J. Hannaher. New York: Harcourt Brace Jovanovich.

———. 1995. *Homo Poeticus: Essays and Interviews,* ed. Susan Sontag. New York: Farrar, Straus and Giroux.

———. 1997a. *The Encyclopedia of the Dead.* Trans. Michael Henry Heim. Evanston, Ill.: Northwestern University Press.

———. 1997b. *Hourglass.* Trans. Ralph Manheim. Evanston, Ill.: Northwestern University Press.

———. 1998. *Early Sorrows: For Children and Sensitive Readers.* Trans. Michael Henry Heim. New York: New Directions.

———. 2001. *A Tomb for Boris Davidovich.* Trans. Duška Mikić-Mitchell. Normal, Ill.: Dalkey Archive.

Klíma, Ivan. 1992. *My Golden Trades.* Trans. Paul Wilson. London: Granta and Penguin.

———. 1993. *Love and Garbage.* Trans. Ewald Osers. New York: Vintage.

———. 1994. *Judge on Trial.* Trans. A. G. Brain. New York: Vintage.

———. 1999a. *Between Security and Insecurity.* Trans. Gerry Turner. New York: Thames and Hudson.

———. 1999b. *Lovers for a Day.* Trans. Gerry Turner. New York: Grove.

———. 1999c. *No Saints or Angels.* Trans. Gerry Turner. New York: Grove.

Klüger, Ruth. 2001. *Still Alive: A Holocaust Girlhood Remembered.* New York: Feminist Press, CUNY.

Krall, Hanna. 1992. *The Subtenant / To Outwit God.* Trans. Jaroslaw Anders. Evanston, Ill.: Northwestern University Press.

Manea, Norman. 1992a. *October, Eight O'Clock.* Trans. Cornelia Golna et al. New York: Grove Weidenfeld.

———. 1992b. *On Clowns: The Dictator and the Artist: Essays.* New York: Grove Weidenfeld.

———. 1994. *Compulsory Happiness.* Trans. Linda Coverdale. Evanston, Ill.: Northwestern University Press.

———. 1996. *The Black Envelope.* Trans. Patrick Camiller. Evanston, Ill.: Hydra.

———. 2003. *The Hooligan's Return: A Memoir.* Trans. Angela Jianu. New York: Farrar, Straus and Giroux.

Perec, Georges. 1988. *W, or The Memory of Childhood.* Trans. David Bellos. Boston: Godine.

Rabinovici, Doron. 2000. *The Search for M.* Trans. Francis M. Sharp. Riverside, Calif.: Aridane.

CONTEMPORARY JEWISH WRITING IN EUROPE

ONE

~

VIVIAN LISKA

Secret Affinities: Contemporary Jewish Writing in Austria

Topography

In the heart of Vienna, slightly off the city center, lies the Judenplatz, an old square lined with baroque facades, restaurants, cafés, and small shops. A 1996 decision to erect a memorial for the 65,000 Austrian Jews murdered by the National Socialists led to the square's renovation, revealing a many-layered architectural palimpsest of Austrian Jewish history and culture. Important discoveries included the foundations of a synagogue where hundreds of Jews were burned in a pogrom on March 12, 1421—the same day that Nazi troops would enter Vienna 517 years later. A sixteenth-century Latin inscription on a plaque states that the "Hebrew dogs" deserved their fate. On an adjacent facade a sumptuous golden emblem of the imperial monarchy decorates what is now the Verfassungsgerichtshof, the republic's courthouse of the constitution. House no. 244, in which Mozart composed *Così fan tutte,* testifies to the image of Vienna as city of music and festive living. Located off the center of the square, a statue dating from the twenties that was relocated to the Judenplatz in the late sixties depicts a larger-than-life Gotthold Ephraim Lessing, the quintessential Enlightenment dramatist, who preached religious tolerance and universal equality. On the opposite side of the square a small museum features a multimedia presentation of the life of Vienna's Jews in the Middle Ages, as well as an interactive database archiving the Nazi extermination of Austrian Jews. The same building houses a renovated synagogue and an Orthodox Zionist youth organization. The square's most recent and prominent addition is Rachel Whiteread's monument commemorating Austrian Jews exterminated by the National Socialists. This "Nameless Library," as the monument is called, consists of a concrete block depicting on its surface shelves of books with their spines facing inside and a permanently locked double door enclosing an empty area that remains forever inaccessible. As the American art critic Robert Storr has stated, this void at the core of the memorial represents the "hollow at the city's heart" (quoted in Young 1999).

The Judenplatz can, in many ways, be regarded as a symbolic topography of the historical, political, and cultural framework for a reading of contemporary Austrian Jewish literature. The square evokes five centuries of repeated persecution and a state and church–sanctioned anti-Semitism that led up to the near extinction of Austria's Jewish population under National Socialist rule. The artistically mediocre Lessing statue is a reminder of the interwar period known as "red Vienna" and of the late sixties, when leftist movements feebly attempted to revive a philosophical and political Enlightenment that never really gained a foothold in this predominantly Roman Catholic country. The incongruity of the monarchist emblem on the facade of the constitutional court building can be read as an architectural embodiment of the lip service that the postwar republic paid to democratic values even as it kept alive various practices and attitudes of its absolutist past.[1] The memorial by the British artist Rachel Whiteread, commissioned by the Viennese municipality, testifies to the belated public acknowledgment of Austrian participation in the Holocaust, a guilt not officially voiced before the "Waldheim affair" in 1986, while the renovated synagogue points to the precarious revival of Jewish life in postwar Vienna. Finally, the square's urban setting and its typically Viennese restaurants and cafés embody the cosmopolitan atmosphere of the capital, with its many semiprivate spaces, where, since the mid nineteenth century, Jewish and non-Jewish artists and intellectuals mingled and sustained the city's often impressive cultural life.[2]

That a monument commemorating the Holocaust was unveiled in the year 2000 points to the fact that it took fifty-five years for Austria to acknowledge its active involvement in the National Socialist murder of Jews. Many of its residents, especially those living on property confiscated from Jews, opposed the memorial and were supported in their resistance by Jörg Haider, the leader of the extreme right party. Significantly, many members of the small Viennese Jewish community were also against the memorial because they believed it would immortalize a shameful, humiliating past that should best be forgotten. This common struggle against Whiteread's monument points to another theme repeatedly invoked in the works of Austrian Jewish writers, namely, the effort by both Jewish survivors and non-Jews to maintain the blanket of silence in place since the end of the war. The perpetrators and survivors obviously had different reasons for wanting to preserve this silence, yet the unacknowledged guilt of the former and the shame of the latter joined hands in consolidating the specifically Austrian "Opferlüge,"[3] the lie that Austria was Hitler's first victim rather than a partner in the National Socialist vendetta against the Jews. Finally, fears of anti-Semitic vandalism, expressed in the debates preceding the erection of the monument and supported by repeated disfigurements of Jewish-related buildings in Vienna, correspond to another topic raised by the younger generation of Austria's Jewish writers, namely, a sense of lingering hostility against Jews among the general population of Vienna. The electoral success in 1999 of the extreme right party, which led to its participation in the coalition government with conservatives, increased those fears, prompting many Jewish intellectuals—among them most of the Vienna's "second generation" of authors—to manifest their concerns in essays, interviews and, to a lesser extent, in their artistic and literary works (Charim and Rabinovici 2000; Menasse 2000).

Just as the Holocaust memorial occupies the center of the square, living traces of the Holocaust occupy a central position in contemporary Austrian Jewish literature. This parallel goes beyond thematic issues. One of the more significant aspects of the Judenplatz is its juxtaposition of different forms of cultural memory. The archeological site, museum, synagogue, multimedia installation, figurative statue, conceptual memorial, and—beyond these actual media—the interaction between the square's loaded meanings and the quotidian, urban environment in which they are embedded can all be read as metaphors for different modes of relating to Jewish history, tradition, and culture. Reflections on these modes and their implications for literature permeate the work of such major Austrian Jewish authors as Robert Schindel, Robert Menasse, and Doron Rabinovici, but also, to a lesser extent, that of Waltrud Mitgutsch, Peter Stephan Jungk, Elfriede Jelinek, Ruth Beckermann, and Vladimir Vertlib.[4] Excavating the past, storing archival evidence, communicating past experiences, mimetically representing lives and stories and, most of all, creating a monument to the memory of the dead are concerns in terms of— and often against—which these writers repeatedly formulate their own poetics and, more generally, their understanding of the possibilities available for literature in this context.

Significantly, the most artistically intentional and also the most enigmatic medium referred to in the constellation of the Judenplatz is the shape and name of the memorial itself. Rachel Whiteread's choice of the closed library and its shelves suggests a core that cannot be entered and evokes the necessarily mediated and indirect nature of remembrance from a contemporary perspective. With its cut pages facing outside, the memorial's inverted books suggest a repository of stored knowledge or a collection of narrated experiences of the past. At the same time, they make room for the projection of new stories onto them, stories that will inevitably inscribe themselves in the interstices and against the background of the old ones. As they create such stories, Austrian Jewish authors of the second generation search for an approach that Robert Schindel, in his novel *Gebürtig (Born-Where)*, calls "a committed but not devouring relationship [to the past]" (1995, 243).[5] Their works intimate that neither empathy with the suffering of the parents nor hatred of the perpetrators should determine the present to the point of de-legitimizing its weight and importance. Most of these works insist that it is only by bringing the present into the picture or, rather, into the writing of the past that a true commemoration of the Holocaust by the generation of the survivors' children can take place.

Contemporary Austrian Jewish authors share a focus on the recent historical trauma with other European Jewish writers—especially German Jewish writers—belonging to the same generation. In both Austria and Germany many young Jewish intellectuals and artists turned to their origins, identity, and tradition after becoming disillusioned by the various leftist movements of the eighties. In both countries the experience of previous generations and the impact of the Holocaust made any direct access to the Jewish tradition impossible. Yet the second generation of Austrian Jews rarely displays its Jewishness as straightforwardly and uncompromisingly as Jews in other countries. As several critics have noted, recent Austrian Jewish literature is characterized by an unusual complexity and indeterminacy. In her introduction to the anthology *Jewish Voices, German Words,* Elena Lappin, sister of the German Jewish writer Maxim Biller, remarks that "Austrian Jews are not as explicitly ('antagonistically') Jewish as German Jews" and supports her statement with a reference to Robert Menasse, in whose work she finds a "subdued presentation of Jewish topics" (1994, 15). In his groundbreaking study of contemporary Jewish literature entitled *Junge jüdische Literatur* (Young Jewish Literature), Thomas Nolden discusses Robert Schindel—in contradistinction to Biller—as the primary example of the "aesthetics of mediation" and the indirect treatment of the past in works by authors of the second generation (1995, 91–94). In a similar spirit, Andreas B. Kilcher ends his essay comparing Biller and Rabinovici with the remark that "while Biller's exterritoriality is based on a neatly defined Jewish otherness, Rabinovici builds his marginality on a ruptured, wounded and precarious Jewish identity, whose cultural position is precisely not clearly definable" (2002, 146).

To a great extent, these authors' approaches to Jewish issues typically reflect the specificity of Austria's historical, cultural, and literary context and manifest themselves in thematic as well as formal compositional and stylistic aspects of their work. Their indirect and non-antagonistic attitude expresses itself most concretely in the works' insistence on the need to confront the past through, rather than against, an affirmation of the present. In the same spirit, these works embrace Jewish concerns while avoiding a closed and unified concept of Jewish identity and encourage an awareness of the Austrian Jews' burdened yet fruitful interaction with the country's non-Jewish environment. These topics find their literary corollary in a heterogeneous and radically non-transcendental poetics that invokes the Jewish tradition as a lively, life-affirming attitude toward everyday human existence.

Confronting the Past:
"A committed but not devouring relationship"

One reason that Austrian Jewish authors are less antagonistically "Jewish" than, say, many German Jewish authors lies in the different ways that Germany and Austria dealt with the Holocaust during the postwar years. While Germany—especially following the student revolts of the late sixties—practiced an overt if often problematic "Vergangenheitsbewältigung" (mastering of the past), both Jews and non-Jews in Austria hushed up the past for a longer time. It was not until 1986—when it was revealed that Kurt Waldheim, the former UN secretary-general, had covered up his activities during World War II, with Austrians reacting to the international outcry by electing him president—that Austria's role in Nazi war crimes was openly discussed. The long silence allowed the unacknowledged guilt of the perpetrators and the repressed trauma of the survivors to linger and, according to many writers, to proliferate in the form of unconscious *ressentiments* and pathological neuroses.

Consequently Austrian literature of the second generation often figures the past as a spectre, ghost, or phantom that links the guilt of the perpetrators to the shame of the survivors. As early as 1946 Ilse Aichinger, addressing the Austrian population in her famous essay "Aufruf zum Misstrauen" (A Summons to Mistrust, 1999), warned of the hidden monster lurking in the innermost recesses of each individual. Similarly, Elfriede Jelinek's novel *Die Kinder der Toten* (Children of the Dead, 2000) features "Untote," souls that cannot find rest and embody a past that has never been confronted. In the afterword to *Born-Where*, the English translation of *Gebürtig,* Michael Roloff calls Schindel's book a "generational novel of ghosts" (1995, 288). In the epilogue to *Papirnik,* Doron Rabinovici's collection of short stories, the survivor Lola Varga collects accounts of the past as if they were pieces of a "memory puzzle": "She conjures up the names in us, the cities and countries, the streets and pathways, the places of being and the sites of death, the spots of murder and the hiding-places of survival" (1994, 125). It is noteworthy that it is "*in* us" that she lets these names appear; clearly here, too, the work

of memory consists in letting the past emerge from an inner hiding place. However, Rabinovici suggests that this work, once made public, is in danger of being
recuperated and instrumentalized. Lola Varga is ultimately celebrated for being
a survivor and is invited to give public lectures as a guest of honor. She is in the
subject of press conferences, municipal officials give speeches praising her memoirs, and yet, as the last sentence of the epilogue intimates, there is no substance
behind the show: no one wants to know what actually happened.

Mullemann, the central figure in Rabinovici's novel *Suche nach M. (The
Search for M,* 1997), is literally a phantom who haunts the city of Vienna.
Wrapped in bandages that both protect and hide a mysterious skin disease
symbolizing the wounds of the past, the phantom compulsively adopts and
thereby exposes the guilt that is woven into the very fabric of his environment.
This phantom turns out to be a disguise worn by Dani Morgenthau, the son of
survivors who kept silent about the past. Dani, a paradigmatic representative
of the "second generation," is described as "a clump of pains made of numerous
deaths and nothing more than a bundle of commemoration" (2000, 76), whose
self risks disappearing under the stifling effect of his parents' wounds, which
have inscribed themselves into his skin. Rabinovici insists that it is the task of
the second generation to uncover the hidden past, yet he simultaneously warns
that an exclusive and obsessive concern with this past may turn into a neurosis
compounded of guilt and revenge: "The search for the culprit turned into an
addiction" (31). Mullemann's obsession increases as he is hunted down by those
who consider him a threat to the status quo. While some members of the current generation of non-Jewish Austrians admit that the effects of his presence
in the city could benefit all, the grandfathers who were implicated in the
crimes want to do away with the unsettling revenant. Rabinovici describes
these effects by toying with the semantic field of the phantom's bandages:

> Fathers muttered about the "bandage creature" living off the crimes of others and
> showing up everywhere in the country. He planted his traps and entangled every-
> one in his plans. It was not merely a matter of a phantom criminal, but of the web
> of politics, the entanglements of high finance, the embroilment of parliament
> that had steered and restrained the people for decades. . . . But a few grandfathers
> warned that if all that should be brought out into the open there would be terri-
> ble consequences. If these things began to unwind, the very bindings holding the
> community together would dissolve. (125)

The complicity of silence endorsed by the grandfathers is the glue that holds
Austrian society together. Arieh, Dani's friend and, like him, a hypersensitive
and neurotic son of survivors, develops a nose for smelling guilt and compulsively goes after it. Dani, or Mullemann, takes a different approach. In mim-
ing the words that should belong to the guilty ones, Mullemann does not ac-

cuse them as an opponent; rather, he undoes the fabric of lies from within. The phantom's subversive power, however, fades as soon as Mullemann becomes famous. Once his identity becomes public, the uncovered guilt is absorbed all too quickly into a false, commercialized discourse of reconciliation. With satiric verve Rabinovici caricatures Mullemann's eventual notoriety, transforming him into a hero, a "Zorro in white." He gets fan mail and his appearance inspires fashion designers and amusement park attractions: "Mullemania everywhere" (1997, 259). Meanwhile, Dani is absorbed into his Mullemann identity and no longer exists as an individual in his own right. Toward the end of the novel Arieh, the other persecutor of the guilty, renounces his pursuit of old criminals and drafts a letter encouraging Dani to do the same, to drop his disguise and let go of the past, become himself and live his own life. However, Arieh destroys this letter when he realizes that Mullemann's disappearance would play into the hands of the former Nazis, who want to cover up their past. He later writes another message in which he suggests that Dani undo the bandages brought to him "by his touching parents" (1997, 265),[6] who expect him to embody "the resurrection of the Jews, their beliefs, their way of thinking and their dignity" (2000, 46). However, he insists that this discarding of the disguise should not be equated with forgetting. In a dialectic turn, Rabinovici describes the unwrapping of Mullemann's bandages as an alternative form of commemoration: "Not to be tied down by the shackles of time like a mummy, to reject all the techniques of preservation, to shed the layers, undo the knots, to go after the knotting together, to feel for the lumps, to unlace and remove the straps: this is the work of memory" (2000, 181). The passive form of being tied down is replaced by actions. Commemoration, Rabinovici suggests, does not consist in passively indulging in a compulsive identification with the former perpetrators and victims but rather in an active unraveling of the past that involves the living self of the one who commemorates. This imperative can be formulated in Walter Benjamin's words as an attempt to "shake off the past from one's back in order to get it into one's hands" (1988, 312). In his final letter Arieh announces to Dani that he will write a book about Mullemann, which is the very book we are reading.

Meanwhile Mullemann seeks relief from his wounds with his non-Jewish mistress, the art expert Sina Mohn, who understands Dani's traumatized psyche and can undo his bandages. The final words of the novel suggest both an awareness of the ineluctable and binding presence of the past and a way out of its traumatic entanglements. Siebert, one of the non-Jewish figures sympathetic to Mullemann, turns to the window, "look[s] through the bars into the open spaces and smile[s] gently" (Rabinovici 2000, 187).

Like *Suche nach M.,* Robert Schindel's novel *Gebürtig* (*Born-Where,* 1992b) describes how children of perpetrators and survivors approach the past. Schindel variously depicts the fragility of a position that can resist both excessive identification with the victims and false conciliatory gestures toward the world that perpetrated and hid the crimes. In a section of his novel that shares many similarities with Rabinovici's epilogue to *Papirnik,* Schindel sketches a scene in which a survivor is honored by Austrian officials for purely self-serving purposes. The Viennese municipality decides to bestow the highest honors on Hermann Gebirtig, a writer and former Viennese resident who was forced to flee Vienna for New York at the time of the Anschluss. In reality, Gebirtig returns to his native city only because a young, politically committed woman convinced him to testify against a former Nazi criminal. While Gebirtig is being decorated and celebrated by the Viennese officials, the Nazi torturer is acquitted. Although Schindel clearly points up the corruptness of the Austrian juridical system in its treatment of former Nazi criminals, the last pages of the novel suggest the futility of thinking of the past primarily in terms of revenge.

In the novel's epilogue, the main character, Danny Demant, figures as an actor in a Holocaust film. Suffering from the freezing weather during the film's shooting, Demant tells himself: "It hits me that the anti-Semites should be the extras. Let them stand there not an hour and a half; but, say, sit and stand for three hours in the snow like that at minus twenty-two centigrade. On the other hand, if they freeze, our kind still won't warm up, not then, and today a tea will do" (1995, 284).[7] Although antagonism is obviously not Schindel's style, he does not call for a smooth reconciliation. The past remains like a "glass wall" between the children of the victims and those of the perpetrators. Their relationships, which play an important role in the novel's many subplots, represent attempts to find ways of living with the burden of the past. Although these relationships remain precarious, the last dialogue between Danny and Christiane, the novel's principal couple, suggests that the non-Jewish woman's final expression of sympathy for all things Jewish makes a continuation of their relationship possible. As in Rabinovici's *Suche nach M.,* one of the main subplots of Schindel's *Gebürtig* ends with a letter and the announcement of a book. This time, however, the reference is not to Schindel's own novel but to the confession made by Konrad Sachs, the son of a former Nazi. It is from the perspective of the perpetrator's children that a different approach to the past is here envisaged. Sachs insists that after telling the truth about his father's activities as a Nazi torturer, he in no way feels "healed or whatever is meant by that word, but merely in a good starting position" (271).

Like Rabinovici's and Schindel's work, Robert Menasse's colorful novel *Vertreibung aus der Hölle* (Expulsion from Hell, 2001) reveals the pervasiveness of an insufficiently acknowledged past. The novel opens with a class reunion twenty years following graduation, during which Victor, the son of a Jewish survivor, recites the NSDAP membership numbers of his former teachers, who are present at the gathering. In response to this revelation, the elderly men depart in furious indignation. It turns out that Victor made up these numbers, but to some extent he unknowingly got it right: two of the teachers had been Nazi collaborators. Although the scene implies that Victor's fictive accusation nevertheless uncovered a real truth, like Rabinovici Menasse also maintains an ironic attitude toward his own obsession with the Nazi past. Once again this stance should not be seen as a conciliatory gesture: the gap between children of Jewish survivors and Austrian perpetrators is never fully bridged, not even between Victor and the woman he is courting. Their reactions to the silenced past of their parents continue to differ (Menasse 2001, 137). When Victor asks this woman what her parents did in the war, she answers: "What my parents did at the time? They lived. In their time. Now they are dead. And my name is Hildegund" (25). Like Schindel and Rabinovici, Menasse mistrusts conciliatory gestures. The person who does make such a gesture is Victor's alter ego from the past, the young rabbi Manasseh, whose parents survived the Spanish Inquisition and who wrote a theological tract called "Il Conciliador" (340), in which all contradictions are smoothed out and harmonized. He thereby gains fame and honor in the eyes of his non-Jewish environment. The historical Menasseh "lifts a millstone from the neck of the Christian world" (418). Victor, on the other hand, acts defiantly toward the old Nazis. Rather than imagining that the rabbi's harmonious solutions might be possible in our time, the modern Menasseh offers much less, suggesting only that Victor and Hildegund, the son of a survivor and the "typically Austrian Nazifamilychild" (191), will continue trying to find each other. Like Sina Mohn, who will eventually heal Mullemann's wounds, and like Schindel's Christiane Kalteisen, Menasse's Hildegund is the non-Jewish woman who helps the male Jewish protagonist understand that his relationship with non-Jews is possible, but only within the context of a full confrontation with his Jewish heritage. The works by Menasse, Schindel, and Rabinovici—together with passages in Anna Mitgutsch's novels *Abschied aus Jerusalem* (Lover, Traitor: A Jerusalem Story, 1995) and *Haus der Kindheit* (House of Childhood, 2000), as well as those in Vladimir Vertlib's fictionalized accounts of exile and emigration in *Die Abschiebung* (The Expulsion, 1995) and *Zwischenstationen* (Transit Stations, 1999)— all describe the traumatic consequences of the Holocaust on former Austrian collaborators, Jewish survivors, and the children of both groups. The unexpected return of the repressed past often expresses itself in sudden clashes, misunderstandings, and hostilities experienced by second-generation Jews in their encounters with non-Jews. However, while the public gestures of regret and reconciliation by Austrian officials are unmasked as a hypocritical show, the present claims its own right and weight in the guise of tentative manifestations of love and sympathy between individuals from both groups. These cautious attempts at a renewed closeness in individual relationships can occur only in the acknowledged shadow of the past and away from public scrutiny, confirming Gershom Scholem's prediction that "fruitful relationships between Jews and Germans"—or, in this case, Austrians—"must be prepared in hidden places" (1970, 45).

However, even as they insist on the crucial task of uncovering the repressed past, the Austrian Jewish writers of the second generation imagine this imperative as a complex enterprise full of psychological, existential, and political traps. Their point of departure lies in the awareness that although the gap between past and present cannot be bridged, this impossibility creates a space for the literary imagination to embrace the concerns of the present along with the confrontation with the past. In his epilogue to *Papirnik* Rabinovici muses that Lola Varga—who busies herself collecting stories of victims and survivors and rewriting from memory the books destroyed in the Nazi book burnings—is about to extend her focus by including herself: "In her most recent texts it almost seems as if she finally remembers her self, as if she remembered new stories that were never heard before" (1994, 127).

Jewish Non-Identity: "You are I when you are in the not-I"

The specific cultural constellation of Austria is another important reason why Austrian Jews—and, consequently, Austrian Jewish writers—are less explicitly and less antagonistically Jewish than their German counterparts. In *Modernité viennoise et crises de l'identité* (Modernity and Crisis of Identity: Culture and Society in Fin-de-Siècle Vienna, 1990), Jacques le Rider locates one possible origin of a truly modernist concept of the self as fragmented and unstable in the crisis of Jewish identity in turn-of-the-century Vienna. Le Rider shows how authors and thinkers like Hofmannsthal, Weininger, Freud, and others turned this crisis into a fruitful inspiration for their artistic and intellectual work. The Holocaust intensified the crisis and simultaneously made the authors of the second generation aware of their ineluctable Jewish origin and background. The works of this generation's authors show an increased identification of Jewishness with a crisis-ridden, ruptured, porous concept of identity, thus situating them squarely within the Viennese artistic and intellectual tradition of the early twentieth century. In his study of contemporary Austrian Jewish literature, Matthias Konzett argues convincingly that "both Jewish ethnic and Austrian national identity never achieved stable coordinates in recent Austrian history" (1998, 77). Because the Habsburg Empire comprised a great diversity of ethnic and cultural groups, where neither Jews nor non-Jews developed a closed, homogeneous collective self-image, the boundaries between them were less clearly demarcated than in the more homogeneous German society. Unlike the German Reich, the Austro-Hungarian monarchy gave many of its Jews the impression that they could be patriots without relinquishing their Jewishness. Konzett explains the specificity of contemporary Austrian Jewish literature as a late consequence of this cultural constellation. He shows how writers such as Jelinek, Schindel, and Rabinovici resist the pitfalls of identity politics and its temptation to re-create closed, stereotypical categorizations[8] even as they openly identify themselves as Jews. In his discussion of individual works by these authors, Konzett explores correspondences between the destabilization of closed identity constructions and such formal aspects as Jelinek's "interwoven discourse configurations" or Schindel's "multi-plot novel" (81).

In line with these more general poetic devices analyzed by Konzett, a close reading of a passage from a dialogue in *Gebürtig* reveals how Schindel's use of language deconstructs unified concepts of identity. After spending the night together—and at the very moment their different backgrounds hinder their relationship—the Jewish lector Danny Demant playfully asks his girlfriend Christiane what she would like to be. Christiane answers that she would like to be either a man or a woman—"or I want to be somehow I" (1995, 36). Danny replies: "You are I when you are in the not-I" (1995, 36).[9] Two elements in this exchange actually perform the seemingly paradoxical reversal contained in this sentence. Possibly echoing Fichte's nonsubstantial conception of the subject, Danny is also quoting or, rather, misquoting a verse from Paul Celan's poem "Lob der Ferne" (Ode to Distance). However, Celan's words "I am you, when I am I" (1983, 1:33) suggest that the boundaries of the self should not dissolve in an encounter with the Other since the "I" can only be addressed as a real "you" as long as it does not lose itself in this Other. Schindel transforms the quotation into its opposite and has Danny suggest to Christiane that she is truly herself only when she does "lose" herself in him. This rather banal statement about the mutual entanglement of individual selves in a love relationship simultaneously refers to Schindel's own writing. Rather than claiming to be the self-identical origin of his words, the formulation implies that he finds his own voice precisely by quoting Celan, by speaking through the words of another and thereby losing himself in them. Meanwhile Schindel also subtly undermines Christiane's wish to be "herself" through the very words she uses to express this desire. In the odd structure of her sentence, in which the object is placed after the verb—in German it would have to be "ich will irgendwie ich sein" (I want to be somehow I)—one can detect a Yiddish ring. Christiane is unwillingly caught in the "Nicht-ich" of her Jewish interlocutor. What this passage performs at the individual level occurs in many of the novel's scenes where collective identities are discussed. In a dialogue between Danny Demant and Masha Singer, the young Jewish woman insists on the difference between the fragmented identity of Jews and that of non-Jewish Austrians, whom she sees as rooted, whole, and united: "They [the Austrians] remain locals. The victors. And me they cut off. And I exist in fragments. And what I am is foreign to me." Demant objects to this distinction and suggests that the Austrian is likewise fragmented and no longer exists as a unified whole. Almost hysterical, Masha replies: "But the Danube connects them" (Schindel 1995, 8). Some three hundred pages later Gebirtig, who has returned to Vienna for the first time since his forced exile before the war, enters a tobacconist's shop and asks for a cigarette brand called "Donau" that he bought for his father as a child. The same shopkeeper who sold these cigarettes before the war replies: "Donau we don't have anymore. . . . Oh, they don't make them anymore." Lost in thought, Gebirtig repeats: "So the Donau doesn't exist anymore" (245). In this exchange, linked to Masha's remark about the unifying powers of the Danube, Schindel implies that today—at least in Vienna—even the legendary river has lost its unifying force. Since the war, both Jewish and non-Jewish citizens of Vienna have become fragmented and no longer constitute unified entities. Although Schindel continues to emphasize the difficulty of overcoming the "glass wall" separating Viennese Jews and non-Jews, he places his hope for the future in the awareness that the war has undone all belief in coherent and closed social, ethnic, and national groups. In the absence of such unified and homogeneous entities, antagonistic relationships that formerly existed between them should have become obsolete.

Adopting a similar approach, the Austrian-American critic Matti Bunzl reaches a perhaps overly optimistic conclusion about the actual situation in Vienna. Bunzl, who invokes the Frankfurt School to support his idea that the Holocaust was the result of an exclusionary modernity, believes that we now live in a "decisively postmodern moment" characterized by a "constitutive pluralism" that has allowed an "affirmative [Jewish] emergence into Vienna's public sphere" (2000, 169). However, Bunzl fails to distinguish between the real political situation in Austria and the conjectures found in works by Austrian Jewish writers. In these works the absence of antagonistic attitudes between Jews and non-Jews is not, as Bunzl would have it, a diagnosis of the present situation but is instead a literary strategy that critically addresses the current state of affairs. The image of an open, diversified, pluralistic society is less a description of Vienna's actual state than a hopeful alternative imagined in the postmodern writings of Austrian Jewish authors like Menasse, Rabinovici, and Schindel.

One of Schindel's better-known poems about Vienna entitled "Vineta I" (1992a, 53) explores the possibilities of this alternative. It opens with the laconic statement "Ich bin ein Jud aus Wien" (I am a Jid from Vienna) and goes on to make an explicit distinction between Austria and Vienna. Although he calls Vienna the former "Welthauptstadt des Antisemitismus" (world capital of anti-Semitism), a city that has now become the "Vergessenshauptstadt" (capital of forgetting), he stresses: "Dies Wien liegt dennoch nicht im Österreiche" (Yet this Vienna does not lie in Austria). Unlike the alpine country, where idyllic, nationalistic images of the sun setting behind mountaintops consolidate a false yet harmless and harmonious sense of *Heimat* (homeland), Schindel's Vienna is itself in exile: "Ach, diese Stadt ist nicht fürs Alpenglühen da / Sondern sie lebt, wie ich, längst in der Diaspora" (Ah, this city is not there for alpine glows / But rather lives, like me, in the Diaspora).

Schindel's identification with the Austrian capital is possible only because of its alienation, its rupture with the "homeland" Austria. Schindel flees the treacherously idyllic, picture-postcard Austria but takes Vienna with him into exile. The capital becomes "his" city, distinguishing itself from the homebound, homogeneous country. The poem's first words, which affirm the Jewish identity of the speaker, and its last word, "Diaspora," which connotes the Jewish experience of exile and dispersion, lend a Jewish frame to the poem without, in turn, "reterritorializing" Jewishness. Jewish existence and Vienna intersect where they are both homeless and unbound. This attitude confirms Dieter Lamping's view that Schindel situates his Jewishness outside any closed national or ethnic identity and that he exposes himself to the unresolved tensions inherent in his situation as an Austrian Jewish writer. Even more important is Lamping's emphasis that this tension "takes place in and through poetry" (2002, 42). In "Vineta I" the word "Diaspora," the nonplace where Vienna "lives," rhymes on "da." This seemingly innocuous little word at first gives the impression of an awkward, "empty" rhyme. A closer look at the verse reveals that "da" is actually the prefix of the verb "sein." In contrast to the foreign word "Diaspora" (dispersion) and its prefix "dia," signifying a split or rupture, "da" indicates an emplacement and links "being" with a specific location, in this case the Austrian Alps. While the glowing alps thus suggest the disclosure of "Da-sein," connoting a Heideggerian existence rooted in the soil of a "homeland," the verb of the last verse ending on "Diaspora" is "leben," living, life. The Viennese Jewish experience that indeed arises "in and through" Schindel's poetry is deployed in the discreet linguistic opposition between "Dasein" und "Leben," between rootedness and exile, between the stillness and passivity required for an authentic existence suggested in the Heideggerian term "Dasein" and the more banal "Leben," the unstable and disorderly quotidian existence. In associating such ordinary existence with exile, Schindel links his refusal of a homebound, nationalistic identity with the subversion of an aesthetics of the sublime that runs through his entire oeuvre.

The banality of Schindel's final rhyme on "da" in conjunction with the sublime experience of the glowing mountains is typical of the purposeful clash of "high" and "low" speech prevalent in the works of many of these writers. Menasse's *Vertreibung aus der Hölle,* for example, offers striking stylistic discrepancies between the dignified historical narrative of Rabbi Manasseh, situated in the fifteenth century, and the colloquial tone of Victor's story about his participation in the student movements of the 1970s.[10] Similarly, the title story of Rabinovici's collections of short stories entitled *Papirnik* mixes references to numinous cabbalistic beliefs with images of Marlene Dietrich acting as "Die blaue Lola." Rather than explicitly promoting positions and counter-positions, Austrian Jewish literature playfully undermines the aura of the sublime and the sacred traditionally attached to topics dealing with origin, identity, and authenticity. This irreverence has its antecedents in earlier Austrian Jewish writing and, more generally, in Austrian literature as such.

A Poetics of Everyday Life: "Shema Israel, my feet are cold"

The influence of a long artistic and intellectual Austrian Jewish tradition of individualistic and subversive dissent, rather than collective and direct opposition, can indeed be regarded as the third reason why contemporary Austrian Jewish authors are arguably "less explicitly and antagonistically Jewish" than one might expect. Wit and satire, combined with self-irony and playful linguistic experiment rather than stern political commitment and dogmatic ideological critique have characterized Jewish and non-Jewish writing in Austria since the days of the celebrated nineteenth-century popular dramatists Johann Nestroy and Ferdinand Raimund. In the interwar and postwar years, parody, comedy, and cabaret performances were the privileged arenas where Jewish Viennese artists like Felix Grünbaum, Ernst Waldbrunn, and Karl Farkas gave voice to their political and social discontent.

More generally, the focus of modern Austrian literature is often described in terms of an epistemological skepticism and a poeticized crisis of language more concerned with the duplicity of words and the ineffability of reality than with ideological contents and calls for justice, equality, and rebellion. In a controversial essay published in 1979, Ulrich Greiner associated the Austrian literary tradition with an anarchic individualism in which reflections on the act of writing replace revolutionary action, and resistance against the existing political discourse expresses itself in opaque or playful aesthetic experiments (48–49). In its exploration of literary means to uncover manipulative discourses and unsettle established assumptions through irreverent parodies and satiric distortions, contemporary Jewish Austrian writing continues this older Austrian tradition, enriching it with Jewish humor, jocular exaggeration, and an ironic attitude toward its own "hang-ups" and obsessions. The result is an inimitable—and barely translatable—marriage of Yiddish *chutzpah,* or Jewish audacity, with Viennese *Schmäh,* the charming yet far-from-harmless humor characteristic of colloquial speech. Except for Elfriede Jelinek's work and some surrealistic elements in Rabinovici's fiction, the general mode of contemporary Austrian Jewish prose is more realistic than experimental. Its realism, however, is interspersed with narrative complexities, jokes, word games, self-reflexive loops, and intertextual references that rupture the surface of the often highly artificial plots and lend these works a typically postmodern heterogeneity. The predominantly idiosyncratic and frequently uneven tone smoothes out antagonistic edges and—particularly in relation to Jewish issues—multiplies positions that mutually discredit one another to the point of undermining them all. It is, however, precisely in this spirit that contemporary Austrian Jewish writing participates in those tendencies within postmodern literature that construct a critical counterdiscourse against all claims to certitude through multiple voices and polycentric perspectives. The casual tone and seeming lightness repeatedly encountered in these works deflates all self-righteous or sanctimonious gestures.

This effect manifests itself in works by Menasse, Rabinovici, and particularly Schindel in contexts and forms that simultaneously reveal their most serious concern, namely, the tension between a secular modernity to which they subscribe wholeheartedly, on the one hand, and Jewish history, identity, and basic religious creeds, on the other. In different ways and through different means, the styles and strategies of these Austrian Jewish authors set them apart from literary approaches to Jewish history and tradition prevalent in the preceding generation. Their tone of colloquial irreverence and playful artifice counters the poetic language of poets like Nelly Sachs or Paul Celan, who endow the past with the aura of a negative sublime and invoke Jewish tradition in terms of an absent or negative yet nevertheless awesome transcendence. Celan's poetry engages in a dialogue with the dead of Auschwitz and searches for ways of poetically resisting the erosion of time. This is paradigmatically expressed in the hypnotic verse from his poem "Vor einer Kerze" (Before a Candle): "Du bleibst, Du bleibst, Du bleibst einer Toten Kind" (You remain, you remain, you remain a dead-one's child), which magically conjures the halting of time and defines the poetic self wholly in terms of the past (1983, 1:110). This denial of the present and of the literary forms that accompany it is questioned by the authors of the second generation, who also question the impossible hope of staying connected with the dead through the poetic word, a conjuration of the magic word that, in Celan's formulation in his Meridian-speech, stands in the "light of utopia" (1983, 3:199). The work of Schindel, Menasse, and Rabinovici purposely undermines such utopian expectations. Dorothee Kimmich eloquently describes this refusal in her discussion of Robert Schindel's *Gebürtig:* "No one here waits for a new, unscathed language, no one awaits redemption, but they all toughly, ironically, bitterly, funnily, sometimes romantically, then again cynically, often failingly, but persistently seem to fumble for an everyday language that would at least be bearable. . . . At no point does language become endowed with a redemptive function" (1996, 105).

While Celan's poetic project participates in an art that, in the words of

Jean-François Lyotard, "doesn't say the unsayable, but rather says that it cannot say it" (quoted in Kimmich 1996, 45), contemporary Austrian Jewish authors have accepted the paradoxical notion that although the unsayable is unsayable, it is possible—perhaps even imperative—to keep on talking. One of the strongest lines in Schindel's novel makes this demystifying gesture explicit. Irreverently distorting the weighty oxymoron "zwei Mundvoll Schweigen" (two mouthfuls of silence) from Celan's poem "Sprachgitter" (1983, 1:167), Schindel has Danny Demant say: "Ich hätte noch gern ein Maul voll Schweigen, aber der Vorrat ist auf" (1992b, 183), which translates as: "I would like another snout full of silence, but the supply is used up" (1995, 146). Instead of an auratic silence meant to reach beyond words in order to overcome the inevitable failure of language to grasp the abysmal catastrophe, contemporary Jewish Austrian literature is talkative in the extreme and wavers concerning the key in which this talking occurs. Kimmich perfectly captures the atmosphere that reigns not only in *Gebürtig,* to which she refers, but in many other works by contemporary Austrian Jewish writers: "The whole world is a stage, where even authors and critics can no longer distinguish between tragedy and comedy. . . . Talking almost always leads to misunderstandings and yet it is what makes participation in life possible. . . . [And] they all talk across each other, with each other, against each other. . . . The garrulousness is legendary and some of the witnesses are, in Lyotard's sense of the word, 'inauthentic'" (1996, 104). In Menasse's *Vertreibung aus der Hölle,* the question "Is it a comedy, is it a tragedy?" (2001, 485) repeatedly interrupts the incessant dialogues and conversations. Historian Victor Abravanel, the novel's protagonist, explicitly rejects the claim to authenticity in reference to the silent gaps in survivor testimonies when he questions "this blind trust in the gaps of memory" (2001, 389). Authenticity is indeed no longer the issue: "Nothing about me is genuine? I should hope so," says one of Schindel's narrators in *Gebürtig,* "what's genuine, the cat can have it" (1995, 11). In a dialogue between Danny Demant and Christiane in the same novel, it is the non-Jewish woman who says: "When we talk everything is lost, or more accurately: everything is named and becomes known." "I don't understand," replies her Jewish lover as he rejects this mystifying refusal of words: "Are you one of those who always claim that all feelings are talked to death? . . . But I like talking. I want things that are known and things that are named" (35). Later Christiane accuses him or, rather, "them," the Jews, of "talking and talking," of "always talking about Auschwitz" (159).

Beyond its nonsacrosanct treatment of the past, this affirmation of everyday speech expresses an allegiance to the quotidian here and now and to a renewed lust for life that also manifests itself in the way contemporary Austrian Jewish authors relate to religious rituals and beliefs. This attitude manifests itself most strikingly in relation to one of the basic Jewish creeds, namely, the expected arrival of the Messiah. Although in "Vineta I" Schindel invokes the Diaspora—which, according to Jewish tradition, points to the anguished waiting for a redeemed time in the future—his poem carries no such implication. In fact, Schindel's entire work, and contemporary Austrian Jewish literature in general, is radically worldly and anti-messianic. For example, Robert Menasse's *Vertreibung aus der Hölle* shows Rabbi Manasseh's belief in a coming redemption to be as pitiful an illusion as Victor's faith in the Hegelian notion of a gradual deployment of the "world spirit." His ancestors are described as "famous politicians, poets, scholars. And one checked in each generation: the Messiah? No! Highly talented people, but no human God" (2001, 412). The novel is constructed along parallel plots in which the lives of the historical Rabbi Manasseh and the contemporary historian Victor Abravanel echo each other continuously. However, at the end of the novel the two life stories diverge on this crucial point. Before he dies, Rabbi Manasseh loses himself in phantasms about his role as redeemer—or at the very least a messenger of the Messiah. In the last lines of the novel his death is described as an apocalyptic explosion of the rising sun that suddenly breaks through his window, but the explosion merely signifies his death. Like Rabbi Manasseh's life, Victor's story also ends with an explosive light, but the difference in content and tone between the two experiences reflects the spirit in which the novel dismisses eschatological expectations. Shortly before the end, Victor is discovered sitting in a bar with Hildegund: "Suddenly it became very bright, the light flared up with a blinding intensity in the midst of cold flames; no, it was only a spot that had wandered through the bar as an invitation to dance" (483). This bar, where the apocalyptic light of redemption turns out to be nothing more than an invitation to dance, is called Eden, which, as Victor laconically remarks, absurdly yet significantly rhymes with "reden" (talking) (480).[11]

Similarly, in *Suche nach M.* Rabinovici dismisses the idea of religious redemption together with an aesthetics of suffering. The art expert Sina Mohn associates Mulleman's obsession with pain and wounds with a baroque tradition based on the Catholic idea of redemption through suffering. The iconography of "those bandaged-up forms wrapped in gauze and racked with pain" (2000, 136), which she recognizes in the works of Viennese avant-garde artists—such as Hermann Nitsch and Arnulf Rainer, members of the "Wiener Aktionisten"—in turn makes her think of an earlier art form widely practiced in Austria:

> [Sina Mohn] knew of various, particularly local avant-garde traditions which emphasized the painting-over of portraits, the depiction of pain, injuries, scars, blood orgies as well as bandages and masks. She could talk about her associations and the roots of these bloody subjects. She was familiar with Catholic depictions of Christian saints pierced with arrows, impaled on stakes, nailed to

crosses, roasted on fires, and battered by stones. These were bodies in extreme pain that found their way to redemption through martyrdom. (136)

Rabinovici suggests that an aesthetic wallowing in wounds would emulate this baroque tradition. The end of the novel shows that Mullemann, the Jewish son of survivors, is not redeemed through suffering but rather is healed thanks to the loving care of Sina Mohn.

In one of the most grotesque yet also most memorable scenes in the entire corpus of contemporary Austrian Jewish literature, Schindel weaves together the major strands related to Jewish history, culture, and tradition and places them under the sign of his poetics of everyday life. In the last lines of *Gebürtig* Danny Demant is still shivering in the freezing cold during the shooting of the concentration camp film. He senses that it is this bodily discomfort in the present that creates a link "von damals nach heute" (1992b, 353), "from then until today" (1995, 285). Standing next to him, Doctor Klang, a man in his seventies, recites in a barely audible voice an irreverent imitation of the most basic Jewish credo articulated in the prayer "Shema Israel," transforming its original words "Hear, O Israel, the Almighty is our God, the one and only" into "Sch'ma Jisruel, kalt is ma in die Fiss, Sch'ma, die Fiss so kalt, oj is ma kalt in die Fiss Israel. Sch'ma Jisruel, in die Fiss is ma soi koit in die Fiss adonai" (1992b, 353), which roughly translates as "Sch'ma Jisruel, cold is me footsie; Sch'ma, footsies so cold, oy me ma footsies Israel. Sch'ma Jisruel, in the footsies is me so coldy, adonai" (1995, 353). Overhearing this disrespectful complaint introduced into the holiest of Jewish prayers, Demant reflects: "There, I think to myself, when the feet finally warm up and the head stays wonderfully cool, it can happen that there comes not the Messiah, but a beautiful feeling" (1995, 353). Schindel's narrator calls this distorted prayer—a polyglottic mix of old and new Hebrew, Yiddish, German, and Viennese dialect[12] that asserts the primacy of life at its most worldly, universal, and basic level—a revelation of "das innere Wesen des jüdischen Gebets" (1992b, 353), "the innermost essence of Jewish prayer" (1995, 353).[13] It is the only instance in Schindel's entire oeuvre—and perhaps even in the whole of contemporary Austrian Jewish literature—where something is described as "essentially" Jewish.

A Time and a Place

The scene is the Judenplatz on a cool Friday evening during the fall. The tourist season is over. Groups of Orthodox Jews in festive clothes cross the square in the direction of the renovated synagogue. Shoppers are on their way home. Residents of the buildings surrounding the square return to their homes. The shops are closed for the night, with the cafés and pubs dimly lit. Spotlights illuminate several points of interest on the square. A slightly yellowish light keeps the Holocaust memorial visible. Its white walls are partially covered with grime, while its simple shape and moderate size lend it an air of self-importance. Neither oppressive nor auratic, it just stands there with a sense of unobtrusive dignity. Resting on its pedestal, several candles illuminate the commemorative inscription, a few faded flowers lie next to the incised names of the concentration camps where Austrian Jews were murdered. Although most people simply walk past the monument, some notice it. A young couple slows down just long enough to comment on the monument's shape and proportions. A family with children walks around it, the father explaining its significance while the mother tries to keep two little girls from stepping on the pedestal. On the bench next to the memorial two lovers hold hands. A few half-drunk men emerge from a pub. One of them bellows out in Viennese dialect; "Der Platz, was die da g'macht ha'm, der is jetz endgültig im Oarsch," which loosely translates as "They have now screwed up the square for good." The memorial has become part of the square, and the square part of contemporary, everyday Vienna.

NOTES

1. The most notorious examples are the absence of a true opposition party for decades and the corrupt collaboration of the various governmental, industrial, and civic powers known as "Sozialpartnerschaft," or social partnership.

2. For a discussion of the Jewish "Kaffeehausliterat," see Beller 1989, 215–16. It is noteworthy that the three novels I discuss begin and/or end in cafés or pubs. These cafés are either explicitly named or identifiable and refer to existing coffeehouses and restaurants. Rabinovici's novel *Suche nach M.* starts in the Café Prückel, identifiable as such because mention is made of the statue of a famous Viennese anti-Semite that is visible through the window. Rabinovici refers to the notoriously anti-Semitic Viennese mayor Karl Lueger. Robert Schindel's novel *Gebürtig* opens in a pub called the Zeppelin. The novel also mentions other artists' hangouts like the Kalb, the Café Zartl, the Café Eiles, among others. Robert Menasse's novel *Vertreibung aus der Hölle* starts in the restaurant Goldenes Kalb and ends in the Eden Bar. These bars and cafés are actual meeting places between Jews and non-Jews.

3. As recently as 2000 Austrian chancellor Wolfgang Schüssel was quoted in the *Jerusalem Post* (January 7, 2001) as believing that "'the sovereign state of Austria was the first victim of Hitler . . . they took Austria by force. They [the Austrians] were the very first victims,' the chancellor defiantly insisted, referring to the Allied propaganda statement of 1943 which, in an attempt to mobilize domestic resistance against the Nazis, recognized Austria as an occupied country."

4. The present essay discusses the work of Schindel, Rabinovici, and Menasse. This choice can be explained in terms of the essay's focus on what is most specific about contemporary Jewish Austrian literature. The reasons why the other authors lend themselves less readily to an assessment of this specificity differ in each case. Vertlib focuses less on questions of Jewish-Austrian relations and amalgamations than on problems of migration. For Mitgutsch,

the experience of conversion to Judaism lies at the center of her work. Jungk left Austria in the late eighties and barely addresses Jewish-Austrian issues. Beckermann is more a filmmaker and essayist than a writer of fiction. Although Jelinek repeatedly and explicitly situates herself in a Jewish Austrian literary and cultural tradition, her texts invite readings from other perspectives that are more relevant to her work than the point of view adopted in this essay.

5. "Ein verpflichtendes, aber kein verschlingendes Verhältnis [zur Vergangenheit]" (Schindel 1992b, 300). Whenever possible, the quotes from Schindel's *Gebürtig* are taken from *Born-Where,* the English translation by Michael Roloff. Most of the time, however, they had to be considerably modified. For example, Roloff translates "verpflichtend" with "dutiful" instead of "committed" or "responsible." He thereby mistakenly adds a negative connotation to Schindel's term "verpflichtend" (1995, 243).

6. "Rührende Eltern" (1997, 265). The translator's "pathetic parents" exaggerates the slight irony in the word "rührend" and thereby betrays the ambivalence in the description of Dani's parents.

7. "Man soll die Antisemiten doch statieren lassen. Sollen sie nicht anderthalb Stunden, sondern, sagen wir, drei Stunden so sitzen und stehen bei Minus zweiundzwanzig Grad. Andererseits, wenn die frieren, werden Unsereins doch nicht erwärmt, damals nicht, und heut tut's ein Tee auch" (Schindel 1992b, 352). Roloff, for example, translates the last sentence of this quote as: "On the other hand, if we freeze, our kind still won't warm up, not then and not today—the tea won't do it either" (Schindel 1995, 284). This translation conveys the exact opposite of the original.

8. Lisa Silverman analyzes some of Rabinovici's short stories and Christine Guenther discusses his novel *Suche nach M.* in a spirit similar to Konzett's. In both cases the emphasis falls on Rabinovici's strategies of preventing Jewishness from turning into a homogeneous, exclusionary identity. While Silvermann focuses on the ways in which Rabinovici dissolves boundaries between Jews and non-Jews and creates hybrid identities, Guenther shows how he insists on the performative terms according to which national and ethnic identities are constituted.

9. "Ich bist du, wenn du im Nichtich bist" (Schindel 1992b, 48). Roloff's translation misses the point when he translates "Ich bist du" as "I am you" instead of "I you are" (1995, 36).

10. In her excellent review of Menasse's novel, Iris Radisch begs to differ with critics who take the novel to task for this discrepancy, preferring to see in the "fall" from the "high tone" of the historical narrative to the banality of the contemporary plot "a gain in humanity" (2001, 10).

11. In Rabinovici's *Papirnik,* truth itself—the sacred, unsayable word hidden in the book of books, the mysterious word that evokes both the mystical name of God and the Jewish suffering in the Holocaust—becomes readable, knowable, and sayable.

12. "Jisruel" is an East European, Yiddish-inflected pronunciation of the word "Israel." "Adonai" is a fairly recent Hebrew pronunciation of one of the names of God. There is also a shift from the German "kalt" to the Viennese equivalent word for cold, "koit." "Fiss" is Yiddish for "feet."

13. By translating "Wesen" as "character" instead of "essence," the English version (Schindel 1995, 294) misses a crucial dimension of this ending.

WORKS CITED

Aichinger, Ilse. 1946. "Aufruf zum Misstrauen." *Plan* 1 (5): 588.

———. 1999. "A Summons to Mistrust." In *Contemporary Jewish Writing in Austria: An Anthology,* ed. Dagmar Lorenz, 159–61. Lincoln: University of Nebraska Press.

Beller, Stephen. 1989. *Vienna and the Jews, 1867–1938.* New York: Cambridge University Press.

Benjamin, Walter. 1988. "Eduard Fuchs, der Sammler und Historiker." In *Angelus Novus,* 302–60. Frankfurt am Main: Suhrkamp.

Bunzl, Matti. 2000. "Political Inscription, Artistic Reflection: A Recontextualization of Contemporary Viennese-Jewish Literature." *German Quarterly* 73 (2): 163–70.

Celan, Paul. 1983. *Gesammelte Werke.* Vols. 1 and 3. Ed. Beda Allemann and Stefan Reichert. Frankfurt am Main: Suhrkamp.

Charim, Isolde, and Doron Rabinovici, eds. 2000. *Berichte aus Quarantanien.* Frankfurt am Main: Suhrkamp.

Greiner, Ulrich. 1979. "Der Tod des Nachsommers: Über das Österreichische in der österreichischen Literatur." In his *Der Tod des Nachsommers: Aufsätze, Porträts, Kritiken zur österreichischen Gegenwartsliteratur,* 11–52. Munich: Hanser.

Guenther, Christine. "Remembering the Holocaust: The Politics of Postmodern Characterization in Doron Rabinovici's *Suche nach M.*" [unpublished manuscript in author's possession].

Jelinek, Elfriede. 2000. *Die Kinder der Toten.* Reinbek: Rowohlt.

Kilcher, Andreas. 2002. "Extraterritorialitäten: Zur kulturellen Selbstreflexion der aktuellen deutsch-jüdischen Literatur." In *Deutsch-jüdische Literatur der neunziger Jahre: Die Generation nach der Shoah,* ed. Sander Gilman and Hartmut Steinecke, 131–46. Berlin: Schmidt.

Kimmich, Dorothee. 1996. "Kalte Füsse: Von Erzählprozessen und Sprachverdikten bei Hannah Arendt, Harry Mulisch, Theodor W. Adorno, Jean-François Lyotard und Robert Schindel." In *Shoah: Formen der Erinnerung; Geschichte, Philosophie, Literatur, Kunst,* ed. Nicolas Berg et al., 93–106. Munich: Fink.

Konzett, Matthias. 1998. "The Politics of Recognition in Contemporary Austrian Jewish Literature." *Monatshefte* 90 (1): 71–88.

Lamping, Dieter. 2002. "'Deine Texte werden immer jüdischer': Robert Schindels Gedicht 'Nachthalm (Pour Celan).'" In *Deutsch-jüdische Literatur der neunziger Jahre—Die Generation nach der Shoah,* ed. Sander Gilman and Hartmut Steinecke, 29–42. Berlin: Schmidt.

Lappin, Elena, ed. 1994. *Jewish Voices, German Words: Growing Up Jewish in Postwar Germany and Austria.* North Haven, Conn.: Catbird.

Le Rider, Jacques. 1990. *Modernité viennoise et crises de l'identité.* Paris: PUF.

———. 1993. *Modernity and Crisis of Identity: Culture and Society in Fin-de-Siècle Vienna.* Trans. Rosemary Morris. Cambridge: Blackwell / Malden, Mass.: Polity.

Liska, Vivian. 1992. "Gegengebet: Zu Paul Celans Gedicht 'Vor einer Kerze.'" In *Zwiesprache: vier Beiträge zu Paul Celan,* ed. J. De Vos, 91–118. Ghent: SGG.

Lorenz, Dagmar, ed. 1999. *Contemporary Jewish Writing in Austria: An Anthology.* Lincoln: University of Nebraska Press.

Menasse, Robert. 2000. *Erklär mir Österreich.* Frankfurt am Main: Suhrkamp.

———. 2001. *Vertreibung aus der Hölle.* Frankfurt am Main: Suhrkamp.

Mitgutsch, Anna. 1995. *Abschied von Jerusalem.* Berlin: Rowohlt.

———. 1997. *Lover, Traitor: A Jerusalem Story,* trans. Roslyn Theobald. New York: Henry Holt.

———. 2000. *Haus der Kindheit.* Munich: DTV.

Nolden, Thomas. 1995. *Junge jüdische Literatur.* Würzburg: Königshausen und Neumann.

Rabinovici, Doron. 1994. *Papirnik.* Frankfurt am Main: Suhrkamp.

———. 1997. *Suche nach M.* Frankfurt am Main: Suhrkamp.

———. 2000. *The Search for M.* Trans. Francis M. Sharp. Riverside, Calif.: Ariadne.

Radisch, Iris. 2001. "Reden im Eden." *Die Zeit,* October 4, lit. suppl. 56, 10.

Schindel, Robert. 1992a. *Ein Feuerchen im Hintennach.* Frankfurt am Main: Suhrkamp.

———. 1992b. *Gebürtig.* Frankfurt am Main: Suhrkamp.

———. 1995. *Born-Where.* Trans. Michael Roloff. Riverside, Calif.: Ariadne.

Scholem, Gershom. 1970. "Juden und Deutsche." In *Werke,* vol. 2, 20–46. Frankfurt am Main: Suhrkamp.

Silverman, Lisa. "'Der richtige Riecher': The Reconfiguration of Jewish and Austrian Identities in the Work of Doron Rabinovici." *German Quarterly* 72, no. 3 (June 1999): 252–64.

Vertlib, Vladimir. 1995. *Die Abschiebung.* Salzburg: Otto Müller.

———. 1999. *Zwischenstationen.* Vienna and Munich: Deuticke.

Young, James E. 1999. "Memory and Counter-Memory." *Constructions of Memory* (special issue of *Harvard Design Magazine*) 9: 7.

TEXTS AVAILABLE IN ENGLISH

Aichinger, Ilse. 1963. *Herod's Children.* Trans. Cornelia Schaeffer. New York: Atheneum.

———. 1983. *Selected Poetry and Prose.* Trans. Allen H. Chappel. Durango, Colo.: Logbridge-Rhodes.

Beckermann, Ruth. 2006. "Beyond the Bridges," trans. Dagmar C. G. Lorenz. In *Voices of the Diaspora: Jewish Women Writing in Contemporary Europe,* ed. Thomas Nolden and Frances Malino, 23–33. Evanston, Ill.: Northwestern University Press.

Celan, Paul. 2001. *Selected Poems and Prose.* Trans. John Felstiner. New York: Norton.

———. 2002. *Poems of Paul Celan.* Trans. Michael Hamburger. New York: Persea.

———. 2005. *Selections.* Ed. Pierre Joris. Berkeley: University of California Press.

Jelinek, Elfriede. 1990. *Wonderful, Wonderful Times.* Trans. Michael Hulse. London: Serpent's Tail.

———. 1996. *Death / Valley / Summit,* trans. Gitta Honegger. In *Contemporary Drama: Germany,* ed. Carl Weber, 217–63. Baltimore, Md.: Johns Hopkins University Press.

Jungk, Peter Stephan. 1985. *Shabbat—A Rite of Passage in Jerusalem.* Trans. Arthur S. Weinsinger and Richard H. Wood. New York: Random House.

Lorenz, Dagmar C., ed. 1999. *Contemporary Jewish Writing in Austria: An Anthology.* Lincoln: University of Nebraska Press.

Menasse, Robert. 2000a. *Meaningful Certainty.* Trans. David Bryer. London: Calder.

———. 2000b. *Reverse Thrust.* Trans. David Bryer. London: Calder.

———. 2000c. *Wings of Stone.* Trans. David Bryer. London: Calder.

Mitgutsch, Anna. 1997. *Lover, Traitor: A Jerusalem Story.* Trans. Roslyn Theobald. New York: Henry Holt.

———. 2006. *House of Childhood.* Trans. David Dollenmayer. New York: The Other Press.

Rabinovici, Doron. 2000. *The Search for M.* Trans. Francis M. Sharp. Riverside, Calif.: Ariadne.

Schindel, Robert. 1995. *Born-Where,* trans. Michael Roloff. Riverside, Calif.: Ariadne.

TWO

~

STEPHAN BRAESE

Writing against Reconciliation: Contemporary Jewish Writing in Germany

In November 1979 Henryk M. Broder and Michel R. Lang published the seminal anthology *Fremd im eigenen Land: Juden in der Bundesrepublik* (Foreign in One's Own Country: Jews in the Federal Republic). The volume represented an attempt to demonstrate "what the Jews who live in Germany really think and feel, what they find difficult, what they cope with—and, then again, sometimes do not" (1979, 11).

The volume marked a crucial turning point, a caesura in the history of Jews in Germany after 1945 that can serve as a point of departure for a discussion of contemporary Jewish literature written in the German language. The editors' introduction plus the thirty-eight contributions representing different generations and political backgrounds illustrate the unique set of problems still facing Jews residing in Germany more than three decades after the end of Nazi rule. As a whole, the anthology fundamentally criticized West Germany's Zentralrat der Juden (Central Consistory of Jews) for the way it had been handling German-Jewish relations since its establishment in 1950. This criticism went hand in hand with an uncompromising evaluation of German *Vergangenheitsbewältigung,* a process of coming to terms with the past that, according to the contributors, did not entail a radical analysis of the Nazi period and its consequences. The authors also maintained that the Zentralrat had been enlisting prominent Jews to shield the organization from criticism both politically and morally.[1] Such criticism of the German way of relating to Jews ultimately led to the fundamental question: How could Jews continue to reside in Germany some thirty-five years after the military defeat of the Nazi regime and the liberation of the survivors of the death camps?

The desire to present an open discussion of these issues in a manner that might also engage non-Jews, as well as the need to reflect on present Jewish identity above and beyond the official rhetorical, were by no means new impulses. There had been prior indications that the Zentralrat's de facto monopoly on public expression of Jewish standpoints was approaching its end. The year 1978 witnessed the publication of the anthology *Mein Judentum* (My Judaism), edited by Hans Jürgen Schultz, in which twenty Jewish artists and intellectuals shared their thoughts on their experiences as Jews in the wake of the Shoah. For many non-Jewish German readers this was the very first time that someone had called attention to the *present existence* of Jews in Germany (Loewy 1980). With the publication of his grotesque novel *Der Nazi & der Friseur* (The Nazi & the Barber) in 1977, Edgar Hilsenrath had created a stir by satirically undermining the ideological notion of the German-Jewish symbiosis, which was a constitutive feature of Germany's strategy of postwar self-rehabilitation. George Tabori preceded Hilsenrath in 1969 when he staged his play *Die Kannibalen* (*The Cannibals*),[2] which dramatized generational conflicts between fathers and their offspring. The chairman of Berlin's Jewish municipal organization tried unsuccessfully to block its performance (Tabori 1981; Braese 1996; Strümpel 2000).

By the end of the seventies, the politics of the Zentralrat had frequently been criticized, especially by younger members of the Jewish community. Y. Michal Bodemann has shown how the Adenauer administration attempted to instrumentalize the Zentralrat as a means of obtaining moral alibis (Bodemann 1986, 1996). This strategy clearly succeeded. The Zentralrat refrained from protesting against leading figures in Germany's regional and national governments despite their Nazi past, as in the case of Hans Globke in 1953.[3] Occasionally the Zentralrat even issued statements honoring such figures, as it did for Hans Filbinger in 1978.[4]

Criticism directed at the functionaries of the Jewish organizations and their politics was decisively structured by a *Legitimationsdruck,* or "pressure to legitimize" (Nolden 1995, 51), to which every Jew trying to live in Germany was exposed. The highly elaborated ideological standpoint of Zionism—which declared that the project of the Diaspora had failed, and that to live in Germany as a Jew was anachronistic—was certainly one source of this pressure. But having to somehow cope with the loss of millions—whose annihilation had been conceived and politically realized in Germany and whose murderers, together with their helpers' helpers, remained largely unpunished, and who sometimes even held influential positions—raised the pressure considerably. Those who criticized the Zentralrat were not blind to its dilemma of having to operate politically from a most unfavorable position within German society only a few years after the Holocaust.[5] They were driven by an acute awareness of German crimes against Jews as well as the necessity for remembrance. They questioned the conditions of Jewish existence in Germany in the wake of the Shoah and found the approaches of the Zentralrat to be inappropriate.

By the end of the seventies questions concerning the state of living as a Jew in present-day Germany were increasingly being raised in public, with the issue generating much controversy. Ten years later a new body of literature by Jewish authors writing in German emerged, with these questions at its center.

It has been noted that the caesura in public discussion about the existence of Jews in Germany was determined by a shift in generations. Members of the second generation—Jews born sometime between 1945 and the beginning of the 1950s who lack any personal recollection of the war years—are said to have ideas regarding their own existence and expectations toward German society that differ from those of their parents. Yet even a cursory glance at the "pioneers" who determined how Germans and Jews related appears to disprove this assumption. Although George Tabori, who was born in Hungary in 1914—as well as contributors to the previously mentioned anthologies, such as Curt Riess (1902), Günther Anders (1902), Manès Sperber (1905), and Hilde Domin(1909)—belonged to the generation of the parents, they nonetheless took steps to begin a discussion of Jewish existence in Germany. However, it was not until the second generation that the "constituting of a post-Shoah identity," one "that had nothing to do with the original identity of the prewar Jews, whether assimilatory, German-nationalistic or Jewish nationalistic," could succeed (Brumlik 1986, 176; Nolden 1995, 20). This generational gap was based not only on the unbridgeable distance to prewar Judaism and its perceptions; it was also motivated by a rebellion against a specific milieu that had established itself in the Jewish communities during the first postwar decades. Maxim Biller has characterized the inhabitants of this milieu as the "Nachmann-Jew": "The postwar Jew in the manner of Nachmann doesn't want to belong . . . he sets himself apart. He has his own cafes and parades, his own boutiques and leisure rituals, his very own canon of values, which he divides strictly between Jewish and gentile. . . . However, such a fearful, egotistical posture automatically leads to spiritual and mental provincialism. That can't be tolerated by the youth" (1991b, 172–74; Nolden 1994, 57). Biller's characterization of the "Nachmann-Jew" makes it evident that criticism of the Zentralrat was ultimately not aimed at the failings of its individual members but rather at fundamental attitudes held by the generation that the Zentralrat most strongly represented. The younger generation's reservations about their parents' mode of existence were linked to the difficulty of contending with the latter's pervasive silence about the years of persecution. As Thomas Nolden has remarked, "within the reality of the annihilation trauma [a] dialogue between the Jewish generations" could not often occur (1995, 27).[6] The "post-Shoah identity" of the second generation entailed recognizing the isolation of a life within a new "Jewish alleyway" in Germany. It was believed that a future for Jews in Germany could not be built on silence regarding the traumatic past. Biller appended an emphatic appeal to his critique of the "Nachmann-Jew": "So get out of the Jewish alleyway, friends. Immerse yourselves in the fantastic turbulence of the arts, politics, and scientific discourse. Life is out there. We can still learn a lot from the others" (1991, 174). Biller's sarcastic depiction of "the Nachmann-Jew" clearly marks—even accelerates and promotes—the caesura in the relationships between Germans and Jews. Yet the author, who was born in 1960, is himself a proponent of the third generation of Jews in Germany after 1945. Nolden has pointed out that this third generation was spared the experience of left-wing anti-Semitism, which arose within the context of the anti-authoritarian movement around the time of the Six-Day War and during the seventies. Left-wing anti-Semitism had been constitutive for the preceding generation. Certainly it still existed later, but the disappointment of expectations that many Jews had placed in the student movement was already history for the members of the third generation. Nor was this the only situation in which they could "critically look over the shoulders of the representatives of the second generation, setting forth where that age group had advanced a new, contemporary Jewish self-conception" (1995, 55).

Nevertheless, overstating the differences between the second and third generations should be avoided if a clearer understanding of the starting position of Jewish German authors writing in Germany is to be attained. According to Hannes Stein, the "three shocks" (Stein 1998, 404) that decisively influenced contemporary Jewish authors—Bitburg and the Fassbinder scandal in 1985 and the Gulf War in 1991—did not affect these authors in categorically different ways. In their critical and literary undertakings the second and third generations engaged a common "object" by focusing on the generation of those who had personally experienced persecution and destruction. Categorical differences were hardly yielded in the process. Within the context of challenges facing Jewish authors active in Germany today, German contemporary literature continues to underscore the commonality of this focus on a generation that was nearly annihilated.

What was being articulated only sporadically at the end of the seventies gained considerable momentum in the course of the eighties. With the publication of the first issue of the *Beiträge zur jüdischen Gegenwart* (Contributions to

Jewish Presence) in 1986 under the title *Babylon,* the door to a public realm of discourse was pushed open, with future discussion about relations between Germans and Jews in Germany positioned at a new level. The debut issue of the journal included Dan Diner's seminal essay "Negative Symbiose" (Negative Symbiosis), which described interrelations between Jews and Germans in an entirely new manner. The journal's editorial statement was hardly less paradigmatic:

> With *Babylon* we want . . . to try to establish an intellectual discourse about Jewish problems again. We don't so much want to express ourselves as representatives of a—depending on your perspective—religious/social/ethnic minority but rather as universally oriented intellectuals who wish to go beyond the particularities of origins while reflecting on them without denying them. If we have our eye on a tradition, then it is possibly that of "Jewish intellectuals," a role that is perhaps most substantial in the American "Jewish community" but that must again be claimed on German ground. . . . The magazine . . . wants . . . to deal with that which issues forth extensively and universally from, or is respectively ascribed to, Jews and Judaism. (*Babylon* 1986, 7)

Babylon's editors declare their commitment to a universalism that remains aware of the particularities of the subject's origins, attempting to "go beyond . . . while reflecting on" the insights and, possibly, restrictions derived from those origins. This commitment links the project advanced by *Babylon* to a tradition in the history of ideas that many Germans, on both sides of the conservative/liberal fence, tend to associate with the history of the alleged German-Jewish symbiosis. However, a younger generation influenced by the anti-authoritarian movement tends to draw the connection more explicitly with critical theory as developed by Horkheimer, Adorno, and the Frankfurt School. At the same time, the universalism sketched out in the *Babylon* editorial reflects the socialization of a particular generation of German Jews. Like Wolfgang Hildesheimer (born 1916), the author of such landmarks of German postwar fiction as *Tynset* (1965) and *Masante* (1973), the proponents of this generation never experienced the "particularity of their origins" as a constraint on their own artistic and political insights and realizations. On the contrary, they experienced and perceived their particular origins as a primary source of and for their critical awareness and creativity. In *Mein Judentum* (My Judaism), Hildesheimer discussed this feature in connection with homelessness, which, when "viewed from the outside," might appear to be "a characteristic of the Jew," but for him, "viewed from within," symbolized "that homelessness . . . in which we—Jew or not—are all at home. That is the source of all of my creative activity" (Hildesheimer 1987, 220). In the realm of experience from which Hildesheimer emerges, all art worthy of the name stems from a process of intensive self-reassurance about personal subjective history. This process clearly "goes beyond" the level of particularity by way of reflection in order to arrive at universally valid expressions. Was this understanding of Jewish cultural creativity at the time (1986) in keeping with the times? The editors of *Babylon,* who looked not only to Kafka but also to Marx and Freud as proponents of the creative transcendence to which they aspired, assert that their posture is absolutely appropriate. They have no doubt that it yields criteria for effectively "participating in political and social life by articulating that which he [the intellectual] considers right" (*Babylon* 1986, 7). When Barbara Honigmann speculates that "it . . . is perhaps true that being a writer and being a Jew are similar" (1999, 47), or when Maxim Biller characterizes "being Jewish as a compressed form of being human" (Schruff 2000, 67), it appears that individual expressions of second-generation Jewish authors are aligned with the sense of universalism previously described. Yet even a cursory glimpse at contemporary German literature by younger Jewish authors reveals that they were not inclined to ground their writings in the notion of transcending "the particularity of their origins." There is no primary impulse to "go beyond" those particularities by way of reflection in order to stake claims within the realm of the universal, as was the case for Hildesheimer and for the critical scholarly discourse initiated by the editors of *Babylon.* On the contrary, in their texts they insistently speak about themselves *as Jews,* however incomplete this identity might be perceived. More specifically, they write about themselves as Jews *in the concrete German present.* This discursive gesture was amplified by two factors to which the texts were related externally. In Germany's social and literary climate, any form of expression by a "noticeably" Jewish author was automatically viewed as an "expression of a collective and not of an individual consciousness" (Nolden 1995, 67). Regardless of how precisely a Jewish author might write in terms of subjective history, a non-Jewish reader was bound to perceive the expression as being representative for "the Jews" of his or her generation. Such a reading position could only have been strengthened (Nolden 1995) when Esther Dischereit's first prose publication, *Joëmis Tisch* (Joëmi's Table, 1988), appeared with the publisher's appended subtitle "Eine jüdische Geschichte" (A Jewish Story) (Nolden 1995)—this just a few years after the West German culture industry was intent on suppressing the term "Jew" or "Jewish" (Braese 2000). Flap copy added the finishing touches after "the literary marketplace . . . had discovered the discourse of the minority as a new trend" (Nolden 1995, 86).

To be sure, the discursive tendency in German literature by Jewish writers to reflect on being Jewish in the here and now *without* attempting to transcend "the particularity of origin" in a universalistic manner was amplified by the commercial interests of the publishing industry at the time. However, the primary causes behind this gesture were separate from that industry. They were derived from the immediately preceding historical stage of Jewish contemporary literature in Germany. Rebelling against the regulated speech that for decades had obscured every subject under discussion between Germans and Jews, the authors of the second generation were acutely aware that relationships between Germans and Jews simply had to be addressed in a more direct and undisguised manner if the status quo—with which many Jews of the second generation could "not come to terms" (Broder and Lang 1979, 11)—was to be altered. Ultimately the "gruff milieu-naturalism" (Koch 1990, 140) of Rafael Seligmann's novel *Rubinsteins Versteigerung* (The Auctioning of Rubinstein, 1988,) and the "brutish gesture" (Eke 2002, 90) in Maxim Biller's stories were grounded in the desire provokingly to dispense with that mode of nonexchange. This impulse was paired with a motif that Biller himself later identified in the following manner: to the extent that "the emergence of the 'young' literary discourse was understood as a reaction in opposition to the tradition of assimilation" (Nolden 1995, 72), the works and aesthetic concepts of the Jewish authors who were poetically and/or biographically committed to that tradition and its universalistic disposition could no longer figure as ideals. This held all the more true when "the younger generation became increasingly convinced about the necessity of a disassociation from the dominant culture" (Lorenz 2002, 153). Beyond that, a "rupture in the history of reception" (Nolden 1995, 79) separated representatives of the young Jewish literature from the elder authors and the tradition that they maintained in their writings. Neither the subject-historical experience[7] of persecution and destruction nor the question of whether literature after Auschwitz was possible—factors that constitutively determined the literary works of authors such as Celan, Sachs, and Hildesheimer[8]—could serve as starting points for writers of the second generation. They no longer shared the key experience. The question of "whether" had metamorphosed into the question of "how" (Nolden 1995, 139).

Yet a fourth aspect came into play as well. Sander Gilman has pointed out to what extent the West German public sphere had perceived any identification of an author as "Jewish" as a particularity from which no universally valid content could issue forth: "Admittedly, that Jews can write about Jewish topics and nevertheless transcend these contents and become 'real' authors—which, in the terminology of liberalism, means writers with 'universal' topics—would question the liberal notion that all particularism is bad." According to this perspective, a "Jewish writer" is either "an unacceptable, even racist category" (Gilman 1988, 293) or an author of decidedly particularistic representations depicting something like religious or folkloristic customs (Loewy 1980, 614). In this sense, the "category of the 'Jewish writer'"—as Gilman rightly emphasizes—was banished from the West German public sphere. Gilman was thinking of such authors as Saul Bellow, Bernard Malamud, and Philip Roth.

The challenges posed by this variously determined starting point were met by the generation of young Jewish writers in a variety of ways. By not even so much as hinting at any topic other than the current lives of Jews in Germany, the previously mentioned texts by Seligmann and Biller—as well as Lea Fleischmann's *Dies ist nicht mein Land: Eine Jüdin verläßt die Bundesrepublik* (This Is Not My Country: A Jewess Leaves the Federal Republic, 1979)—set examples of a type of writing that demonstratively broke the commandment to adhere to universalism. However, shortly thereafter the American representatives of the "category of the 'Jewish writer'" (as Gilman described it) were looked upon as models. The results were ambivalent. The historical and current social circumstances and conditions of this literature in the United States differed completely from those in Germany.

A highly charged field in and through which contemporary literature written in German by Jews has moved and continues to move is generated by the desire to talk about Jews in the here and now while simultaneously fulfilling the demand placed on literature to accomplish more than merely helping to express the concrete social situation of a "minority,"[9] however complex and burdened that situation might be. A closer look at the writings of five of this literature's most important representatives reveals how these authors variously responded to this desire and navigated through this field.

Maxim Biller was first introduced to the German public as the author of the column "100 Zeilen Hass" (100 Lines of Hate), which was initially published in 1986 in the magazine *Tempo*. While the title leaves little doubt that the impulse of hate is programmatic for the column, it also indicates that the hatred in question might be randomly targeted at whatever topics and/or individuals attract Biller's animosity. The column did, in fact, address an array of subjects, many of which had no specific bearing on relations between Germans and Jews. However, in Biller's later work, as a representative of young Jewish literature, hate became a more specific motif. Indeed, "hate as a source of truth and honesty" (Schruff 2000, 66), "fury as a fermentation of enlightenment" (Eke 2002, 90), and Biller's "brutish gesture" (104) are decisive for his literary production. They are required aspects of an attempt to find "a contra style of writing against the German Jewish discourse of overcoming [the past]" (90). Beyond questions of psychological motivation, the political and cultural status of the hate that Biller brings into play can only be recognized in terms of its opposition to the culture of reconciliation that determined German Jewish relations throughout the postwar period. For instance, the final scene of Lessing's eighteenth-century play *Nathan der Weise* (Nathan the Wise) with its "wordless repetition of all-around embraces" (Lessing 1979, 347) was celebrated not only as allegedly indisputable proof of a onetime German Jewish symbiosis but Nathan's "wise sufferance" was also looked upon,"sometimes implicitly and sometimes explicitly, as a promising precondition for future relations between Germans and Jews (Fischer 2000, 143).[10] In connection with contemporary Jewish literature, to admit hatred into the picture meant, first and fore-most, to break decisively with a precept that had not facilitated any fundamental change in the situation of Jews in Germany for over four decades.

In Biller's collections of short stories entitled *Wenn ich einmal reich und tot bin* (When I Am Finally Rich and Dead, 1990) and *Land der Väter und Verräter* (Land of the Fathers and Betrayers, 1994), "reckoning up with the fathers" (Eke 92) whose "lies . . . destroyed the lives of their sons" (93) is a central concern. In depicting their precarious existence in postwar Germany, Biller draws attention to numerous striking "deadlocks, self-deceptions and bigotries" (Strümpel 1995, 3) in the lives of Jews and non-Jews. As Jan Strümpel has emphasized, if sensi-bilities are stepped on in the process, this is done with the aim of "destroying the 'aura' that makes the Jewish survivor of the Holocaust into a better human being for both Jews and non-Jews" (4).

To this extent, Biller emphatically committed himself to a form of realism he attempted to legitimize in various poetic statements. Understood as a "con-nection between journalism and literature," Biller offensively positioned his con-cept of realism against "bloodless intellectualism" and "the self-gratifying stub-bornness of the old-avant-garde and the nomenclaturalists of literature" (1991, 34). He characterized his concept of realism even more clearly in an attack against the "wimpy literature" of the present, where he sees "dozens of paper corpses . . . that want nothing, hate nothing, love nothing, that can't fall, can't cry, can't kill. Their story lines can't—in the sense of Aristotelian catharsis—shock, sweep away, stir up anybody" (2000a, 49). This aesthetic understanding, which sees catharsis as an indispensable tool of literary elucidation, has rightly been referred to as "premodern" (Eke 2002, 104). Indeed, in reading Biller's works—including his *Harlem Holocaust* (1998) and *Die Tochter* (The Daughter, 2000)—the question arises as to whether such determined avoidance of the in-novations of literary modernity can muster sufficient artistic means to represent the constantly changing forms and effects of the precarious "negative symbiosis" between Jews and Germans that Biller subjects to such scrutiny.

In his novel *Rubinsteins Versteigerung* Rafael Seligmann claimed to have presented the first "fictitious document about the feelings and thoughts of German postwar Jews" (1991, 146). He regarded prior writings of Jews in postwar Germany as having been "hatred-sterile" (78). Relating this to a "vic-tim and reconciler role" that Jews had played, he argued that "this Nathan cli-ché" finally needed to be "sacrificed" (36). Seligmann's first novel, which re-volves around the erotic and sexual desires of a twenty-year-old Jew in present-day Germany, demonstratively dispenses with this formerly binding notion. Sander Gilman's observation that the book projects a "'Rothian' tone" (1995, 49) and allows a "Rothian world" (52) to arise indicates that Seligmann's poetic endeavor might represent a renewal of the "category of the 'Jewish writer'" (Gilman 1988, 271). Yet, as Hartmut Steinecke points out, even in Seligmann's *Der Musterjude* (The Exemplary Jew, 1997), a "grotesque satire with autobiographical traces," the author omits "hardly a platitude or prejudice, spreading out the entire palette of anti-Semitic stereotypes. Certainly, Seligmann is also playing with this, but what selectively comes across as if in jest is tiring in the long run, for in his love of didacticism Seligmann is very German. That is why he explains to the reader quite clearly and repeatedly what he wishes to say to him" (2002, 167). The discourse-political merits of Seligmann's work, which are underscored by the interesting documents collected by the author himself in his book *Mit beschränkter Hoffnung* (With Limited Hope, 1991), should not be overlooked.

Since the eighties, when literature written by Jews in German first began to diversify decisively, other authors of the second generation have developed more advanced artistic means of expressing contemporary Jewish existence. Esther Dischereit is to be counted among the "most linguistically advanced" (Günther 2000, 4) representatives of contemporary Jewish literature. Whereas Maxim Biller is said to have unleashed "a contra style of writing against the German Jewish discourse of overcoming [the past]" (Eke 2002, 90), Dischereit unfolded an entire "contra aesthetics" (Breysach 2002, 111). This differentiation is reflected in the highly refined literariness of her writings, which operate on grounds far removed from the poetic suppositions of, say, Biller and Seligmann. Throughout her writings Dischereit remains fundamentally skeptical about the usefulness of all rational forms of expression. In a 1995 interview she stated: "With the lapsing of time, my notion about the importance of the political-rational word has changed. Today I no longer believe in the immediate enlightening value of words. This had its impact on the literature that I create" (Przyrembel 1995, 365). Dischereit's writing is legible as "radically subjective speech" (Oellers 2002, 75) that exercises a "subversive language game" in the form of a "literary experiment" (Shedletzky 1998, 223, 87). In *Joëmis Tisch: Eine jüdische Geschichte* (Joëmi's Table: A Jewish Story, 1988) this approach permits the expression of "shattered history as presently recalled" in the sense of a "liberation of that which has collected within, what is stored up, what is preserved, what was transformed again and again and will undergo new transformations" (Oellers 2002, 82). Syntax is not always adhered to because, as Norbert Oellers points out, "the rules are deactivated" (86). Such traces of disruption and woundedness are essential features of Dischereit's writing. According to Sander Gilman, "her works themselves are as highly fragmented as she senses Jewish and female identity to be" (1995, 60).

Itta Shedletzky has pointed out that "in Dischereit's texts the shard appears with increasing clarity and differentiation as a metaphor for a basic sense of being" (1998, 203). Shedletzky interprets the shard as "a poetic metaphor in a twofold sense: as a metaphor for the figurate representation of German Jewish–feminine existence in the present, and as a metaphor for poetic language, lyrical writing" (205). The manner in which Shedletzky writes out the metaphor of the shard with respect to the female Jewish figure in Dischereit's play *Ich ziehe mir die Farben aus der Haut* (I Extract My Colors from the Skin, 1992) applies to Dischereit's mode of writing as a whole: "Like the shard, it is injured and causes injury" (211). In Gilman's words: "Jews cannot be 'beautiful' in their representations of their tormented world" (1995, 67).

Committed as she was to literary modernity or, more precisely, to the "post-Shoah modernist German high culture" (Gilman 1995, 61) of, for instance, Christa Wolf's *Kassandra* and the avant-garde lyricism of Friederike Mayröcker, Dischereit was never accused of "dirtying the nest," as was long the case in the internal Jewish debates over the works of Biller and Seligmann. No "reckoning up with the fathers" (Eke 2002, 92) stands at the core of her work, but rather a questioning of the entire "concept of an unequivocal personal identity" (Günther 2000, 3). Certainly, in his seemingly endless conundrums about the identities of his figures Biller also rebels against society's and the readers' desire to be able to assign subjects to a clearly defined position. For Dischereit "language remains the defining moment of the cultural experience" (Gilman 1995, 62). She grasps the *texts themselves* not merely as a tool for the expression of circumstances torn by crisis but as *their very staging grounds.* Since the author radically writes out this poetic premise, the circumstances are made experiential with greater immediacy than in Biller's realism. It appears that the "realistic" manner of writing was indispensable for the inception of contemporary Jewish literature, compelled as it was by an impulse to intervene. However, it was apparently not until the aesthetics of radical modernity were tapped into—as with Dischereit—that the existential reality of Jews in Germany of the second postwar generation could lastingly be anchored within a cultural memory whose formation and forms were integrally linked to the historical experience of Jews in Germany under the sign of modernity.

Barbara Honigmann, one of the most important Jewish authors of the second generation, spent her formative years in the German Democratic Republic. In terms of social and political circumstances, her background was vastly different from those of her contemporaries residing in West Germany. According to the Marxist tradition, historical anti-Judaism and anti-Semitism were perceived as offshoots of a "secondary contradiction" that would dissolve as soon as class issues were overcome in the proletarian revolution. At the same time, communism designates religion as "a wrong consciousness of the world" (Burgauer 1993, 165).[11] Marx himself held Judaism in disdain. A significant number of Jewish citizens of the GDR, many of whom considered themselves communists, had, in a manner of speaking, "surrendered" their Jewish identity. The few tiny communities that existed were under surveillance by the interior secret services. Although anti-Semitic excesses were suppressed, so was reporting about them. In the GDR problems between Jews and Germans could not be publicly addressed.

It was not until Jurek Becker's *Bronsteins Kinder* (Bronstein's Children, 1986) that the existence of Jews in the GDR—their daily lives and the problems they experienced in relating to non-Jewish citizens—were explicitly addressed in a novel. Becker's work introduced to the GDR what Tabori and Hilsenrath had accomplished within West Germany's discourse: a reversal in public utterances about relations between Germans and Jews. Beginning in the mid-eighties, the government of the GDR attempted to improve its relations with Jews both within and beyond its borders, but the country didn't outlive the process.

With the exception of her *Roman von einem Kinde* (Novel of a Child, 1986), Barbara Honigmann's publications appeared after the dissolution of the GDR in 1989–90. Nonetheless, in autobiographically resonant texts such as *Eine Liebe aus nichts* (A Love Made of Nothing, 1991) and *Damals, dann und danach* (Back Then, Then and Thereafter, 1999) Honigmann dealt quite extensively with the conditions of Jewish existence in the GDR, as well as with the diverse attempts to live out a—however blurred—Jewish identity under those restrictive circumstances. Unlike Biller, Seligmann, and Dischereit, Honigmann tapped into the literary traditions of German classicism and romanticism. As she has clearly stated: "I don't just write in German. The literature that formed and educated me is the German literature, and I draw connections to it in all that I write, to Goethe, to Kleist, to Grimm's fairy tales and to German romanticism. And I am well aware that all of these gentlemen were more or less anti-Semites, but that doesn't matter" (1999, 18). While most Jewish authors of the second generation in West Germany perceived these core traditions of German literature as having been contaminated, Honigmann did not allow herself to be inhibited by such reservations. Her proximity to German classicism might reflect the elevated status that the educational system and culture politics of the GDR assigned to that literary heritage. However, the drive toward universal expression that runs through German classicism might well have been appropriated by Honigmann when the focus of her work shifted from reflecting on the situation of Jews in the GDR to recognizing exile as the "basic experience" (Remmler 2002, 49) of her more recent writings. When in her tale *Soharas Reise* (Sohara's Journey, 1996) Honigmann explores how the experiences of flight and persecution differed between Ashkenazi and Sephardic Jews, she leaves no doubt that she is talking about Jews in Europe of the twentieth century. Nonetheless, it is precisely in this story, which recalls the death of a Jewish baby in the Holocaust, that Amir Eshel recognizes a "grammar of historical loss" (2002, 60). As evidence that this "grammar" can also be found in the literature of non-Jewish authors, Eshel cites Hans-Ulrich Treichel's novella *Der Verlorene* (The Lost One, 1998), in which war refugees from eastern Europe mourn the loss of their young son. Eshel finds that both experiences of violent loss resist any transformation into "a coherent, meaningful 'history'"; both traumas reject "any form of mimetic, i.e., organizing and rationalizing representation. . . . That the 'it' won't allow itself to be recounted in the form of an enlightening and enlightenment-oriented narration, i.e., as 'history' . . . bears evidence . . . of the ceaseless search that authors like Honigmann, Treichel, and other representatives of their generation undertook, striving to arrive at poetic forms of expression beyond the tradition of enlightenment that might do justice to this 'it'" (Eshel 72). Granted that Honigmann's writings deal with Jews from Germany (not so much *in* Germany) today, it remains equally apparent that they seek to link themselves with historically concrete realms of experience that are not exclusively Jewish. Karen Remmler has shown that under the particular circumstances of German literary reception after the dissolution of the GDR, such writing was exposed to considerable risks, especially that of being assimilated (2002, 57).

The division of Germany by the allies following World War II was perceived not only by Germany but also globally as "punishment" for the crimes committed by Germany during Nazi rule. Focusing on Berlin, where the division was most obvious, but thinking in terms that apply to the whole of Germany, Sander Gilman writes: "In the fantasy of many Jews, the Wall was somehow constructed as the physical embodiment of the Nazi defilement of the city. . . . What would happen to the sense of Jewish presence when the one living monument to the Shoah and to German guilt for the murder of the Jews, the Wall, vanished?" (1995, 64). Since "official Germany was desperately trying to disassociate itself from the very concept of collective guilt for the Shoah after reunification" (Remmler 2002, 30),[12] one might presume that the event of the Wall being torn down would register strongly in the literature of Jewish authors residing in Germany. Yet in his analysis of the writings of German-speaking Jewish authors of the second generation after 1990, Steinecke maintains that "the German turnabout" represents "a hardly relevant stage of history" (2002, 168). At times the events surrounding the reunification remain "entirely meaningless for the plot" (169)—as is the case in Honigmann's narrative *Soharas Reise.* At times they are "decidedly and almost demonstratively *not*" in any way topical, as in Chaim Noll's *Nachtgedanken über Deutschland* (Nocturnal Ruminations about Germany, 1992) and *Leben ohne Deutschland* (Life Without Germany, 1995). Yet it can also be said of the works that Biller, Seligmann, Dischereit, Fleischmann, Ulla Berkéwicz, Ronnith Neumann, Matthias Hermann, and Gila Lustiger wrote after 1990, that "the reunification and its consequences make for a side topic at most" (Steinecke 2002, 172). With regard to all of these authors, Steinecke finds that

on the whole " for the core issue of their belletristic works—the quest for a Jewish identity—the German developments of the 1990s play a comparatively small
role. Most of the central points of such a quest—Shoah, the silence of the parents'
generation, relations with Jews during 50 years of postwar Germany, daily and
new anti-Semitism, discussion of Israel—are intimately related to German history, but not especially to aspects of that history that came about after the unification or that have become critical since then" (173).

Conversely, the prose of Wladimir Kaminer, which more closely relates to
the events and consequences of the political shift in 1989–90 than the writings
of any other German-speaking Jewish author, is hardly concerned with the
"search for a Jewish identity" that Steinecke recognizes as "a core issue." Kaminer
was born in Moscow in 1967. He is one of the many Jews who immigrated to
Germany after the loosening of border restrictions and the gradual disintegration of the Soviet Union, a development that decisively altered the demographic
situation of Jews in Germany.[13] Adopting the compact literary form of the
feuilleton—as it was, for instance, masterfully rendered by Alfred Polgar in the
twenties but thereafter seldom practiced in German-speaking parts of the world
after 1945—Kaminer writes laconically yet mostly ironically about his experiences as a Russian-Jewish immigrant in Germany during the initial years of reunification.[14] His setting is Berlin, the city that registers the consequences of the
Wall's disappearance and the reunification experience like no other. Assuredly
Kaminer explicates the Jewish background of his very autobiographically situated first-person narrator. Moreover, in the first chapter of his celebrated debut
novel *Russendisko* (Russian Disco, 2000), entitled "Russen in Berlin" (Russians in
Berlin), Kaminer has the narrator recall the restrictions to which his Jewish parents were exposed in Moscow because of their religion. However, Kaminer also
ironically refers to the narrator and his friends, who arrived in Berlin in 1990, as
"the avant-garde of the first wave of emigrants" (2002, 12). In a brief description
of his initial impressions about being in Germany, the author writes: "The first
citizens of Berlin, whom we got to know, were Gypsies and Vietnamese" (25).
These lines immediately establish the perspective that remains formative for
Kaminer's writing: as an always curious, sometimes ethnographically inclined
observer, Kaminer gazes, for the most part lovingly, at a multi-ethnic subculture
of legal and illegal immigrants in a land that stubbornly refuses to recognize its
factual status as a country of immigrants.

In this subculture Jews from Russia are only one group among many. To
be sure, the experiences that once specifically defined contemporary Jewish
literature—such as the institutionalization of German-Jewish relations, the
German mode of *Vergangenheitsbewältigung,* and the torturous question of how
a Jew might lead an existence in the land of those who strove to decimate his
kind—are largely missing in Kaminer's socialization. He was not living in

Germany during the decades between the Adenauer era and the second Gulf War. But now he is. To the same degree that the influx of Russian Jewish immigrants has altered Jewish existence in Germany in social terms, Kaminer's oeuvre appears paradigmatic in literary terms. This is no by means merely because of the demographic impact of Russian Jews immigrating to Germany and the history they bring with them. As precisely and "particularly" as Kaminer paints the experiences of the Russian Jewish narrator, those same experiences are simultaneously recognizable as part of a universal experience: transnational, trans-ethnic, and transcultural movement and encounter in the twenty-first century.

While exile figures as the basic experience of Barbara Honigmann's writing, this experience being inseparably connected to loss, Kaminer's feuilletons, though acutely sensitive to and aware of the immigrants' pain and sadness, decisively hinge on the experience of the fullness and diversity of energies released as the immigrants seek to live their lives. Potentially they all share an attribute that Kaminer makes so very productive in his literature, namely, a clarity of perspective regarding the state of affairs in Germany that comes from living and observing as an outsider. Revelations about the Germans become recognizable in the many projections that Kaminer's alter ego draws upon itself. At one point he is asked to portray a Russian in a film about Stalingrad and, later, to characterize the situation of East European intellectuals in Berlin. Expecting results within a day, an editor for the culture section of a newspaper calls for "anything on the topic of youth culture" (2002, 90). After hours of fruitless pondering and watching MTV, the narrator determines in a follow-up phone call that the editor meant " Jewish culture, not youth culture" (93). Kaminer is quite aware of the fact that the German majority culture continues to try to assign "the Jew" to a specific place—socially, culturally, and in terms of discourse politics. Nevertheless, it appears that there is no Jewish author, writing in German, belonging to the same generation who remains so unaffected by this pressure.

In 1986 the editors of *Babylon* presented the following programmatic notion: "We don't so much want to express ourselves as representatives of a—depending on your perspective—religious/social/ethnic minority, but instead as universally oriented intellectuals who wish to step beyond the particularities of origins while reflecting on them without denying them" (7). The foregoing overview of some of the exceptional works of contemporary Jewish literature has shown that even the most remarkable paradigmatic efforts of Jewish writers belonging to the second generation in Germany were not fully able to realize this universal aim. However, there are indications that this aim has been met through very different poetic approaches: Dischereit's radical modernism, Honigmann's link to German classicism and romanticism, and Kaminer's feuilleton make it appear that the category of the "Jewish writer" has quite unexpectedly remerged again—this time in Germany. In and through their literature these authors speak unambiguously about the existence of Jews in present-day Germany while simultaneously addressing the subject of contemporary society and engaging the reader with the immediacy of their approach.

Translated by Timothy K. Boyd

NOTES

1. See note 4 for an example. Among others, Karl Marx (editor of the *Jüdische Allgemeine Zeitung*) and Hans Joachim Schoeps (a well-known scholar) were often used to validate the claim that West Germany had successfully addressed its Nazi past.

2. For additional information concerning the scandals provoked by Tabori, see Braese 1996. On Hilsenrath see Braese 2001: 429–84.

3. In 1935 Globke had coauthored an official commentary on the Nuremberg Laws. Nevertheless, in 1953 Adenauer appointed him to a prominent position in his administration.

4. In 1978 Werner Nachmann, who served as board chairman of the Central Consistory of Jews in Germany from 1965 until 1988, made a controversial statement honoring Filbinger, who had participated in the National Socialist judicial system of terror.

5. Ralph Giordano discusses the "predicaments and pains of conscience" (1990, 108) that weighed heavily on the Zentralrat during the Globke affair.

6. Dagmar Lorenz has examined the parents' silence in the writings of second-generation Jewish authors; see Lorenz 2002, 147–61. Sounding a contradictory note, Hannes Stein has declared: "The Jews aren't afraid of stories because in their families genocide was talked about" (1998, 406).

7. For an explanation of the Lacanian term "subject-historical," see Briegleb 1992.

8. For a discussion of the works of Paul Celan and Nelly Sachs, see Kremer 2003, 1:215–23 and 2:1067–74. For Hildesheimer, see Braese 2001, 223–320, 365–428, 485–515.

9. See the illuminating discussion in Nolden (1995, 66) of "minority" and "minor literature" as defined by Deleuze and Guattari.

10. Regarding Nathan's refusal to engage in the final embraces, see Simon 1991, 628.

11. Burgauer provides a great deal of information about the situation of Jews in the GDR.

12. The quote has been slightly altered.

13. Already in 1998 the number of Jews residing in Germany had more than doubled compared to 1990. According to Salomon Korn: "Since the German unification, the community of Jews in Germany, whose members had numbered approx. 30,000 up until 1990, grew to 75,000, i.e., 150%, largely due to the immigrants from the former Soviet Union, and it is foreseeable that there will soon be over 100,000" (1999, 151).

14. Regarding the literary form of the feuilleton—which should not be confused with the arts supplements of German daily newspapers—see Polgar 2003. For another current example of the revitalized feuilleton, see Loewy 2002.

WORKS CITED

Babylon. 1986. Editorial.1: 7–8.

Becker, Jurek. 1986. *Bronsteins Kinder.* Frankfurt am Main: Suhrkamp.

Berkéwicz, Ulla. 1992. *Engel sind schwarz und weiß.* Frankfurt am Main: Suhrkamp.

Biller, Maxim. 1990. *Wenn ich einmal reich und tot bin.* Cologne: Kiepenheuer und Witsch.

———. 1991a. *Die Tempojahre.* Munich: DTV.

———. 1991b. "Soviel Sinnlichkeit wie der Stadtplan von Kiel: Warum die neue deutsche Literatur nichts so nötig hat wie den Realismus—Ein Grundsatzprogramm." *Die Weltwoche* 30, July 25: 34.

———. 1994. *Land der Täter und Verräter.* Cologne: Kiepenheuer und Witsch.

———. 1998. *Harlem Holocaust.* Cologne: Kiepenheuer und Witsch.

———. 2000a. "Feige das Land, schlapp die Literatur: Über die Schwierigkeiten beim Sagen der Wahrheit." *Die Zeit,* April 13: 47–49.

———. 2000b. *Die Tochter.* Cologne: Kiepenheuer und Witsch.

Bodemann, Y. Michal. 1986. "Staat und Ethnizität: Der Aufbau der jüdischen Gemeinden im Kalten Krieg." In *Jüdisches Leben in Deutschland seit 1945,* ed. Micha Brumlik et al., 49–69. Frankfurt am Main: Jüdischer Verlag bei Athenäum.

———. 1996. *Gedächtnistheater: Die jüdische Gemeinschaft und ihre deutsche Erfindung.* Hamburg: Rotbuch.

Braese, Stephan. 1996. "Rückkehr zum Ort der Verbrechen: George Tabori in Deutschland." In *Das Politische im literarischen Diskurs: Studien zur deutschen Gegenwartsliteratur,* ed. Sven Kramer, 32–55. Opladen: Westdeutscher Verlag.

———. 2001. *Die andere Erinnerung: Jüdische Autoren in der westdeutschen Nachkriegsliteratur.* Berlin: PHILO.

———. 2002. "Überlieferungen: Zu einigen Deutschland-Erfahrungen jüdischer Autoren der ersten Generation." In *Deutsch-jüdische Literatur der neunziger Jahre: Die Generation nach der Shoah,* ed. Sander L. Gilman and Hartmut Steinecke, 17–28. Berlin: Schmidt.

Breysach, Barbara. 2002. "Dischereit, Esther." In *Metzler Lexikon der deutsch-jüdischen Literatur,* ed. Andreas B. Kilcher, 110–12. Stuttgart.

Briegleb, Klaus. 1992. "Vergangenheit in der Gegenwart." In *Gegenwartsliteratur seit 1968,* ed. Klaus Briegleb and Sigrid Weigel, 73–116. Munich: Hanser.

Broder, Henryk M., and Michel R. Lang. 1979. "Vorneweg." In *Fremd im eigenen Land: Juden in der Bundesrepublik,* ed. Henryk M. Broder and Michel R. Lang, 11–12. Frankfurt am Main: Fischer.

Brumlik, Micha. 1986. "Zur Identität der zweiten Generation deutscher Juden nach der Shoah in der Bundesrepublik." In *Jüdisches Leben in Deutschland nach 1945,* ed. Micha Brumlik et al., 172–77. Frankfurt am Main: Jüdischer Verlag bei Athenäum.

Burgauer, Erica. 1993. *Zwischen Erinnerung und Verdrängung: Juden in Deutschland nach 1945.* Reinbek: Rowohlt.

Dischereit, Esther. 1988. *Joëmis Tisch: Eine jüdische Geschichte.* Frankfurt am Main: Suhrkamp.

Eke, Norbert Otto. 2002. "'Was wollen Sie? Die Absolution?': Opfer- und Täterprojektionen bei Maxim Biller." In *Deutsch-jüdische Literatur der neunziger Jahre: Die Generation nach der Shoah,* ed. Sander L. Gilman and Hartmut Steinecke, 89–107. Berlin: Schmidt.

Eshel, Amir. 2002. "Die Grammatik des Verlusts: Verlorene Kinder, verlorene Zeit in Barbara Honigmanns 'Soharas Reise' und in Hans-Ulrich Treichels 'DerVerlorene.'" In *Deutsch-jüdische Literatur der neunziger Jahre: Die Generation nach der Shoah,* ed. Sander L. Gilman and Hartmut Steinecke, 59–74. Berlin: Schmidt.

Fischer, Barbara. 2000. *Nathans Ende? Von Lessing bis Tabori: Zur deutsch-jüdischen Rezeption von "Nathan der Weise."* Göttingen: Wallstein.

Fleischmann, Lea. 1979. *Dies ist nicht mein Land: Eine Jüdin verlässt die Bundesrepublik.* Hamburg: Hoffmann und Campe.

Gilman, Sander L. 1988. "Jüdische Literaten und deutsche Literatur: Antisemitismus und die verborgene Sprache der Juden am Beispiel von Jurek Becker und Edgar Hilsenrath." *Zeitschrift für deutsche Philologie* 107: 269–94.

———. 1995. *Jews in Today's German Culture.* Bloomington: Indiana University Press.

Giordano, Ralph. 1990. *Die zweite Schuld: Von der Last Deutscher zu sein.* Munich: Droemer Knaur.

Günther, Petra. 2000. "Esther Dischereit." In *Kritisches Lexikon zur deutschsprachigen Gegenwartsliteratur,* ed. Heinz Ludwig Arnold, 1–4. Munich: text + kritik.

Hermann, Matthias. 1998. *72 Buchstaben.* Frankfurt am Main: Suhrkamp.

Hildesheimer, Wolfgang. 1987. "Mein Judentum." In *Mein Judentum,* ed. Hans Jürgen Schultz, 219–29. Munich: DTV.

Hilsenrath, Edgar. 1977. *Der Nazi & der Friseur.* Berlin: Braun.

Honigmann, Barbara. 1986. *Roman von einem Kinde.* Darmstadt: Luchterhand.

———. 1991. *Eine Liebe aus nichts.* Berlin: Rowohlt.

———. 1996. *Soharas Reise.* Berlin: Rowohlt.

———. 1999. *Damals, dann und danach.* Munich and Vienna: Hanser.

Kaminer, Wladimir. 2002. *Russendisko.* Munich: Goldmann.

Koch, Gertrud. 1990. "Corporate Identities: Zur Prosa von Dische, Biller und Seligmann." In *Babylon* 7: 139–42.

Korn, Salomon. 1999. "Auf der Suche nach innerer Festigung: Über die Gefährdung der jüdischen Gemeinden in Deutschland und Europa—Ein Ausblick ins 21. Jahrhundert." In his *Geteilte Erinnerung: Beiträge zur "deutsch-jüdischen" Gegenwart,* 149–57. Berlin: PHILO.

Kremer, S. Lillian, ed. 2003. *Holocaust Literature: An Encyclopedia of Writers and Their Work.* 2 vols. New York: Routledge.

Lessing, Gotthold Ephraim. 1979. *Nathan der Weise.* In *Das dichterische Werk,* vol. 2, ed. Herbert G. Göpfert. Munich: DTV.

Loewy, Ernst. 1980. Review of *Mein Judentum,* ed. Hans Jürgen Schultz. *Jahrbuch des Instituts für deutsche Geschichte* 9: 613–22.

Loewy, Hanno. 2002. *Taxi nach Auschwitz.* Berlin: PHILO.

Lorenz, Dagmar C. G. 2002. "Erinnerung um die Jahrtausendwende: Vergangenheit und Identität bei jüdischen Autoren der Nachkriegsgeneration." In *Deutsch-jüdische Literatur der neunziger Jahre: Die Generation nach der Shoah,* ed. Sander L. Gilman and Hartmut Steinecke, 147–161. Berlin: Schmidt.

Lustiger, Gila. 1995. *Die Bestandsaufnahme.* Berlin: Aufbau.

Neumann, Ronnith. 1991. *Nirs Stadt.* Frankfurt am Main: Fischer.

Nolden, Thomas. 1995. *Junge jüdische Literatur: Konzentrisches Schreiben in der Gegenwart.* Würzburg: Königshausen und Neumann.

Noll, Chaim. 1992. *Nachtgedanken über Deutschland.* Reinbek: Rowohlt.

———. 1995. *Leben ohne Deutschland.* Reinbek: Rowohlt.

Oellers, Norbert. 2002. "'Sie holten mich ein, die Toten der Geschichte': Ansichten über Esther Dischereits 'Joëmis Tisch: Eine jüdische Geschichte.'" In *Deutsch-jüdische Literatur der neunziger Jahre: Die Generation nach der Shoah,* ed. Sander L. Gilman and Hartmut Steinecke, 75–88. Berlin: Schmidt.

Polgar, Alfred. 2003. *Das große Lesebuch.* Zurich: Kein und Aber.

Przyrembel, Alexandra. 1995. "Gespräch mit Esther Dischereit: 'Als Jüdin in Deutschland schreiben.'" *Die Neue Gesellschaft / Frankfurter Hefte* 4: 365–69.

Remmler, Karen. 2002. "Orte des Eingedenkens in den Werken Barbara Honigmanns." In *Deutsch-jüdische Literatur der neunziger Jahre: Die Generation nach der Shoah,* ed. Sander L. Gilman and Hartmut Steinecke, 43–58. Berlin: Schmidt.

Schruff, Helene. 2000. "Biller, Maxim." In *Metzler Lexikon der deutsch-jüdischen Literatur,* ed. Andreas B. Kilcher, 66–68. Stuttgart: Metzler.

Schultz, Hans Jürgen, ed. 1987. *Mein Judentum.* Munich: DTV.

Seligmann, Rafael. 1989. *Rubinsteins Versteigerung.* Frankfurt am Main: Eichborn.

———. 1991. *Mit beschränkter Hoffnung: Juden, Deutsche, Israelis.* Hamburg: Hoffmann und Campe.

———. 1997. *Der Musterjude.* Hildesheim: Claassen.

Shedletzky, Itta. 1998. "Eine deutsch-jüdische Stimme sucht Gehör: Zu Esther Dischereits Romanen, Hörspielen und Gedichten." In *In der Sprache der Täter: Neue Lektüren deutschsprachiger Nachkriegs- und Gegenwartsliteratur,* ed. Stephan Braese, 199–225. Opladen: Westdeutscher Verlag.

Simon, Ralf. 1991. "Nathans Argumentationsverfahren: Konsequenzen der Fiktionalisierung von Theorie in Lessings Drama 'Nathan der Weise.'" In *Deutsche Vierteljahresschrift für Literaturwissenschaft und Geistesgeschichte* 65: 609–35.

Stein, Hannes. 1998. "Schm'a Jisruel, kalt is ma in die Fiß." In *Deutsche Nachkriegsliteratur und der Holocaust,* ed. Stephan Braese et al., 401–411. Frankfurt am Main: Campus.

Steinecke, Hartmut. 2002. "'Geht jetzt wieder alles von vorne los?' Deutsch-jüdische Literatur der 'zweiten' Generation und die Wende." In *Deutsch-jüdische Literatur der neunziger Jahre: Die Generation nach der Shoah,* ed. Sander L. Gilman and Hartmut Steinecke, 162–73. Berlin: Schmidt.

Strümpel, Jan. 1995. "Maxim Biller." In *Kritisches Lexikon zur deutschsprachigen Gegenwartsliteratur,* ed. Heinz Ludwig Arnold, 1–5. Munich: text + kritik.

———. 2000. *Vorstellungen vom Holocaust: George Taboris Erinnerungs-Spiele.* Göttingen: Wallstein.

Tabori, George. 1981. *Die Kannibalen.* In *Unterammergau oder Die guten Deutschen,* 37–138. Frankfurt am Main: Suhrkamp.

Treichel, Hans-Ulrich. 1998. *Der Verlorene.* Frankfurt am Main: Suhrkamp.

TEXTS AVAILABLE IN ENGLISH

Becker, Jurek. 1996. *Jacob the Liar.* Trans. Leila Vennewitz. New York: Arcade.

———. 1999. *Bronstein's Children.* Trans. Leila Vennewitz. Chicago: University of Chicago Press.

Hildesheimer, Wolfgang. 1984. *The Jewishness of Mr. Bloom.* Frankfurt am Main: Suhrkamp.

———. 1987. *The Collected Stories of Wolfgang Hildesheimer.* Trans. Joachim Neugroschel. New York: Ecco.

Hilsenrath, Edgar. 1966. *Night.* Trans. Michael Roloff. Garden City, N.Y.: Doubleday.

———. 1971. *The Nazi & the Barber: A Tale of Vengeance.* Trans. Andrew White. Garden City, N.Y.: Doubleday.

———. 1990. *The Story of the Last Thought.* Trans. Hugh Young. London: Scribners.

Honigmann, Barbara. 2003. *A Love Made Out of Nothing* and *Zohara's Journey.* Trans. John Barrett. Boston: Godine.

———. 2005. "On My Great-Grandfather, My Grandfather, My Father, and Me." Trans.

Meghan W. Barnes. In *Voices of the Diaspora: Jewish Women Writing in Contemporary Europe,* ed. Thomas Nolden and Frances Malino, 123–34. Evanston, Ill.: Northwestern University Press.

Kaminer, Wladimir. 2002. *Russian Disco: Tales of Everyday Lunacy on the Streets of Berlin.* Trans. Michael Huise. London: Ebury Press.

Lappin, Elena, ed. 1994. *Jewish Voices, German Words: Growing up Jewish in Postwar Germany and Austria.* North Haven, Conn.: Catbird.

Lustiger, Gila. 2001. *The Inventory.* Trans. Rebecca Morrison. New York: Arcade.

Tabori, George. 1974. *The Cannibals.* London: Davis-Poynter.

———. 1996. "Mein Kampf." In *Contemporary Drama: Germany,* ed. Carl Weber, 37–85. Baltimore, Md.: Johns Hopkins University Press.

THREE

~

ELRUD IBSCH

Remembering or Inventing the Past: Second-Generation Jewish Writers in the Netherlands

Immediately following World War II the Dutch tried to come to terms with the German occupation by emphasizing the sufferings they had endured while at the same time fostering the hope that their newly acquired freedom would change everything. The war was seen as a struggle between good and evil. Although it was impossible to ignore the fact that there had been collaborators in the Netherlands who were to be punished accordingly, the majority of the Dutch population was thought to have resisted the German occupier and National Socialism. On the whole, the Dutch conceived of their nation's role in the war as benign. It must be granted that there was a fairly well organized resistance movement in the Netherlands which helped many Jews go into hiding and escape deportation. The countless acts of sabotage, counterfeiting identity papers, and sporadic armed resistance are well known. Postwar literature glorified the heroic aspects of the resistance movement. Most of these writings have now been forgotten, not least because authors such as Simon Vestdijk and W. F. Hermans ironically qualified the importance of the resistance movement in their fiction (Anbeek 1986; Hettema 2002).

A rude awakening occurred in the sixties and seventies, when documents gradually surfaced indicating that the number of Dutch Jews who had been deported and murdered was very high in comparison to other European countries (Presser 1965; de Jong 1969–89). In his article on the persecution of Jews in the Netherlands historian Hans Blom writes: "The high percentage of Jews from the Netherlands, around 75%, who perished as a result of Nazi policies is on a par only with the figures for eastern Europe and stands in stark contrast to neighboring western European countries, where the percentages were much lower" (1989, 333). This happened despite a high level of integration of most Dutch Jewry and the fact that the Netherlands had never upheld a clearly anti-Semitic tradition. Blom offers up the hypothesis that the illusion of safety harbored by the Jewish population in the Netherlands was one of the reasons for their vulnerability. Both Blom and von der Dunk (1990) have attempted to explain the shameful situation by referring to particular circumstances, such as the legalistic tradition of the Dutch people, which was at odds with acts of sabotage; the dense population of the country; its geophysical and geographical situation; and the particularly severe occupation policy. Arthur Seyss-Inquart, who belonged to the hardliners of the Austrian Nazi elite, was nominated Reichsbevollmächtigter in the Netherlands. Moreover, recent Jewish immigrants from Germany, who came to the Netherlands after 1933, were poorly integrated and could easily be identified by their German accent.

In the course of the sixties the Dutch lost their innocence. The historical cliché that they did not live in an anti-Semitic nation was overshadowed by a growing awareness that they had failed to show sufficient solidarity with their Jewish compatriots and had unconsciously placed part of the responsibility for their own sufferings on the Jews. The mechanism of "blaming the victim" was at work. As Evelien Gans (2002) has shown, many Dutchmen complained about the ingratitude of the Jews who were in hiding.

The Jewish survivors of the concentration camps who returned to the Netherlands hoping for a new beginning were confronted with disappointments. Their reception was often far from cordial and the Dutch were hardly interested in listening to their experiences in captivity. In a considerable number of cases it was difficult, if not impossible, to reclaim property the Jews had left with friends and neighbors for safekeeping—not to mention the traumatic situations which arose when foster parents, who for several years had protected Jewish children, reacted with barely concealed hostility when Jewish parents reclaimed their children.

After the war the Dutch population, both Jews and non-Jews alike, had the same desire, namely, to forget the past and begin a new life. For the Jews this meant, first and foremost, not to be conspicuous,, not to manifest exceptionality, of which the yellow star had been the deadly symbol. Author Andreas Burnier, pseudonym for Catharina Irma Dessaur, professor of criminology at the University of Nijmegen, recalled that "after liberation I belonged to the generation of Jewish children who had gone into hiding and developed fear and resistance

with respect to all things Jewish. For being Jewish in fact meant, after a decep-
tively nice childhood, to be persecuted" (quoted in Meijer 1998, 51).

Speaking about literature as a specific form of cultural memory, one notes
that the first literary reactions to the traumatic experiences of the Holocaust are
autobiographies written by eyewitnesses. There are, of course, significant differences with respect to the subjective positions, perspectives, and narrative techniques within this genre, but the authenticity and documentary value of these
writings are indisputedly a common factor. Among the Dutch eyewitnesses,
Abel Herzberg and Gerhard L. Durlacher should be mentioned. Herzberg was
imprisoned in Bergen-Belsen. His book *Tweestromenland* (Between Two Streams:
A Diary from Bergen-Belsen, 1989) has been widely translated. Durlacher survived Auschwitz. He broke his silence and began to write only many years after
the war. To recapture life after having been condemned to death was an enormous task which could be fulfilled only after the author had realized that his attempts to suppress his painful memories had failed. Once the silence was broken,
Durlacher published several highly impressive books.

The second and third generations of the victims, however, are faced with a
different situation. They experienced the trauma of the Holocaust as children
growing up with parents who basically tried to hide their past sufferings. The
children had to live with the tension created by being excluded from a crucial
segment of their parents' lives, on the one hand, and their own desire to be included, on the other. Those who became writers later felt compelled to write
their own stories. Here, too, the autobiographical element cannot be denied.
Nevertheless, with the passage of time the commitment to achieve documentary authenticity diminishes. These young writers have gradually attempted
to free themselves from the generic restrictions of the eyewitness, claiming
their own way to remember—or invent—the history of their parents and
grandparents. The Holocaust as a theme becomes "available" for "those who
were not there" (Sicher 1998), a situation which favors strategies of fictionalization. These young writers are free to choose a genre, a poetic program, a new
language, and to explore their own limits of representation. The selection of
genres and the combination of themes are no longer subordinated to an unam-
biguous final meaning. Whether the younger generations should write in a realistic, grotesque, ironic, or postmodernist mode depends on their own preferences. Just as no one will deny them the right to find their own voices, so no
one will deny the reader the right to respond in his or her own way. Unlike
other fiction, the fictionalization of the Shoah refers to undeniable historical
facts, in this case the history of suffering and intellectual disaster which is in-
delibly inscribed in the Jewish cultural memory. Writers must assume that
their representations will be juxtaposed against the factual knowledge of the
events their readers possess. Literary experiments with respect to the Shoah are

based on the assumption that readers possess sufficient historical knowledge; otherwise additional pedagogical instruction seems a necessity.[1]

For the purposes of this essay I have chosen texts by Dutch Jewish writers who were either young children during World War II or were born after the war. One of the consequences of such a selective approach is that the stories of older writers, such as the "grand old lady" Marga Minco, or the well-known diaries of Anne Frank and Etty Hillesum are not dealt with here.

Contemporary Dutch Jewish authors are not minority writers. They are part of the mainstream just like such prewar Jewish writers as Herman Heijermans, one of the founders of Dutch naturalism; Jacob Israel de Haan, one of the first to introduce the theme of homosexuality in Dutch literature; and his sister, Carry van Bruggen, who, through the critical reception by Menno ter Braak, contributed to the introduction of literary modernism in the Netherlands. Together with non-Jewish authors, contemporary Dutch Jewish writers are active in the literary arena and are praised and criticized by Jewish and non-Jewish critics alike. They never write exclusively for a Jewish public. They are read by non-Jews and receive literary prizes by non-Jewish juries. One reason may be that, as in the work of such celebrated non-Jewish authors as Simon Vestdijk and W. F. Hermans, World War II figures as a prominent theme. The same applies to Harry Mulisch, perhaps the most outstanding contemporary writer in the Netherlands, who is partly Jewish yet never conceived of himself as a Jewish author, nor was he classified by critics as belonging to that group. Mulisch was fascinated by German culture, in particular by romanticism as a German phenomenon, and by larger-than-life historical figures such as Hitler and Eichmann. Another reason for the fully integrated position of contemporary Dutch Jewish authors may be that they were not in need of any justification for their participation in cultural life, unlike German Jewish writers, who, as Thomas Nolden (1995) has argued, had lived and worked under the pressure of legitimating their return to Germany.

The majority of the literary texts referred to in this essay bear the hallmark of autobiographical writing, which remains close to the narrative principles of psychological realism. This applies in particular—but not exclusively—to the work of female writers. However, such ostensible fictional and formal innovations as experiments with time and space, fragmented or multiple identities, as well as other aspects of postmodernist writing have until recently only be found in the writings of male authors.

Remembering the Jewish Experience

The following principal themes may be found in the predominantly autobiographical texts:

The obligation to succeed in life. Parents who survived the concentration camps or had been in hiding see in their children the validation of their own past and future lives. They have great expectations for them to succeed in life and are convinced that they will express a sense of gratitude and devotion to their parents, who enabled them to live. In a sense, the children are living "memorial candles."

The past is silenced. In order not to impede the expected success of their children, as well as to forget their own sufferings, parents hardly speak about what they have gone through. They shelter their children from their traumatic past. The children, however, often feel embarrassed by the lack of information about their parents' wartime experiences, a situation which easily becomes a source of intergenerational conflict.

Emotional problems with a new father or mother. If only one parent survived, he or she may decide to remarry and have children with the new partner. The children who suffered through a double separation—first from their own father or mother, then from their foster parents after the period spent in hiding—encounter difficulties in accepting a new father or mother, who is often non-Jewish and is reluctant to listen to the stories about a tragic past.

The desire to bury Jewish identity. The attempt not to be recognized as a Jew leads to an aggressive denial of one's Jewish identity in some cases.

In her autobiographical work *Het jongensuur* (The Time of the Boy, 1969), which tells the story of a child in hiding, Andreas Burnier emphasizes not the Jewish identity of the young girl she is describing but rather the contradiction between her wish to be a boy and the reality of being a girl. With respect to her character's Jewishness, Burnier merely states that this identity had been forced upon her by others.

Brief aan mijn moeder (Letter to My Mother), by Ischa Meijer (1943–1995), was published in 1974. This forthright analysis of the consequences resulting from the humiliations and sufferings endured by an infant and his parents in Westerbork and Bergen-Belsen was received with great ambivalence. Meijer unmasks the idea, maintained by many civilized and religious people, that suffering can have a purifying effect on human beings. The long "letter" written by the adult son represents a vehement complaint against his mother. The words she has spoken to him are set off in italics, a formal feature which conveys the impression of an irrevocable past. The son is incapable of detaching himself from her words—or from her motherhood. The common past in the camps, which had strengthened the ties between mother and child, had simultaneously reduced the distance that is a necessary precondition for the proper education of a child. The attitude of the parents toward their son is ambiguous. On the one hand, the child is the undeniable proof of their survival and source of their hopes. On the other hand, he is looked upon as a witness to their humiliations. As he confesses: "The hatred which unites you [i.e., father and mother] and which has its roots in a dark past of which I had been the witness, was—consciously or unconsciously—transferred to me without compassion: I knew too much" (48–49). There was never any discussion of their shared experiences.

The novel *Voor bijna alles bang geweest* (Living in Fear), by Lisette Lewin, was published in 1989 as the debut work by the then fifty-year-old writer. All four themes previously mentioned are combined in her tale. The mother of Emma Morgenblatt, the main character, was murdered. Her father survived and married a non-Jewish woman. In order not to shock his new wife, the father is unwilling to speak about the traumatic past endured by himself and his family, leaving his daughter with a sense of rootlessness. Reluctantly Emma had left the house of her gentile foster parents, where she had lived in hiding during the war and where she felt at home, and now considers the members of her surviving Jewish family as strangers. She develops a strong resistance against Judaism and dislikes being identified as a Jewish girl because of her physiognomy. Her Jewish background fills her with shame as a student, and she cannot accept the fact that her friends (who are both Jewish and non-Jewish) expect her to be interested in the cultural and historical contexts of Judaism. Emma does not succeed in establishing a stable relationship with men. After a period of addiction to alcohol, she finally ends up as a psychiatric patient. Lisette Lewin cites Rousseau in order to explain why she felt the need to relate the story of her shattered identity: "Je sais bien que le lecteur n'a pas grand besoin de savoir tout cela, mais j'ai besoin, moi, de le lui dire" (I know very well that the reader has no great desire to know all this, but I feel the need to express it). Like Ischa Meijer, for Lisette Lewin the text functions as a form of therapy. The style of both authors is emotional and direct.

Emotionality and directness are characteristics of what I call "therapeutic writing." As young children both Meijer and Lewin had undergone traumatic experiences which, as Dori Laub argues, take place beyond "normal reality."[2] Consequently, writing is regarded as a means of regaining the parameters of "reality" as well as a sense of self-acceptance. This, however, did not allow these authors to dissociate themselves from their painful memories and to switch to an extensive stylistic elaboration, including irony and the tempering possibilities of fiction.

Compared with Lewin, Chaja Polak describes feelings and emotions in a more indirect way. A survivor who hid during the war, in *Tweede vader* (Stepfather, 1996) she tells the admittedly autobiographical story of a girl named Fanny who apparently is unable to establish an emotional relationship with her stepfather, whom her mother married after her first husband was killed in the camp. The novel begins as follows: "A man falls in love with a woman, whose name is Salka [mother of Fanny]. He knew her already but he meets her again" (7). Concealed beneath this outwardly neutral description is the child's fear that the intimacy of the mother-daughter relationship will be disturbed. However, there is still more. The grown-up Fanny, now the divorced mother of a son, reflects on the past in order to discover the truth behind her relationship with her stepfather. It is not jealousy that prevented her from admitting that she actually liked him but rather her fear of betraying her biological father, whom she had never really known. She sees herself as the only person who is unconditionally devoted to her father, now that her mother has remarried and given birth to twins. Her faithfulness does not leave room for another person even if this proves painful for herself and the other. With great effort Fanny tries to keep her stepfather at a distance, although she senses that he likes her and wants to be a father to her. Following his untimely death, she asks herself: "Why had nobody ever told me that I could have loved Dries [the stepfather] without doing anything wrong with respect to the memory of my own father?" (59). Within the family the past had been silenced. Her mother and Dries had never told her that they had been interned in the camp together with her father, Leo, Salka and Leo because they were Jews and Dries because he was a Communist. The novel is alternately written in the first and third person, depending on whose feelings are being reported, Fanny's or those belonging to others.

Chaja Polak's stylistic qualities are remarkable. Without being too explicit, she succeeds in convincing the reader that the three main characters—Fanny, Dries, and Salka— love each other despite the emotional resistance evidenced by the child. The ambiguity of longing for love, on the one hand, and resisting love, on the other, is stylistically sustained throughout the text and heightens its literary quality.

Chaja Polak's novel *Over de grens* (Beyond the Border, 2001) was a finalist for the prestigious Libris prize. The novel is comprised of chapters that function as distinct short stories without a narrative continuum. The character named Rosa, who is a child in the first story and a divorced woman in the last one, provides the necessary connective tissue. Once again faithfulness toward human beings who did not survive the genocide is among the main themes. In one of the stories, for example, Rosa learns that she is looked upon as a substitute child by her parents and was named after her murdered sister. She finally understands why her father had never called her by her name. Although naming a child after a deceased family member is part of the Jewish tradition, in the case of Holocaust victims this tradition elicits embarrassing and painful memories. Another story relates how a man remains faithful to a young girl whom he had promised to marry when they were children. She never returned after her deportation. Although Rosa senses that this man appreciates her company and likes talking to her about his early love, she simultaneously feels that he can never be her lover: their relationship exists exclusively within the boundaries established by the memory of his former girl friend.

The last example drawn from among the group of authors born before or during the war is the poet and playwright Judith Herzberg, daughter of Abel Herzberg.[3] In her play *Leedvermaak* (The Wedding Party, 1991), which was also made into a film, Holocaust survivors appear to have successfully forgotten the past and are living a comfortable life. The play is set in the seventies and recounts how couples marry, divorce, and remarry—the ex-wives and their former husbands remain friends and are each other's party-guests—which is no problem at all. However, at the wedding party of Lea, the play's main protagonist, the strained relations between Lea's mother and her non-Jewish foster mother during her period of hiding prove that the past can never be denied. Herzberg sharply observes and ironically describes the various characters. Unlike Polak, whose analytical descriptions do not result in irony, Herzberg employs commonplaces and stereotypes that function as ironic echoes. Her stylistic repertoire includes everyday descriptions, bureaucratic advice, and commonplace talk (for example, the philo-Semitic opinions of the foster-mother). However, despite the author's apparent intellectual mastery of the past, a subtle emotional subtext nevertheless remains. For instance, it surfaces when Lea says: "If I had a child I'd take it with me, I'd keep it with me, I'd take it everywhere I went. I'd soothe it just by holding it against me. I can't imagine it: let's give the child to someone else" (105). Clearly there is no irony intended here.

Turning to authors born after the war, Carl Friedman,[4] a female author, published her first novel *Tralievader* (Nightfather) in 1991.[5] The main character, the father, is the very antithesis of other father figures discussed thus far. Whereas in the previous texts the silenced past often appeared to be a source of conflict, the tension gnerated in Friedman's *Nightfather* are to the result of the father's continuous talking about his camp experiences. The novel consists of brief chapters depicting the daily lives of the children, whose moments of carefree childhood are repeatedly overshadowed and spoiled by their father's recollections about the concentration camp in which he was detained. During mealtimes, while playing games, or while driving in the car—in short, at all family gatherings—the father uses the slightest pretext to recount his traumas, with the result that all daily objects and perceptions lose their innocence. The narrative perspective is that of the daughter, a girl of primary school age. The father, of course, speaks the language of an adult eyewitness, including code words used in the concentration camp. The resultant lopsided communication is responsible for numerous misunderstandings. The children take the expressions he uses literally or are unable to grasp their semantic range. As a literary procedure, however, the the unequal cognitive abilities of the young children and their father convincingly illustrates the abyss that separates normal family life from the abnormal living conditions in the concentration camp.

In the course of the novel the father increasingly assumes the role of the narrator. The language and the life of the children disappear, as it were, behind the verbiage and past history of the father.

Jessica Durlacher, daughter of Gerhard Durlacher and wife of Leon de Winter (whose work is discussed below), achieved success both in the Netherlands and in Germany with her novel *De dochter* (The Daughter, 2000). Notwithstanding the title, which seems to favor an autobiographical reading, the daughter in question is not the daughter of Gerhard but a fictional character. Of course, autobiographical elements are not completely absent from the novel, but they are reflected in the psychological traits of some of the characters rather than on the narrative level. The plot, which is not free from clichés, can be summarized briefly. A young woman who adores her father, believing him to be a survivor of the Holocaust, discovers that he is a liar and has lived under a false identity and, consequently, that she is the daughter of a perpetrator. Without explaining herself, she decides to leave Max, her lover, who happens to be the son of a survivor.

What makes the novel a near masterpiece, however, is not the plot but the narrative perspective and the stylistic abilities of the author. The narrator of the novel is Max—a wise decision in that it permits a female author to free herself from the constraints of her gender identity. At the same time, this choice offers her the possibility of maintaining a certain distance, a space of strangeness, between herself and Sabine, the main female character. From the very beginning of their friendship, Max finds Sabine's behavior somewhat puzzling and cannot understand her fully. For example, he cannot grasp why she insists on talking about the traumas of the Holocaust, emphasizing the Jewish identity of their families, and founding their relationship on the shared history of the genocide. Both Sabine and his own father break the silence which had sheltered the Holocaust experience from Max's world. The motif of silencing the past, which is a recurrent one in the writings of the younger generation, belongs to the life experiences of Jessica Durlacher. In an earlier essay she wrote: "After the publication of his [her father's] book we were bewildered and even offended. All these things about himself, about his parents, about the camps, he suddenly could communicate to others" (1994, 11). Max's father, who had never previously talked about his traumatic experiences, suddenly begins to talk about them following the visit of his sister, Judith, and even more so after her death and funeral in Jerusalem. Max's relationship with his father changes in the sense that he now understands that his father's life had been deeply influenced by his experiences in the camp and that he is much more vulnerable than his son had ever imagined.

Sabine repeatedly tells Max the story of (what she then still believes to be) her "heroic" father. She relates how a boy in hiding at a farm falls in love with a Jewish girl who is also living there. Driven by jealousy, the son of the farmer tries to make love to the girl, but she does not accept him. Finally, the farmer's son commits a heinous act by revealing that there are Jews at the farm, who are subsequently arrested and deported.

Following her sudden disappearance after discovering that her father is a liar, Sabine resolves to end her relationship with Max. In a letter she entreats him not to make any effort to find her. When, after several years, they happen to meet at the Frankfurt Book Fair, they sense that they are still in love with each other. However, an elderly man named Sam, an American Jew born in the Netherlands, not only accompanies Sabine but also lives not far from her home in California. Max is uncertain about their relationship and feels that any inquiries are impossible. Something unreliable and unexplained threatens the friendship between Max and Sabine even during his subsequent visit to the United States. Only when he reads the manuscript of Sam's autobiography—Max, in the meantime, has become a publisher and is considering bringing out the book on the Dutch market—does he uncover the secret: Sam was the Jewish boy in hiding; while Sabine's father was the traitor, the son of the farmer. The novel's conclusion suggests that the worlds of the child of the victim and that of the perpetrator are not completely separate. There is a telephone call during which silence predominates. Max is given the final words: "Sabine, can you forgive me?"

Arnon Grunberg represents the youngest authors of the second generation. He is the enfant terrible of the group and attracts young readers in particular. He loves to be in the limelight and thrives on provocation as a writer. He has stated that he is not interested in the problem of Jewish identity and feels those readers are misguided who think that he is addressing this problem in *Blauwe maandagen* (Blue Mondays, 1994). However, readers of this novel will find it difficult to agree with this statement. *Blue Mondays* deals with sex and alcohol, domestic quarrels, and school-related issues, but although the narrator-cum-protagonist refuses to appropriate the traumatic war experiences of his parents as an explanation for his own misbehavior, beneath the surface of confrontation and cynicism lie his attempts to survive (as a Jew) in an environment which he basically cannot trust. Is this not a fundamental problem of Jewish identity? For example, when his mother asks him why he is always so cynical, he replies: "I wasn't being cynical, I was being truthful. It's too bad the truth can end up sounding cynical, which is why you're often better off lying" (130). For Grunberg torrents of words are a means of preserving one's life. One of the whores the narrator frequents suggests: "Stop talking all the time. You don't have to go on about everything." Whereupon he replies: "I'm not much use unless I can talk" (138). This response can be taken as the author's poetic credo.

Beyond Psychological Realism:
Fictionalizing the Jewish Experience

If, after a period of silence, Holocaust survivors are capable of tentatively reex-
periencing their past within the categories of time, place, and sequence, they
may find the words to tell their life stories. At this point memory, the *mental
repetition* of a past experience, functions as a source of knowledge and communication. This type of repetitiveness is, of course, not identical with the actual
past experience since the chronological distance introduces selectivity and subtle transformations. The written manifestation of memory is autobiography. I
reserve the concept of *memory* for the reminiscences of those who themselves
experienced the concentration camps. For the remembering of the second and
third generations I propose the term *remembered history.* Since children (and
grandchildren) of survivors cannot mentally repeat the experiences of the
camps, they depend on the memorial narratives of their parents or other eyewitnesses. If there is no obvious storyteller, they have to search for traces in
books, visual images, and at the official *lieux de mémoire.* Remembered history
is the main source of remembrance for those authors discussed thus far.

Another stage in the process of writing the Holocaust is the *imagined history.*
As I previously mentioned, there are young Jewish authors who have managed to
free themselves from the traditional restrictions of Holocaust writing and have
narrated events which, if they happened at all, were transformed through pro-
cesses of de- and recontextualization. In many cases their fantasy contradicts
rather than echoes official historiography. Leon de Winter, Marcel Möring, and
Nol de Jong represent Jewish history and identity in a manner that can be characterized as postmodern from a literary-historical perspective.

In his novel *La Place de la Bastille* (1981) Leon de Winter explicitly turns
to a postmodernist philosophy of history. Beginning with his novel *Kaplan*
(1986), de Winter's writings (e.g., *SuperTex, Hoffman's honger, Zionoco, De hemel
van Hollywood, God's Gym*)—all of which deal with the theme of Jewish identity—became less sophisticated and consequently more accessible. The number of his readers is still growing, although some professional critics complain
about such concessions in his later work to gain a wider public.

Paul de Wit, the protagonist and narrator of *La Place de la Bastille,* is a
high school teacher of history who in his spare time does historical research.
Specifically, he is writing a book on Louis XVI's flight from the Tuileries. During a visit to the Bibliothèque nationale in Paris, de Wit comes to the conclusion that archives offer no real meaning and represent mere collections of use-
less papers: "History does not exist" (16). Traveling back to Amsterdam, he
entertains the notion that he will cease to work on the history of the French

king in accordance with traditional scholarly methods. He develops the idea of a hypothetical history which takes into account the possibility of unpredictable effects: "History has no meaning, it has no goal; history is an amorphous body; some unreliable facts have formed a false chain of causes and effects, only to offer justification to historians and validate their ideologies. Causes are supposed to exist because there were events. But on the list of facts the fascinating element of *coincidence* never appeared, the element capable of deriding causalities and exposing the lessons of the past as absurdities" (27).

In his novel de Winter uses the concept of *coincidence* not only on the reflective level but also as a structural principle on the narrative level. Coincidence determines both the professional historiography and the personal history of the protagonist. "La Place de la Bastille: A Case Study on the Role of Coincidence in History" is the projected title of the book the protagonist intends to write. As part of Parisian topography, however, La Place de la Bastille is the place where, in the novel, a a photo was taken of Pauline, the woman he happened to meet during a visit to the library and with whom he had a love affair. The picture is to exert a lasting influence on de Wit's life. Behind Pauline, on the left, a man is glimpsed whose face resembles that of the protagonist not merely in his own eyes but also according to others. Historiography and biography merge: one single coincidental element emerges and the course of history or life is altered as a consequence. De Wit is obsessed by the idea that he has a brother, that he, an orphan whose parents were murdered in the camps, has something like a family, a past. The emptiness of his past—nobody had ever talked to him about his parents—could be replaced by a family history if only he could find his brother. From the moment of the discovery of the man in the picture, de Wit spends his time looking for his brother, a search which eventually proves futile despite the assurances of a midwife that his mother had given birth to twins.

Although both the professional historian and the individual human being try to free themselves from the absolute value of the factual, neither is successful. De Wit wished to tack on a happy ending to the history of Louis XVI as well as his own life story. This ultimate failure is already suggested by the title of the novel, which refers to the topological reality of lost revolutionary promises in history. (The title also recalls Patrick Modiano's novel *La Place de l'Étoile*, 1968).[6] One could argue that the only one who is successful is the author of the novel *La Place de la Bastille*. He is in command of the narration; his fantasy accomplishes what neither scholarship nor human intention and emotion are capable of. It is a function of fiction— the combination of aesthetic arrangements and intellectual conjectures—to provide a space for dreams as well as to witness their collapse.

Marcel Möring is the author of a number of novels that have garnered favorable critical response—including prestigious literary prizes. *In Babylon* (1997) is, according to most critics, his masterpiece thus far. Here Möring breaks away from the oppressive influence of the Shoah. The Jewish identity of the protagonist, Nathan Hollander, is no longer exclusively determined by the Holocaust but rather by Jewish history and rituals belonging to a more remote past than that of the recent catastrophe. The chronology of the novel spans the seventeenth to the end of the twentieth centuries; the topology from the east (Poland) to the western United States (New Mexico). The geographical center, however, is located in the Netherlands. The author relates the history of the Levie family, alias Hollander, as one of travelers, choosing Isaac Deutscher's words "Trees have roots. Jews have legs" as his epigraph. In the seventeenth century Magnus Levie, a clockwork maker, left eastern Europe and first settled in the eastern part of the Netherlands. In the course of a successful career, the family finally settled in the western part of the country, specifically in the city of Rotterdam. Centuries later Nathan Hollander, one of the descendants, inherited the house of his uncle Herman. The latter had stipulated that Nathan should write his uncle's biography. Together with his niece, Nina, illegitimate daughter of Zeno, his brother, Nathan arrives at the house, which they discover is haunted. They are isolated for quite a while because of heavy snowfalls. Trying not to freeze or starve to death—some of their adventures recall motifs drawn from the gothic novel—Nathan writes the history of his Jewish family. He loses all sense of time and place, with the boundaries separating the world of the dead from the living members of his family blurred. He travels back and forth in space and time. Nathan communicates with Chaim and Magnus, the founders of the family, who reveal their secrets to him. Möring succeeds in connecting past and present in surprising parallel scenes, thus creating a universal presence of Jewish life transcending the Shoah. Chronology is of little importance in his eyes: "Chronology is for sequence, chaos is for comprehension" (325).

Of course, the Shoah is not completely absent, which would have been impossible in a story recounting several generations of a Jewish family. It is Uncle Herman who saved the family by convincing his brother to emigrate and providing the necessary facilities. Having founded his life on rationality, he understood the danger of National Socialism from the very beginning. The emigration of the Hollanders to the United States permitted the author to de-emphasize the European catastrophe.

During moments of uncertainty and lack of creativity, Nathan seriously considers abandoning the project. He reasons that it is not a terrible thing to live without a family history. Nina, however, is highly irritated by this attitude and reproaches him for talking like extremely rich people, who claim that money is not all that important. As the illegitimate daughter of Zeno, who conceived of himself as the Messiah, she is in dire need of her own history and expects her uncle to reveal it to her.

The Shoah is part of the biography of Uncle Herman and remains in the background. Nathan discovers why his uncle had such a solid knowledge of German history and culture and displayed a surprising interest in German affairs. An American scientist, Herman belonged to an army unit that liberated Bergen-Belsen. There he caught a glimpse of the inferno. He subsequently returned to Germany on several occasions, believing that one should force it to come to terms with its guilt: "The curse of Germany is romanticism. They've romanticized their own nonexistent past. They've romanticized a future. Let's not give them the chance to romanticize their guilt as well" (274).

Notwithstanding the perennial force of Jewish ritual, the history of the Hollander family is marked by discontinuity. Not only the Shoah but also other disruptions within the family tradition leave behind a deep uncertainty with respect to the identity of the characters. Is it true that Nathan is the son of Emmanuel or could it be that Uncle Herman is his real father? (390–91). Who are Nina's parents? Is Zeno indeed her father? Is the erotic encounter between Nathan and his niece in the snowbound house—expected by the reader by virtue of several hints and allusions—not a serious break in continuity? Even the assistance offered by Chaim, Nathan's forefather, who in a dream tells him the story of Lilith in order to integrate Nathan's incestuous act into Jewish mythology, does not make things any better. The new Jewish identity founded on the existence of the state of Israel, is also not very helpful: Why should we all live in one and the same country? So that our enemies can find us more easily? Why must we remain together and marry one another? These are the types of questions Nathan asks himself.

At the end of the twentieth century, the grand narrative of Jewish life—its rituals, its nomadic existence, including Diaspora and exile, but also its new beginning in the new land—reveals undeniable points of rupture. The author/narrator—who is able to bridge large chronological and topological distances and who knows both the past and the future—is well equipped to ask the question which the reader must eventually answer: Does the grand narrative of Jewish identity still exist?

The last work to be discussed is *Joods labyrinth* (Jewish Labyrinth, 2000), by Nol de Jong, a psychologist. This debut novel is a satirical criticism of a Jewish identity that defines itself exclusively in terms of the genocide. It comprises both a realistic and a grotesque discourse. The former is dominated by the well-known motif of the child as an iconic image of survival and a symbol of the future. However, the boy in this case has never felt himself part of the community of parents, family, and friends who survived the Holocaust. His parents and their generation had appropriated all the suffering of the world and nothing was left for him, who belonged to a postwar universe. He felt as though he had been exiled to an "island of happiness," and that he had no right to experience sadness. On the one hand, he was assumed to know nothing about the catastrophe, yet, on the other, he was expected to show the greatest consideration for the adults who had suffered so much. He was named after his murdered uncles, yet he was expected to be successful in life. As a grown-up, Otto Aron distances himself from his Jewish background. Together with his non-Jewish wife and his half-Jewish children, he lives the life of a Dutch middle-class family man. At a certain moment, however, he feels that he should recapture something of his Jewish past and applies for the position of director of the First Jewish Insurance Company. He is accepted, although the board knows that he is not observant—in the fictional context a tacit requirement for entry into the organization. His functioning in the company and its consequences form the background of a grotesque story involving Otto's arrest and imprisonment in a jail in which he is the sole inmate, with personal guards keeping watch. The crime he was accused of involved neglecting the tradition and the genocide as the very foundations of Jewish identity, which also serve as the guiding principles of the company. As director he had wanted to modernize and reorganize the company, to point it to the future. The public prosecutor, egged on by the Orthodox rabbi at the insurance company, whose authority appears to be much greater than that of the director, accused him of Jewish self-hatred. In the ongoing dialogue of accusation and (self-)defense, the problematic relationship between tradition and innovation is discussed at length. Aron denies that dignity is the exclusive preserve of the survivors. When he is finally acquitted of the charge and is on his way home, he knows that he will say to his wife: "I am at home, Tess; if you only knew how much I feel at home" (317).

In 2004 both Arnon Grunberg and Jessica Durlacher published novels that were well received by the critics. Grunberg's *De joodse Messias* (The Jewish Messiah) was praised as a masterpiece of storytelling, a remarkable mixture of tragedy and satirical comedy. Durlacher's novel *Emoticon,* which was almost immediately compared with *De joodse Messias,* received a bit less acclaim. Although they were impressed by Durlacher's courage in dealing with a rather controversial theme, literary critics were less emthusiastic about her laborious, effortful attempt to fashion the novel. In their novels Grunberg and Durlacher left the Holocaust at a distance. The compulsive identification of a boy of German descent with Judaism in Grunberg's *Messiah* and the terrorist attack in Durlacher's *Emoticon* doubtlessly relate to the genocide, but this remains implicit rather than explicit. The two authors are among the first Dutch writers to choose Israel as the topological center of a relatively large segment of their narrative.

This overview, which was prefaced by a short historical introduction, concludes with a summary of a sociological report entitled *De joden in Nederland anno 2000: Demografisch profiel en binding aan het jodendom* (Jews in the Nether-

lands in the year 2000: Demographic Profile and Commitment to Jewishness),
which recounts the story of the highly successful efforts of Dutch Jewry at the
end of the twentieth century (Solinge and de Vries 2001). The level of education
of these Dutch Jews is remarkably high. More than half of those interviewed
have studied at a university or an advanced vocational school. Compared with
the general Dutch population, the rate of Jewish academics is four times higher
than that of non-Jews. Although the percentage of Jewish academics (3%) was
higher than that of non-Jews even before the war, the difference after the war has
still continued to grow. There are various reasons for this phenomenon. One sociological explanation holds that during German occupation the chance of survival among the intellectual and economic elite was higher than that among the
working class, which was almost totally annihilated. The average level of professional status among Jews is also higher (55 on a scale ranging from 13 to 89,
compared with 45 for the Dutch population as a whole). The same applies to personal income, which is 30 percent higher than that of Dutch non-Jews. This statistical analysis implies that by the end of the twentieth century the self-consciousness of the Jewish population has grown considerably compared with the
period immediately after the war. Although these statistics apparently confirm
the success of postwar Dutch Jewry, occasionally the sociological report also uncovers a significant negative aspect, namely, the instability of domestic partnership among Jews as revealed by the demographic profile. Historically there had
been considerable resistance to divorce. Nowadays, however, Jews divorce more
frequently than non-Jews. The high educational level accounts for only a small
fraction (10%) of the explanation behind this trend. Secularization may be another reason, but traumatic experiences should also not be excluded.

The second part of this demographic study is concerned with the emotional ties Jews hold toward their religion and culture (the sociocultural bond)
and their commitment to a Jewish identity as a consequence of anti-Semitism
and the genocide. Jews born before 1925 as well as those born between 1925
and 1944 largely belong to the group that is committed to Judaism as a consequence of the genocide. Moreover, within the cohort of those born between
1925 and 1944 feelings of loneliness due to a separation from their parents are
frequently mentioned.

De joden in Nederland anno 2000 is based on reliable research. The methods and language of the social sciences have their indisputable merits. The dis-
advantage of large surveys, however, is in the loss of the individual. Archival
and statistical data cannot give us access to individual emotions. Surveys are
not the place where experiences approaching the unspeakable can be expressed.
It is the language of literature that has the potential to explore the limits of
what can be said. It is capable of dealing with ambiguity, irony, and metaphor,
with hidden feelings and lies. Literature is at its best when personal deviations

from the generalizations of history and sociology are at stake. Of course, history and sociology can be helpful to the literary scholar. For example, in the aforementioned sociological study the generation of Dutch Jews born between 1925 and 1944 occupy a special position: their commitment to Judaism appears to be based on the experiences of anti-Semitism and genocide. These are "realities" that tolerate restricted literary strategies but not flights of the imagination. Reading the texts of writers belonging to this generation, one is forced to conclude that they cannot free themselves from inhumane persecution. Most of them rely on *memory* or *remembered history* as the basis for their autobiographical works. The younger generation, by contrast, openly reject the determinism of war and genocide. This is what Arnon Grunberg and Nol de Jong do, but also Leon de Winter, who does not reduce the past to historical facts but instead interprets it in terms of his fantasy.

What is the future of Jewish literature in the Netherlands? One assumes that Dutch Jews will continue to make important contributions to Dutch culture. What about the specifically Jewish character of their work? It does not appear likely that the Shoah will ever lose its influence in terms of defining Jewish identity. At this very moment the struggle for Jewish identity outside Europe is deeply connected with the European catastrophe in the first half of the twentieth century. In the future the Shoah, although unique in Jewish and German history, will become part of a larger historical context and of a literary universe where invention, fantasy, and experiment are welcomed. We, as readers, should not be afraid of that, although we might bear in mind the words of Geoffrey Hartman: "To allow the limits of representation to be healing limits yet not allow them to conceal an event we are obligated to recall and interpret, both to ourselves and those growing up unconscious of its shadow" (1992, 334).

NOTES

1. I have dealt with this aspect more extensively in Ibsch 2004.

2. "The traumatic event, although real, took place outside of the parameters of normal reality, such as causality, sequence, place, and time. The trauma is thus an event that has no beginning, no ending, no before, no during, and no after. This absence of categories that define it lends it a quality of 'otherness,' a salience . . . outside the range of comprehension, of recounting, and of mastery" (Felman and Laub 1992, 69).

3. Abel Herzberg, a lawyer, survived Bergen-Belsen together with his wife while their three children were in hiding. During the Eichmann trial Herzberg acted as a Dutch reporter. Among other books, he is the author of the previously mentioned autobiographical work *Between Two Streams*.

4. Despite recent rumors questioning the Jewish identity of Carl Friedman, I see no reason not to mention her work, which, after all, belongs to Dutch Holocaust literature.

5. Her later novel *Twee koffers vol* (The Shovel and the Loom, 1996) was made into the movie *Left Luggage.*

6. The title refers both to the famous square in Paris—during the war it was a hub of Gestapo activities—and to the yellow star Jews were forced to wear. As in *La Place de la Bastille* the search for traces of the past is the central theme.

WORKS CITED

Anbeek, T. 1986. *Na de oorlog: De Nederlandse roman, 1945–1960.* Amsterdam: De Arbeiderspers.

Blom, J. C. H. 1989. "The Persecution of the Jews in the Netherlands: A Comparative Western European Perspective." *European History Quarterly* 19: 333–51.

Burnier, Andreas. 1969. *Het jongensuur.* Amsterdam: Em. Querido.

Dunk, H. W. von der. 1990. *Voorbij de verboden drempel: De Shoah in ons geschiedbeeld.* Amsterdam: Prometheus.

Durlacher, Gerhard L. 1985. *Strepen aan de hemel.* Amsterdam: Meulenhoff.

———. 1991. *Stripes in the Sky.* Trans. Susan Massotty. London: Serpent's Tail.

———. 1991. *De zoektocht.* Amsterdam: Meulenhoff.

———. 1993. *Quarantaine.* Amsterdam: Meulenhoff.

———. 1993. *Quarantine.* Trans. Susan Massotty. Rotterdam: Story International.

———. 1998. *The Search.* Trans. Susan Massotty. London: Serpent's Tail.

Durlacher, Jessica. 2000. *De dochter.* Amsterdam: De Bezige Bij.

———. 2004. *Emoticon.* Amsterdam: De Bezige Bij.

———, ed. 1994. *De olifant en het joodse probleem.* Amsterdam: Arena.

Felman, Shoshana, and Dori Laub. 1992. *Testimony: Crises of Witnessing in Literature, Psychoanalysis, and History.* New York: Routledge.

Friedman, Carl. 1991. *Tralievader.* Amsterdam: Van Oorschot.

———. 1995. *Nightfather.* Trans. Arnold and Erica Pomerans. New York: Persea.

Gans, Evelien. 2002. "'Vandaag hebben ze niets—maar morgen bezitten ze weer tien gulden': Antisemitische stereotypen in bevrijd Nederland." In *Polderschouw: Terugkeer en opvang na de Tweede Wereldoorlog; Regionale verschillen,* ed. Conny Kristel, 313–353. Amsterdam: Bert Bakker.

Grunberg, Arnon. 1994. *Blauwe maandagen.* Amsterdam: Nijgh en Van Ditmar.

———. 1997. *Blue Mondays,* trans. Arnold and Erica Pomerans. New York: Farrar, Straus and Giroux.

———. 2004. *De joodse Messias.* Amsterdam: Vassallucci.

Hartman, Geoffrey H. 1992. "The Book of the Destruction." In *Probing the Limits of Representation: Nazism and the "Final Solution,"* ed. Saul Friedlander, 318–34. Cambridge, Mass.: Harvard University Press.

Herzberg, Abel. 1989. *Tweestromenland.* Amsterdam: Querido.

———. 1997. *Between Two Streams: A Diary from Bergen-Belsen.* Trans. Jack Santcross. London: Tauris.

Herzberg, Judith. 1991. *Leedvermaak.* In *Teksten voor toneel en film, 1972–1988,* 397–495. Amsterdam: De Harmonie.

———. 1997. *The Wedding Party.* In *Dutch and Flemish Plays,* trans. Della Couling et al., 63–120. London: Nick Hern.

Hettema, Douwe. 2002. "Nederlandse verzetshelden en joodse onderduikers: De Duitse bezetting in de romanliteratuur." In *Polderschouw: Terugkeer en opvang na de Tweede Wereldoorlog; Regionale verschillen,* ed. Conny Kristel, 355–77. Amsterdam: Bert Bakker.

Ibsch, Elrud. 2004. *Die Shoah erzählt: Zeugnis und Experiment in der Literatur.* Tübingen: Niemeyer.

de Jong, L. 1969–89. *Het Koninkrijk der Nederlanden in de Tweede Wereldoorlog.* 13 vols. The Hague: Nijhoff. Vol. 14: The Hague: SDU.

de Jong, Nol. 2000. *Joods labyrinth.* Breda: De Geus.

Lewin, Lisette. 1989. *Voor bijna alles bang geweest.* Amsterdam: Nijgh en Van Ditmar.

Meijer, Daphne. 1998. *Joodse traties in de literatuur.* Amsterdam: De Bijenkorf.

Meijer, Ischa. 1974. *Brief aan mijn moeder.* The Hague: Bert Bakker.

Möring, Marcel. 1997. *In Babylon.* 1997. Amsterdam: Meulenhoff.

———. 2000. *In Babylon.* Trans. Stacy Knecht. New York: William Morrow/HarperCollins.

Nolden, Thomas. 1995. *Junge jüdische Literatur: Konzentrisches Schreiben in der Gegenwart.* Würzburg: Königshausen und Neumann.

Polak, Chaja. 1996. *Tweede vader.* Amsterdam: Vasallucci.

———. 2001. *Over de grens.* Amsterdam: Vassallucci.

Presser, J. J. 1965. *Ondergang: De vervolging en verdelging van het Nederlandse Jodendom, 1940–1945.* 2 vols. The Hague: Nijhoff.

Sicher, Efraim. 1998. *Breaking Crystal: Writing and Memory after Auschwitz.* Urbana: University of Illinois Press.

Solinge, Hanna van, and Marlene de Vries, eds. 2001. *De joden in Nederland anno 2000: Demografisch profiel en binding aan het jodendom.* Amsterdam: Aksant.

de Winter, Leon. 1981. *La Place de la Bastille.* Haarlem: De Knipscheer.

TEXTS AVAILABLE IN ENGLISH

Durlacher, G. L. 1988. *The Search.* Trans. Susan Massotty. London: Serpent's Tail.

———. 1991. *Stripes in the Sky.* Trans. Susan Massotty. London: Serpent's Tail.

———. 1992. *Quarantine.* Trans. Susan Massotty. Rotterdam: Story International.

———. 1993. *Drowning: Growing Up in the Third Reich.* Trans. Susan Massotty. London: Serpent's Tail.

Friedman, Carl. 1995. *Nightfather.* Trans. Arnold and Erica Pomerans. New York: Persea.

———. 1996. *The Shovel and the Loom.* Trans. Jeannette K. Ringold. New York: Persea.

———. 1998. *The Gray Lover: Three Stories.* Trans. Jeanette K. Ringold. New York: Persea.

Grunberg, Arnon. 1997. *Blue Mondays.* Trans. Arnold and Erica Pomerans. New York: Farrar, Straus and Giroux.

Herzberg, Abel. 1997. *Between Two Streams: A Diary from Bergen-Belsen.* Trans. Jack Santcross. London: Tauris.

Herzberg, Judith. 1997. *The Wedding Party.* In *Dutch and Flemish Plays,* trans. Della Couling et al. London: Nick Hern.

Möring, Marcel. 2000. *In Babylon.* Trans. Stacy Knecht. New York: William Morrow / HarperCollins.

de Winter, Leon. 1995. *Hoffman's Hunger.* Trans. Arnold and Erica Pomerans. London: Andre Deutsch.

FOUR

~

EVA EKSELIUS

Bonds with a Vanished Past: Contemporary Jewish Writing in Scandinavia

The Jewish communities in the Scandinavian countries represent an extremely small demographic minority. ("Scandinavia" formally comprises Sweden, Norway, and Denmark but, as is the case here, often includes Finland.) Sweden, whose Jewish population keeps increasing, has the largest concentration of Jews—some 18,000 out of a total population of 9 million—whereas Catholics and Muslims are each about ten times as numerous as Jews. Denmark, Norway, and Finland have about half the population of Sweden (each with 4.5 to 5 million inhabitants), but while there are 8,000 Jews in Denmark, there are only 1,500 in Norway and 1,200 in Finland. Given the size of the Jewish population, the large number of contemporary Jewish authors is astonishing.

The literature of Scandinavian writers of Jewish origin reflects their relationships toward the past, with its long history of Jewish assimilation into a Protestant yet exceedingly modern secular society. The Shoah and the previous incidents of persecution brought new waves of Jewish immigrants; their experiences constitute the dark core of many of the narratives told by Jewish writers active in Sweden. In the writings of Danish Jewish authors, the period of German occupation and the dramatic evacuation of virtually all of Denmark's seven thousand Jews to Sweden remain recurrent themes.

In many of the stories by authors born during or after the Shoah, the Jewish world appears to have vanished, with only faint and fragile memories remaining. The plot often centers on the protagonist's attempt to reconstruct an image of a past that he or she—as well as the authors themselves—never knew.

Survivors of the Shoah have borne witness to the atrocities both in memoirs and autobiographical novels. However, those authors who belong to the next generation often describe having to confront a wall of silence surrounding the trauma of the Shoah. The shadow of the Holocaust is despicted as ever-present, but the traumatic experiences of war, persecution, and concentration camps are communicated only through fragments of conversations, or by means of letters or notes found by those who remain. The attempt to penetrate this wall of silence and to create a narrative out of these shattered pieces of information reflects the desire to reconnect with a broken Jewish tradition and to reestablish a link to a vanished Jewish world.

There are also those writers who feel well grounded in Judaism and Jewish thought. They are often nonfiction writers concerned with aspects of Jewish ethics related to issues of global and social justice, gender, and the political situation in the Middle East. In their writing they respond to the challenges of Jewish philosophy by bringing it into contemporary political discourse.

Jewish writing in Scandinavia has to be viewed in the light of the history of the Scandinavian Jews. Even if "Portuguese" Jews were already living in Copenhagen in the seventeenth century, Jews did not represent a significant minority in the Scandinavian countries until the nineteenth century. In 1775 the first Jew was allowed to settle in Sweden without first becoming a Christian. He soon received permission to let another ten Jewish men and their families join him. In 1815 there were 785 Jews residing in the country; by 1870 their numbers had increased to 3,000. Many of these Jews were highly skilled, and enjoyed royal protection. Their descendants soon acquired wealth and prestige within the commercial, financial, and industrial sectors where they were permitted to work.

Well-to-do merchants, manufacturers, and factory owners dominated the first generations of Jews in Sweden. Material wealth rather than scholarship and piety led to social rank and prestige. To consolidate the fragile acceptance of the Jews and to counteract anti-Semitism, some of the wealthiest Jews donated large sums for philanthropic purposes or to support the arts. A few generations later the Jewish community had produced some of the country's most prominent scholars.

Several of Sweden's most well known families—Josephson, Philipson, Lamm, Hirsch, Bonnier, Wahren, Markus, Mannheimer, Schück, Heckscher, Abrahamson, Benedicks—were descended from these pioneer Jewish immigrants. Influenced by the accomplishments of the Enlightenment and of emancipation, many sought total assimilation. As Per Wästberg has commented with respect to his ancestor Axel Hirsch, "Stockholm and its archipelago were their home district, not the desert and olive groves in Palestine. In appearance and origin they were Jews, but the soul, the habits, and the cultural heritage were Swedish" (2002, 30). Karl Otto Bonnier, one of the founders of the publishing house that bears his name, considered himself "purely Swedish" and defended his right as a Jew to speak and feel as a Swede. Opposing those of his peers who would subsequently embrace Zionist ideas, Bonnier insisted that it would be "totally absurd, unscientific and against reality," that a Swedish Jew should feel any kinship with his ancestors (quoted in Gedin 2003, 383).

Most Jews remained within the social circle of Jewish families not because of common religious beliefs but rather out of loyalty to their lineage. Some individuals or branches of families became Christian through conversion or continuous intermarriage. In time most Jews became assimilated and secularized while still maintaining a strong sense of Jewish identity.

No Jewish ghettos existed since there were very few poor Jews. Some Jewish beggars and peddlers could be found in the towns and the countryside. They had often entered the country illegally and were met with resistance by both the authorities and the Jewish communities. This social structure may explain why Sweden did not harbor the prevailing and lasting anti-Semitism that existed in many other European countries. This is not to say, however, that anti-Semitism did not exist; there were indeed local outbreaks of mob violence, especially in 1838, when stones were thrown into the homes of prominent Jewish families in Stockholm. Hatred was often expressed in pamphlets and press campaigns, and anti-Jewish stereotypes surfaced in the writings of some of Sweden's most famous intellectuals, including August Strindberg. Nevertheless mob action was met with massive protests and public support of the Jews, both in terms of parliamentary legislation and at public demonstrations. Greeted with enthusiasm by both liberals and conservatives, Sweden's parliament granted the Jews emancipation in 1870 (Valentin 1964).

A similar development could be seen in Denmark, and in Norway, which remained part of the Danish-Norwegian kingdom (1814–1905) until the union with Sweden. The social network of Denmark's Jewish community was somewhat wider, and the religious conflicts between Orthodox and progressive circles more bitter. Conversions to Christianity left deep scars within some Jewish families.

Emigration of Jews from eastern Europe to Scandinavia in significant numbers did not begin until the late nineteenth and early twentieth centuries. After the escalating Russian pogroms, a wave of new immigrants entered Denmark, Norway, and Sweden. Most of them came from the lower middle classes and had worked as small-scale traders, artisans, retailers, and peddlers. Whereas the "old" Jewish families emphasized their patriotism and ties to their new Nordic home country, many of the newcomers spoke Yiddish and held on to their traditional Orthodox belief and lifestyle—at least for several decades. Relationships among the different social classes were occasionally tense; the newcomers were treated with contempt by the upper classes, while the assimilated and wealthier families worried that the arrival of eastern European Jews would give rise to anti-Semitism.

After World War II, thousands of Jews immigrated to Sweden as refugees from or survivors of the Shoah. A second wave of immigration followed the political events in Hungary in 1956 and the escalating anti-Semitism in Poland around 1968, bringing many Hungarian and several thousands Polish Jews to Sweden. By 1970 "approximately 14,000 Jews—twice as many as in 1933—lived in Sweden" (Dencik 2003, 81).

In Denmark at the turn of the nineteenth century the flood of immigrants from eastern Europe had doubled its Jewish population. Many of the newcomers settled in the slums of the inner city of Copenhagen, where their presence gave a foreign and exotic *Yiddishkeit* to the area. Socialist agitators of the Bund were active, as were many cultural organizations. Fearing the potential impact of Russian revolutionaries, and supported by a xenophobic public opinion, immigration to Denmark was halted completely in 1917.

Finland has had a very different history of Jewish settlement. Whereas in the other Scandinavian countries the first waves of newcomers came from northern and central European countries, where their immigration was voluntary, most Jews in Finland came from Russia, where their immigration was generally compulsory. Until 1809 Finland was part of Sweden, following which it became an autonomous grand duchy of the Russian empire. It remained a part of Russia until the Great War and the Russian Revolution of 1917. Russia's Jews faced extreme difficulties during the last decades of the nineteenth century. Young Jewish boys had to serve fifteen to twenty-five years in the Russian army, and were often forcibly recruited. Hundreds of young Jewish soldiers were stranded in Finland when the army was demobilized. As a result, most Finnish Jews today are descendants of these Russian Jewish soldiers; others later joined them from Russia, Poland, and Lithuania. In recent years Jews from the former Soviet Union, Poland, and elsewhere in eastern Europe have sought sanctuary in Finland.

The history of the Jews often appears only sporadically in contemporary Jewish writing in Scandinavia, either rendered as fragmented memories of a world long vanished or concealed within the dark shadows of the Shoah. To penetrate the wall of silence, to reassemble disparate memories in order to reconstruct the past tends to be the aim of many Scandinavian Jewish authors.

The trauma of persecution and genocide still dominates historical discussion even though the losses suffered by Scandinavia's Jewish population were small in comparison with those of other European countries. No Scandinavian country ever deported any Jews who had settled there legally, although many Jews from Germany were refused entry and asylum. Sweden managed to stay out of the war and offered refuge to some five thousand Danish Jews. Due to the steadfastness of the Finnish authorities, Finnish Jewry was also spared the horrors of the Shoah, while half of Norway's eighteen hundred Jews were deported after the defeat of Norway's resistance forces in 1942. Still, the Nazi genocide remains a constant presence in many works of the post-Shoah writers, who often portray it as an unspeakable horror.

Sweden

Contemporary Jewish writing in Sweden includes authors spanning several generations. Among the older generation of writers mention should be made of Georg Klein, Per Wästberg, and Erland Josephson, all of whom were born before World War II and are still actively involved in shaping Sweden's cultural life. Cordelia Edvardson, Zenia Larsson, and Hédi Fried are all survivors of the Shoah; their autobiographical fiction has had a profound impact on their audiences. Last but not least, one should mention Peter Weiss (who died in 1982), one of Europe's greatest postwar playwrights and novelists.

Cordelia Edvardson holds a unique position in Swedish public life as both a witness of Auschwitz atrocities and a long-term reporter from Israel. She was born in Berlin in 1929, the illegitimate daughter of the famous German writer Elisabeth Langgässer and the well-known political scientist Hermann Heller. Her mother later married a Christian and Cordelia was raised a Catholic. At the time she knew nothing about her Jewish origin on either side of her family. (Elisabeth Langgässer's father was a Jewish convert to Catholicism.) In the thirties Cordelia, considered to be the only Jew in the family, was forced to wear the yellow star without understanding why. She was later sent to Terezin and then to Auschwitz. After the war, she was taken to Sweden. Her famous *Bränt barn söker sig till elden* (Burned Child Seeks the Fire, 1984), which has been translated into several languages, tells the story of her childhood. Despite her immigration to Israel in 1974, she continues to exert a powerful influence on contemporary Jewish-Swedish-Israeli-Palestinian discourse. She regularly reports from Israel for one of Sweden's large daily newspapers and is the author of many volumes of fiction, essays, and poetry.

Zenia Larsson, who was born in Poland in 1922, experienced a breakthrough in the early sixties with a series of novels dealing with her time in Bergen-Belsen and the periods preceding and following her deportation. Like many of the Holocaust survivors residing in Sweden, she had arrived in one of the Red Cross buses commandeered by the Swedish prince Folke Bernadotte (who was eventually murdered in Jerusalem).

The psychologist and writer Hédi Fried, born in Rumania in 1924, has re-counted the story of her life in the novel *Skärvor av ett liv: vägen till och från Auschwitz* (Fragments of a Life: The Road to and from Auschwitz, 1992) and its two sequels. Magda Eggens, born in Hungary in 1924, is a Holocaust sur-vivor who has recounted her experiences of deportation and concentration camps in *Om stenarna kunde tala* (If the Stones Could Speak, 1997) as well as in several books for young readers. Ferenc Göndör (born in Hungary in 1928), Emerich Roth (born in Czechoslovakia in 1924), and Ebba Sörbom (born in Yugoslavia as Ruzsica Schreiber in 1927) have all recounted their life stories and experiences in various concentration camps. The traumatic effect of the Shoah on children has recently been studied by Suzanne Kaplan, based on in-terviews with Holocaust survivors in Sweden in *Barn under Förintelsen—då och nu* (Children in the Holocaust—Now and Then, 2003) and in her earlier dis-sertation "Child Survivors in the Holocaust" (2002).

Georg Klein, who was born in Hungary in 1925, managed to escape the deportation of Hungarian Jews to Auschwitz and fled to Sweden. In addition to being an internationally recognized scientist and cancer specialist, he is also a prominent writer with a number of essay collections to his credit, most of which concern ethical, political, and philosophical issues. In his memoir *I stäl-let för hemland* (In Place of a Homeland, 1984), he has chronicled his experience of persecution.

Per Wästberg, who was born in 1933, is one of the most prolific—he has au-thored some fifty books—and prominent writers of his generation. In addition to being a member of the Swedish Academy, he has held important positions in the media, having served as editor in chief of the daily *Dagens Nyheter* and presi-dent of International PEN. He is also a recognized authority on African society and African literature. A recent publication is a biography dedicated to one of his ancestors, *Axel Hirsch: Folkbildare och filantrop* (Axel Hirsch: Public Educator and Philanthropist, 2002), who was both a leading member of Stockholm's Jewish community and a dedicated anti-Zionist who advocated assimilation.

Erland Josephson, who was born in 1923 to another established and as-similated Jewish family, is one of Sweden's most distinguished actors, whose international reputation is equally strong. In several of his books, such as *En berättelse om herr Silberstein* (A Story about Mr. Silberstein, 1957), he specifically addresses Jewish issues.

In 2005 Morton Narrowe, the chief rabbi emeritus of Stockholm, pub-lished his memoir *En tretvinnad tråd: amerikan, jude, svensk* (A Three-Twined Thread: American, Jew, Swede), which portrays the young American rabbi ar-riving in Stockholm with the ambitious desire to modernize a traditional Jew-ish community with a succession of elderly German scholars as their rabbi.

Peter Weiss, who was born in 1916, gained worldwide fame for his penetrating dramas *Die Verfolgung und Ermordung Jean Paul Marats* (The Persecution and Assassination of Jean Paul Marat, 1964) and *Die Ermittlung* (The Investigation, 1965a), the latter based on the proceedings at the Auschwitz trials. Weiss is the son of a Hungarian father of Jewish origin (a convert to Catholicism) and a Swiss mother. The family left Germany before the war, bound first for England and then for Sweden, where Weiss became a naturalized citizen. His first published works were written in Swedish, but he soon returned to writing in German, his native language. His multivolume novel *Ästhetik des Widerstands* (Aesthetics of Resistance, 1975) addresses the role of aesthetics in the struggle against fascism. It was published in an English translation in 2005, an indication of the increasing interest in Weiss's writing.

Lars Gustafsson, who was born in 1936, is a poet, novelist, and essayist, whose international acclaim as a fiction writer has overshadowed his more controversial political writings. He is a "Jew by choice," having converted to Judaism in 1982 and lived for many years with his American Jewish family in Austin, Texas. Jewish themes are, with a few exceptions, not prominent in his writing, but a note of metaphysical reflection can be traced throughout his work. *Bernard Foys tredje rockad* (Bernard Foy's Third Casting, 1986) is a sophisticated thriller that intertwines elements of the cabbala with the story of an assistant rabbi to the chief rabbi of Stockholm's Great Synagogue. In his essay "Att åta sig att vara jude" (To Take Upon Oneself to Be a Jew, 1994) Gustafsson describes Judaism as the true basis of Western values, from which Christianity has extracted and developed only parts. Contrary to Christian thought, which stresses faith, Gustafsson stresses that Judaism emphasizes duty, with Jewish speculation more a matter of law than ontology.

Leif Zern, born in 1939, is one of Sweden's most lucid essayists and prominent critics. He has published several books on drama, literature, and theater. Endowed with a penetrating sensitivity, he analyses and uncovers the hidden structure and various layers of meaning in a piece of art, be it a drama by Shakespeare, a film by Ingmar Bergman, or a live theatrical performance. In one of his essays (2004) he has presented an affectionate portrait of his Orthodox father, Simon Zernjaffsky, and has provided a glimpse of his own childhood, which involved weekly studies of his father's old Hebrew prayer books.

Tobias Berggren, who was born in 1940, is one of Sweden's great postwar poets. His mother was born into one of Sweden's most prominent Jewish families (the Bonniers). Utilizing motifs based upon Vilnius and Israel, Berggren's poetry reflects the quest for the lost Jewish culture that once flourished in Europe. His libretto for *Requiem: De ur alla minnen fallna* (Requiem: Those from All Memories Fallen, 1992) by the Swedish composer Sven-David Sandström has been compared to "Babi Yar," the poem by Yevgeny Yevtushenko set to music by the Russian composer Dmitri Shostakovich. Berggren's text for the

Requiem is a modernist poet's cry of rage and pain, emerging from a deep empathy and identification with those silenced by the Holocaust. Based on historical documents, it refers to the deportation of eighty thousand French Jews. The text provocatively reverses the features of the Christian mass. The "Dies Irae," the Day of Wrath, does not depict the anger of God on Judgment Day but rather everyday life of a humanity drawn to violence. Likewise, the "Communio" section of the mass is a travesty of the communion at Christ's Last Supper, which is now invaded by death and sexuality. Obscene words and scenes are used to disclose the inadequacy of language. The representations of horror and feeling of nausea captured by highly emotive language are intended to awaken the listener's moral conscience (Pettersson 2004).

Peter Mosskin was born in 1945, the older son of a Jewish Russian immigrant father and a Christian mother of Swedish origin. His father used to tell his sons about his St. Petersburg childhood within an aristocratic Russian family. Not until his father was an old man and Peter had determined to write a novel about his Russian past did he learn that these stories were pure fantasy. His father, who had come to Sweden as a child, was actually the son of a poor Russian Jewish tailor. In three novels—*Skänk åt den fege en hingst* (Give to the Coward a Stallion, 1994), *Glöm inte bort att jag finns* (Don't Forget That I Exist, 1997), and *Där stäppen tar slut* (Where the Steppe Ends, 2000)—Mosskin reimagines the life of his humble Jewish ancestors. Just as his father had to make use of Tolstoy's novels to create the fantasy of a noble past, so the son had to turn to literature—specifically the works of Isaac Bashevis Singer and Sholem Aleichem—to create the narrative of his family and ancestors.

Joakim Philipson, who was born in 1958, comes from one of Sweden's oldest Jewish families with a long history of assimilation. (One of his cousins is a well-known clergyman in Sweden's Protestant community.) His attitude toward his Jewish heritage is, however, very different from that of Mosskin. While the latter tries to re-create the physical, tactile dimensions of a vanished world, Philipson adopts a more philosophical approach. His debut novel *Tecknet och tystnaden* (The Sign and the Silence, 1991) is presented as a translation of a collection of notes found in a horsehair mattress at a Russian hospital during the twenties. The plot concerns a Jewish painter who is working on a portrait of Lenin. From this starting point, the novel develops into a combination of thriller and essay on ethical, aesthetic, philosophical, and religious issues.

Even if Philipson, like Mosskin, takes his inspiration from Russian tall tales, he is primarily interested in existential and religious questions. This is even more evident in his second novel. Set in Paris in the fifties, *Jakobs röst* (The Voice of Jacob, 1996) presents the story of Jacques Lévy, a young Orthodox Jew who is preparing for Rosh Hashanah. The author surrounds his protagonist with people who hold differing attitudes toward political ideologies and Jewish tradition: his father is a socialist who is secretly reading the Jewish mystics; his brother considers those ideas to be mumbo-jumbo; and his friend finds holiness in the visual arts. Competing with Marxist ideology, Orthodox Judaism becomes the focus of Lévy's life.

Many of the writers who were born after the Shoah have turned to the traumatic experiences of their parents as subject matter for their literary work. In 2005 Lena Einhorn's *Ninas resa* (Nina's Journey) received the August Prize, Sweden's most prestigious literary award. The book is based on interviews with her mother, who, with the active assistance of her brother, escaped deportation and managed to flee to Sweden. Einhorn has rendered her mother's experience—she was one of the few survivors of the Warsaw ghetto—in a combination drama and documentary film bearing the same title. The film also won as best Swedish film of 2005. The portrayal of her mother's escape is just one of several drama-documentaries Einhorn has devoted to the plight of Jews during the Nazi persecution. She has also documented the courageous attempts of the Lithuanian Jew Gilel Storch, who, through secret strategic alliances, managed to save thousands of Jews from the concentration camps and was one of the key figures in Raoul Wallenberg's rescue operations in Budapest. Einhorn has also made a documentary entitled *The Riddle of "I"* about the German-language poet Nelly Sachs, who sought refuge in Sweden in 1940 and who, together with Samuel Joseph Agnon, was awarded the Nobel Prize in literature in 1966.

Stefan Einhorn, the younger brother of Lena, was born in 1955. Like his sister and their parents he received training in the medical profession (Their father, Jerzy Einhorn, was a well-known cancer specialist, politician, and Holocaust survivor who recounted his memories in *Utvald att leva* [Chosen to Survive, 1996]). Stefan Einhorn's nonfictional essay *En dold Gud: om religion, vetenskap och att söka Gud* (A Concealed God: Religion, Science, and the Search for Truth, 1998) grapples with the possibility of proving the existence of God. His novel *Den sjunde dagen* (The Seventh Day, 2003) deals with a man who engages in existential conversations with his father, who, before dying, attempts to pass on the Jewish tradition to his son.

Anita Goldman, who was born in 1953, and Göran Rosenberg, who was born in 1948, are writers whose parents were refugees (Goldman) or survivors (Rosenberg) of the Shoah. Both hold prominent positions as journalists and essayists with leading magazines and newspapers, have published widely on social and political issues, and play a significant role in Sweden's public discourse on Israel, where both of them have lived.

In *Det förlorade landet: en personlig historia* (The Lost Land: A Personal History, 1996) Rosenberg shares his reflections on Israel, where he had gained a new perspective on the modern Jewish experience. Following the suicide of his father (a survivor incapable of overcoming severe depression), Göran, his mother, and his sister made their aliyah to Israel in 1962, when he was thirteen years old. He quickly learned Hebrew and became a committed Zionist pioneer, a common practice among Israeli schoolchildren. In the book he recalls his shock upon realizing that Palestine was never the uninhabited desert that he had been led to believe; the stones on the hills were the remnants of Palestinian villages that predated the arrival of Jewish pioneers. In his role as a journalist and publisher, Rosenberg continued to analyze social and political conflicts and to pursue the goal of finding a just solution to the Middle East conflict. *Plikten, profiten och konsten att vara människa* (Duty, Profit and the Art of Being Human, 2003) is the title of a collection of essays in which Rosenberg argues against a "morality of profit" in favor of an "ethics of duty" based upon an understanding of our interdependence and responsibility toward one another.

Both Göran Rosenberg and Anita Goldman have dealt with Jewish thought and history in their writings. In *Det förlorade landet* Rosenberg follows Zionism and the messianic tradition throughout history. Anita Goldman is a feminist who, intrigued by the faint female presence in the Bible and the Talmud, has pursued her interests in such nonfiction works as *Våra bibliska mödrar* (Our Biblical Mothers, 1988b) as well as in fictional form. *Den sista kvinnan från Ur* (The Last Woman from Ur, 1988a) focuses on Sarah, wife of Abraham, while *Orden som brändes* (Burning Words, 1994) recounts the life of Bruria, the first woman scribe in rabbinic times. Like Rosenberg, Goldman has commented extensively on life in modern Israel, particularly in *Jag bor bredvid paradiset* (I Live Next to Paradise, 2001), as well as in her book on the first intifada entitled *Stenarnas döttrar* (Daughters of the Stones, 1991). Her most recent work to date, *Guds älskarinnor: om hängivna kvinnor i en livrädd värld* (Lovers of God: On Devoted Women in a Terrified World, 2005), portrays a number of women (and one man) who are all radical and spiritually passionate in their love of God. One is the Dutch intellectual Etty Hillesum, killed in Auschwitz, who explored the limits of free love and spiritual devotion. Her experiences are documented in her diary, which has been translated into many languages.

Anita Goldman's sister, Marianne Goldman, who was born in 1952, is a playwright who has produced works for both stage and screen. She focuses on Jewish characters, which she places in contemporary Swedish situations. Her works have met with critical acclaim, especially her play *Försoningsdagen* (The Day of Atonement, 1998). In this play, which provoked intense debates among Jewish audiences, she portrays the neuroses, hypocrisy, and aggression of a Jewish family and their community, who finally achieve reconciliation and atonement. The play takes place during a dreamlike, if not nightmarish, synagogue service during Yom Kippur. Marianne Goldman has also authored the script for the film *Freud flyttar hemifrån* (Freud Leaving Home, 1991), which tells the story of a rebellious daughter (called Freud) and her Jewish family,

whose life is thrown into turmoil when they learn that the mother is termi-
nally ill with cancer.

Nathan Shachar, who was born in 1951, immigrated to Israel as a young
student and since then has been working as a correspondent for a leading Swedish newspaper. His *Vilsenhetens förklädnader: essäer om myter, modernitet och tradition
i Mellanöstern* (The Disguise of Being Astray: Essays on Myths, Modernity and
Tradition in the Middle East, 1996) deconstructs traditional concepts of ethnicity, religion, nationality, and culture as the foundation of identity. He demonstrates how all these factors have become intermingled in the Middle East and
how only myths and legends keep alive the notion of "a people" as a homogeneous entity. His most recent work, *Blodseld och nordisk längtan: Oscar Levertin och
hans tid* (Fiery Blood and Nordic Yearning: Oscar Levertin and His Times, 2006),
portrays the Jewish poet Levertin, a leading writer and literary critic in Sweden
around the turn of the twentieth century.

Unlike many of their peers, Rosenberg and Goldman—and, to a certain
extent, Shachar—are intensely involved in contemporary ethical and political
questions rather than the traumatic Jewish past. Rosenberg, in particular,
challenges himself and his readers to address difficult questions relating to
present-day Jewish identity, such as the following: What are the moral implications of being a Jew and how should they be applied to the situation in the
Middle East? When is the role of the victim no longer adequate? Should the
notion of diaspora and the assumed centrality of Israel as the Jewish homeland
be reevaluated?

Annika Thor has dealt with Jewish themes primarily in novels written for
younger audiences. Born in 1950 into one of the older Jewish families in Gothenburg, she gained international success with a series of novels for adolescents inspired by the research of Swedish historian Ingrid Lomfors, who investigated the
fate of five hundred Jewish refugee children sent to Sweden shortly before the
war. The series chronicles the life of two young Jewish sisters who leave Vienna
in 1939 to escape the war and are placed with two different puritanically Christian Swedish families on a barren island of the archipelago. Thor manages to relate a sensitive story about loss, loneliness, and longing. The emerging catastrophic events in Europe are depicted indirectly through rumors and letters
that repeatedly announce that the arrival of the parents has been delayed. The
concise description of the rural, pious life on the island makes the loss of the
urban, modern Jewish middle-class life of Vienna even more painful. By avoiding any mention of the horrifying events surrounding the war and the camps,
the novels paradoxically make them even more present.

Another successful writer for younger readers is Rose Lagercrantz, who
was born in 1947. Her novel *Flickan som inte ville kyssas* (The Girl Who Didn't
Want to Kiss, 1995) reconstructs her father's route through Nazi Europe, flee-

ing from Germany to Prague and Poland and back to Prague again before finding asylum in Sweden.

Susanne Levin, who was born in 1950, has published four autobiographical novels: *Leva vidare* (Go On Living, 1994), *Som min egen* (Like My Own, 1996), *Suggan i dômen* (The Sow in the Cathedral, 1998) and *Tillbaka till Király utca* (Back to Király utca, 2000). These four novels feature a young woman growing up in a family where the mother is one of the few survivors of a Jewish family from Hungary. The horror of her Jewish past is communicated to the daughter only through fragmentary conversations held in lowered voices by adults who speak in a foreign language to prevent the children from understanding. Jewish holidays are celebrated without any explanation of their meaning. *Suggan i dômen* examines and discusses anti-Semitic attitudes, while in the fourth novel the grown-up daughter accompanies her mother on a journey to her native Hungarian village of Király utca.

In *Systrarna Blaumans hemlighet* (The Secret of the Blauman Sisters, 1987), Suzanne Gottfarb, who was born in 1948, tells the story of twin sisters who survived the experiments of Dr. Josef Mengele. Neither of the sisters can articulate the pain of the past, preferring that it be consigned to oblivion. The novel discusses what it means for a girl to grow up in such an atmosphere of secrecy and denial. In her second work of fiction, *Hur familjen Green slutligen fick sitt skräprum utrymt* (How the Green Family Finally Got Their Lumber Room Vacated, 1998), Gottfarb adopts a farcical tone and juxtaposes the holiness of the city with the banalities of everyday life in Jerusalem.

Jacques Werup, who was born 1945, has published more than thirty works, including novels and poetry collections. He is also a jazz musician, singer, and cabaret performer. His novel *Shimonoffs längtan* (Shimonoff's Yearning, 1983) tells the story of the life of a young Sephardic Jew named Elias Shimonoff—the portrait of the protagonist was inspired by the life of Werup's Bulgarian-born grandfather—who leaves his native Bulgaria at the beginning of the twentieth century in order to live an adventurous life in various places in Europe. He ends up in Malmö, in southern Sweden, which is also the native city of the author. Although it had stayed out of the war, to Shimonoff Sweden does not offer a sense of security as he still expects Nazi sympathizers to turn up at any moment.

Lennart Kanter, who was born in 1956, made his literary debut at twenty-one. His latest novel *David Kahans sista ord* (David Kahan's Last Words, 1981) features a Jewish writer in his thirties who spends his last days in a hospital as a result of an inoperable malignant brain tumor. Before he finally loses the faculty of speech ("the Word") he tape-records the story of his life. In all three of Kanter's novels one can hear vague echoes of the past: in the background there are legendary Jewish relatives who arrive on foot from Russia or flee Nazi Germany for Norway.

Born in 1940, the illegitimate daughter of a Christian Swedish mother, Marianne Ahrne grew up without knowing anything about her father. Her novel *Fader okänd* (Father Unknown, 1998) recounts her search for him. He turns out to be a Jew of Czech origin who subsequently converted to Catholicism. Ahrne portrays the father's capricious nature, accepting and encouraging yet at the same time rejecting her when they finally meet. In her late teens and early twenties she shows him her first tentative efforts at writing, which he dismisses with contempt. Ahrne herself later converted to Judaism.

Tomas Böhm, who was born in 1945, is a professional psychoanalyst and writer who has published several novels in addition to several nonfiction books on psychological issues. His novel *The Vienna Jazz Trio* (2000) features a Jewish musician of Viennese background who has settled in California, where he is interviewed about his life as a pianist and writer. His story leads back to cosmopolitan Vienna of the twenties and early thirties, where socialism and psychoanalysis are seen as the significant ideas of the times, with jazz as their corresponding musical equivalent. Both Sigmund Freud and Wilhelm Reich turn up in the novel. In a psychoanalytic session with Reich, Judaism is found to be the "lost object," the broken connection that will be restored by a late-in-life circumcision. The real implication of the rite, however, remains open to debate: "Why did he do this? He had not become more religious. No one had told him to! Leah thought it was crazy. But he wanted to do it." The protagonist goes on to explain: "Just imagine, now I am part of the covenant; it always was a bit strange to me not to be circumcised, even if I don't believe in the religious superstructure, but it was like having no membership card" (92–93).

It is worth noting that almost all the works by the fiction writers discussed thus far reflect an attempt to reconnect with a vanished Jewish past, often representing experiences of loss and trauma. Relatively few of them draw on contemporary Jewish life as a main theme, suggesting that the Shoah remains at the core of present-day Jewish identity.

One of the few to tap into contemporary Jewish life was Madeleine Kats, who was born in 1932 and died in 1990. In *Taggig frukt* (Thorny Fruit, 1965) she chronicled her stay at an Israeli kibbutz and addressed the conflict between being a supporter of the Zionist project while at the same time living a secular existence as an assimilated modern Swedish Jew.

Those Jewish writers in Sweden who address notions of the Jewish tradition beyond the sufferings related to persecution seem to prefer the essay and other nonfictional forms in their writing. Aside from Rosenberg, Shachar, Edvardson, and Goldman, Ludvig Igra is another important contributor to present-day Jewish discourse. Born in Poland in 1945 to parents who managed to escape persecution, he grew up in Sweden, where he became a renowned psychoanalyst. Igra died in 2003 while still at the beginning of his career as a writer. His book *Den tunna hinnan mellan omsorg och grymhet* (The Thin Membrane Between Care and Cruelty, 2001) elaborates on the concepts of good and evil by utilizing an incident experienced by his father right after Germany's surrender as a starting point: the father rejects the offer of taking revenge against a group of German soldiers captured by the Red Army. Igra uses his father's choice as a model for his psychoanalytically informed theory of the origins of destructiveness and benevolence, as well as an explanation for the cruelties committed during wartime.

Jackie Jakubowski, who was born in 1951, is an essayist preoccupied with Jewish thought. Of Sephardi origin, he had left his native Poland just before the anti-Semitic incidents of 1968 and 1969. Presently editor in chief of *Judisk krönika* (Jewish Chronicle), a highly respected magazine of Jewish culture in Sweden, he has published several volumes of essays. As is apparent from the title—*Judiska prövningar och omprövningar: tankar om makt och minne, diaspora och Israel, vänner och antisemiter, kaos och humor* (Jewish Considerations and Reconsiderations: Thoughts about Power and Memory, Diaspora and Israel, Friends and Anti-Semites, Chaos and Humor, 1992)—his essays cover a wide spectrum of mostly secular Jewish themes, although some are theological in nature. In his book *Ljudet av alef: judiska tankar om hemmahörande, minne, identitet, Gud och diasporan* (The Sound of Aleph: Jewish Thoughts about Belonging, Memory, Identity, God and the Diaspora, 2000), he describes the Jewish tradition as reverberating with the sound of aleph, the first letter of the Hebrew alphabet. It is a letter without a sound; it cannot be pronounced by itself but is necessary for the pronunciation of other letters. In his most recent book *Bortom beit: judiska tankar om öde och tid, oändlighet och godhet, blod och arv* (Beyond Beit: Jewish Thoughts about Fate and Time, Infinity and Benevolence, Blood and Heritage, 2005) he focuses on the increasingly porous borders between science and religion and examines how concepts of God can be understood in the light of modern scientific discoveries.

Born in 1973, Nina Solomin is one of Sweden's youngest Jewish authors and journalists. In her book *Ok, amen: om kärlek och fientlighet i chassidernas New York* (Okay, Amen: On Love and Hostility in the New York of the Hasidim, 2001), she chronicles everyday life among Brooklyn's Satmar Hasidim. Although herself a Jew, she feels toward them the same mixture of curiosity and alienation any young secular Swedish woman would.

In Sweden Yiddish is one of the very few officially recognized minority languages. As elsewhere in Europe, the number of people who speak or even understand Yiddish is decreasing rapidly. One of the few writers proficient in Yiddish is Salomon Schulman, a pediatrician who is also a well-known commentator on East European Jewry and on *Yiddishkeit*. Born in Sweden in 1947, Schulman comes from a Yiddish-speaking family (his parents are Holocaust survivors) from Poland. Schulman has introduced Yiddish writers like Abraham Sutzkever, Itzik Manger, and others to Swedish readers. In *Ur själens getto: en judisk dagbok*

(From the Depths of the Soul: A Jewish Journal, 2002), a collection of newspaper columns and causeries, Schulman displays a burlesque style of his own. He is also the author of a book on Yiddish history and culture entitled *Jiddischland: bland rabbiner och revolutionärer* (Land of Yiddish: Among Rabbis and Revolutionaries, 1996), which features poets and musicians, dybbuks and cabbalists, and saints and whores coexisting side by side. In a joint venture with singer/ actress Basia Frydman, he has translated popular Swedish and other Western songs into Yiddish. He believes that such work with Yiddish keeps him connected to a dying tradition: "Through my Yiddish I maintain a fragile thread to the past. In the special tone of every word I can experience the scents from a world that is no more but to which I ultimately belong" (1996, 256).

Joanna Bankier and Jackie Jakubowski are the coeditors of an anthology of essays entitled *Judisk identitet* (Jewish Identity, 1993). Jakubowski opens the discussion by quoting Emmanuel Levinas: "To investigate one's Jewish identity means to have already lost it" (7). A number of Jewish intellectuals in Sweden are listed as contributors, among them Böhm, Igra, Gustafsson, and Philipson. Several have confirmed that their Jewish identity is rather vague, and that its essence still remains to be defined. Many of the contributors regard themselves as neither entirely Swedish nor exclusively Jewish, claiming the "borderland" between the two as their emotional abode.

At a public debate in Stockholm, the Israeli author and playwright Joshua Sobol insisted that Jewish identity could never be determined by fixed rules or strict boundaries. He maintained that Jewishness involved gravitating toward a bedrock of Jewish tradition whose core is comprised of the Tanakh and the Talmud, the Prophets and the cabbala, the Halacha (Jewish law) and the mystical tradition, the Jewish holidays, and the religious rites. Sobol insisted that being Jewish was a matter of choice between approaching this center versus mantaining one's distance.

Denmark

On April 9, 1940, German forces overran Denmark. The Danes capitulated immediately. During the first months of the occupation, synagogues were allowed to remain open and Zionist organizations could continue to operate. As a result, Danish Jews had trouble believing the rumors about what was happening to Jews living in other parts of Europe.

However, on August 29, 1940, things changed dramatically. German soldiers entered Copenhagen, Danish soldiers and officers were taken prisoner, the government was dissolved, and the parliament was shut down. The Germans confiscated lists with names and addresses of members of the Jewish community and arrested Chief Rabbi Max Friediger.

At that point the Danish public showed a great solidarity with the Jews, who were the primary target of the new Nazi regime. A resistance movement was mobilized to warn Danish Jews about the mounting threat. Ambulances were sent to pick them up and hide them in hospitals under false names. Entire families were aided by members of the clergy or hidden in the homes of gentiles. In October 1943, the month of "the Action," Danes from all walks of life helped their Jewish compatriots escape by boat to neutral Sweden. About 90 percent of the approximately 7,000 Jews in Denmark were secretly transported to safety by this means. Sadly, 472 were captured and deported to Terezin, where 49 died.

Contemporary Jewish authors in Denmark often revisit these events in both their autobiographical and fictional works. "The Danes saved the Jews," Herbert Pundik has proclaimed in his recollections. "The Danes formed a human wall of daring and silence around the rescue operation" (1994, 38). Pundik, who was born in 1927, is a second-generation immigrant whose Orthodox grandfather came to Denmark from the Ukraine following the pogroms. For decades Pundik has maintained a leading position as an intellectual and a writer. Editor in chief of a large Danish newspaper, he has commented prolifically on foreign politics and passionately on the complex situation in Israel and the Middle East. He now resides in Tel Aviv and maintains contact with Denmark in his role as foreign correspondent. The first volume of his memoirs, *Det er ikke nok at overleve* (It Is Not Enough to Survive, 2005), was followed by a second volume, *Du kan hvis du tør: erindringer* (You Can If You Dare, 2006). Pundik reminisces about his youth in Copenhagen, his rescue and arrival in Sweden as a thirteen-year-old, and his return to Denmark as a member of the Danish Brigade, which had been founded by refugees in Sweden to help liberate their country. Several years later he joined the Hagana and took part in the Israeli war of independence. Once considered a hawk, he has assumed a more dovish posture in calling for an Israeli state with equal rights for all its citizens, including both Arabs and Jews.

Several survivors who found refuge in Denmark following the war have published their memoirs. Iboja Wandall-Holm was born in 1923. In *Farvel til århundredet: en fortælling om Europa* (Farewell to a Century: A Tale about Europe, 2000) she describes her flight from an orphanage, experience in Auschwitz, studies in communist Prague, and her arrival in Denmark. She has also published several collections of poetry and translated poems from Slovak into Danish.

Olly Ritterband was born in 1923 and came to Sweden and Denmark after having survived Bergen-Belsen and Auschwitz. Her diary, *Ét ord er et skrig: Auschwitz, 1944–45* (A Word Is a Scream: Auschwitz, 1944–45), was also published in French. Her work *Jeg ville overleve* (Will to Survive, 1984) was published in an English-language edition in 1990.

Lui Beilin, who was born in 1919, has also recorded the story of his escape to

Sweden. He is the son of Samuel Beilin, the famous publisher, lecturer, and activist of the Bund, the Yiddish socialist movement. Lui Beilin has described his father in *Min jiddishe far—og jeg* (My Yiddish Father—and I, 2001). Bent Melchior, the former chief rabbi of Copenhagen, who was born in 1929, collected his memories in a volume entitled *Så vælg da livet* (Choose Life, 1997).

Finn Abrahamowitz was one of many Danish Jews who were taken to Sweden as a child in order to avoid Nazi persecution. He was born in 1939, the son of a Jewish father, whose ancestors came from Minsk, and a Christian mother. He has published a number of mostly nonfiction books focusing on psychological and psychiatric issues, as well as works of fiction. *Da jeg var lille, var Danmark stor: til minde om oktober '43* (When I Was Small, Denmark Was Large: In Remembrance of October 1943, 2003) recounts the events of October 1943, while *Jesus: en biografi* (Jesus: A Biography, 2002) focuses on whether Jesus was an observant Jew, concluding that he was.

Born in 1956, Peter H. Fogtdal belongs to the second generation of Jewish writers. Like many others, his works focus on war-related experiences. In his novel *Drømmeren fra Palæstina* (The Dreamer from Palestine, 1998) he reconstructs the story of his grandfather, David Huda, who left Palestine as a young child and later joined the Danish resistance movement, all the while being chased by the Gestapo. Fogtdal's recent novel *Flødeskumsfronten* (The Whipped Cream War, 2001) features an Austrian lieutenant whose meeting with the Danish Jew "David Huda" revives repressed memories of when he was in charge of propaganda in the Austrian army and served as a soldier at the Eastern front.

Suzanne Brøgger, who was born in 1944, is undoubtedly Denmark's most renowned Jewish writer and a member of the Danish Academy. She made a spectacular debut in 1973 with *Fri os fra kaerligheden* (Deliver Us From Love, 1976), a passionate apology *against* love, marriage, nuclear families—and nuclear weapons. In the novel she describes transvestites as guerrilla fighters for sexual equality and tells a story about herself of being raped and abused by a dozen policemen in Uzbekistan. Rejecting a single genre, the novel, according to the author's prefatory note, is presented as "fragments of reports, essays, interviews *and fiction*" (my italics). This mixture of genres has become a trademark of her work, which combines autobiography, essay, and fiction to create a unique style. Her novel *Jadekatten: en slaegtssaga* (The Jade Cat: A Family Saga, 1997), set in the era of the Nazi occupation, chronicles five generations of a Danish Jewish family whose wealth and social prominence is not enough to save its members from danger. The narrative begins with the story of a poor Jewish immigrant named Isidor Løvin, the son of a lace maker. Løvin came from Poland to Denmark in the early 1800s, where he founded the quintessentially Danish Aalborg liquor factory. Having consciously set themselves apart from the "Ghetto Jews," the family members are shocked to realize that although they are indistinguishable from the rest of the Danish bourgeoisie, they are nevertheless subject to Nazi persecution. Their attitude to the creed of their ancestors is depicted in the image of a young women's copy of the *Khumash,* the Five Books of Moses: "Rubbish, Nonsense, Bubble, Trash, Excuses, Wiseacre, False prophets" is scrawled all over the pages, "and all the laws of burnt offerings, harvest offerings, and thanksgiving offerings are crossed" (38). Reality catches up with the family, however, and they have to flee to Sweden.

Pia Tafdrup, who was born in 1952, is one of the most renowned poets in Denmark and a member of the Danish Academy. Her auspicious debut involved a collection of poems, *Når der går hul på en engel* (When There Is a Hole in an Angel, 1981), in which the loss of innocence figures as a primary theme. She has published a number of poetry collections, some plays, and a collection of essays explaining her poetics entitled *Over vandet går jeg: skitse til en poetik* (Over the Water I Walk: Outline of a Poetics, 1991). Tafdrup's parents never spoke of their Jewish background. In *Territorialsang: en Jerusalemkomposition* (Territorial Song: A Jerusalem Composition, 1994), the author breaks the taboo of silence shielding her parents' past. While the female body in all its sensuousness and sexuality is a major theme of her poetry, there is also a strong metaphysical dimension. In *Hvid Feber* (White Fever, 1986), she articulates the melancholy feeling of being a stranger in the world, and in her book on poetics she speaks about her poetry as being torn between two poles: hunger for life and fear of death, between emotion and thought, language and muteness.

One of her recent poems is *Dronningeporten* (Queen's Gate, 1998). In a postscript to the book she explains the choice of title. During a visit to Jerusalem she realized that none of the names of the eight gates in the old city walls carried any female connotations. Thinking that there must be a way for women to enter the world, she coined the name "Queen's Gate" for this imagined opening. In the collection, images of pain, stone, and parched land contrast with water in its myriad forms—drop, lake, river, well, sea, bath, rain, body fluids, and rainbow—while the ongoing intifada becomes an emblem for the drought in Jerusalem.

Compared to their co-religionists in the neighboring countries surrounding the Baltic Sea, Scandinavian Jews have enjoyed an exceptionally peaceful coexistence with the Christian majority. Janina Katz, who was born in 1939, is one of about twenty-five hundred refugees who came to Denmark from Poland in 1969 to escape the witchhunt undertaken by the Communist regime. Katz, who has been called a Polish Jewish author writing in Danish, only made her debut in 1991. To date she has published some fifteen volumes, including poetry, novels, and short stories. One of her novels, *Mit liv som barbar* (My Life as a Barbarian, 1993), tells the story of the unspoiled Polish childhood of an imaginative child of a Jewish and Catholic family who grows up surrounded by pain and suffering.

Katz's autobiographical novel *Putska* (1997) captures what it felt like as a young woman among students and intellectuals in socialist Poland of the turbulent sixties. *Den glade jødinde og andre historier* (The Happy Jewess and Other Stories, 1998) is a collection of short stories in which Jewish melancholy is balanced by surreal magic realism and the grotesque.

Morten Thing, who was born in 1945, is a cultural historian and essayist. His father was a well-known Danish political activist and a member of the resistance, while his mother came from an observant Orthodox Jewish family. Having focused mainly on political issues from a radical left-wing perspective, Thing has turned to questions concerning Jewish history and identity. In several collections of essays—*Den historiske jøde* (The Historical Jew, 2001), *Jiddishland i København* (Land of Yiddish in Copenhagen, 2005), and *Næste år i Jerusalem* (Next Year in Jerusalem, 1999)—he concentrates on modern Jewish immigration to Denmark, mentioning some of its prominent personalities and discussing the essence of Judaism and the meaning of being Jewish today. He raises provocative issues, such as whether Jews should be considered "a people" and whether the state of Israel should be seen as the "solution" to the "Jewish question."

Gerz Feigenberg, who was born in 1956, made his debut as a novelist in 1980. During his teens his family immigrated to Israel, only to return to Denmark two years later. In the novel *Bastard* (1985) he portrays a family cloaked in secrets that are partly revealed through the accounts of the aging grandmother and partly thanks to a bundle of letters received by the narrator, which tell the story of a young Jewish man encountering the prejudices of the cultural elite of Copenhagen in the early thirties.

Daniel Dencik, who was born in 1972, belongs to the most recent generation of Danish Jewish writers. He grew up in a Swedish Jewish family residing in Copenhagen and is fluent in both Danish and Swedish. *Solvinden* (The Sun Wind, 2005), his fourth book and second collection of poetry, touches upon the theme of being both Jewish and of binational origin. He has also written the script for the film *Ghetto*, a Jewish-Arabic Romeo and Juliet love story that takes place in the Jewish school in Copenhagen where Dencik himself was once a pupil.

Norway

Of all the Scandinavian countries, Norway has the smallest number of Jews—some fifteen hundred in total. Before World War II there were eighteen hundred, most of them immigrants from eastern Europe, all but two hundred Norwegian citizens.

From 1915 to 1940 Jewish cultural life in Oslo blossomed. Despite the small Jewish population, there were several Jewish theater groups performing in Yiddish. In addition to Jewish choirs, there were also cultural and academic organizations. In 1940 it all came to an end when Denmark and Norway were occupied by Nazi Germany. During the German occupation, almost half the Norwegian Jews (770) were sent to Auschwitz, where 760 of them were killed. The Norwegian underground movement succeeded in smuggling the remaining Jews to safety in Sweden.

Born in 1912, Leo Eitinger immigrated to Norway in 1939 but was deported to Auschwitz and Buchenwald in 1942. He returned to Norway, one of only a handful of survivors, and devoted the rest of his life to the study of concentration camp survivors. A psychiatrist by training, he is considered a cofounder of victimology. In addition to his numerous scientific works, he has written and edited books about anti-Semitism and xenophobia, including *Fremmed i Norge* (Stranger in Norway, 1981), *Mennesker blant Mennesker* (Human Among Humans, 1985), and (with Hallvard Rieber-Mohn) *Retten til å overleve* (The Right to Survive, 1976). He also played a decisive role in the human rights movement in Norway before he died in 1996.

Eva Scheer, who was born in 1915, should be mentioned in this context as she has published both fiction and nonfiction on Jewish themes. Aside from autobiographical works, she has written books on Jewish migration history and on the Jewish heritage as expressed in folktales and legends. Scheer died in 1999.

Mona Levin, who was born in 1939, is a Norwegian journalist who, at the age of three, was carried in a rucksack through the woods to Sweden. She has published a biography of her father, the pianist Robert Levin, entitled *Med livet i hendene* (With Life in the Hands, 1983), as well as several other works.

Unlike contemporary Jewish writers in other Scandinavian countries who utilize their family background as a motif in their fiction, this is not a common practice in Norway. Øystein Wingaard Wolf, who was born in 1958, is often seen as the only fiction writer who "comes from a Jewish family." He himself, however, has corrected this misleading impression by noting that only his father is Jewish. Yet he "tends and irrigates his Jewish roots" ("Jiddisch—levende eller døende?" 1990, 51). East European Jewish culture and questions of present-day Jewish identity are recurrent themes in his books. *Dodi Ashers död* (The Death of Dodi Asher, 1986) is the story of two Jewish women whose families have disappeared in the Ukraine during the war. *Kongen er i himmelen* (The King Is in Heaven, 1989) is a novel about a young man named David who suddenly discovers that his mother is Jewish, which prompts him to learn more about Jewish history and identity. The poetry collection *En fremmed våker over min sjel* (A Stranger Watches Over My Soul, 1991) deals with philosophical and religious questions, especially one's relationship to God. The title story of *Vi kom gjennom ørkenen* (We Came Through the Hurricane, 1997) describes the lives of five Jewish friends who undertake a journey to Israel in order to confirm their Jewish identity. Although Wingaard Wolf often touches upon tragic themes, he emphasizes that "joy is a Jewish obligation," and that it must be upheld in the face of painful Jewish suffering ("Jiddisch—levende eller døende?" 1990, 51). His most recent volume of poetry, *Bønner til en tvilling* (Prayers for a Twin, 2004), focuses on the relationship between the sexes, with numerous references to the author's Jewish background, Jewish mythology and religion, and the seemingly never-ending conflict between Israel and the Palestinian people.

Finland

Finland, like Sweden, was one of the few European countries not occupied by Nazi Germany. Jewish immigrants to Finland came solely from the east, from countries of the former Russian empire or from the Soviet Union. These immigrants brought with them a familiarity with the Yiddish-speaking shtetl, including its oral and literary traditions. This heritage reverberates most distinctively in the voice of the novelist Daniel Katz, who was born in 1938 into a family of Russian origin. Katz and Jakobson are the only writers among Finland's Jewish authors who write in Finnish. Karmela Bélinki and Mikael Enckell belong to the Swedish-speaking minority, representing only 6 percent of Finland's population.

Daniel Katz conveys the distinctive tone and diction of *Yiddishkeit*. In contrast to those Scandinavian writers who seek to grasp fading memories of a vanished world, his narratives appear deeply rooted in a living Jewish tradition. Katz has published a number of novels, several of which have been translated into other languages. He has also written plays for the theater, radio, and television. The novel *Kun isoisä Suomeen hiihti* (My Father Owned a Cornet, 1971) tells the story of how the narrator's grandfather, a noncommissioned officer in the Russian army, came to Finland in the wake of the Russo-Japanese War. Like all of Katz's novels, it is told in a burlesque, ironic style that treats the characters with humorous affection. In *Orvar Keinin Kuolema* (The Death of Orvar Klein, 1976), he relays the history of the first Jewish immigrants in Finland with black humor, with the protagonist, Orvar Klein, ending up—at least temporarily— back in Siberia. There is a melancholy irony in these picaresque stories, where the poor Jew is at the mercy of the absurdities and caprices of life, and is ultimately rescued from tragedy only by the lightness of the humoresque.

Karmela Bélinki, who was born in 1947, is an essayist and radio journalist who has published several essay collections, including *Tikva—Hopp* (Tikva— Hope, 1987) and *Brev till Sarah* (Letters to Sarah, 1996), which address Jewish themes. Her work is driven by a desire to unmask hidden forms of racism and anti-Semitism, to explain Yiddish culture and language, and to criticize Jewish Orthodoxy for preventing women from assuming leading positions in the community and the synagogue. She stands up for Halacha, the Jewish law, and for Israel and Zionism, while also stressing the alliance between Finnish

Jews and Finland. She received her doctorate in religious studies with a dissertation on the image of the Jew in Finnish literature entitled "Shylock i Finland: judarna och Finlands litteratur, 1900–1970" (Shylock in Finland: The Jews and the Literature of Finland, 1900–1970, 2000). *Det gröna apoteket* (The Green Pharmacy, 2005) tells of the fate of the Baltic Jews during and after World War II. The title alludes to the family-run pharmacy in the Lithuanian town of Kaunas. Except for her grandmother, who was married in Finland, only one member of the family survived.

Max Jakobson, who was born in 1923, grew up in a Jewish family originally from Kurland, Latvia. He has forged a brilliant career as a diplomat and is also known as an astute political observer, having even been slated to become secretary-general of the United Nations. Jakobson has published a number of books on political, historical, and diplomatic issues, the most recent being a two-volume study of current political history entitled *20. vuosisadan tilinpätös* (Closing the Books of the 20th Century, 1999–2001), which is interspersed with reminiscences of his Jewish childhood.

Although Mikael Enckell, who was born in 1932, does not come from a Jewish family—he is the son of the modernist poet Rabbe Enckell—he should nevertheless be mentioned as an important contributor to Finland's discourse on Jewish issues. Trained as a psychoanalyst, as a literary critic and essayist he sides with a group of American Jewish literary critics—Geoffrey Hartman, Harold Bloom, Robert Alter, and Susan A. Handelman—who have distanced themselves from the purist ideals of new criticism in favor of a more associative and ambiguous way of interpreting literary texts harking back to the tradition of the Talmud and the Midrash.

In the preface to his book *I den frågandes själ* (In the Soul of the Inquirer, 1993) Enckell calls attention to the fact that there is a new wave of interest in Jewish issues among Jews as well as throughout the world. Although he fears that this may be just a fad, he is inclined to believe that it is the sign of a true renaissance. Could it be, he asks himself, that the generations born during and after the war now feel an urgent need for healing and reparation? Is there a rhythm in the historical memory that calls for a change in attitude toward the Jewish catastrophe of the years 1933–45? Enckell sees the revived—or newly sparked—interest in the trauma of the Shoah as part of a historical process of healing that can serve as a link to the tradition of Jewish thought.

The most characteristic feature of contemporary Jewish fiction in Scandinavia is the continuous presence of the war and the Shoah. While many members of the older generation of Jewish writers bear witness to the atrocities, the post-Shoah generations often endeavor to penetrate the wall of silence that has encapsulated the trauma, to reassemble disparate pieces of the past and fragmentary memories in order to re-create the vanished world of their Jewish parents and ancestors.

Is the current obsession with the Holocaust, sixty years after the end of the war, a sign of a historical and collective healing process, as Mikael Enckell suggests, or is it a symptom of a process of assimilation that has left a generation of writers devoid of any Jewish heritage other than the enshrined memories of persecution and genocide?

To a certain extent, both notions seem to be at work. The healing of a trauma of historical dimensions requires a period of time that can only be measured in terms of generations. The absence in contemporary Jewish literature of a visible and dynamic Jewish tradition as well as any discussion of the intrinsic values of Judaism is probably more a consequence of secularization than of "assimilation." The process of secularization has gained support not only through the hegemony of "rationalist" thought (which is considered antagonistic to religion) but also as a result of the difficulties of Judaism in Europe to adapt to modernity. The trauma of the Holocaust seems to have instilled an anguish and fear of development and change, as though any modification of Jewish life and rituals (like those concerning the role of women) might obliterate the last immaterial remains of Jewish life. This resistance to change and to the challenges of modern life and thought (which helps maintain Jewish Orthodoxy's dominance in Europe) continues to widen the gap between those who choose to live within religious Jewish tradition and those who choose to remain outside it. The latter seems to be the choice of most Jewish writers.

Contemporary Jewish writing addresses and reflects this situation. It tells us that in a secular world the borderline separating "Jewish" and "non-Jewish" is porous and not definitive. The perspective of both is often that of an outsider observing a vanishing world of traumatic events and fading memories. The threshold between the "secular" and the "religious," conversely, remains difficult to cross.

The nonfiction produced by present-day Jewish intellectuals in Scandinavia—authors as different as Göran Rosenberg, Herbert Pundik, Mikael Enckell, Morten Thing, Karmela Bélinki, Jackie Jakubowski and Anita Goldman— adds another dimension to this discussion. These essayists view both the knowledge and traditional approaches of rabbis, scholars, and philosophers as valid contributions to contemporary discourse. The tradition of Jewish thought is openly embraced, with Jewish ethics emerging as an energizing factor in the often heated discussion of political issues.

WORKS CITED

Abrahamowitz, Finn. 2002. *Jesus: en biografi.* Copenhagen: Høst.
———. 2003. *Da jeg var lille, var Danmark stor: til minde om oktober '43.* Copenhagen: Høst.

Ahrne, Marianne. 1998. *Fader okänd.* Stockholm: Norstedt.

Bankier, Joanna, and Jackie Jakubowski, eds. *Judisk identitet.* 1993. Stockholm: Natur och Kultur.

Beilin, Lui. 2001. *Min Jiddishe Far—og Jeg.* Copenhagen: C. A. Reitzel.

Bélinki, Karmela. 1987. *Tikva—hopp.* Otalampi: Sahlgren.

———. 1996. *Brev till Sarah.* Otalampi: Sahlgren.

———. 2000. "Shylock i Finland: judarna och Finlands litteratur, 1900–1970." Ph.D. diss, åbo akademi.

———. 2005. *Det gröna apoteket.* Helsinki: Sahlgren.

Berggren, Tobias, and Sven-David Sandström. 1992. *Requiem: De ur alla minnen fallna.* Caprice Records, CAP 22027.

Böhm, Tomas. 2000. *The Vienna Jazz Trio.* Stockholm: Natur och Kultur.

Brøgger, Suzanne. 1973. *Fri os fra kaerligheden.* Copenhagen: Rhodos.

———. 1976. *Deliver Us from Love.* Trans. Thomas Teal. New York: Delacorte.

———. 1997. *Jadekatten: en slaegtssaga.* Copenhagen: Gyldendal.

———. 2004. *The Jade Cat.* Trans. Anne Born. London: Harvill.

Dencik, Daniel. 2005. *Solvinden.* Copenhagen: Gyldendal.

Dencik, Lars. 2003. "Jewishness in Postmodernity: The Case of Sweden." In *New Jewish Identities: Contemporary Europe and Beyond,* ed. Zvi Gitelman, Barry Kosmin, and András Kovács, 75–105. Budapest: Central European University Press.

Edvardson, Cordelia. 1984. *Bränt barn söker sig till elden.* Stockholm: Bromberg.

———. 1997. *Burned Child Seeks the Fire: A Memoir.* Trans. Joel Agee. Boston: Beacon.

Eggens, Magda. 1997. *Om stenarna kunde tala.* Stockholm: Rabén & Sjögren.

Einhorn, Jerzy. 1996. *Utvald att leva: minnen.* Stockholm: Bonnier.

Einhorn, Lena. 2005. *Ninas resa: en överlevnadsberättelse.* Stockholm: Prisma.

Einhorn, Stefan. 1998. *En dold Gud: om religion, vetenskap och att söka Gud.* Stockholm: Forum.

———. 2002. *A Concealed God: Religion, Science, and the Search for Truth.* Trans. Linda Scheck. Philadelphia, Pa.: Templeton Foundation Press.

———. 2003. *Den sjunde dagen.* Stockholm: Forum.

Eitinger, Leo. 1981. *Fremmed i Norge.* Oslo: Cappelen.

———. 1985. *Mennesker blant Mennesker: en bok om antisemittisme og fremmedhat.* Oslo: Cappelen.

Eitinger, Leo, and Hallvard Rieber-Mohn, eds. 1976. *Retten til å overleve: en bok om Israel, Norge og antisemittismen.* Oslo: Cappelen.

Enckell, Mikael. 1993. *I den frågandes själ? Essäer i judiska ämnen.* Helsingfors: Söderström.

Feigenberg, Gerz. 1985. *Bastard.* Copenhagen: Lindhardt and Ringhof.

Fogtdal, Peter. 1998. *Drømmeren fra Palæstina.* Copenhagen: Lindhardt og Ringhof.

———. 2001. *Flødeskumsfronten.* Copenhagen: Lindhardt og Ringhof.

Fried, Hédi. 1992. *Skärvor av ett liv: vägen till och från Auschwitz.* Stockholm: Natur och Kultur.

———. 1995. *Livet tillbaka.* Stockholm: Natur och Kultur.

———. 1996. *Fragments of a Life: The Road to Auschwitz.* Trans. Michael Meyer. London: Hale.

———. 2000. *Ett tredje liv: från jordbävning i själen till meningsfull tillvaro.* Stockholm: Natur och Kultur.

Gedin, Per I. 2003. *Litteraturens örtagårdsmästare: Karl Otto Bonnier och hans tid.* Stockholm: Bonnier.

Goldman, Anita. 1988a. *Den sista kvinnan från Ur.* Johanneshov: Hammarström och Åberg.

———. 1988b. *Våra bibliska mödrar.* Stockholm: Natur och Kultur.

————. 1991. *Stenarnas döttrar.* Stockholm: Bonnier.

————. 1994. *Orden som brändes.* Stockholm: Natur och Kultur.

————. 2001. *Jag bor bredvid paradiset.* Stockholm: Natur och Kultur.

————. 2005. *Guds älskarinnor: om hängivna kvinnor i en livrädd värld.* Stockholm: Natur och Kultur.

Goldman, Marianne. 1998. *Försoningsdagen.* Manuscript. Stockholm: Draken Teaterförlag.

Gottfarb, Suzanne [Suzannah]. 1987. *Systrarna Blaumans hemlighet.* Stockholm: Bromberg.

————. 1998. *Hur familjen Green slutligen fick sitt skräprum utrymt: berättelser från Jerusalem.* Nora: Nya Doxa.

Gustafsson, Lars. 1986. *Bernard Foys tredje rockad.* Stockholm: Norstedt.

————. 1988. *Bernard Foy's Third Casting.* Trans. Yvonne L. Sandstroem. New York: New Directions.

————. 1994. "Att åta sig att vara jude." In *Judisk identitet* (1993), ed. Joanna Bankier and Jackie Jakubowski, 83–93. Stockholm: Natur och Kultur.

Igra, Ludvig. 1994. "Gränsöverskridandets folk." In *Judisk identitet* (1993), ed. Joanna Bankier and Jackie Jakubowski, 17–36. Stockholm: Natur och Kultur.

————. 2001. *Den tunna hinnan mellan omsorg och grymhet.* Stockholm: Natur och Kultur.

Jakobson, Max. 1999–2001. *20. vuosisadan tilinpätös.* Vol. 1: *Väkivallan vuodet.* Vol. 2: *Pelon ja toivon aika.* Helsinki: Otava.

Jakubowski, Jackie. 1992. *Judiska prövningar och omprövningar: tankar om makt och minne, diaspora och Israel, vänner och antisemiter, kaos och humor.* Stockholm: Bromberg.

————. 2000. *Ljudet av alef: judiska tankar om hemmahörande, minne, identitet, Gud och diasporan.* Stockholm: Natur och Kultur.

————. 2005. *Bortom beit: judiska tankar om öde och tid, oändlighet och godhet, blod och arv.* Stockholm: Atlantis.

"Jiddisch—levende eller døende?" 1990. *Aftenposten, Morgen,* May 2: 51.

Josephson, Erland. 1957. *En berättelse om herr Silberstein.* Stockholm: Bonnier.

————. 1995. *A Story about Mr. Silberstein.* Trans. Roger Greenwald. Evanston, Ill.: Northwestern University Press.

Kanter, Lennart. 1981. *David Kahans sista ord.* Stockholm: Norstedt.

Kaplan, Suzanne. 2002. "Child Survivors in the Holocaust: Affects and Memory Images in Trauma and Generational Linking." Ph.D. diss., University of Stockholm.

————. 2003. *Barn under Förintelsen—då och nu: Affekter och minnesbilder efter extrem traumatisering.* Stockholm: Natur och Kultur.

Kats, Madeleine. 1965. *Taggig frukt: att leva i Israel.* Stockholm: Bonnier.

Katz, Daniel. 1969. *Kun isoisä Suomeen hiihti.* Porvoo: Söderström.

————. 1971. *Min farfar hade en kornett.* Trans. Anna Bondestam. Stockholm: Geber.

————. 1976. *Orvar Kleinin kuolema.* Porvoo: Söderström.

————. 1978. *Orvar Kleins död.* Trans. Ralf Parland. Stockholm: Rabén & Sjögren.

Katz, Janina. 1993. *Mit liv som barbar.* Copenhagen (Valby): Vindrose.

————. 1997. *Putska.* Copenhagen (Valby): Vindrose.

————. 1998. *Den glade jødinde og andre historier.* Copenhagen (Valby): Vindrose.

Klein, Georg. 1984. *I stället för hemland.* Stockholm: Bonnier.

Lagercrantz, Rose. 1995. *Flickan som inte ville kyssas.* Stockholm: Bromberg.

Larsson, Zenia. 1960. *Skuggorna vid träbron.* Stockholm: Rabén & Sjögren.

————. 1961. *Lång är gryningen.* Stockholm: Rabén & Sjögren.

————. 1962. *Livet till mötes.* Stockholm: Rabén & Sjögren.

Levin, Mona. 1983. *Med livet i hendene.* Oslo: Cappelen.

Levin, Susanne. 1994. *Leva vidare.* Stockholm: Natur och Kultur.

———. 1996. *Som min egen.* Stockholm: Natur och Kultur.

———. 1998. *Suggan i dômen.* Stockholm: Natur och Kultur.

———. 2000. *Tillbaka till Király utca.* Stockholm: Natur och Kultur.

Lomfors, Ingrid. 1996. "Förlorad barndom—återvunnet liv: de judiska flyktingbarnen från Nazityskland." Ph.D. diss., University of Gothenburg.

Melchior, Bent. 1997. *Så vælg da livet: erindringer.* Copenhagen: Gyldendal.

Mosskin, Peter. 1994. *Skänk åt den fege en hingst.* Stockholm: Bonnier.

———. 1997. *Glöm inte bort att jag finns.* Stockholm: Bonnier.

———. 2000. *Där stäppen tar slut.* Stockholm: Bonnier.

Narrowe, Morton H. 2005. *En tretvinnad tråd: amerikan, jude, svensk.* Stockholm: Bonnier.

Pettersson, Thorsten. 2004. "Dödsmässan bekräftar vår mänsklighet." *Svenska Dagbladet,* January 24.

Philipson, Joakim. 1991. *Tecknet och tystnaden: anteckningar funna i en tagelmadrass; första gången utgivna på svenska, i översättning av Joakim Philipson.* Stockholm: Bonnier.

———. 1996. *Jakobs röst.* Stockholm: Bonnier.

Pundik, Herbert. 1994. "The Escape of 1943." In *A Guide to Jewish Denmark,* ed. Karen Lisa Goldsmith Salamon, 26–43. Copenhagen: Reitzel.

———. 2005. *Det er ikke nok at overleve: erindringer.* Copenhagen: Gyldendal.

———. 2006. *Du kan hvis du tør: erindringer.* Copenhagen: Gyldendal.

Ritterband, Olly. 1984. *Jeg ville overleve.* Copenhagen: Haase.

———. 1990. *Will to Survive.* Trans. Séan Martin. Copenhagen: Frihedsmuseets Venners Forlags Fond.

———. 1998. *Ét ord er et skrig: Auschwitz, 1944–45.* Copenhagen: Aschehoug.

Rosenberg, Göran. 1996. *Det förlorade landet: en personlig historia.* Stockholm: Bonnier.

———. 2003. *Plikten, profiten och konsten att vara människa.* Stockholm: Bonnier.

Shachar, Nathan. 1996. *Vilsenhetens förklädnader: essäer om myter, modernitet och tradition i Mellanöstern.* Stockholm: Atlantis.

———. 2006. *Blodseld och nordisk längtan: Oscar Levertin och hans tid.* Stockholm: Atlantis.

Schulman, Salomon. 1996. *Jiddischland: bland rabbiner och revolutionärer.* Nora: Nya Doxa.

———. 2002. *Ur själens getto: en judisk dagbok.* Nora: Nya Doxa.

Solomin, Nina. 2001. *Ok, amen: om kärlek och fientlighet i chassidernas New York.* Stockholm: Wahlström & Widstrand.

Stenberg, Peter, ed. 2004. *Contemporary Jewish Writing in Sweden: An Anthology.* Lincoln: University of Nebraska Press.

Tafdrup, Pia. 1981. *Når der går hul på en engel.* Copenhagen (Valby): Borgen.

———. 1986. *Hvid feber.* Copenhagen (Valby): Borgen.

———. 1991. *Over vandet går jeg: skitse til en poetik.* Copenhagen (Valby): Borgen.

———. 1994. *Territorialsang: en Jerusalemkomposition.* Copenhagen (Valby): Borgen.

———. 1998. *Dronningeporten.* Copenhagen: Gyldendal.

———. 1999. "Six Poems from *Territorialsang.*" Trans. Roger Greenwald. In *New Zealand–Scandinavian Conference on Ethnicity and Migration: North and South,* ed. Ivo Holmqvist, 104–13. Västerås, Sweden: Mälardalen University.

———. 2001. *Queen's Gate.* Trans. David McDuff. Tarset, U.K.: Bloodaxe.

Thing, Morten. 1999. *Næste år i Jerusalem.* Copenhagen: Aschehoug.

———. 2001. *Den historiske jøde.* Copenhagen: Forum.

———. 2005. *Jiddishland i København: den jødiske invandring, 1905–1914.* Copenhagen: Nemos Bibliotek.

Thor, Annika. 1996. *En ö i havet*. Stockholm: Bonnier Carlsen.

———. 1997. *Näckrosdammen*. Stockholm: Bonnier Carlsen.

———. 1998. *Havets djup*. Stockholm: Bonnier Carlsen.

———. 1999. *Öppet hav*. Stockholm: Bonnier Carlsen.

Valentin, Hugo. 1964. *Judarna i Sverige*. Stockholm: Bonnier.

Wandall-Holm, Iboja. 2000. *Farvel til århundredet: en fortælling om Europa*. Copenhagen: Gyldendal [originally published as *Morbærtræet* in 1991].

Wästberg, Per. 2002. *Axel Hirsch: Folkbildare och filantrop*. Stockholm: Svenska Akademien, Norstedt.

Werup, Jacques. 1983. *Shimonoffs längtan*. Stockholm: Bonnier.

Weiss, Peter. 1964. *Die Verfolgung und Ermordung Jean Paul Marats dargestellt durch die Schauspielgruppe des Hospizes zu Charenton unter Anleitung des Herrn de Sade: Drama in zwei Akten*. Frankfurt am Main: Suhrkamp.

———. 1965a. *Die Ermittlung*. Frankfurt am Main: Suhrkamp.

———. 1965b. *Jean Paul Marat förföljd och mördad så som det framställs av patienterna på hospitalet Charenton under ledning av herr de Sade*. Trans. Britt G. Hallqvist. Lund: Cavefors.

———. 1965c. *Rannsakningen: oratorium i 11 sånger*. Trans. Britt G. Hallqvist. Malmö: Cavefors.

———. 1966a. *The Investigation*. Trans. Jon Swan and Ulu Grosbard. New York: Atheneum.

———. 1966b. *The Persecution and Assassination of Marat as Performed by the Inmates of the Asylum of Charenton under the Direction of the Marquis de Sade*. Trans. Geoffrey Skelton. Verse adaptation Adrien Mitchell. London: John Calder.

———. 1975. *Die Ästhetik des Widerstands*. Frankfurt am Main: Suhrkamp.

———. 1976–81. *Motståndets estetik*. Trans. Ulrika Wallenström. Stockholm: Arbetarkultur.

———. 2005. *The Aesthetics of Resistance*. Trans. Joachim Neugroschel. Durham, N.C.: Duke University Press.

Wingaard Wolf, Øystein. 1986. *Dodi Ashers død*. Oslo: Cappelen.

———. 1989. *Kongen er i himmelen*. Oslo: Aschenhoug.

———. 1991. *En fremmed våker over min sjel*. Oslo: Aschenhoug.

———. 1997. *Vi kom gjennom ørkenen*. Oslo: Aschenhoug.

———. 2004. *Bønner til en tvilling*. Oslo: Aschenhoug.

Zern, Leif. 2004. "Porträtt av kritikern som ung." *Dagens Nyheter*, July 28.

TEXTS AVAILABLE IN ENGLISH

Brøgger, Suzanne. 1976. *Deliver Us from Love*. Trans. Thomas Teal. New York: Delacorte.

———. 2004a. *"A Fighting Pig Is Too Tough to Eat" and Other Prose Texts*. Trans. Marina Allemano. Norwich, U.K.: Norvik.

———. 2004b. *The Jade Cat*. Trans. Anne Born. London: Harvill.

Edvardson, Cordelia. 1997. *Burned Child Seeks the Fire: A Memoir*. Trans. Joel Agee. Boston: Beacon.

Fried, Hédi. 1996. *Fragments of a Life: The Road to Auschwitz*. Trans. Michael Meyer. London: Hale.

Gustafsson, Lars. 1988. *Bernard Foy's Third Casting*. Trans. Yvonne L. Sandstroem. New York: New Directions.

Josephson, Erland. 1995. *A Story about Mr. Silberstein*. Trans. Roger Greenwald. Evanston, Ill.: Northwestern University Press.

Ritterband, Olly. 1990. *Will to Survive.* Trans. Séan Martin. Copenhagen: Frihedsmuseets Venners Forlags Fond.

Stenberg, Peter, ed. 2004. *Contemporary Jewish Writing in Sweden: An Anthology.* Lincoln: University of Nebraska Press.

Tafdrup, Pia. 1989. *Spring Tide.* Trans. Anne Born. London: Forest Book.

———. 1999. "Six Poems from *Territorialsang.*" Trans. Roger Greenwald. In *New Zealand–Scandinavian Conference on Ethnicity and Migration: North and South,* ed. Ivo Holmqvist, 104–13. Västerås, Sweden: Mälardalen University.

———. 2001. *Queen's Gate.* Trans. David McDuff. Tarset, U.K.: Bloodaxe.

Weiss, Peter. 1966. *The Investigation.* Trans. Jon Swan and Ulu Grosbard. New York: Atheneum.

———. 1984. *The Persecution and Assassination of Marat as Performed by the Inmates of the Asylum of Charenton under the Direction of the Marquis de Sade.* Trans. Geoffrey Skelton. New York: Atheneum.

———. 2005. *The Aesthetics of Resistance.* Trans. Joachim Neugroschel. Durham, N.C.: Duke University Press.

FIVE

~

BRYAN CHEYETTE

Imagined Communities: Contemporary Jewish Writing in Great Britain

Jewish writing in Britain has a long and multiple history that is only now being retold.[1] Starting at the beginning of the nineteenth century, the origins of this literary tradition have been variously understood in relation to the Anglo-Jewish emancipation struggle, as a key aspect of Victorian women's writing, and in the light of conversional desires of English liberal culture (Valman 2007 and Cheyette and Valman 2004). Within these varied contexts, British Jewish writers were primarily mediators who were buffeted and bowed by the common expectations of Victorian society. Writing between the 1820s and the 1850s—a time when Anglo-Jewry was attempting to gain full political and civil rights, these authors were called upon to represent their nascent community in the best possible light as worthy citizens. With only about 35,000 Jews residing in England and Wales in 1851, one should not underestimate the sense of minority literature being produced under severe pressure from the majority culture.

After Jews were finally granted full political and civil rights, there was still a distinct unease about whether they could fulfill the emancipationist contract and ultimately transform themselves into "Englishmen of the Mosaic Persuasion." This renewed anxiety was primarily due to an influx of around 150,000 Jewish immigrants from eastern Europe between 1881 and 1914. Historians have described this transformation of Anglo-Jewry in terms of the complex nexus of class, community, and nation. Within this fluid and constantly changing context, the Anglicization of migrant Jews was given the highest priority by a centralized and assimilated Anglo-Jewish elite (Feldman 1994). Jewish writers were able to reassure a British readership that "Jewishness" was limited to the private sphere. The towering figure of Israel Zangwill (1864–1926) undoubtedly produced the best known and most influential portraits of immigrant Jews within these communal terms.[2]

This irrevocable split between English and Jewish culture, between the "ghetto" and the "melting pot," characterizes a good deal of Zangwill's writing. What is clear from his literary politics is that it was impossible for Zangwill to imagine an Englishness which could in any way accommodate a Jewish past.[3] The sharp division between the assimilation of the "melting pot" and his narrow "ghetto" territorialism points up the dangers of conforming, as an insider, to the restrictive choices permitted within English national culture. The latter were foisted on British Jewish writers and continued to deform their literary output long after Zangwill was forgotten.

Alongside the largely conformist tradition of Zangwill were more transgressive writers such as Amy Levy (1861–89), Julia Frankau (1864–1916), and Isaac Rosenberg (1890–1914). All three challenged the assumptions of an English national culture and Anglo-Jewry's complacent self-image. In the case of Levy and Frankau, it is clear that their role as avowed "outsiders" came close to realizing the liberatory potential of their early Victorian foremothers Grace Aguilar (1816–47), Celia and Marion Moss (1819–1873 and 1821–1907, respectively), and Charlotte Montfiore (1818–1854). Isaac Rosenberg originated a form of diasporic British Jewish writing that, with its images of in-betweenness, of simultaneously belonging and not belonging, prefigures much of postwar British Jewish literature.

The figure who most closely followed Zangwill as an Anglo-Jewish insider was the novelist Louis Golding (1895–1958). Like his predecessor, he continued to present mainly sympathetic images of Anglo-Jewry which conformed to communal expectations. In his best-selling novel *Magnolia Street* (1932) he records the clash between Jews and gentiles in a provincial town and their eventual reconciliation. This vision of harmony clearly struck a chord at a time when an Anglo-Jewish elite was constantly embarrassed by the poor and unassimilated sons and daughters of immigrants. Nearly a century after the struggle for emancipation, Anglo-Jewry was still desperately attempting to prove that it was worthy of the rights and freedoms extended to it. However, it was this crushing need to present favorable images of Jews to the outside world which deformed much British Jewish writing and remained at the top of Anglo-Jewry's communal agenda throughout the interwar years (Waterman and Schmool 1995).

Postwar British Jewish Literature

At the end of 1958, in a series of articles entitled "The Men Behind the Pen," the London-based *Jewish Chronicle* called on the "younger generation of Jewish writers in England" to discuss their attitudes toward "Judaism and the Jewish community."[4] To the chagrin of its readership, all of the authors interviewed displayed either indifference or animosity toward Anglo-Jewry. As the only surviving European Jewish community after the war, Anglo-Jewry numbered 450,000 strong and had a literary culture whose roots went back more than a century. Despite this fact, all of the authors interviewed were ignorant of writing within a continuous cultural tradition. For instance, Alexander Baron declared: "I don't think there's any real cultural life in the Jewish community" (quoted in Cheyette 2004, 701–2). Sadly, like many British Jewish writers Baron stopped writing fiction in the seventies after an initially promising beginning. From the outset the playwright Peter Shaffer refused to engage imaginatively with his Jewishness, or "Yiddishkeit," describing it as "the most boring thing in the world." Even such prize-winning British Jewish authors as Gerda Charles have had astonishingly brief literary careers.

It is no coincidence that, unlike their American counterparts, the best Jewish writers in Britain—such as Harold Pinter, Peter Shaffer, Gabriel Josipovici, and Anita Brookner—have until recently created few Jewish characters or addressed explicitly Jewish subject matter. In the decades immediately after the war, many postwar British Jewish writers had advanced the expansion of British culture as much by their social position as through their ethnicity. The playwrights Arnold Wesker and Bernard Kops, for instance, enabled working-class voices and Yiddish folk traditions to enter the mainstream.

Wesker's early trilogy *Chicken Soup with Barley* (1958), *Roots* (1959), and *I'm Talking About Jerusalem* (1960) made a considerable impact and led to a rethinking of post-imperial Britain. Wesker's drama records the breakup of the close-knit Jewish community in London's East End and its resulting estrangement from the commercial values of modern industrial society. Wesker thus challenges one of the abiding myths of Anglo-Jewry, namely, that the trajectory of poor immigrant Jews was above all away from the "ghettos" and into the "suburbs," in other words away from Jewishness and toward Englishness. Wesker, however, was aware that his plays were overly didactic, contrasting the idealism of the characters with the harsh realities surrounding them. His transition from class warrior to ethnic writer can be seen most clearly in his play *The Merchant* (1976;

since renamed *Shylock*), which is an impressive reworking of Shakespeare's *Merchant of Venice* from Shylock's viewpoint. The shift from class to ethnicity also has a wider historical resonance in contemporary Britain, given the general breakdown of univocal explanations and the location of identity outside the nation-state. Many of the writers discussed in this chapter repeat the move from the modernity of liberal progress to the postmodern critique of these assumptions.

Along with Kops, Wesker, and Wolf Mankowitz, a significant number of interwar proletarian novelists preceded the "new wave" of British Jewish writers in the fifties. Novelists such as Simon Blumenfeld and William Goldman produced hard-hitting autobiographical works which concentrated on the powerless and impoverished East End Jewish community. The master chronicler of the East End in the postwar era was Emanuel Litvinoff, who, in the preface to his *Journey Through a Small Planet* (1972), made clear that he was primarily engaged in an act of re-creation and memorialization in a bid to reclaim a past which had long since been forgotten. He noted that from the very beginning those who "survived" the East End were "moving eagerly into the universe of the future and had no wish to look back at the retreating past" (9). The Jewish East End, in other words, was destroyed as much by the cultural amnesia of those who left as it was by the bombs of the German Luftwaffe.

Harold Pinter reverses the literary careers of Wesker and Litvinoff and turns aspects of his life history *into* an assimilationist modernism. Pinter was also born in London's East End, and one can view the modernist deracination of his plays as an implicit comment on his shared loss of community. His autobiographical novel *The Dwarfs* (1990) was originally written between 1952 and 1956, although it belies its origins. European literature and philosophy, as well as the fiction of James Joyce, overwhelm this youthful bildungsroman, which shows that from the beginning Pinter wished to transfigure his particular background and identity (Esslin 1977, 121–30). While the novel is dotted throughout with Yiddish jokes, as well as references to the Talmud, circumcision, and "the gas chamber," Pinter is at pains not merely to reproduce the social and cultural milieu of Hackney. Given that much of the Jewish East End was destroyed during the war, Pinter's tabula rasa does have a real historical subtext. The intense seriousness of the gifted Jewish men in the novel also indicates something of the flavor of Pinter's background without simply being reduced to that background.

In *The Birthday Party* (1958), produced soon after *The Dwarfs* was written, Goldberg, Pinter's most unequivocal Jewish figure, simultaneously articulates both an unreal and nostalgic Englishness as well as a fixed Jewishness. At one point he extols the virtues of "a little Austin, tea in Fullers, a library book from Boots" (86) in a self-consciously artificial construction of an idealized English past. But within a few lines he acts as if Stanley's grotesque "birthday

party" is not unlike an Anglo-Jewish family *simcha:* "Stanley, my heartfelt con-
gratulations. I wish you, on behalf of us all, a happy birthday. I'm sure you've
never been a prouder man than you are today. Mazeltov! And may we only
meet at Simchahs!" (86).

Englishness and Jewishness are crucially brought together in relation to a
contrived and illusory past. Goldberg's underlying menace goes hand in hand
with his sentimentality; an Anglo-Jewish insider will know that the phrase "may
we only meet at Simchahs" is rather ominous since it is routinely said at funerals.
Throughout the play Goldberg's blatant self-contradictions concerning his upbringing expose both his Englishness and Jewishness as specious fabrications, a
refusal to come to terms with the past. As Goldberg delineates them, these cross-
cultural identities are no longer opposites but mirror images of each other. Their
equally distorted vision of a flawless community ultimately threatens to overwhelm Stanley's sense of self, which partially explains his breakdown in the final
scenes of the play. After *The Birthday Party,* Pinter did not explicitly represent his
complex Jewishness again. That his oeuvre is now at the center of English national culture contrasts with the relative isolation of his East End contemporaries
of the fifties, such as Wesker and Kops, who also helped to transform a complacent English drama of reassurance. Although Pinter clearly had to leave out a
great deal in order to enter the pantheon of English literature, the more recent
play *Ashes to Ashes* (1997), can be said to evoke the Holocaust. The price of such
radical assimilation, where the act of writing becomes either a literal or symbolic
form of conversion, is to be considered next.

Beyond Englishness

Many prolific British Jewish women writers converted to Christianity, such as
Cecilly Sidgwick and Julia Frankau in the Edwardian period and G. B. Stern and
Naomi Jacob in the forties. This embrace of a supposedly superior aesthetic order
indicates just how literally these writers internalized the assumption that Jews
were profoundly materialistic and outside of the pantheon of culture. In the
postwar period the best-known figure who converted from Judaism to Catholicism was Muriel Spark, whose hybrid background—part English, part Scottish,
part Protestant, part Jewish—has enabled her to become an essentially diasporic
writer with a fluid sense of self (Cheyette 2000).

Ruth Prawer Jhabvala can similarly be thought of as a diasporic writer whose
fiction encompasses several continents and cultures and whose tightly controlled
aesthetic form rigidly contains her Jewishness. Prawer Jhabvala is not a convert
in a religious sense, but she has partially adopted the Indian subcontinent and
culture as her own. Born in Cologne of German Jewish parentage, she emigrated
to London at the age of twelve, just before the outbreak of war. In 1951 she mar-

ried Cyrus S. H. Jhabvala, returning with him to his home in Delhi. Since 1975 she has lived mainly in New York and London. Prawer Jhabvala is best known as a novelist of contemporary India, but one can argue that her fiction, although set in India, is a way of indirectly encompassing the loss of her family and childhood friends. In the preface to her collection of stories entitled *Out of India* (1986) Prawer Jhabvala speaks of the unendurable dilemma of living and writing in a country where the majority of the population is starving. The sense of being surrounded by the horror of millions of people dying needlessly—which makes her characters want to escape into spiritual obfuscation and eventually destroys their feeling of well-being—can be thought of as a way of speaking about the Holocaust (Shepherd 1994).

What the literary history of Anglo-Jewry reveals, above all, is the dual pressure on British Jewish writers either to universalize their Jewishness out of the public sphere (which takes the extreme form of conversion) or to particularize it in preconceived images. This reductive "either/or" has until recently deformed much of the literary output of Anglo-Jewry into either tame satire or crude apologetics. One should not, however, underestimate the extent to which Jews have been regarded as the Other in Britain. In the past few years a host of studies have explored the varying constructions of "the Jew," which have saturated English national identity since the medieval period (Freedman 2000). The dead hand of this history has, I believe, taken its toll on postwar British Jewish literature. This can be seen most noticeably in the continuation of a culture of apology which attempts to portray Jews in more "positive" terms. There is, in other words, a strong sense in which English society still saps the confidence of Jewish writers. Along with other ethnic minorities, as many have argued, British Jews "were invited to take their place, and become spectators of a culture already complete and represented for them by its trustees" (Dodd 1986, 22). Ever since Israel Zangwill refused to be shut up in the ghetto, as he put it, Jewish writers in Britain have been made to feel distinctly uncomfortable with respect to their Jewishness.

The popular writers Maisie Mosco and Rosemary Friedman have written Jewish family sagas in the eighties as a direct response to the negative stereotype of the Jew in English culture. Friedman's trilogy, in particular, is designed to "explain" a range of Anglo-Jewish life to the outside world, whether it be aspects of Judaism, the Holocaust, or present-day Israel. When asked what motivated them to write their family sagas in the first place, both Mosco and Friedman invariably reply that it is to counter images of "Shylock," "Fagin," or "Svengali," all of which still circulate in contemporary Britain. Both see their fiction as rectifying these images by correcting an unbalanced portrait of "the Jew." They write, in other words, in order to present Jews in a favorable light—what Philip Roth, speaking of Leon Uris, has called "public relations" fiction (1985).

Needless to say, all this has little to do with Jewishness and everything to do with the Englishness of the wider culture. It is almost as if Jewish writers in Britain have had to combat an all-encompassing Englishness throughout their careers—and quite often Englishness wins out. As a consequence, a number of British Jewish writers, such as Gerda Charles or Alexander Baron, have given up the fight and have fallen into silence. These "walking wounded" can be contrasted with those writers who have managed to find strategies to combat an overbearing Englishness fixed in the past. Such narrative strategies vary, from the radical interrogation and rewriting of the dominant culture by Bernice Rubens, Michelene Wandor, and Howard Jacobson to Anita Brookner's self-conscious refusal to engage with this culture.

Dannie Abse and Bernice Rubens share a common Welsh background, which means that they avoided a stultifying Englishness throughout their childhoods. In addition to their mutual location within a wider Britishness, these writers can be regarded as the great survivors of the defunct "new wave" of the sixties. Rather like the multiple selves of the Catholic convert Muriel Spark or Prawer Jhabvala, these writers have access to a range of ethnic, cultural, and professional identities that enable them to explore specific aspects of their hybrid upbringing. A doctor by training, Abse's poetry is as much about his life as a physician as anything else. He is equally regarded as both a Welsh, Jewish, and "Golders Green" poet (Cohen 1983). Because her fiction encompasses family life in general, Rubens has resisted the label "Jewish writer." Nevertheless, she has consistently explored her Jewish upbringing and has recently attempted to encompass the Diaspora as a whole.

The claustrophobic particularity of Rubens's fiction can be contrasted with such other proponents of the "new wave" as Frederic Raphael, who universalize their Jewishness as a form of alienation. At the same time, Rubens resists the tendency to classify Anglo-Jewry in reductive terms, as do other "new wave" writers such as Gerda Charles. Instead of documentary realism, Rubens has embraced a more symbolic mode already present in the poetry of Amy Levy and Isaac Rosenberg (Daiches 1973, 77–93; Rubens 2005). This is an understandable reading of Rubens's prolific literary output since she is well known for avoiding any descriptive passages in her works. However, the emphasis on the symbolic in her fiction belittles the extent to which she, like her predecessors, explicitly challenges the dominant norms of both Anglo-Jewry and English national culture. Her writing takes the "positive" stereotypes of what it means to be a respected citizen in Britain—upward mobility, family values, and an untroubled sense of community—and turns them on their heads. Her subject matter, especially in her early fiction, is concerned with the disabling nature of family and communal expectations, which tend to cripple her fragile characters emotionally. While her fiction can be divided into "Jewish" and "non-Jewish" (or even "English" and "Welsh") motifs, there is a good deal of thematic crossover in her novels. By situating her dysfunctional families in a range of contexts, her novels critique the social values in general and not merely within the Jewish community. In this way, Rubens both universalizes her particular Jewish identity and particularizes a supposedly universal culture.

Other authors focus on specific myths and fantasies or key texts—insofar as they are part of the larger national and communal narratives of Englishness and Jewishness—and radically interrogate them. Written from an explicitly feminist position, the stories of Michelene Wandor rework or transfigure commonplace assumptions of what it is to be a Jew—or a woman—in England. Her "Song of the Jewish Princess" (1989) explores a common myth of Jewish femininity in order to understand its liberating potential. Wandor's feisty "Jewish Princess," a female counterpart to the Wandering Jew, contrasts starkly with the compliant, endlessly malleable Jewish woman prevalent in conversionist rhetoric. What happens, Wandor asks, when you replace the common public images of the male Jew with their supposedly domesticated female counterparts? Although she still uses popular mythology, the location of the "Jewish Princess" in a public, historicized realm is paradoxically liberating. By situating her mythic figure in the fifteenth century, around the time of the Jewish expulsion from Catholic Spain, she places Jewish women at the center of historical narratives. Wandor's reworking of the "Jewish Princess" in relation to the subversive spirituality of Lilith is also reflected in the later fiction of Bernice Rubens (Behlau and Reitz 2004).

In contrast to the woman-centered fiction of Michelene Wandor, Howard Jacobson is an aggressively masculine writer who, from this perspective, has confronted head-on the thorny question of Englishness. His first two comic novels, *Coming From Behind* (1983) and *Peeping Tom* (1984), both directly resist a definition of Jewishness based on an excessive regard for the Englishness of others. Jacobson's protagonists specifically undermine the oppressive language of culture which divides the world into those who are beautiful or civilized and those who are ugly or uncivilized, like the "Jew." He exposes the means by which English culture has attempted to civilize Jews or other minorities in order to make what is ugly beautiful again. His subject is thus the psychic damage which this causes to British Jews.

When Jacobson's *Coming From Behind* and *Peeping Tom* were first published, he was mistakenly acclaimed as Britain's answer to Woody Allen or Philip Roth. Jacobson, however, is a quintessentially English writer. He was born in Manchester, in the industrial north of England, and was educated at Cambridge University. At the same time, Jacobson was excluded both from the Manchester Jewish community (he was not wealthy enough) and English culture (he was not English enough). His juxtaposition of reverence for English culture and irreverence as a comic outsider is characteristic of his fiction. This doubleness meant that *Coming From Behind* and *Peeping Tom* are not, strictly speaking, "Jewish" novels but are more accurately described as "anti-Gentile novels." Jacobson's protagonists define themselves as the opposite of English gentility (in both senses of the word). In *Coming From Behind,* Jacobson's campus novel, Sefton Goldberg is Jewish because he hates goyische soccer, the English countryside, small towns and midland polytechnics, British trains, students, Cambridge, women, homosexuals—you name it. He is not Jewish because he attends synagogue services.

In *Peeping Tom* Jacobson cleverly turns this negative definition of self into the subject of his novel by directly confronting his opposite, the Victorian rural novelist Thomas Hardy. In the end Barney Fugelman discovers that he needs Thomas Hardy's "goyische greenery" to exist. On the one hand, Hardy is Barney's antagonist in the novel: "Pity the poor Jew. Let him gentrify and ruralize himself all he likes . . . he will never know what it is to take a turn around the garden" (186). But Barney *is* also Hardy, or at least his reincarnation. He becomes Hardy because he is part of a culture which he feels is not really his own. In other words, Jacobson's fictional personae define themselves negatively in terms of their supposed gentile Other. The danger for Jacobson is that this turns his Jewish characters into a vacuum, with nothing of positive value apart from their hatred of the outside world. His later work—*The Very Model of a Man* (1992), *Roots Shmoots: Journeys Among Jews* (1993), and *The Mighty Walzer* (1999)—attempts to fill the vacuum of his earlier character's acknowledged nonidentity. *Peeping Tom* is ultimately a study in cultural masochism. What Jacobson highlights is the extent to which Jews, who had come to love English culture, were caught in a double bind. He argues that although Jews participate in this culture—through the English language—they still have a precarious foothold in it. This is a particularly painful contradiction for Jacobson, who thinks of himself as a Leavisite, the custodians of culture. However, as a "Jew" he can always be expelled from that which he loves.

Although the radical interrogation and reworking of the prevalent myths of Englishness is obviously most welcome, it does have its limitations. All of the writers previously discussed are ultimately bounded by certain dominant images of "the Jew," however radically they are rewritten. To escape this limitation, Anita Brookner explicitly refuses to engage with the dominant culture according to these terms and tends to set her novels on the Continent. On one level Brookner is a prime example of a mainstream British Jewish writer who has written out virtually any reference to her Jewishness. Only with *The Latecomers* (1988) and *A Family Romance* (1993) is the Jewishness of her characters made explicit. Although Brookner writes stylistically as an English insider—in the tradition of Jane Austen, George Eliot, and E. M. Forster—her heroines are all cultural or ethnic outsiders. There is also a self-consciousness about Brookner's reluctance to engage directly with her Jewishness in her fiction, which raises crucial questions about the nature of the silence imposed on ethnic voices (Sylvester 2001).

By bringing together a disparate group of authors and categorizing them as "British Jewish," one clearly runs the risk of reducing these writers to a monolithic ethnicity. Some critics have categorized British Jewish writers in terms of their relation to the "East End" and "North West" of London. However, one cannot understand a writer such as Brookner in terms of these city limits since she narrates, above all, from the outside in and thereby challenges the received cultural boundaries of Englishness.[5] Brookner writes in an ostensibly conventional mode of realism, subtly evoking the great tradition of English letters while also expanding into a European context dominant images of Englishness. Her precarious position—as neither an insider nor an outsider, neither Jewish nor English—can be likened to that of Harold Pinter. Like Brookner, after *The Birthday Party* Pinter universalized his Jewishness, making it impossible to reduce it to a set of images. Until she wrote *A Family Romance,* Brookner similarly refused openly to portray her characters as Jewish outsiders, although this does not apply to the way she presented herself in various interviews.

As her novel *The Latecomers* demonstrates, Brookner's reluctance to make her Jewishness usable in her fiction was above all a self-conscious strategy. In an article on contemporary British Jewry, she defines "latecomers" as thirties German Jewish émigrés to Britain. Two such "latecomers," Thomas Hartmann and Thomas Fibich, are at the heart of this novel, although their status as émigrés remains teasingly inexact. If Hartmann and Fibich are "latecomers" to England, then this assumes a line of earlier arrivals. However, this is an immigrant story which Brookner pointedly refuses to tell. Her narrative method has, in this sense, been rightly described as a "refusal of emplotment" (Skinner 1992, 137; Brookner 1989, 44; Haffenden 1985, 60). Although Hartmann and Fibich are both child refugees from nazism who lost their families during the Holocaust, Brookner uses the word "Jew" only once in her novel. Not unlike the painfully incomplete storytelling of the Israeli writer Aharon Appelfeld, what is left unsaid in *The Latecomers* becomes the subject of the novel. To this extent Brookner makes overt the silence which surrounds Jewishness within English national culture, as opposed to challenging it head-on like Rubens, Wandor and Jacobson.

The Émigrés

It is no coincidence that many of the Jewish writers who thrive in Britain were not born there. As émigrés, these writers do not have to transcend an Englishness that was imbibed with their mother's milk. Because they do not need to engage with the cultural fixity of the British past, these writers have a skeptical and detached relationship both to the past and to national cultures in general, which is not to say that they have reacted in the same way to the experience of migration and exile. Some, such as George Steiner and Ronit Lentin, have directly engaged with their personal histories in both their fiction and criticism. Others, such as Gabriel Josipovici and Eva Figes, have created a more general modernist and feminist aesthetic which only implicitly addresses their particular history. Dan Jacobson's fiction lies somewhere between these two polarities, having moved from directly embracing his specific background to creating more universalized imaginary homelands.

In his influential essay "Our Homeland, the Text" George Steiner contends that the "dwelling . . . ascribed to Israel is the House of the Book" and that the "centrality of the book does coincide with and enact the condition of exile" (1996a, 305). Steiner is the émigré writer par excellence. Born in Paris in 1929 to Viennese parents, he was brought to the United States in 1940 to escape the Nazi occupation of France and has lived in Britain intermittently since 1950. His teaching, however, has occurred mainly in Geneva, Switzerland, and he remains at home in many different European traditions. Steiner's ideal of a textual homeland has been criticized by Cynthia Ozick for giving precedence to a surface aestheticism that is defined as "a-thing-that-subsists-for-its-own-sake-without-a-history" (1984, 225). Steiner, however, is well aware of the tension between his extraterritorial homeland and the particularities of history, which he defines as "the dialectical relations between an unhoused at-homeness in the text . . . and the territorial mystery of the native ground, of the promised strip of land" (1996a, 305). The struggle between the historical specificities of the past and a transcendent sense of exile is, to a large extent, the theme of much of Steiner's fiction and cultural criticism.

Steiner has always been a writer-critic and is, above all, a self-translator. He writes philosophical essays as if they were a species of poetry and fiction as if it was philosophy. Many of the lifelong obsessions of his extraordinarily compelling set of essays entitled *Language and Silence* (1967), were imaginatively prefigured in his early stories, collected under the title *Anno Domini* (1964). The primacy of translation, explored at length in *After Babel* (1975a), has rightly been understood as a structuring metaphor in *The Portage to San Cristobal of A.H.* (1981) (Sharp 1994). With an ambiguity that is still troubling Steiner puts into the mouth of an aged Hitler ("A.H.") words which he himself had used a decade earlier in his work *In Bluebeard's Castle* (1971). In this way Steiner is able to explore the dark side of his own reasoning. His more recent novella and stories, collected under the title *Proofs and Three Parables* (1992), continues this pattern of self-questioning. Written at about the same time as his *Real Presences: Is There Anything "in" What We Say?* (1989), these fictions make human the "wager on transcendence" which Steiner has long since called for as an antidote to our current "postcultural" nihilism. His fiction, now collected into a substantial volume, provides a persuasive internal commentary on his more familiar critical writings.[6]

Throughout his career Steiner has been obsessed with the unbearable ambiguity—or "dialectic"—between the aesthetic and the barbaric, or metaphor and history, which is illustrated in *A Conversation Piece* (1985). In this parable we are told that "God" and "un-nameable evil" are "utterly alike," and that the "difference between them is only that of a rain-drop in the sea" (106). Only this cabbalistic understanding of the terrible intimacy between God and the devil enables Steiner to use the Hitler figure in *The Portage to San Cristobal of A.H.* to explore the underside of his own thinking. Steiner and his Hitler ("A.H.") both believe that Jews are the "conscience" (124) of the world and that this has caused a lethal resentment which has culminated in the Shoah. And yet by embodying the redemptive homeland of the text—at its most creative and lasting in an extraterritorial central Europe—diasporic Jews have personified a life-giving self-transcendence. Viewed in this light, Jewish transcendence is both a form of moral validation and a death warrant. *The Portage to San Cristobal of A.H.* and *A Conversation Piece* take risks with such heart-rending chasms of meaning in order to let the reader decide where the truth lies.

On a smaller scale, the Israeli-Irish writer Ronit Lentin has also devised a narrative framework somewhere between metaphor and history in order to come to terms with the trauma of the past. Lentin was born in Haifa and settled in Dublin shortly after the Six-Day War. Her parents came from Rumania, with her mother emigrating to Palestine in 1941. *Night Train to Mother* (1989) is a fictionalized autobiography which attempts to transfigure and reclaim her mother's history. Lentin has noted the way in which the Israeli national identity of her childhood prevented her from coming to terms with her family's history in much the same way that Englishness has obfuscated other minority histories (1990). Her novel attempts to capture the minutiae of four generations of Rumanian Jewish women in a bid to break down the spurious universality of a nationalized and masculinized Israeli identity.

Lentin's family saga is framed as a momentary performance falling somewhere between autobiography and fiction. Above all, she does not want to create another mythologized ethnicity to replace the "sabra arrogance" (218) of her alter ego. *Night Train to Mother* refuses the narrative a limited point of origin which is, by definition, predicated on a continuous line of history. As a writer defined by her inner exile, her women-centered stories are both a means of restoring the past as well as self-conscious and limited acts of memorialization.

Gabriel Josipovici and Eva Figes create more generalized images of displacement and loss in their modernist fiction, which is characterized by a refusal to turn past trauma into simple stories. As with Steiner and Lentin, both of these writers have a profound sense of dislocation and of writing in a language which they were not born into. Born in France in 1940, Josipovici emigrated to Egypt with his mother shortly after the Nazi occupation. Educated in Cairo and Oxford, he has taught comparative literature at Sussex University since 1963. His fiction and criticism are steeped in a European tradition of literary modernism which, in recent years, has increasingly been influenced by the Greek classics and the Bible. His delicate, vulnerable novellas atempt to make art of the everyday and discover, as he puts it in *Contre-Jour: A Triptych after Pierre Bonnard* a "thousand subjects for every moment of time" (1986, 76). While his pointedly fluid and exilic Jewishness has always been a key aspect of his outstanding critical works—such as *The World and the Book* (1971) and *The Book of God* (1988)—it has only recently been addressed in his fiction.

The move from the cosmopolitanism of his early fiction to a more explicitly Judaic understanding of the world illustrates the limitations of a universalizing modernism which has historically assimilated Judaism rather ambivalently. Which is not to say that Josipovici's Jewishness is in any way fixed or easily formulated (Josipovici 1993; Josipovici 1988; Fludernik 2000). The epigraph to his work *In a Hotel Garden* is taken from the Midrash on Genesis (39:7): "Potiphar's wife too wished to belong to the history of Israel" (1993, 6). Josipovici's "history of Israel," in other words, eschews well-worn images and clichés of what it means to be a Jew. For this reason his novel is principally concerned with the difficulties of both representing and reproducing the past. Ben, the protagonist, thinks he is understanding the history of a Jewish family that was touched by the Holocaust, but Josipovici's fiction is never quite as certain as his rather innocent characters.

In fact, Ben eventually comes to belong to Josipovici's contemporary "history of Israel" even though he is not himself Jewish. When on holiday in the Italian Alps, he meets Lily, the granddaughter of a family of Italian Jews. Lily remembers a story that her grandmother told her about a rendezvous in a hotel garden with a distant cousin who, she later learns, died during the war. The cousin fell in love with the grandmother but married someone else. She thus refused to answer any of his letters. Lily decides to return to her grandmother's meeting place in an attempt to commune with her. As the novel progresses, Ben gradually reenacts the story of Lily's grandmother and thus continues her family's history for another generation.

One must not, however, ignore just how fragile and transitory Lily's retelling of her grandmother's story is. Ben relates his encounter with Lily to friends, yet he also virtually turns her desire to visit the site of her grandmother's unrequited love affair into an overly simple story. That her grandmother's cousin was killed along with his family during the war makes *In a Hotel Garden* a post-Holocaust novel on one level. However, it is somewhat reductive to think of Josipovici's modernist fiction merely in these terms. Throughout Lily remains undecided about the nature of her visit to the hotel garden and the import of her grandmother's memories. At times she believes that "everything" would be "resolved" (107) by entering the garden, while at other times she remains skeptical of this absolute sense of past and present coming together. Here Lily, like Goldberg in Josipovici's previous novel *The Big Glass* (1991), negotiates between a Christian "ache for redemption" (54) and a Judaic uncertainty. This markedly Hebraic imprecision concerning Lily's transcendent resolution of past, present, and future is pointedly juxtaposed with an English disdain for dwelling on Nazi atrocities. Toward the end of the novel Ben's friend Fran becomes exasperated with Lily's story and complains that she is "fed up with people being obsessed by the Holocaust. It's done and we've got to move on" (125). Her husband remarks that "its different if you're Jewish" (125), and these competing versions of the past are highlighted throughout.

Jewishness is presented here as an imaginary Diaspora held together by the deceptive power of memory and genealogical storytelling. Lily herself exemplifies this version of Jewishness, although Josipovici is at pains not to reduce it to a fixed myth. For this reason Lily often quotes another line from the Midrash: "Absalom gloried in his hair—therefore he was hanged by his hair" (42). She pointedly cites this line from the Midrash to avoid any overly simple transfigurations of her past into easily comprehensible patterns. In this way *In a Hotel Garden* becomes both myth and history, simultaneously located in the past and the present.

The haunting images of displacement and plangent note of distress can also be found in the poetic fiction of Eva Figes. A refugee from nazism, Figes was born in Berlin and escaped to London with her parents in 1939 following her father's imprisonment in Dachau. While most of her short novels do not directly address this history, many are suffused with a poignant sense of dislocation. For instance, Stephan Konek, the protagonist of *Konek Landing* (1969) is a stateless orphan displaced by war whose humanity is put at risk by the need to survive in a nameless country full of victims and executioners. The determinedly non-naturalistic *Ghosts* (1988) explores the consciousness of an elderly woman looking back over the "ghosts" of another country and of her younger self. Like Josipovici, who is also influenced by the works of Kafka and Beckett, Figes has increasingly combined pained images of fragmentation with a lyric intensity. Above all, she has eschewed a cosy English realism as incapable of dealing with her childhood experiences. Her fiction is not directly autobiographical, although on a deeper level it obviously relates to a profound sense of rupture and of having an irredeemable past.

Only in her memoirs *Little Eden: A Child at War* (1978a) and *Tales of Innocence and Experience* (2003) does Figes engage directly with her adolescence in Germany and her fraught migration to Britain as a seven-year-old. Aside from these memoirs, plus her first quasi-autobiographical novel *Equinox* (1966), her Jewishness remains an unfigured source of anxiety. In an article written at the same time as *Little Eden,* Figes described herself as a "European wrestling with a different reality. A piece of shrapnel lodges in my flesh, and when it moves, I write" (1978b, 14). This crippling disruption contrasts starkly with the need for historical continuity in Britain after the war, which Figes has located in both the conventions of English political life as well as its artistic forms. Her influential work *Patriarchal Attitudes* (1970) was one feminist's response to a gendered conservatism in England. Her fiction can also be viewed as a more subtle aesthetic reaction to an overly cautious and narrow English literary culture.

What is paradoxical about *Little Eden* is that it is precisely the wholesome conservatism of English society which made it such a comfort to the adolescent Figes. Her memoir tells the story of her childhood evacuation to rural England and her subsequent rite of passage when she learns about the Holocaust and the deaths of immediate family members. For Figes the discovery of her Jewishness goes hand in hand with her loss of innocence. After a particularly difficult time with her understandably preoccupied mother, the thirteen-year-old Eva is told to go to the local cinema and to see a newsreel account of the liberation of Bergen-Belsen slave-labor camp. Her reaction to the horrendous pictures is telling: "At last I knew what it meant to be a Jew, the shameful secret that had been hidden from me for so many years. . . . Now I knew. I was not a child any longer" (131).

What *Little Eden* and *Tales of Innocence and Experience* make clear is that the untroubled narcissism of English society is, for those with a traumatized past, a double-edged sword. As she states elsewhere, "England does not share the European experience. German troops did not march down Whitehall; men were not rounded up and shot or sent to labor camps" (1978, 14; Conradi 1983). Living in England and absorbing its cheery continuity with the past can thus be a necessary relief, as Figes illustrates in *Little Eden* when, at the end, she desperately seeks to escape back into her rural English idyll. In *Tales of Innocence and Experience,* it is the dark side of childhood fairy tales that are used to illustrate this ambiguous relationship to Englishness. Other childhood accounts of German émigrés growing up in Britain during the war are less sanguine about even this level of relief from past traumas (Brauner 2001; Lawson 2005).

Dan Jacobson left South Africa in his twenties and has for over five decades mainly lived and worked in London, where he is a university professor. Jacobson's move from an unproblematic realism to myth-infused history culminated in *The God-Fearer,* a novel described explicitly as "Another history! Another past for the human race!" (1992, 65). It is, above all, an otherworld where the dominant proselytizing religion in Europe is no longer Christianity but Judaism. *The God-Fearer* radically rewrites European history in order to show the ways in which the past continually needs to be remade. In this novel it is the minority "Christer" people—"the followers of Yeshua, Jesus, the Christus, the Natzerit [*sic*], whatever they liked to call him?" (18)—who suffer pogroms, prejudice and expulsions. Without the advent of Christendom, Old Testament God-Fearers or followers of the one true God govern medieval Europe. This inversion of history is accompanied by a series of alternative homelands and mythic figures, such as Manasse, Sar of the Upperland, who are superimposed on more familiar historical landscapes. Although Kobus, Jacobson's octogenarian protagonist, has a good deal of trouble remembering even his deceased wife's name, the one thing that he is sure of is that the past alone could not be "forever without ambiguity" (53). Out of the "wreckage of what was left of his mind" (68–69) Kobus—like the reader—spends most of the novel trying to make sense of his ambiguous past.

In his work *The Story of the Stories: The Chosen People and Its God* (1982) Jacobson was at pains to show that the chosenness of the biblical chosen people was a man-made myth, as opposed to a God-imposed truth. Kobus is a "bookbinder," not unlike Steiner's proofreader, because he embodies the theological need to canonize or fix stories that are inherently changeable. For this reason Jacobson has a good deal of fun in *The God-Fearer* dramatizing a multitude of possible national stories and imagined communities that are not a part of received history. The strength of the novel is that these abiding concerns are not merely of intellectual interest. Kobus's "pain of recollection" (84) is felt throughout as he envisions his existence as a "kind of postscript to a life that was already concluded" (3). That he is dominated by his "errant, grotesque, utterly absurd" (126) memories is finally realized in the ghostly young "Christer" children, who, as the novel progresses, begin to absorb him. These "phantom lives," taken from Henry James's novella *The Turn of the Screw* (1898), fatally disrupt the certainties that Kobus has about himself and the chosenness of his people. By playfully sketching a fantasy world made up of "non-historic peoples," as he put it in his novel *Hidden in the Heart* (1991, 189), Jacobson shows how our notions of the past are both arbitrary and variable. As we have seen, while émigré writers react differently to the experience of dislocation and exile, they all crucially transcend a dominant culture and rewrite both its past as well as its present.

Diasporas of the Mind

What is clear from reading the works of British Jewish writers over the past twenty-five years is that to succeed as a creative writer in England one has to become—at least symbolically—an émigré or outsider. Because a Jewish past has been written out of British national culture, Jewish writers have had to look to the Diaspora or Israel for their sites of Jewishness. On one level this extraterritoriality might be considered a form of postmodern fiction. However, the very fact that these writers want to historicize their Jewishness and not merely universalize it points to an implicit critique of a too generalized postmodernism. Although these British-born novelists and poets all create diasporas of the mind in a bid to subvert a wide range of national certainties, they nonetheless remain wedded to their particularist identities, however fluid and capricious they may be. Clive Sinclair and Simon Louvish focus as much on Israel and the Middle East as on the Diaspora, which distinguishes them from Ruth Fainlight and Elaine Feinstein. The women-centered fiction and poetry of Fainlight and Feinstein contrasts with that of their male counterparts, who write from an overtly masculine perspective. Unlike Eva Figes or Michelene Wandor, however, these two women writers do not have an explicitly feminist aesthetic.

The issue of gender is always in tension with the question of ethnic and national identity. In these latter terms, Clive Sinclair has rightly been described as instigating a "quiet but profound revolution" in Anglo-Jewish letters. In his two early collections of short stories entitled *Hearts of Gold* (1979) and *Bedbugs* (1982) he pointedly attempted to write fictional texts divorced from the English literary heritage. Sinclair has consequently located his "national" history as a Jew in Israel, the United States, and eastern Europe. He describes his fiction as a self-consciously failed "attempt to distill the essence of other places. To make myself temporarily at home" (Cheyette 1984). Continuing this theme in his *Diaspora Blues: A View of Israel*, Sinclair defines himself as having a "dual loyalty [to] the language of England and the history of Israel" (1987, 65), arguing that for a writer there is "something to be gained from having a language but no history, a history but no language" (53). Compared with his alienation from England, his unrequited love affair with Israel has provided him with a "narrative" in which to situate himself. The sources for his work are both national *and* transnational. His characters consequently shift from place to place, with history changing its meaning so as to remake events (Hanson 1985; Bradbury 1987; Woolf 1995; Brauner 2001).

The crossing of all temporal and spatial boundaries so as to transcend his English birthplace—which is displaced onto the Continent, the United States, and Israel—has posed an interesting dilemma for Sinclair. On the one hand, as the story "Bedbugs" demonstrates, the history of the Holocaust is deemed to be outside the moral purview of his protagonists. When asked to teach poetry dating from World War I to German students, Joshua, Sinclair's protagonist, fantasizes about teaching a parallel course called "Rosenberg's Revenge," which would primarily highlights Nazi atrocities. Isaac Rosenberg's poem "Louse Hunting" is evoked in this story as a metaphor for the Shoah as Joshua and a German student burn the bedbugs infecting their living quarters. All of Sinclair's stories concern the dangers of turning such historical metaphors into reality. Joshua finally acts as if he has the right to exact "revenge" on behalf of the Nazi victims, but by the end of the story he is clearly deranged.

The reference to Rosenberg is significant here since Sinclair is making explicit a British Jewish literary canon different from that of the insider and documentary realist Israel Zangwill. Only the poet Jon Silkin has explicitly written in this tradition (Lawson 2005). Crucial here is the fact that Sinclair is careful not to universalize Rosenberg's extraterritoriality. Sinclair's protagonists are often made delirious by their impossible displacement of an "English" identity onto a wider Diaspora. In his story "Ashkenazia" (1982) Sinclair takes such solipsism to its extreme limit by inventing an "imaginary homeland" untouched by genocide. Situated somewhere in central Europe, Ashkenazia, a fictitious Yiddish-speaking country (which later reappears in Dan Jacobson's novel *The God-Fearer*), is defined as a language community outside of history: "Many of my fellow countrymen do not believe in the existence of God. I am more modest. I do not believe in myself. What proof can I have when no one reads what I write? There you have it; my words are the limit of my world. You will therefore smile at this irony; I have been commissioned by our government to write the official English-language *Guide to Ashkenazia*" (238).

By the end of the story, all that remains of Ashkenazia is a "field of wooden skeletons," with Sinclair's demented persona truly bound by his words: "Now the world will listen to me, for I am the guide to Ashkenazia. I am Ashkenazia" (248). Viewed on one level, this conflation of selfhood with nationhood is the necessary solipsistic response of an author who displaces the national culture of his English birthplace onto a useful fiction. For the post-Holocaust writer, however, such aestheticized "imaginary homelands" cannot merely be constituted by words alone. A purely textual "Ashkenazia" is an act of artistic megalomania precisely because Sinclair's narrator thinks that he can bring these "skeletons" to life.

Sinclair's prize-winning collection of stories entitled *"The Lady with the Laptop" and Other Stories* (1996) continues to invent purely imaginary national homelands—such as "Ishmalyia" in his story "The Iceman Cometh"—while simultaneously subjecting his aestheticized diaspora to the contingencies of history. More recently, the novel *Meet the Wife* (2002) continues to examine the boundaries between life and death and past and present in a bid to assert the power of artistry yet also to acknowledge the insurmountable borders which the aesthetic cannot cross.

Reimagining histories and debunking received mythologies and taboos, especially with regard to Israel and the Middle East, is also the subject of much of the fiction of Simon Louvish. Louvish was born in Glasgow in 1947 and at the age of two was taken to Israel, where he was educated. After serving in the Six-Day War as a military cameraman, he returned to Britain in 1968, where he has lived ever since. Like the Irish-Israeli Ronit Lentin, the Scottish-Israeli Louvish is a hybrid cross-cultural voice whose literary influences range from the Latin America novel to North American science fiction and Israeli popular satire. His uncategorizable novels eschew conventional forms, which stifle much fiction in Britain, and push the boundaries of what supposedly constitutes literary fiction. His version of magic realism in his novel sequence—ranging from *The Therapy of Avram Blok* (1985) to *The Days of Miracles and Wonders* (1997) and *The Cosmic Follies* (2004)—is an endlessly mobile hodgepodge of memory, fantasy, history, graffiti, parody, and Israeli street humor. All of Louvish's "Blok-busters" exhibit the same exuberant overflowing accretion plus a central figure, Avram Blok, who seeks to contain these multiple histories and find a much-needed sense of place.

In his first Blok novel, *The Therapy of Avram Blok,* a lunatic asylum in Jerusalem serves as a metaphor for a world where the line between fantasy and political reality has increasingly become blurred. The novel puns on whether Israel remains an asylum, that is, a refuge, or is just plain lunatic. Refusing to use a linear narrative, Louvish structures his Blok novels in terms of historical cycles which encompass World Wars I and II, the Shoah, and the Israeli wars. In this way Louvish leaps about in time while still—depressingly—dealing with the same themes. In addition to transgressing temporal boundaries, where dead figures come back to life, Louvish also crosses ever-changing spatial boundaries. Avram Blok, the author's alter ego, thus travels throughout the world in a desperate but failed attempt to obtain some kind of rational perspective. Louvish's second Blok novel, *City of Blok* (1988), which encompasses the election of Menachem Begin in 1977 and the war with Lebanon of 1982, has Louvish's protagonist pursued by the shadowy Department of Apocalyptic Affairs. At one point the fragmented, restless, perpetually mobile Blok sums up his desperation when he states that he does not care about the future since "the past has taken over the present" (361). And yet, like an inverted Dorian Gray, Blok succeeds in remaining pure and innocent while all around him become corrupt. Forced into the maelstrom of Middle Eastern politics, Blok encounters Jewish fascists, Palestinian resistance fighters, and Israeli peaceniks—in short, a world "composed of a thousand splinters." To prove that he has the courage of his convictions, Louvish published *What's Up God?* (1995), a satirical account of what the apocalyptic age might look like after the Messiah has arrived. He has also written comic thrillers, such as *The Death of Moishe Ganef* (1986) and *The Silencer* (1991), to give his themes a more recognizable form. His diasporic Jewishness, akin to Salman Rushdie's Indian-ness, has extended the range and vocabulary of the English-language novel to encompass global concerns and a sense of morality beneath the rubble.

In her prose fiction and poetry Elaine Feinstein also locates herself in a diasporic realm beyond a restrictive Englishness. Her poetic novels are generally set in an imaginary but historically specific central Europe. Interestingly enough, when she does write directly about her British antecedents, as she does in *The Survivors* (1982), she is unable to go beyond the restrictions inherent in the conventional novelistic form of the family saga. Her writing, in other words, needs a liberating extraterritoriality to eclipse the parochial representations and received images of an apologetic Anglo-Jewry. Her poetry, conversely, is flexible enough for her to deal directly with her immediate family and friends yet also ranges through myriad voices and topics.

As a woman Feinstein has situated "magical" father-enchanters at the heart of her narratives and has principally historicized the domestic sphere. In this way, her female alter egos reject the dominant sexual values of English national culture. By contrast, Sinclair and Louvish attempt to masculinize their personae in opposition to the powerlessness of Diaspora life. Far from being liberating, Feinstein's father-enchanters are always thoroughly ambiguous, breathing "life" into her female protaganists while at the same time threatening to make them "dead with dependence." In *The Shadow Master* (1978), the seventeenth-century Jewish false messiah Sabbatai Zevi is the ultimate historical expression of this double-edged enchantment. In *The Border* (1984) and *Loving Brecht* (1992), Feinstein situated Walter Benjamin and Bertolt Brecht, respectively, in this "magical" role. If the source of this life-giving "magic" is the "music of words", as she suggests in *The Circle* (1970, 164), then male writers are a peculiarly disabling embodiment of this imaginative "refuge" for her female personae (Kenyon 1991; Behlau and Reitz 2004; Neumeier 1998).

In *The Border* Walter Benjamin—"a Marxist who is not a materialist" (57)—is presented as a "mystical" synthesizing figure which the novel deliberately deconstructs. Set in Vienna before the Anschluss, this work is written as a triptych in diary and epistolary form, allowing for three equally passionate accounts of an erotic triangle. Far from a single male consciousness, the multiple, hallucinatory sense of reality in this novel—which turns history into the domestic and vice versa—is foregrounded even when the main characters are faced with the threat of nazism. The Spanish border at Port Bou, where Benjamin actually committed suicide in 1940, finally signifies both his tragically fixed place in history and the internal fissures that are writ large in the novel. This is acknowledged in the form of *The Border,* which reads an arbitrary version of its own story back from a contemporary perspective.

Like Feinstein, the poet and short story writer Ruth Fainlight has domesticated the political and historical realm and defamiliarized what is usually thought of as the domestic sphere. Born in New York of Austro-Hungarian and British parents, Fainlight has lived in England since the age of fifteen. Her writing is divided between her immediate personal concerns— what it means to be a "Jew, woman, poet" in Britain—and the location of an identity outside of these categories. For instance, in "A Child's Fear of Spiders" Fainlight initially relates this fear to the image of her parents copulating, then onto two swastikas, and finally to the concept of absolute power. Many of Fainlight's poems are based on individual vignettes of people she has observed, which is also the basis of two volumes of stories, *Daylife and Nightlife* (1971) and *"Dr. Clock's Last Case" and Other Stories* (1994). In her quasi-autobiographical story "A Wizard Robe Patterned with Stars and Moons" (1994), Fainlight locates this childlike naïveté in a New York school at the time of World War II. As with the memoirs of Emanuel Litvinoff and Eva Figes, Fainlight's juxtaposition of the language and outlook of childhood with the horror of war is telling.

By situating a variety of texts, as well as national and global perspectives, in their fiction and poetry, Fainlight and Feinstein, like Louvish and Sinclair, establish the possibility of reimagining a European past in terms of imaginative wordplay as well as the insurmountable borders of history. This is not, as some have argued (Shechner 1990), merely a "journey of self-integration" (100) into the European past for the Jewish writer. On the contrary, it is the lack of a sense of "integration" into another history which these British Jewish writers highlight in their fiction. In other words, they evoke an indeterminate Jewishness precisely in order to help us rethink the presumed certainties of the present.

New Voices

By the end of the twentieth century, British Jewish writing no longer conformed to the dominant expectations of English or Anglo-Jewish culture. The ability of these writers to refuse the opposition of nation and exile, authenticity and inauthenticity indicates the extent to which they could challenge a conservative multiculturalism which mistakenly valorizes closed cultures, roots, and traditions. In contrast to their Victorian predecessors, for whom British history was synonymous with world history, an increasingly impoverished sense of national destiny has resulted with the end of British imperial rule. Because the values of imperial Britain are no longer disseminated worldwide, mainstream British writers lack confidence about their place in the world and are uncertain about what constitutes English history and identity. According to these terms, British Jewish writers share a good deal in common with their postcolonial counterparts, which include Caryl Philips, Anita Desai, Salman Rushdie, Kazuo Ishiguro, Zadie Smith, and Hanif Kureishi. The work of these writers, which also utilizes Jewish history, exposes a radically different sense of the past and rewrites an alternative Englishness from the margins. It is for this reason that contemporary Jewish and postcolonial fiction in Britain is a study in fragmentation. No longer do writers learn from the previous generation, nor do they have a settled sense of place or identity (Connor 1996).[7]

Thus, even what defines a "new voice" is peculiarly problematic. For instance, Alan Isler published his prize-winning first novel *The Prince of West End Avenue* (1994) at the age of sixty. The strength of this novel was evident in how it moved effortlessly from the comic to the tragic mode and combined raucous New York humor with the bleak undertow of European history. Isler's narrative skill is revealed by giving his Anglo-American narrator many different cultural registers, which mischievously catches the reader unawares. Seen in this light, Isler is both a British and American writer (he lives in New York) as well as a welcome "old-new" voice.

The Anglo-American Jonathan Wilson, conversely, was born in London and educated in Jerusalem and New York. These tripartite settings are reflected in his collections *Schoom* (1993) and *An Ambulance Is on the Way: Stories of Men in Trouble* (2005). Unlike Isler, Wilson writes in a multitude of contexts reflecting the boundlessness of the English-born diasporic writer. No longer is history contained within national territories; it is everywhere both local and global. His novels *The Hiding Room* (1995) and *A Palestine Affair* (2004) encompass Jerusalem over an eighty-year period, while his story "From Shanghai" (collected in *Schoom*) brings together the Far East, Nazi Europe, and postwar Britain. In this tale an obsessive uncle, who emigrates to Britain from Shanghai in the fifties, turns out to have lost his wife and child in the World War II. The transformation of his collection of Hans Andersen into a shrine for his family both encircles and transcends his varied histories.

Jonathan Treitel's extraterritorial fiction and poetry is reflected in his restless and unsettling narrative technique. The ability to launch a story like a spinning top so that it eventually comes back to a fixed point characterizes many of Treitel's tales. Although born in London, Treitel was educated in California and has lived and worked in San Francisco and Tokyo. Like Wilson, Treitel can be regarded as a second-generation diasporic writer whose sense of place and identity has always been situated outside national boundaries. His first novel, *The Red Cabbage Café* (1990), is set in Russia in 1922, but his stories generally have no fixed sense of time or place, ranging from personal intimacies to historical landscapes. As with many of the writers discussed, Treitel's fiction skillfully blends fantastical wordplay with actual events or historical figures. This heady combination results in a new kind of writing, as can be seen in his *Arafat's Elephant: Stories* (2002) and *Freud's Alphabet: A Novel* (2003) (published under the pseudonym "Jonathan Tel"), which reconfigures both the inner and outer world by moving in and out of dream and reality, fiction and history.

In this new writing, the authenticity of experience no longer determines how we read or what is written since it is precisely the assumption of authenticity that is being undermined. Although it has not personally affected her, in her *Holocaust Trilogy* (1996) playwright Julia Pascal communes wholeheartedly with the Shoah. Viewed collectively, her three plays reflect an unapologetic and obsessive identification with the ghosts which she believes still haunt European culture. Along with Diane Samuels's more understated and subtle *Kindertransport*

(1992), there is a strong sense in which different pasts—here the Shoah and women's history—collide to form new wholes. This can be seen in Linda Grant's important first novel *The Cast Iron Shore* (1996) which places her heroine, Sybil Ross, at the center of many of the key events of the twentieth century. The novel drifts across continents—the United States, Vietnam, the Balkans, England—in an ambitious attempt to bring together both political idealism and personal commitment. No longer does the male figure assume the mock-heroic role of being buffeted by forces beyond his control. For the first time Grant has placed a woman at the heart of Western history in *The Cast Iron Shore* and *Still Here* (2002), extending this theme to Israel/Palestine in *When I Lived in Modern Times* (2000).

Most recent British Jewish writers are not merely unapologetic in their Jewishness but can be characterized as Jews "with attitude" who disrupt all conventions. In this assertive spirit, William Sutcliffe's debut novel *New Boy* (1996) has uniquely made gay Jewish identity a key motif. Equally significant, the playwright Steven Berkoff has explored the extreme violence inherent in a masculine Jewish identity in many of his expressionist plays. As with *The Cast Iron Shore*, Elena Lappin's collection of stories *Foreign Brides* (1999) utilizes material that has hitherto been considered the exclusive province of male Jewish writing. Lappin's personal history has included residences in Prague, Berlin, Haifa, and New York. Now based in London, she has written determinedly British Jewish stories. At their most compelling, the contemporary British Jewish writers I have discussed defy the authority of England and the Anglo-Jewish community and disrupt the usual categories in which they have been authenticated. At its best, much contemporary British Jewish literature is written against fixed boundaries that are increasingly being contested and are thus more fluid than ever. All of the writers are risk takers who will eventually help replace narrow national narratives and gendered identities with broader, more plural diasporic fictions.

NOTES

1. This chapter is a modified and updated version of my introductory essay to *Contemporary Jewish Writing in Britain and Ireland: An Anthology* (Lincoln: University of Nebraska Press / London: Peter Halban, 1998). I am grateful to Thomas Nolden for editing this text for this collection. Since its initial publication in 1998, there has been a substantial growth in nineteenth- and twentieth-century Anglo-Jewish literary criticism in Britain, the Continent, and the United States. I have updated the notes and bibliography to give a sense of the new work in Anglo-Jewish literary studies over the past decade, although much is still forthcoming. There are many more monographs and edited collections on individual British Jewish authors. British Jewish women's writing and representations of the Jewess are particularly in evidence. There is a renewed and welcome focus on British Jewish poetry—although more work is still needed in the

area of British Jewish drama. There are also a number of important recent studies comparing Jewish writing in Britain and the United States. My own work over the past decade has become increasingly comparative. As the last section of this chapter indicates, I am particularly interested in bringing together Jewish and postcolonial writing in Britain.

2. For a counterargument see Rochelson 1998, 11–44.

3. I use the term "Englishness," as opposed to a more inclusive "Britishness," since this identity is based on a fixed and homogeneous sense of self rooted in the past. While some of the writers surveyed in this chapter have more autonomous Welsh, Irish, or Scottish identities—or are émigrés—the majority have had to write against the dominance of an oppressive Englishness.

4. See Brian Glanville, "Young Jewish Writers and the Community." In *Jewish Chronicle,* December 19, 1958: 19; December 26, 1958: 13; January 2, 1959: 17; January 9, 1959; and January 16, 1959: 19.

5. See Sicher 1985 for a reductive reading of British Jewish writing in these terms and Brauner 2001 for a useful corrective.

6. See Steiner 1975b and 1989. His fiction has been collected in Steiner 1996b. For a longer account of Steiner's fiction, see Cheyette 1999.

7. For a fuller discussion of this argument, see my book *Diasporas of the Mind: Literature and Race after the Holocaust* (2007).

WORKS CITED

Behlau, Ulrike, and Bernhard Reitz, eds. 2004. *Jewish Women's Writing of the 1990s and Beyond in Great Britain and the United States.* Mainz: Wissenschaftlicher Verlag.

Bradbury, Malcolm. 1987. *No, Not Bloomsbury.* London: Arena.

Brauner, David. 2001. *Post-War Jewish Fiction: Ambivalence, Self-Explanation and Transatlantic Connections.* Basingstoke, U.K.: Palgrave.

Brookner, Anita. 1988. *The Latecomers.* New York: Pantheon.

———. 1989. "Aches and Pains of Assimilation." *The Observer,* April 23.

———. 1993. *A Family Romance.* London: Jonathan Cape.

Charles, Gerda, ed. 1963. *Modern Jewish Stories.* London: Faber and Faber.

Cheyette, Bryan. 1984. "On the Edge of the Imagination: Clive Sinclair Interviewed by Bryan Cheyette." *Jewish Quarterly* 3–4: 26–29.

———. 1993. *Constructions of "the Jew" in English Literature and Society: Racial Representations, 1875–1945.* Cambridge: Cambridge University Press.

———. 1999. "Between Repulsion and Attraction: George Steiner's Post-Holocaust Fiction." *Jewish Social Studies* 5 (3): 67–81.

———. 2000. *Muriel Spark: Writers and Their Work.* Horndon, U.K.: Northcote House.

———. 2004. "British-Jewish Writing and the Turn Towards Diaspora." In *The Cambridge History of Twentieth-Century English Literature,* ed. Laura Marcus and Peter Nicholls, 700–715. Cambridge: Cambridge University Press.

———. 2007. *Diasporas of the Mind: Literature and Race after the Holocaust.* New Haven, Conn.: Yale University Press.

———, ed. 1996. *Between "Race" and Culture: Representations of "the Jew" in English and American Literature.* Stanford, Calif.: Stanford University Press.

———, ed. 1998. *Contemporary Jewish Writing in Britain and Ireland: An Anthology.* Lincoln: University of Nebraska Press / London: Peter Halban.

Cheyette, Bryan, and Nadia Valman, eds. 2004. *The Image of the Jew in European Liberal Culture, 1789–1914.* London: Vallentine, Mitchell.

Cohen, Joseph, ed. 1983. *The Poetry of Dannie Abse: Critical Essays and Reminiscences.* London: Robson.

Connor, Steven. 1996. *The English in History, 1950–1995.* London: Routledge.

Conradi, Peter. 1982. "Elaine Feinstein: Life and Novels." *Literary Review* (April): 24–25.

———. 1983. "Eva Figes." In *Dictionary of Literary Biography.* Volume 14: *British Novelists Since 1960,* ed. Jay L. Halio, 298–302. Detroit, Mich.: Gale.

Daiches, David. 1973. "Some Aspects of Anglo-American Jewish Fiction." In *Jewish Writing Today, 1953–1973,* ed. Jacob Sonntag, 88–93. London: Vallentine, Mitchell.

Dodd, Philip. 1986. *Englishness and Culture, 1880–1920,* ed. Robert Colls and Philip Dodd. London: Croon Helm.

Esslin, Martin. 1982. *Pinter: The Playwright.* Rev. ed. London: Methuen.

Fainlight, Ruth. 1971. *Daylife and Nightlife.* London: Andre Deutsch.

———. 1994. *"Dr. Clock's Last Case" and Other Stories.* London: Virago Books.

Feinstein, Elaine. 1970. *The Circle.* London: Hutchinson.

———. 1978. *The Shadow Master.* London: Hutchinson.

———. 1982. *The Survivors.* London: Hutchinson.

———. 1984. *The Border.* London: Hutchinson.

———. 1992. *Loving Brecht.* London: Hutchinson.

———. 1994. "Making Dailiness Exotic." *Jewish Quarterly* 155: 64–65.

Feldman, David. 1994. *Englishmen and Jews: Social Relations and Political Culture, 1840–1914.* New Haven, Conn.: Yale University Press.

Figes, Eva. 1966. *Equinox.* London: Secker and Warburg.

———. 1969. *Konek Landing.* London: Faber and Faber.

———. 1970. *Patriarchal Attitudes: Women in Society.* London: Faber and Faber.

———. 1978a. *Little Eden: A Child at War.* London: Faber and Faber.

———. 1978b. "The Long Passage to Little England." *The Observer,* June 11: 14.

———. 1988. *Ghosts.* London: Hamish Hamilton.

———. 2003. *Tales of Innocence and Experience: An Exploration.* London: Bloomsbury.

Fludernik, Monika. 2000. *Echoes and Mirrorings: Gabriel Josipovici.* Frankfurt am Main: Peter Lang.

———, ed. 2003. *Diaspora and Multiculturalism: Common Traditions and New Developments.* Amsterdam: Rodopi.

Freedman, Jonathan. 2000. *The Temple of Culture: Assimilation and Anti-Semitism in Literary Anglo-America.* New York: Oxford University Press.

Glanville, Brian. 1958–59. "Young Jewish Writers and the Community." *Jewish Chronicle,* December 19, 1958: 19; December 26, 1958: 13; January 2, 1959: 17; January 9, 1959; and January 16, 1959: 19.

———. 1960. "The Anglo-Jewish Writer." *Encounter* 24 (2): 62–64.

Grant, Linda. 1996. *The Cast Iron Shore.* London: Picador.

———. 2000. *When I Lived in Modern Times.* Harmondsworth, U.K.: Penguin.

———. 2002. *Still Here.* Boston: Little, Brown.

Jacobson, Howard. 1983. *Coming From Behind.* New York: St. Martin's Press.

———. 1984. *Peeping Tom.* London: Chatto and Windus.

———. 1992. *The Very Model of a Man.* London: Viking.

———. 1993. *Roots Schmoots: Journeys Among Jews.* London: Viking.

———. 1999. *The Mighty Walzer.* London: Jonathan Cape.

Haffenden, John, ed. 1985. *Novelists in Interview.* London: Methuen.

Hanson, Clare. 1985. *Short Stories and Short Fictions, 1880–1980.* London: Macmillan.

Isler, Alan. 1994. *The Prince of West End Avenue.* Bridgehampton, N.Y.: Bridge Works.

Jacobson, Dan. 1982. *The Story of the Stories: The Chosen People and Its God.* London: Secker and Warburg.

———. 1991. *Hidden in the Heart.* London: Bloomsbury.

———. 1992. *The God-Fearer.* London: Bloomsbury.

Josipovici, Gabriel. 1971. *The World and the Book: A Study of Modern Fiction.* Stanford, Calif.: Stanford University Press.

———. 1986. *Contre-Jour: A Triptych after Pierre Bonnard.* Manchester, U.K.: Carcanet.

———. 1988. *The Book of God: A Response to the Bible.* New Haven, Conn.: Yale University Press.

———. 1991. *The Big Glass.* Manchester, U.K.: Carcanet.

———. 1993. "Going and Resting." In *Jewish Identity,* ed. David Theo Goldberg and Michael Krausz, 309–21. Philadelphia, Pa.: Temple University Press.

Kenyon, Olga. 1991. *Writing Women: Contemporary Women Novelists.* London: Pluto.

Lappin, Elena. 1999. *Foreign Brides.* New York: Farrar, Straus and Giroux.

Lawson, Peter. 2005. *Singers of the Diaspora: Anglo-Jewish Poetry from Isaac Rosenberg to Elaine Feinstein.* London: Vallentine, Mitchell.

———, ed. 2001. *Passionate Renewal: Jewish Poetry in Britain since 1945.* Nottingham, U.K.: Five Leaves.

Lee, A. Robert, ed. 1995. *Other Britain, Other British: Contemporary Multicultural Fiction.* London: Pluto.

Lentin, Ronit. 1989. *Night Train to Mother.* Dublin: Attic.

———. 1990. "Childhood Landscapes." *Jewish Quarterly* 138: 48–51.

Lerman, Anthony. 1987. "'Diaspora Blues': Real or Imagined." *Jewish Quarterly* 128.

Litvinoff, Emanuel, ed. 1972. *Journey Through a Small Planet.* London: Joseph.

———. 1979. *The Penguin Book of Jewish Short Stories.* Harmondsworth, U.K.: Penguin.

Louvish, Simon. 1985. *The Therapy of Avram Blok.* London: Heinemann.

———. 1986. *The Death of Moishe Ganef.* London: Black Swan.

———. 1988. *City of Blok.* New York: Collins.

———. 1991. *The Silencer.* New York: Interlink.

———. 1995. *What's Up God? A Romance of the Apocalypse.* New York: Random House.

———. 1997. *The Days of Miracles and Wonders: An Epic of the New World Disorder.* New York: Interlink.

———. 2004. *The Cosmic Follies.* London: ICA and BlokBooks.

Neumeier, Beate, ed. 1998. *Jüdische Literatur und Kultur in Grossbritannien und den USA nach 1945.* Wiesbaden: Harrassowitz.

Ozick, Cynthia. 1984. *Art and Ardor: Essays.* New York: Knopf.

Pascal, Julia. 1996. *Holocaust Trilogy.* London: Oberon.

Pinter, Harold. 1990. *The Dwarfs.* New York: Grove Weidenfeld.

———. 1993. *The Birthday Party.* Ed. Margaret Rose. London: Faber and Faber.

———. 1997. *Ashes to Ashes.* New York: Grove Press.

Prawer Jhabvala, Ruth. 1979. "Disinheritance." *Blackwoods* (April): 319–30.

———. 1986. *Out of India: Selected Stories.* New York: Morrow.

Rochelson, Meri-Jane, ed. 1998. *Israel Zangwill's "Children of the Ghetto": A Study of a Peculiar People.* Detroit, Mich.: Wayne State University Press.

Roth, Philp. 1985. *Reading Myself and Others.* Rev. ed. Harmondsworth, U.K.: Penguin.

Rubens, Bernice. 2005. *When I Grow Up: A Memoir.* Boston: Little, Brown.

Samuels, Diane. 1992. *Kindertransport.* New York: Plume.

Sharp, Ronald A. 1994. "Steiner's Fiction and the Hermeneutics of Transcendence." In *Reading George Steiner,* ed. Nathan A. Scott and Ronald A. Sharp. Baltimore, Md.: Johns Hopkins University Press.

Shechner, Mark. 1990. *"The Conversion of the Jews" and Other Essays.* London: Macmillan.

Shepherd, Ronald. 1994. *Ruth Prawer Jhabvala in India: The Jewish Connection.* Delhi: Chanakya.

Sicher, Ephraim. 1985. *Beyond Marginality: Anglo-Jewish Literature after the Holocaust.* New York: State University of New York Press.

Silkin, Jon. 1972. *Out of Battle: The Poetry of the Great War.* London: Routledge.

Sinclair, Clive. 1979. *Hearts of Gold.* London: Allison and Busby.

———. 1982. *Bedbugs.* London: Allison and Busby.

———. 1987. *Diaspora Blues: A View of Israel.* London: Heinemann.

———. 1996. *"The Lady with the Laptop" and Other Stories.* London: Picador.

———. 2002. *Meet the Wife.* London: Picador.

Skinner, John. 1992. *The Fictions of Anita Brookner.* London: Macmillan.

Sonntag, Jacob. 1980. *Jewish Perspectives: 25 Years of Jewish Writing.* London: Secker and Warburg.

Steiner, George. 1964. *Anno Domini: Three Stories.* New York: Atheneum.

———. 1967. *Language and Silence: Essays, 1958–1966.* London: Faber and Faber.

———. 1971. *In Bluebeard's Castle: Some Notes Towards the Re-definition of Culture.* London: Faber and Faber.

———. 1975a. *After Babel: Aspects of Language and Translation.* New York: Oxford University Press.

———. 1975b. *Extraterritorial: Papers on Literature and the Language Revolution.* Harmondsworth, U.K.: Penguin.

———. 1981. *The Portage to San Cristobal of A.H.* London: Faber and Faber.

———. 1985. *A Conversation* Piece. Cambridge, U.K.: Granta.

———. 1989. *Real Presences: Is There Anything "in" What We Say?* London: Faber and Faber.

———. 1992. *Proofs and Three Parables.* London: Faber and Faber.

———. 1994. "A Responsion." In *Reading George Steiner,* ed. Nathan Scott and Ronald A. Sharp, 275–85. Baltimore, Md.: Johns Hopkins University Press.

———. 1996a. *No Passion Spent: Essays, 1978–1995.* London: Faber and Faber.

———. 1996b. *"The Deeps of the Sea" and Other Fiction.* London: Faber and Faber.

Suttcliffe, William. 1996. *New Boy.* Harmondswoth, U.K.: Penguin.

Sylvester, Louise. 2001. "'Troping the Other': Anita Brookner's Jews." *English* 50 (196): 47–58.

Treitel, Jonathan. 1990. *The Red Cabbage Cafe.* New York: Pantheon.

———. 2002. *Arafat's Elephant: Stories.* Washington, D.C.: Counterpoint.

———. 2003. *Freud's Alphabet: A Novel.* Washington, D.C.: Counterpoint.

Valman, Nadia. 2007. *The Jewess in Nineteenth-Century British Literary Culture.* Cambridge: Cambridge University Press.

Wandor, Michelene. 2005. "Song of the Jewish Princess." In *Voices from the Diaspora: Jewish Women Writing in Contemporary Europe,* ed. Thomas Nolden and Frances Malino, 135–45. Evanston, Ill.: Northwestern University Press.

Waterman, Stanley, and Marlena Schmool. 1995. "Literary Perspectives on Jews in Britain in the Early Twentieth Century." In *Writing Across Worlds: Literature and Migration,* ed. Russell King, John Connell, and Paul White. London: Routledge.

Wesker, Arnold. 1958. *Chicken Soup with Barley.* Harmondsworth, U.K.: Penguin.

———. 1959. *Roots.* Harmondsworth, U.K: Penguin.

———. 1960. *I Am Talking about Jerusalem.* Harmondsworth, U.K.: Penguin.

Wilson, Jonathan. 1993. *Shoom.* London: Lime Tree.

———. 1995. *The Hiding Room.* London: Secker & Warburg.

———. 2004. *A Palestine Affair.* New York: Pantheon.

———. 2005. *An Ambulance Is on the Way: Stories of Men in Trouble.* New York: Random House.

Woolf, Michael. 1995. "Negotiating the Self: Jewish Fiction in Britain since 1945." In *Other Britain, Other British: Contemporary Multicultural Fiction,* ed. A. Robert Lee, 124–41. London: Pluto.

SIX

~

THOMAS NOLDEN

À la recherche du Judaïsme perdu: Contemporary Jewish Writing in France

The process of *réjudaïsation,* or Jewish revival, reached its zenith in France in 1979 and 1980, profoundly affecting the attitudes among the 600,000 French Jews who presently constitute the largest Jewish community in the Western world after the United States.[1] This embrace of Jewish heritage marked the end of a long-standing tradition of Jewish emancipation in France dating back to the French Revolution, when for the first time in modern history Jews became emancipated. *Juifs* thus became *israélites,* that is, highly acculturated citizens. During and following the eighties, this assimilationist trajectory was reversed. The notion of Jewish invisibility has given way to self-conscious and self-confident articulations of Jewish particularity. Thus, French Jewish historian Annette Wieviorka could conclude: "Whether one likes it or not, the republican model is behind us. There are no longer Frenchmen of the Jewish faith in our country" (2000, 26).

The "New Jewish Question"—to borrow the title of Shmuel Trigano's book—reemerged in the national consciousness over the course of the eighties. Journals like *Esprit* and *Histoire* presented special issues, such as "The Jews in Modern Times" and "The Jews in France," and an editorial in the then newly founded journal *Combat pour la diaspora* proclaimed: "The Diaspora must find its own voice" (1979, 1). In 1980 the French Jewish sociologist Dominique Schnapper presented her important study *Juifs et israélites* (Jewish Identities in France). In 1979 her colleague Claudine Vegh had published her conversations with children of deportees entitled *Je ne lui ai pas dit au revoir* (I Never Told Him Goodbye). Lastly, in 1980 journalist Luc Rosenzweig edited his *Catalogue pour des juifs de maintenant* (Catalogue for Today's Jews), in which he introduced the notion of a new "cacophony" of Jewish voices: "Those who listen to Jewish voices today are perhaps surprised by the cacophony of contradictory discourses which emerge from this turbulent world" (7).

That same year critic Alain Finkielkraut—like Rosenzweig, Trigano, and Schnapper a member of the younger generations of Jews—presented his seminal essay *Le Juif imaginaire* (The Imaginary Jew, 1980), a self-critical exploration of the fallacies he pinpointed in the identity discourse prevalent among his peers. Simultaneously Rosenzweig made yet another provocative move by calling his new collection of interviews with young Jews *La Jeune France juive* (Young Jewish France, 1980), a title deliberately reminiscent of Edouard Drumont's notorious anti-Semitic 1886 pamphlet.

The creation of a "néo-diasporisme culturel" (Mandel 1980, 95) during the eighties was accomplished primarily by the children and grandchildren of the generations directly affected by the Shoah and—to be sure—by the children of immigrants from France's former colonies and territories in North Africa. Their collective attempt to reappropriate and emphasize their *judéité* (to use Albert Memmi's term) manifested itself in a renewed interest in religious observance, political activism against anti-Semitism and racism, the definition of new forms of communal discourse, historical research and philosophical inquiries, and, last but not least, in artistic forms—especially in the creation of what has been called "jeune littérature juive" (young Jewish literature), "littérature des générations d'après" (literature of the post-Shoah generations), or "nouvelle littérature juive" (new Jewish literature).

In the wake of the process of politicization that had favored social affiliations over cultural, ethnic, and religious ties, this return to Jewish heritage followed impulses that originated within both the Jewish community—especially the influx of Sephardic Jews from the Maghreb—and the French nation at large. Alarmed by patterns of denial and anti-Semitic attacks, uneasy with their parents' choice of acculturation, and encouraged by the attitude prevalent among the Jewish immigrants from the Maghreb, the post-Shoah generations responded with assertive criticism. Bombings of Jewish sites in the early eighties as well as the desecration of the Jewish cemetery in Carpentras in May 1990 shook France and challenged the public to reevaluate the dangers to which the Jewish population was exposed some forty-five years after the end of the Vichy regime. One could even argue that the public deconstruction of Vichy France reached its apogee only when the governments of Jacques Chirac and Lionel Jospin finally officially acknowledged the complicity of the French in the persecution of Jews. France's difficulties in acknowledging its problematic past forms the subject matter of texts in which angry young Jews take stock of the toll this national apathy has cost. Cécile Wajsbrot has the protagonist of her novel *La Trahison* (The Betrayal) reflect, not without bitterness: "Thus, she saw her life as an effort, a permanent attempt to detach herself from this history that imprisoned her, the war and the deportation, the attitudes of those surrounding her, which prevented her from really feeling at home in a nation in which she had in fact been born, because of the collaboration, the denunciation, but also because of the silence which still endured today, because of this fierce desire to turn the eyes away, to look elsewhere" (1997, 114). The *mémoire juive* that in the late fifties had begun to contest unspoken assumptions of the *mémoire collective française* and to break the silence of France's involvement in the genocide also led to a questioning of the attitudes of many of the older Jews, who initially had responded to the shock of the Vichy years by holding on to the very project of acculturation that Vichy had terminated so brutally. Thus, the second generation of Jews had to set out to find their own ideas not only about gentile society but also about the experiences and choices of their parents and grandparents. They enjoyed the experience of a societal development in which the arrival of immigrants from the former colonies and protectorates would corrode the monocultural hegemony of French civilization. A new appreciation of regional concerns, ethnic particularity, and minority traditions was about to undermine Jacobin French centralism. Moreover, the growing presence of Muslim immigrants challenged the notion of France as "the Church's eldest daughter," a largely monoreligious—that is, Catholic—country. The universalist conception of the nation was shattered by the *nouveaux philosophes,* many of them of Jewish origin and not at all reluctant to use metaphors drawn from the Hebrew Bible in their works. When, in 1981, "le droit de la différence" (the right to be different) became the slogan of presidential campaigns, the question regarding whether Jews should refer to themselves as "les juifs français" rather than "les français juifs" gained new meaning (Halbronn 1996, 64).

What Is Jewish Writing? The Critical Debates

The corresponding discussion of the phrases "Jewish writer of the French language," "French writer of Jewish origin," and "French Jewish writer" was first undertaken not by the postwar generations of authors but as early as 1965, in a roundtable discussion organized by the Union des étudiants juifs de France (Union of Jewish Students of France).[2] The varied backgrounds of the discussants serves as a good indication of the diverse projects these authors had been pursuing. Anna Langfus (born in 1920 in Poland), Piotr Rawicz (born in 1919 in Poland), Arnold Mandel (born in 1913 in the Alsace region), and Albert Memmi (born in Tunisia in 1920) all testified to the confluence of various national backgrounds (primarily eastern Europe and the Maghreb) and languages within Jewish writing in the immediate postwar period. The issues raised by these authors differed in several respects from those debated by writers ten, twenty, or thirty years later. For immigrant authors born outside of the realm in which French represented the language of belles lettres per se, the attribute "French Jewish" hardly offered a valid description of their situation as writers. (For example, Elie Wiesel's work *La Nuit* [Night, 1958] first appeared not in French but in Yiddish, and Albert Cohen spent most of his time living in Switzerland rather than France.) In addition, Langfus insisted on the religious dimension as a necessary part of Jewish writing, while Memmi doubted that the given modes of reception—a largely gentile audience unfamiliar with Jewish traditions—would allow authors to write Jewish literature since it would not be understood by their readers. The centrality of the Shoah, however, was recognized by almost all of the authors of this generation, who would often provide written testimony of the *univers concentrationnaire,* to use a neologism introduced by David Rousset in 1946.

Unhindered by the aesthetic reservations that the philosopher T. W. Adorno had voiced in 1955 on the other side of the Rhine, "French imaginative writing 'after Auschwitz,'" according to critic Elaine Marks, "was obsessed with the death camps" (1996, 85). This "littérature du génocide" (Ruszniewski-Dahan 1999, 9) met with the appreciation of the literati. André Schwarz-Bart's epic of the Jewish people, which ends with the destruction of the Polish shtetl, and Langfus's accounts of persecution and resistance were awarded the prestigious Prix Goncourt in the late fifties and early sixties, respectively. A highly sardonic piece like Romain Gary's *La Danse de Gengis Cohn* (The Dance of Gengis Cohn, 1967) remained an exception in the overwhelmingly realist literary production of the time; its counterparts only exist in the very early works of the Hungarian Jewish playwright George Tabori and the German Jewish novelist Edgar Hilsenrath, which, interestingly enough, were conceived not in Europe but in the United States.

Jewish writing in the first decades following the Shoah continued a tradition of writing by Jewish authors which was driven neither by any kind of "nostalgia for times gone by and vanished places" nor insistent on the preservation of the "memory of the deceased" (Lévy 1998, 55). A writer like Nathalie Sarraute, for example, held on to the tradition of indifference toward one's Jewish affiliation, which dates back to Marcel Proust and continues today—for example, in the works of the young best-selling author Emmanuèle Bernheim. That the definition of Jewish writing cannot be dependent solely upon ethnic belonging is also documented by the recent literary debut of Justine Lévy, who in her prose hardly addresses Jewish matters. Conversely, Bernard-Henri Lévy, her father, has fully participated in the recent "pluralization of ways to be Jewish" (David 1993, 27) in both in his philosophical and fictional works.

Whereas in 1974 the notion of Jewish writing in France was still being contested by most of the authors involved in a debate primarily featuring the writers of the *génération d'après,* eight years later—more distant from the political imperatives of the student rebellion—a new debate could appreciate what now was perceived as the *symptôme massif* of an emerging body of Jewish writing in France authored by post-Shoah writers. In 1982 the editorial staff of the then newly founded journal *Traces* dedicated an entire issue to the question "Qu'est-ce que la littérature juive?" (What Is Jewish literature?). The critics could now appreciate a long list of writers who all quite directly addressed their topics from a Jewish perspective and who no longer primarily concerned themselves with representations of the genocide. Many of them were born not in France but in the Maghreb and were eager to introduce the idioms of the *mellahs* and *haras* to the French literature with which they had been intimately familiar in their youth.

The discussions in *Traces* marked the positions taken in the debate on the shape of Jewish writing in present-day France. The literary critic Rachel Ertel was the first to apply Deleuze and Guattari's notion of a "minor literature" to the comparative study of contemporary Jewish writing. Looking at Kafka writing in German as a Jew living in Prague, Deleuze and Guattari had coined the term "deterritorialization" to describe a situation in which a major language—in this case German—is used by a minority in a territory where the major language has been surviving only "for strange and minor uses" (Deleuze and Guattari 1986, 17). According to Deleuze and Guattari, the revolutionary force of minor literature derives from the attempt by the deterritorialized writer to instill in this "paper language" a "new intensity" in order to "arrive at a perfect and uniform expression, a materially intense expression" (19). In addition, they suggest that in a minor literature "everything takes on a collective value. Indeed, precisely because talent isn't abundant in a minor literature, there are no possibilities for an individuated enunciation that would belong to this or that 'master' and that could be separated from a collective enunciation. . . . What each author says individually already constitutes a common action, and what he or she says or does is necessarily political, even if others aren't in agreement" (17). Ertel sees "deterritorialization" as characteristic of the works of the Jewish writers from the Maghreb and notes that although contemporary Jewish literature is highly complex and its texture not captured by "une définition unidimensionelle" (a one-dimensional definition), its legitimacy as a literary phenomenon cannot be doubted (1982, 91).

In her contribution to *Traces* Janine Gdalia—then the editor of the series *Judaïques* (Judaisms), published by Lattès and an affiliate of the Fédération Sepharde (Sephardic Federation)—insisted on a broad and inclusive description of the emerging Jewish literature in France that would take into account the multiplicity of voices both within this literature and among individual authors: "Jewish writing? Writing of difference, of suffering; the mark of an assumed or inherited manifold experience, the symptom of an acute eye, focused on the world, traces of an occasionally haunted, melancholy perspective. Jewish writing would know how to render in its meandering this human experience made up of specific faith in a universal aspiration, to take into account this reasoning, which, though it does not belong exclusively to the Jew, is nevertheless very familiar to him" (1982, 91). For Gdalia the most intriguing feature of this literature is a new interest in memory and the past. This fascination with the past is manifested in the phenomena of both the *nouveaux Ashkenazim* (new Ashkenazim) rediscovering the *Yiddishkeit* their parents had left behind, and of young Sephardic writers looking back to the times when different cultures and ethnicities mingled in the cities of the Maghreb. She explained this historical curiosity as a response to the exhaustion of the great ideas and ideological projects that had characterized the late sixties and seventies.

According to the critic Lazare Bitoun (who was born in 1944 in Casablanca), the works of the newly self-assertive "Juif de France" (French Jew) removed the self-imposed invisibility of the literature by the "Français de confession israélite" (Frenchman of the Israelite faith). The writer no longer makes "se faire oublier" (himself forget), nor writes solely for Jewish audiences. Rather, the new motto is "se faire entendre" (make oneself heard) as a participant in a highly heterogeneous literary project reflecting the diversity of attitudes prevalent among young Jews: "Today's young Jewish literature is without contest the heir to all these tensions. It is the intersection of cultural currents: Jewish and French; Ashkenazi and Sephardic; bourgeois, religious, or militant. It unites them or is torn apart in the process, but in any case it creates a new space for original expression. It is this unity and this diversity that one must recognize" (1982, 82). Bitoun observed that behind the many voices of contemporary Jewish literature there is, after all, one genre dominating the imagination of the young writers, namely, autobiography. There is also a common point of departure, proceeding from the here and now of French society. Differences within this "minority ensemble in a hegemonic language" arise primarily with respect to the language. Whereas French-born Jews have unhindered access to "correct French," writers born outside France display a bilingualism comprised of French learned in French high schools abroad and Judeo-Arabic—and, one should add, Judeo-Spanish. This, Bitoun noted, has contributed enormously to the rejuvenation of the French literary idiom.

Provocative Beginnings

A historical survey of contemporary Jewish literature in France has to commence with a look at the works of two enfants terribles who, in the late sixties and early seventies, entered the stage with enormously provocative books that portrayed the life of two very different extreme Jewish picaros. In his 1968 novel *La Place de l'étoile* Patrick Modiano has his young Jewish protagonist, Raphaël Schlemilovitch, blatantly transgress all political, ideological, and aesthetic boundaries of the "années noires" (dark years) to advance his career as a "juif collabo."[3] The son of a collaborator, the lover of Hitler's Eva Braun, and an admirer of the writers sympathizing with Vichy, Schlemilovitch proudly proclaims that the future of Jewish writing rests solely on his shoulders. Neither he nor his author suffers from any "anxiety of influence." On the contrary, the novel welcomes both the Jew Marcel Proust and the anti-Semite Louis-Ferdinand Céline as ghostwriters for the story of Schlemilovitch's own life. They function as the godfathers for *La Place de l'étoile,* a novel by an angry young man who makes his literary debut trying to outdo the grand names of a literary history which has repeatedly proven to be politically ambiguous. Shocking those who only reluctantly accepted the "mode rétro" he initiated, Modiano had his protagonist pose as a "juif anti-sémite" (1968, 25) aiming to create "a Jewish Waffen S.S. and a legion of Jewish volunteers against Bolshevism" (26).

In his autobiography *Souvenirs obscurs d'un juif polonais né en France* (Dim Memories of a Polish Jew Born in France, 1975) political activist, self-styled guer-rilla, and writer Pierre Goldman examined the combative course his life had taken from the explicit perspective of Jewish experience and situated his identifi-cation with the cause of the suppressed in the third world within his own exis-tential particularity as a Jew born to Polish members of the resistance (Nolden 2003). In his novel *L'Ordinaire Mésaventure d'Archibald Rapoport* (The Ordinary Misadventure of Archibald Rapoport, 1977) he offered the following portrait of his alter ego: a young Jew who breaches all societal contracts of the postwar era by setting out to kill representatives of the state at random, trying in vain to commit acts of resistance upon which he can mount a claim for glory and for an afterlife in literature. Archibald Rapoport is a Jew who restlessly embarks on a merciless rampage to execute the political and social pillars of the French estab-lishment, carrying out a mission determined by his father's fate: "My father died on a Vichy scaffold and I want to fight . . . I want to kill fascists" (53).

Goldman's novel is a remarkable examination of the motivations and con-finements of an extreme life experienced—and, as it were, released—in the realm of imaginary deviance rather than in reality. In this regard, the peculiar coexistence of autobiography and novel in Goldmann's modest oeuvre—at thirty-five he was murdered by right-wing extremists—resembles the coexistence of autobiographical and fictional discourse in Georges Perec's *W, ou le souvenir d'enfance* (W, or The Memory of Childhood, 1975).

Thus, the beginnings of Jewish writing after 1968 are marked by the works of agnostics who had barely been exposed to the religious practices of Judaism. Their Jewishness, or *judéité,* to use the terminological differentiation offered by Albert Memmi in his *Portrait d'un juif* (Portrait of a Jew, 1962), intersects historically—but hardly religiously or culturally—with the rich traditions of Judaism. For Ashkenazi writers, the Shoah—or, more precisely, their parents' experience of the Shoah—is one of the focal points of their fiction. Whereas the writing of the former generation of Ashkenazi Jews was primarily a literature of the genocide, the literary production of the succeeding generation finds its impetus in the past of its parents. Goldman crafts accounts of contemporary Jewish resistance to expose the fallacies of the *Israelites* and most expressively shatters the notion of Jewish invisibility. Conversely, Myriam Anissimov (born in 1943 in a refugee camp in Switzerland) portrays the children of the victims as incapable of action, caught between the guilt of the survivors and the lack of models of resistance with which to identify. She describes the syndrome of "telescoping," that is, the emotional handing down by family members of traumatic experiences, which preoccupies many authors for years to come.

Autojudéographies

Georges Perec's beginnings as a Jewish author also date back to the mid-seventies, to his experiments with autobiographical genres, which, aside from *W, ou le souvenir d'enfance,* include *Je me souviens* (I Remember, 1978) and *Ellis Island: Description d'un projet* (Ellis Island: Description of a Project, 1979), co-authored with Robert Bober. In an interview Perec elaborated in a remarkable manner on the relationship between his writing and his Jewishness: "I think I began to feel Jewish when I set about telling the story of my childhood and when the plan developed, long deferred, but increasingly inevitable, to trace the history of my family through the memories that my aunt had passed on to me" (Perec and Le Sidaner 1979, 9). I would like to borrow the peculiar term *autojudéographie* from the title of an autobiographical essay by the fairly unknown Robert Ouaknine because it aptly describes an important feature of second-generation Jewish writing. The autobiographical texts by Perec and the fictional writing by many authors of the "générations d'après" reflect the struggle to fill the vacuum of Jewish traditions and the task of articulating the silence that had engulfed the traditions terminated by the Shoah or erased by a long history of acculturation. In his lipogrammatic novel *La Disparition* (The Disappearance, 1969), Perec had signaled this silence by the omission of the letter *e* throughout the entire text, suggesting that language is no longer complete, that it has also suffered greatly. In his novel *Ellis Island* Perec acknowledged what Finkielkraut had alluded to in his *Imaginary Jew:*

> Somewhere, I am foreign in relation to something of my own;
> somewhere, I am "different," but not
> different from others, different from "my own people" . . . (1995, 59)

"Autojudeography," then, is a form of "écriture de soi" that recaptures and reaffirms the bonds with the past, with forms of Jewish life lived by previous generations, while simultaneously supplementing the nation's collective memory with fragments of lost Jewish memory. To do so it has to break the silence that has imperiled efforts to hand down traditions and share stories about the past within the Jewish community. This literature attempts to reassess what it means to be Jewish after the fires by affirming its ties to its people. Writing turns out to be one of the essential means of achieving this affirmation, and as such it has to start counteracting the conformist reticence of the established community, be it the community of the family or the community of French postwar Jewry. In the preface to his study *Les Juifs, la mémoire et le présent* (The Jews, Memory, and the Present, 1981) Jewish historian Pierre Vidal-Naquet confirms that the phenomenon of "autojudeography" is not at all confined to the writing of fiction or to "écriture de soi": "Paradoxically enough, I will say gladly that it is less because I am Jewish that I wrote these pages than the opposite: it is in writing this book, plus several other works, that I became Jewish, a voluntary Jew, if you will, or a Jew by reflection" (1981, 11–12). It is the very act of writing rather than the fact of ethnic belonging that creates the unique attitude toward the Jewish tradition and the Jewish people displayed in the works of these younger generations of authors. The proclivity toward the autobiographical (*auto*) and the self-reflexive preoccupation with the nature of writing (*graphie*) provide, as it were, the narrative frame within which the notion of Jewishness (*judéo*) appears.

This feature of contemporary Jewish writing characterizes individual texts—Gérard Wajcman's elliptic novel *L'Interdit* (The Forbidden, 1986); the autobiographies of Serge Koster, Alain Fleischer, and Jean-Luc Allouche; Antoine Spire's coming-of-age novel *Le Silence en héritage* (The Legacy of Silence, 1988)— and also defines the trajectory of the entire oeuvre of individual authors, such as that of Henri Raczymow, who is one of the most prolific contributors to contemporary Jewish writing in France, as well as one of its foremost critics.

Writing against Silence and Forgetting

A powerful literary tribute, Raczymow's *Contes d'exil et d'oubli* (Tales of Exile and Forgetting, 1979) brought together the past of the shtetl and the present of Belleville. Raczymow (who was born in 1948) began his literary career in 1973, although he published three novels before he wrote his first "Jewish" book. His early works did not speak to his cultural and ethnic background as an Ashkenazi Jew born in France after the war (Astro 1994; Fine 1985; Hirsch 1997). Moreover, these books were written in the governing stylistic paradigms of the time. Raczymow eventually realized that his—and his Jewish peers'—distinctive point of departure was one which he would eventually have to address in his writing.

The literary critic Marianne Hirsch suggested the term "postmemory" to identify the starting point of such authors as Perec and Raczymow. According to Hirsch, postmemory is "distinguished from memory by generational distance and from history by deep personal connection," and its "connection to its object or source is mediated not through recollection but through an imaginative investment and creation" (22). It was the lack of any personal memory of the decisive events of twentieth-century Jewish history that prompted many Jewish writers to take up their pens in the late seventies and early eighties, when the members of the older generations were no longer available as witnesses of the Shoah, the "années noires," and of decolonization. In this regard, Pierre Nora's notion that "generational memory is stocked with remembrances not so much of what its members have experienced as of what they have not experienced" (1992, 525) aptly describes the point of departure common to Raczymow and his peers.

In his *Contes* Raczymow addressed this point of departure head-on. Matthieu Schriftlich, the narrator of the section entitled "Préhistoire," is disturbed by the "absence of memory," which leads him to urge his grandfather to describe life in the Polish provinces before the war and to break the silence in which the past has been trapped. The setting—Belleville in the fifties—provides an apt location for Matthieu's gathering of the collective saga of the shtetl, not least because this modern community is about to undergo profound changes in the seventies (with the arrival of immigrants from the Maghreb), when the story is being told. The narrative construction of the *Contes,* which approaches the world of the shtetl through multilevel citations, shields the text from the risks of folklorization and nostalgic sentimentalism which the critic Régine Robin has identified as the perils of any process of "retours identitaires" (1989, 129).

In a text like Raczymow's *Contes,* autojudeography and literary ethnography almost merge. Indeed, ethnography as an observer's account of the practices of an ethnically defined community is a form that has gained prominence in contemporary Jewish writing. Many writers of Maghrebi origin render scenes from the life led by their ancestors in the Jewish ghettos of North Africa by noting the cultural, societal, and historical differences that set them apart as observers from the Jewish worlds inhabited by their ancestors. For example, in his story "Le Fils du serpent" (The Son of the Snake, 1981) Ami Bouganim (who was born in 1951 in Mogador) alludes indirectly to his impetus for telling stories when he has one of his characters voice his vexation over his gradual loss of memory, which threatens irrevocably to erase the world of the ghetto. He wants to provide answers for those whose curiosity has been piqued and whose pride in their Sephardic heritage will not be relinquished:

> The others knew nothing of Morocco but the wounded appearance of their parents, their drained looks, their old Jewish memories. At certain gatherings I recounted to them, to those who knew better how the Polish lived in a ghetto than the Moroccans in a *mellah*, Mogador. I spoke to them of Rabbi Pinhas, of Rabbi Mard'haï, of Rahamim and all the others. "What became of them?" . . . they asked. I explained the atmosphere that reigned on the rue des Épices, in the synagogues where the Jews carried on and on in hymns, because the prayer blended into the song, in the *mellah*, on the days of the great murmurs. (22)

Authors who spent only their early childhood years in the Maghreb or who were born in France to immigrant parents take up the task of recording what their parents and grandparents left behind and of articulating what their forbears cannot because of the *mutisme* that makes it impossible for the older immigrants to articulate the pains that the process of decolonization and the experience of displacement have inflicted on them. In her novel Des gens infréquentables (Bad Company, 1996) Algerian-born writer Marlène Amar has her narrator re-create the short life of her cousin, Samuel, with whom she had lost contact after arriving in France. The story "begins with silence" (21), which is broken only when the narrator begins to inquire about Samuel's fate as well as the experience of her extended family. To break the silence and in to understand, she becomes a journalist and poses questions until her family members begin to talk: about persecution in the form of Arab pogroms; the emigration from the North African desert; the humiliating experience of the immigrants; the abuses suffered by the Ashkenazim; the fallacies of re-migration; the spaces, smells, views, people, and feelings left behind. It is the self-imposed task of the young woman to get people to speak who have previously not shared any of these stories: "My mother did not speak. When I questioned her, she said that she did not know or that she no longer remembered. For a long time I believed that she really had forgotten everything. The silence lasted for years" (22). Once she begins to talk to her daughter, cruel images of pogroms back in Algeria are conjured up, which the narrator records almost impassively. Family history is presented against the background of historical events at large. The reader is introduced to people who have gotten "lost in a France too large" (20) and whom nobody would deign to approach since they are considered "bad company" even by their non-Sephardic co-religionists.

Breaking the silence of the parent is for writers of Maghrebi descent an act that also poses stylistic questions. In their use of the French language some choose to perfect a stylistic notion that aspires to the celebrated French literary standards of clarity, lucidity, and precision, stylistically paving a path to what Annie Goldmann (1995) has described as the lure of French literary culture, which fascinated the young writer from the shores of North Africa.

For writers like Marlène Amar or Chochana Boukhobza the challenge is to create within these conventions an idiom that can render justice both to the rhetorical traditions of French letters and to the cultural, ethnic, and linguistic experience of the Maghreb. Others—like Katia Rubinstein, Marco Koskas, and Gil Ben Aych— instead capture the overdetermined situation of the Sephardic writer in a linguistic "mélange" and stylistic "patchwork."

Gil Ben Aych, who left Algeria with his family in 1956, has written all his books in French, and yet he has acknowledged that he simply translated them from the native languages of his childhood. This process of translation, however, does not filter out all the remnants of the languages to which the author has been exposed. Thus, his works offer a stylistic homage to the linguistic and cultural worlds of characters whose ties to Algeria remain strong. In his early novel *L'Essuie-mains des pieds* (The Hand Towel for Feet, 1981), this homage manifests itself in a record of culinary customs which, as the literary historian Guy Dugas has pointed out, alludes to deep memories residing in the body, connecting sensual experiences from childhood with the sphere of the family and the home (1990, 148).[4] The novel is presented as the account of a young boy, Nanou, in chapters which all bear the names of culinary dishes. From the perspective of an eleven-year-old narrator, odors and meals have the same relevance as the relatives who are trying to get their feet on the ground in Champigny.

Ben Aych's novel *Le Voyage de Mémé* (Mémé's Voyage, 1982), intended for a young readership, recounts how the grandmother of an immigrant family traveled on foot the long distance between Paris and the suburb of Champigny. His novel *Le Livre d'Étoile* (Étoile's Book, 1986), presented as an oral narrative by the same grandmother, Étoile, describes her journey from Algeria to France, capturing in long passages the breathless parlando of the old woman, who has been persuaded by her children to leave her home country. Imitating the associative, redundant, and ungrammatical patterns of spoken language, the author disappears, as it were, behind the voice of the old Arabic-speaking Jew, whose diatribes against the Western industrialized world metamorphose into a stream-of-consciousness recording of the pain inflicted on her by exile.

In *Balace Bounel* (Bounel Palace, 1979), the debut novel by Marco Koskas (who was born in 1951), there is no external organizing principle that guides the reader through this almost anarchic tale of a multistory tenement building owned by the Bonan family of Nabeul. The gestalt of the novel resembles a multicolored rug in which the many tales and anecdotes drawn from the everyday life of the owners and their employees have been tightly woven together, meshing the inside of the tenement building with the world outside. The spatial sense offered by *Balace Bounel* differs profoundly from the "closed conformism of the cubes in Ryvel's *hara*" (Roumani 1984, 261), although the works of the Tunisian Jewish writer Raphaël Lévy (who was born in 1898) have influenced Koskas's literary fashioning of oral storytelling.

Another variety of ethnographically informed narrative can be found when writers of Ashkenazi background turn to the everyday life of the survivor communities populated by older Jews born in eastern Europe. Here, too, the task is manifold, including enunciating the pain of the ancestors, who have been rendered speechless by an experience of persecution too traumatic to articulate. For example, the young protagonist of Claude Gutman's novel *Les Larmes du crocodile* (Crocodile Tears, 1982) revisits the community centered around the cultural events organized by the Amis israélites de Montreuil. The narrator-protagonist looks with both estranged puzzlement and tender admiration at a long-lost Jewish world that has nevertheless been preserved by a handful of East European survivors who have all changed their names "to sound more French than the French" (26).

New Books of Memory: Alain Gluckstein and Myriam Anissimov

The notion of recording the lost world of the shtetl is not only an important theme of contemporary French Jewish letters but also a stylistically relevant principle, with Ashkenazi authors revisiting the forms of Yiddish storytelling. While Cyrille Fleischman distills subtle melancholic vignettes from the vanishing milieu of Yiddish-speaking émigrés in his short stories, his younger colleague Gilles Rozier, in his novel *Par-dela les monts obscures* (Beyond the Dark Mountains, 1999) engages in intertextual play with Sholem Aleichem's tale "The Little Redheaded Jews," which in itself can be read as a fictionalized form of ethnographic literature. Nonliterary forms of writing within the Yiddish tradition have also informed contemporary Jewish fiction. Most prominently, the *yizker bou'h*—the memorial book commemorating the Polish Jewish communities before the Holocaust—has been discovered as a narrative matrix for literary projects wanting both to render justice to the notion of origin and to acknowledge that the latter is solely a construct of the imagination. Like many of the stories by Fleischman, Alain Gluckstein's novel *Nos grands hommes* (Our Great Men, 1997) is concerned with the past and the present of Yiddish literature. Like Fleischman, Gluckstein addresses the demise of this part of Jewish writing with a sense of humorous and at times melancholic nostalgia.[5] Unlike Fleischman, however, Gluckstein uses a grand design for his novel, with intricate, constantly shifting narrative perspectives and forms, including excerpts from texts in various genres. Set in Paris in 1980, the novel engages in a dialogue not only with the art of Yiddish storytelling but also with the genre of the memorial book. Gluckstein brings to this dialogue a postmodern interest in toying with tradition and in mixing genres. Although at the end of the novel the old narrator, Berl, burns a Yiddish-language manuscript by one of his deceased friends because he was unable to decipher or understand it—and because it had made him fall asleep—a younger generation nevertheless continues in the literary traditions of Judaism.

Viewing Jewish literature by the older generations as an outdated project, the novel propels its own literary self-awareness into the realm of the ironic by displaying how successfully and creatively it can perpetuate a tradition to which it is about to bid farewell. It playfully draws on central motifs and aspects of Jewish folklore and history, using the wheeling and dealing of a *landsmanschaft* as a microcosm which also speaks to the current interest in writing Jewish history and literature. One of the shtetl/immigrant writers in the novel cuts off his ties to the past so completely after the war that he dispenses with his Jewish name, his accent, and his devotion to rituals of Jewish life in the East and embarks on an illustrious career as a writer of indistinguishable ethnicity and interest.

Although the novel does not condemn such a life of literary acculturation, it places assimilation in a rich context of highly hybridized, creative emanations of the cultural productions of Jews. Moreover, it even alludes to the power of handed-down forms of Jewish narratives over non-Jews, as illustrated by the work "Guéfilté Nem" by Berl's Asian-born adopted daughter, Rita (her title conflates the name of the classic Yiddish dish with one drawn from Vietnamese cuisine). Kenneth Avruch's suggestion that contemporary Diaspora Judaism is made "not of tradition, but of traditionalizing" (quoted in Boyarin 1991, 158) reverberates in the ironic literary constellations that are introduced in this mazelike text about Jewish writing written by Jews and non-Jews alike.

The self-reflexive irony that can be found in ethnographic forms of contemporary Jewish writing is mostly absent in the genealogically oriented forms of "jeune littérature juive." While "mnemography" in general, including the ethnographic modes, responds to the imperative of *zakhor,* genealogically oriented narratives are dedicated to the memory of family members who can no longer articulate their experiences. The literary act of remembering is the attempt to remember family histories fragmented by the Shoah. The writer often appears as the ancestor's delegate, one who will commit to writing what would otherwise remain untold. Such delegatory constructions are found primarily in texts by women writers, as in the works of Myrian Anissimov or Collette Fellous. In accordance with the paradigm of *écriture féminine,* the daughter documents the experience of the mother and thus pays homage to the female experience and perspective. At the same time, however, Jewish writers go beyond the conventions of women's literature by accomplishing in a literary manner what in religious form is achieved by the kaddish offered by male offspring.

Anissimov's most recent novel *Sa majesté la Mort* (Her Majesty Death, 1999) intertwines—as do many of her previous works of fiction—the narratives of the parents and grandparents with stories from the life of the author-narrator. Reconstructing the past by searching for photographs and documents, reading letters, and listening to the stories of her mother, the author-narrator faces an almost insurmountable challenge: "Almost all of the members of our family had disappeared before my birth. They were born in Szydlowiec, in Poland, near Radom, where the Jews were sequestered by the Germans before their deportation and liquidation in the gas chambers and the Treblinka extermination camp in 1942" (13). Here Anissimov creates a forum in which she stages crucial moments of her own life, asserting her own presence in this book of family remembrances. Switching back and forth between scenes from the ancestors' lives in Poland and the survivors' lives in French exile, plus vignettes from her own early childhood spent in hiding under the auspices of a nun, Anissimov carries on a narrative that she began to tell as early as 1992 in *Dans la plus stricte intimité* (Family Only).

The book is, as it were, a commissioned piece instigated by the author's mother: "She decided that I would be the guardian of her memory, of the memory of all of her people, the living and the dead" (15). Instead of reducing her own role to that of an archivist, from the beginning the daughter establishes her own place both in the history of the family and in history at large. The vectors of Anissimov's prose, however, always pull the narrative from the present of 1997–98 back toward the past, where she discovers, among other things, fragments of the Yiddish language which she claims as her own. "A Yiddish Writer Who Writes in French" is the title of an essay in which Anissimov proudly accepts a linguistic legacy on which many of her books reflect melancholically. The "hybrid language" of her books, the author explains, results from the "fertile ground of the conflict between French and Yiddish" (2005, 37). Although Yiddish presents an important linguistic and cultural backdrop for Anissimov's books, one can barely find traces in them of any elements reminiscent of the traditions of Yiddish storytelling. Neither the Haggadah nor the artistically rendered—and therefore secularized—forms of traditional folk narrative are present in her work; nor are anecdote, parody, and parable forms in which this author is interested. Her art of storytelling—unlike the work of Gluckstein, Fleischman, or Raczymow—enlists imagination into the service of historical reconstruction rather than permitting it to commit the kind of acts of "creative betrayal" for which, according to literary critic David G. Roskies, modern representatives of Yiddish storytelling are known (1995, 295). Anissimov's work is geared toward the autobiographical while constantly searching—like a historian—for the traces of the lives of her ancestors, as if neither of these stories could be told separately.

Family Portraits

Striking stylistic differences set an author like Anissimov apart from her younger colleague Eliette Abécassis (born in 1969), who, as a member of a generation further removed from the trauma of the past, can employ more playful narrative forms to address the complexities of contemporary Jewish identity. In her two novels *Qumran* (Qumran Mystery, 1996) and *L'or et la cendre* (Gold and Ashes, 1998), Abécassis is similarly preoccupied with the relationship between older and younger Jews, yet she sets her exploration of such patterns of filiation within the framework of detective novels, charged with dense references to theological and historiographical debates. *L'or et la cendre,* her second novel, presents an intimate picture of a family imploding due to forces exerted almost fifty years earlier by Nazi perpetrators. The young protagonist's father had to bear the loss of his parents and siblings, yet he refused to share his thoughts and feelings with his children, among them the young sculptor Lisa, who puts the dilemma of her own formative years in the form of a succinct question: "How can you have your adolescent crisis and revolt against a father who was at Auschwitz and who has never recovered from it, because one can't recover from it?" (186). A highly articulate woman, she constantly debates the planned Berlin Holocaust Memorial, the presence of Carmelite nuns on the site of the Auschwitz camp, the canonization of Edith Stein, the role of Swiss banks in the war, and, above all, the theology of evil. Settled in her Marais apartment, she vents her rage against a God who did nothing to prevent the gassing of six million Jews and who—if He existed—deserved to have suffered in Auschwitz as well. There are few authors whose work is as clearly situated within the aftermath of the Enlightenment as is that of Abécassis—a spirit of dialogical exploration of the truth, of the mutual illumination of opposing attitudes toward the big questions of life presented in the form of a suspenseful *roman policier* featuring grotesque if not bloody crimes.

The family tableaux created by male and female authors are prisms of the history of persecution, discrimination, and exile. First questioning the myth of the *grande nation* born of the ashes of resistance to fascism and later, following decolonization, the notion of a tolerant society that treats its subjects equally, the younger generations of Jews discovered the humiliation imposed upon their forefathers and parents by their gentile compatriots both on European and North African soil. In their writing they create a fictional space where all the participants from various generations meet once again. They create a forum for readdressing the unarticulated issues of their own coming of age, a stage where the family drama of their youth can be recast, altered, and occasionally resolved through the power of retrospective understanding. In their scripts for encounters between old and young, they steer a course between their desire for an autonomous notion of the self and their recognition that the formation of the self takes place within an intergenerational process in which ethnic givens constantly have to be reconfigured.

Setting their portraits of young Jews against the backdrop of family histories, some writers (Antoine Spire, Patrick Modiano, Marco Koskas, Nickie Golse) feature children as relentless critics overturning the decisions made by elders. Still other writers (Myriam Anissimov, Norbert Czarny) depict them living harmoniously alongside their parents to show that, despite the predicaments of history, the power of the Covenant remains as strong as the family contract. Preserving the unrecorded fates of the victims and articulating what exists behind the silence of mute immigrants are fictional means of re-membering truncated families. To create narratives that reinvest a family legacy of resistance with new meaning is a way of doing justice to the past, even if these narratives (like those of Pierre Goldman or Eliette Abécassis) show how difficult it is to keep sight of what it means to do justice to the present and to the self under the weight of these legacies.

The assertion by literary critic Anny Dayan-Rosenman that contemporary Jewish writers in France "remain strangely silent about the place and time in which they are writing" (1998, 341) needs to be questioned. Rather than revisiting the biblical figures and sites at the origins of Judaism, retracing the history that led French Jewry to the Vichy deportations, and recalling the memories of their kin's exodus from the Maghreb, these writers quite decisively turn their own and their readers' attention to the more recent era of Jewish life in France. In lieu of memories, they create fictional worlds in which the young respond to contemporary echoes of the past and to reverberations of the past experienced in the present. Their literature is thus a writing born of a void, a literature about a void, and at times a literature against a void. Not surprisingly, the literary motif of the secret pervades much of this writing—secrets of historical impact yet also those of rather small importance, to allude to the title of one of the novels by the young writer Agnès Desarthe. Detectives set out to solve racist hate crimes (Abécassis, Weill Raynal), tourists to solve mysteries (Jacques), and scholars to piece together the puzzle of literary history (Gluckstein). Sons and daughters repeatedly set out to uncover their parents' pasts in order to discover the traces of their pain and suffering (Anissimov, Fellous, Boukhobza), as well as other parts of their lives that they had not shared with their offspring (Amar, Spire, Koskas, Rozier). The notion of displacement gains prominence in the writings of the authors of

Maghrebi origin in order to document their complex relationship as outsiders to the French-born Jewish establishment, to French society (in which Muslim immigrants outnumber Jews by a wide margin), and to the former centers of North African Judaism that their parents had to leave.

The coexistence of writers of Sephardi and Ashkenazi backgrounds and of writers of different generational affiliations with their particular historical experiences, attitudes toward Judaism, and relationship to French culture has created a rich and vibrant literature. This literature has abandoned identity politics and, given its multitude of voices, now participates in discourses that address both Jewish concerns and those of French society at large.

NOTES

1. This chapter summarizes many observations and readings contained in my book *In Lieu of Memory: Contemporary Jewish Writing in France.* See Nolden 2006.

2. The proceedings were documented in the journal *Les Nouveaux Cahiers,* which was founded the same year.

3. Modiano's work has been well researched and documented, in contrast to most other French Jewish writers.

4. See also Fortunée Hazan-Aramar, *Saveurs de mon enfance* (1987); Jacqueline Cohen-Azuelos, *Fleur de Jasmin* (1999); and, from the point of view of ethnography, Joëlle Bahloul, *Le Culte de la table dressée* (1983).

5. Fleischman's story "Le Petit Bureau d'à côté," for example, features an episode from the life of a Yiddish writer whose work is finally being translated and reviewed in a French journal, albeit in the same issue that will include his obituary.

WORKS CITED

Abécassis, Eliette. 1996. *Qumran.* Paris: Ramsay.
———. 1997. *L'Or et la cendre.* Paris: Ramsay.
Amar, Marlène. 1996. *Des gens infréquantables.* Paris: Gallimard.
Anissimov, Myriam. 1992. *Dans la plus stricte intimité.* Paris: Editions de l'Olivier.
———. 1995. "A Yiddish Writer Who Writes in French," trans. Thomas Nolden. In *Voices of the Diaspora: Jewish Women Writing in Contemporary Europe,* ed. Thomas Nolden and Frances Malino, 33–39. Evanston, Ill.: Northwestern University Press.
———. 1999. *Sa majesté la Mort.* Paris: Gallimard.
———. 2005. "A Yiddish Writer Who Writes in French." In *Voices from the Diaspora: Jewish Women Writing in Contemporary Europe,* ed. Thomas Nolden and Frances Malino, 33–39. Evanston, Ill.: Northwestern University Press.
Astro, Alan. 1994. "Editor's Preface: Jewish Discretion in French Literature." Special issue, "Discourses on Jewish Identity in Twentieth-Century France," ed. Alan Astro. *Yale French Studies* 85: 1–17.
Bahloul, Joëlle. 1983. *Le Culte de la table dressée: rites et traditions de la table juive algérienne.* Paris: Métailié.

Ben Aych, Gil. 1981. *L'Essuie-mains des pieds.* Paris: Presses d'aujourd hui.
———. 1986. *Le Livre d'Étoile.* Paris: Seuil.
Bitoun, Lazare. 1982. "Israélites hier, juifs aujourd'hui." *Traces* 3: 79–88.
Bouganim, Ami. 1981. *Récits du Mellah.* Paris: J.-C. Lattès.
Boyarin, Jonathan. 1991. *Polish Jews in Paris: The Ethnography of Memory.* Bloomington: Indiana University Press.
Cohen-Azuelos, Jacqueline. 1999. *Fleur de Jasmin: images et saveurs du Maroc.* Aix-en-Provence: Edisud.
Combat pour la diaspora. 1979. Editorial: 6.
David, Renée. 1993. "Le Renouveau juif laïque en France." *Les Nouveaux Cahiers* 114: 22–27.
Dayan-Rosenman, Anny. 1998. "Mémoire, écriture, identitaire minoritaire." In *Les Juifs de France: de la Révolution française à nos jours,* ed. Jean-Jacques Becker and Annette Wieviorka, 329–62. Paris: Liana Levi.
Deleuze, Gilles, and Félix Guattari. 1975. *Kafka: Pour une littérature mineure.* Paris: Minuit.
———. 1986. *Kafka: Toward a Minor Literature.* Trans. Dan Polan. Minneapolis: University of Minnesota Press.
Dugas, Guy. 1990. *La Littérature judéo-maghrébine d'expression française.* Paris: L'Harmattan.
Ertel, Rachel. 1982. "Une littérature minoritaire." *Traces* 3: 88–91.
Fine, Ellen S. 1985. "New Kinds of Witnesses: French Post-Holocaust Writers." *Holocaust Studies Annual* 3: 121–36.
Finkielkraut, Alain. 1980. *Le Juif imaginaire.* Paris: Seuil.
Fleischman, Cyrille. 1994. *Rendez-vous au métro Saint-Paul.* Paris: Le Dilettante.
———. 1995. *Nouveaux rendez-vous au métro Saint-Paul.* Paris: Le Dilettante.
Gdalia, Janine. 1982. "Un age d'or." *Traces* 3: 91–93.
Gluckstein, Alain. 1997. *Nos grands hommes.* Paris: Seuil.
Goldman, Pierre. 1975. *Souvenirs obscurs d'un juif polonais né en France.* Paris: Seuil.
———. 1977. *L'Ordinaire mésaventure d'Archibald Rapoport.* Paris: Julliard.
Goldmann, Annie. 1995. "Langue et création littéraire." *Pardès* 21: 55–59.
Gutman, Claude. 1982. *Les Larmes du crocodile.* Paris: Mercure de France.
Halbronn, Jacques. 1996. "La Problématique identitaire des juifs français." In *Hier Juifs "progressistes" aujourd'hui Juifs . . . ? Quelle identité juive laïque construire?* Colloque organisé par les Amis de la Commission Centrale de l'Enfance, Sorbonne, 11 et 12 février 1995, 49–79. Paris: Les Amis.
Hazan-Aramar, Fortunée. 1987. *Saveurs de mon enfance: la cuisine juive du Maroc.* Paris: Laffont.
Hirsch, Marianne. 1997. *Family Frames: Photography, Narrative, and Postmemory.* Cambridge, Mass.: Harvard University Press.
Koskas, Marco. 1979. *Balace Bounel.* Paris: Ramsay.
Lévy, Clara. 1998. *Écritures de l'identité: les écrivains juifs après la Shoah.* Paris: Presses Universitaires de France.
Mandel, Arnold. 1965. "Qu'est-ce que la littérature juive?" *Les Nouveaux Cahiers* 2: 34–36.
———. 1980. "Le néo-diasporisme culturel." *L'Arche* 282 (September–October): 94–98.
Marks, Elaine. 1996. *Marrano as Metaphor: The Jewish Presence in French Writing.* New York: Routledge.
Memmi, Albert. 1962. *Portrait d'un juif.* Paris: Gallimard.
Modiano, Patrick. 1968. *La Place de l'étoile.* Paris: Gallimard.
Nolden, Thomas. 2003. "Pierre Goldman and the Beginnings of *jeune littérature juive.*" *French Forum* 28 (3): 57–76.

———. 2006. *In Lieu of Memory: Contemporary Jewish Writing in France.* Syracuse, N.Y.: Syracuse University Press.

Nora, Pierre. 1992. "Generation." Trans. Arthur Goldman. In *Realms of Memory: Rethinking the French Past,* ed. Pierre Nora, 499–531. New York: Columbia University Press.

Perec, Georges, and Robert Bober. 1979. *Ellis Island: Description d'un projet.* In *Catalogue pour des juifs de maintenant,* ed. Luc Rosenzweig, 51–54. Special issues of *Recherches: Revue du Cerfi* 38.

———. 1995. *Ellis Island.* Trans. Harry Matthews. New York: New Press.

Perec, Georges. 1975. *W, ou le souvenir d'enfance.* Paris: Denoël.

———. 1978. *Je me souviens.* Paris: Hachette.

Perec, Georges, and Jean-Marie Le Sidaner. 1979. "Entretien." *L'Arc* 76: 3–10.

Raczymow, Henri. 1979. *Contes d'exil et d'oubli.* Paris: Gallimard.

———. 1982. "Aujourd'hui, le roman juif?" *Traces* 3 (1982): 71–78.

Robin, Régine. 1989. *Le Roman mémoriel: de l'histoire à l'écriture du hors lieu.* Montreal: Préambule.

Roskies, David G. 1995. *A Bridge of Longing: The Lost Art of Yiddish Storytelling.* Cambridge, Mass.: Harvard University Press.

Rosenzweig, Luc, ed. 1979. *Catalogue pour des juifs de maintenant.* Special issue of *Recherches: Revue du Cerfi* 38.

———. 1980. *La Jeune France juive: conversation avec des juifs d'aujourd'hui.* Paris: Libres-Hallier.

Roumani, Judith. 1984. "The Portable Homeland of North African Jewish Fiction: Ryvel and Koskas." *Prooftexts* 4 (3): 253–67.

Rozier, Gilles. 1999. *Par-delà les monts obscurs.* Paris: Denoël.

Ruszniewski-Dahan, Myriam. 1999. *Romanciers de la Shoah: Si l'écho de leur voix faiblit . . .* Paris: L'Harmattan.

Schnapper, Dominique. 1980. *Juifs et Israélites.* Paris: Gallimard.

Spire, Antoine. 1988. *Le Silence en heritage.* Paris: Robert Laffont.

Trigano, Shmuel. 1979. *La Nouvelle question juive: l'avenir d'un espoir.* Paris: Gallimard.

Vegh, Claudine. 1979. *Je ne lui ai pas dit au revoir: des enfants des déportés parlent.* Paris: Gallimard.

Vidal-Naquet, Pierre. 1981. *Les Juifs, la mémoire et le présent.* Paris: Maspero.

Wajcman, Gérard. 1986. *L'Interdit.* Paris: Denoël.

Wajsbrot, Cécile. 1997. *La Trahison.* Candeilhan, France: Zulma.

Wieviorka, Annette. 2000. "Le Judaïsme laïque n'a pas d'avenir." In *Nous, juifs de France,* ed. Olivier Guland and Michel Zerbib, 7–30. Paris: Bayard.

TEXTS AVAILABLE IN ENGLISH

Abécassis, Eliette. 1998. *The Qumran Mystery.* Trans. Emily Read. London: Orion.

Amar, Marlène. 2005. "On the Edge of the World," trans. Marjolijn de Jager. In *Voices of the Diaspora: Jewish Women Writing in Contemporary Europe,* ed. Thomas Nolden and Frances Malino, 5–12. Evanston, Ill.: Northwestern University Press.

Anissimov, Myriam. 1999. *Primo Levi: Tragedy of an Optimist.* Trans. Steve Cox. Woodstock, N.Y.: Overlook.

———. 2005. "A Yiddish Writer Who Writes in French," trans. Thomas Nolden. In *Voices of the Diaspora: Jewish Women Writing in Contemporary Europe,* ed. Thomas Nolden and Frances Malino, 33–38. Evanston, Ill.: Northwestern University Press.

Bénabou, Marcel. 1998. *Jacob, Menahem and Mimoun: A Family Epic.* Trans. Steven Rendall. Lincoln: University of Nebraska Press.

Bober, Robert. 1998. *What News of the War.* Trans. Robin Buss. Harmondswoth, U.K.: Penguin.

Cixous, Hélène. 1997. "My Algeriance, in other words, to depart not to arrive from Algeria," trans. Eric Prenowitz. *Tri-Quarterly* 100: 259–79.

Finkielkraut, Alain. 1980. *The Imaginary Jew.* Trans. Kevin O'Neill and David Suchoff. Lincoln: University of Nebraska Press.

Gary, Romain. 1968. *The Danse of Gengis Cohn.* Trans. Romain Gary. New York: World.

———. 2004. *White Dog.* Chicago: University of Chicago Press.

Goldman, Pierre. 1977. *Dim Memories of a Polish Jew Born in France.* Trans. Joan Pinkham. New York: Viking.

Halter, Marek. 2003. *The Book of Abraham.* Trans. Lowell Bair. New Milford, Conn.: Toby.

Kahn, Annette. 1991. *Why My Father Died: A Daughter Confronts Her Family's Past at the Trial of Klaus Barbie.* Trans. Anna Cancogni. New York: Summit Books.

Memmi, Albert. 1962a. *The Pillar of Salt.* Trans. Edouard Roditi. New York: Orion.

———. 1962b. *Portrait of a Jew.* Trans. Elisabeth Abott. New York: Orion.

———. 2003. *The Colonizer and the Colonized.* Trans. Howard Greenfeld. London: Earthscan.

Modiano, Patrick. 1971. *Night Rounds.* Trans. Patricia Wolf. New York: Knopf.

———. 1974. *Ring Roads.* Trans. Caroline Hillier. London: Gollancz.

———. 1999. *Dora Bruder.* Trans. Joanna Kilmartin. Berkeley: University of California Press.

———. 2005. *Missing Person.* Trans. Daniel Weissbrot. Boston: Godine.

Perec, Georges. 1988. *W, or The Memory of Childhood.* Trans. David Bellos. Boston: Godine.

———. 1995. *Ellis Island.* Trans. Harry Matthews. New York: New Press.

Raczymow, Henri. 1995. *Writing the Book of Esther.* Trans. Dori Katz. New York: Holmes & Meier.

Rozier, Gilles. 2005. *Love Without Resistance.* Boston: Little, Brown.

———. 2006. *The Mercy Room.* Trans. Anthea Bell. Boston: Little, Brown.

Schwarz-Bart, André. 1960. *The Last of the Just.* Trans. Stephen Becker. New York: Atheneum.

SEVEN

~

CHRISTOPH MIETHING

Ital'Yah Letteraria: Contemporary Jewish Writing in Italy

When asked about contemporary Italian Jewish literature, Stefano Levi della Torre, one of Italy's leading Jewish intellectuals, answered that there was none. He was, of course, wrong in reaching this conclusion but correct in suggesting some differentiations. First, there are in Italian literature important works that deal with what may broadly be called "cultura ebraica," be they written by Jewish or non-Jewish authors. However, to categorize such works as "Italian Jewish literature" presupposes an interest in cultural particularism that is not in keeping with the Italian Jewish tradition. Second, within the last forty years two outstanding writers, Primo Levi and Giorgio Bassani, have been identified as specifically Italian Jewish authors. Neither Italo Svevo, nor Alberto Moravia, nor Natalia Ginzburg—all well-known writers of Jewish background—would have accepted this categorization. Third, there is no contemporary writer who could be compared to Levi or Bassani, nor are there works of outstanding quality to suggest that a new literary tradition is in the making. Fourth, had it not been for the Holocaust, neither Levi's nor Bassani's oeuvre would have been written. After all, Levi was a survivor and Bassani was a member of the anti-fascist resistance. They were witnesses and transformed their experiences into literature. Today the Holocaust as a literary theme is the

common denominator for most works classified as "Italian Jewish." This criterion is of historical interest but may not necessarily be of aesthetic value.

So what is meant by the "Italian Jewish tradition" and what are its defining features? Among Europe's Jewish communities, Italian Jewry stands out
in its strong awareness of the continuity of its existence. Since Roman times
Jews have lived in Italy. There was never a general expulsion of Jews, as was
the case in England, France, Spain, and Germany. There were no pogroms. Anti-
Semitism was not as virulent as in other countries. As Frederic M. Schweitzer
has written: "In stark contrast to Austria, France, and Germany, there was no
political anti-Semitism in Italy in the decades before 1914, since the clericals,
under papal injunction, refrained from organizing themselves as a political
party. Racism, such as that of Gobineau . . . had to be imported" (2002, 263).
Also, in Italy a strong, locally defined, mostly urban Jewish culture has always
existed. Its main centers were Rome, Milan, Turin, Trieste, Venice, and
Livorno, but there were Jewish communities in many other smaller towns and
cities. Since the Italian nation-state only came into being in the late nineteenth
century, regional identity was all that mattered for all Italians, as well as for
Italian Jews. The number of Jews living in Italy never exceeded one hundred
thousand (today there are some thirty thousand), but this relatively small
number can look back on a long, unbroken record of its presence.

Any attempt to elucidate Italian Jewish self-awareness and the distinctive-
ness of Italian Judaism felt most particularly by authors born after World War II
has to be substantiated by the history of Italian Jewry (Luzzatto 1992, 149–56).
Crucial for understanding the development of Italy as well as Jews is the fact
that from the time of the Roman Republic onward—that is, well before the
Christian era—religion was primarily a political and only secondarily a religious
issue. Christianity in Italy was created as an institution, and politics was handled
within the dialectic of *res publica* and *res privata.* Here the spirit of citizenship was
first developed, founded on craftsmanship and trade rather than on dynastic affiliation or religious denomination. The individualization of religious experience
(i.e., "Protestantism") never acquired any great importance. Moreover, there were
no religious wars in Italy. From the Middle Ages until the twentieth century
Italian statehood has been at the mercy of the competing interests of the ecclesi-
astical and secular pursuit of power. Some of the most important Italian banks
are still owned by the Vatican. Precisely this precarious state of the polity—the
centuries-long juxtaposition of regional political concerns and Catholic preten-
sions to universality—created the free space in which a nondogmatic, not rab-
binically ruled way of Jewish life could develop.

What makes the situation of Italian Judaism different from all others—
perhaps even unique—is that to be Italian and to be Jewish are viewed as complementary components of a single identity. The Holocaust has not eradicated

the heritage of the Risorgimento. In the wake of the French Revolution, no other group within the Italian population engaged itself so unconditionally in Cavour's projected creation of a unified nation-state. It is not by chance that there is a myth of the "crogiolo ebraico italiano" (Italian Jewish melting pot). This implies that the non-Jewish surroundings are felt to be a constituent part of the Jewish community. For over two thousand years in some parts of Italy (Jews were expelled in the southern region, which was under Spanish rule in 1492) Jews were able to live virtually free from fear to a degree unheard of in other parts of Europe. According to historian Renzo de Felice: "The Italian Jews, free and equal to all other Italian citizens, were undisturbed and favored by the state whenever the practice of their religion and the respect for their traditions in an essentially Catholic country were in danger of being jeopardized" (2001, 10).

The reason for this was that in Italy the Christian religion, as a political institution, was relatively stable and thus less inclined to exert pressure upon the Jewish community. At the same time, within the Jewish community there was comparatively little pressure to regulate communal behavior. The power the rabbis could invoke as judges of Jewish normative practices was accordingly diminished. In contrast to the Ashkenazi world, efforts to create enclosed, specifically Jewish communities never seemed pressing. In this respect, it is one of the oddities of history that the concept of the "ghetto" emerged within Italy. The ghetto in Venice was established in the 1530s in the context of the Counter-Reformation, the causes of which lay outside Italy. When, in 1553, the Talmud was put on the Index and hundreds of copies were publicly burned, the danger Italian Judaism had to face remained comparatively small. From the outset Italian Jews lived in urban and cultural communities alongside their non-Jewish fellow citizens.

It may have been this lack of rabbinic-Talmudic dogmatism which in Italy caused the Haskalah, as a reform movement of Jewish thinking, to remain without great impact (Foa 1999, 235). Italian Judaism had no need of "Enlightenment" since Jewish hieratic erudition was one of its sources. Thus, Italian Judaism is based on a different experience of time and space than American and Israeli Judaism, caught up as it is in the problem of traditional versus modern. Furthermore, the Renaissance, as the progressive rediscovery of the ancient world, was shaped, among others, by Italian Jewish scholars and artists—Menachem Recanati, Yehuda Romeno, Moshe da Rieti, Leone Ebreo, Azarya de Rossi—plus many others who never considered their work a "renaissance." The dichotomy between ancient and modern constitutive for an "enlightened" consciousness has its historical antithesis in the continuity of Italian Judaism. In this regard, in his *Essere ebrei in Italia* (Being Jewish in Italy) Stefano Jesurum (who was born in 1951) proposed the thesis that the only remaining descendants of the ancient Romans are the Jews of Rome (1987, 9).

Sociologically speaking, for a long time Jewish society had been more homogeneous in Italy than anywhere else. Solidly embedded in the Italian urban tradition, the Jews had established themselves as part of the *borghesia media,* the middle and upper-middle class. The social stratification which in modern times had grown—for instance, in Germany—and separated a traditionally rural and newly proletarianized strata of the Jewish population from a smaller group of well-to-do Jewish citizens did not exist here. And there was never immigration in great numbers. The low percentage of Jews within the population may well have promoted their integration into Italian society. Italian Jews were free to choose their profession. There were no "ethnic" constraints governing social ambition. The Catholic Church, which was always anti-Judaic, could be tolerant as long as it could think of itself as the only organizing body of social life. This changed during the Risorgimento, the time of Italian nation-building of a laic state, which furthered the cause of the Jews. Acording to Alexander Stille:

> In Italy, the struggle for the creation of a united modern Italian state and the struggle for emancipation of Italian Jews were virtually synonymous. It is an important historic accident that the forces of reaction in Italy—the Austrian Hungarian Empire (which dominated most of northern Italy), the Papal States (which occupied central Italy), and the Spanish Empire (which controlled southern Italy)—were also the main opponents to Italian unity. And it is highly significant that King Carlo Alberto, the head of the Savoy dynasty, which would become Italy's royal family, literally signed the decree granting religious freedom to the Jews in 1848 on the battlefield of Voghera before going off to fight Austrian troops. (2005, 25)

Thus, external conditions normally led Italian Jews to consider themselves an integral part of the surrounding society. According to historian H. Stuart Hughs, "By 1914 the process of assimilation had gone very far indeed. Eight years later, when Mussolini came to power, it had gone farther still: in contrast to so many Italians who had harbored neutralist or even defeatist sentiments about their country's intervention in the First World War, the Jewish middle class, not unpredictably, had ranked as superpatriotic" (1983, 23).

There had, of course, always existed a strong sense of family coherence, but since the nineteenth century interreligious marriage had occurred with increasing frequency. Inevitably the problem of mixed marriages endangered Jewish identity. Social integration furthered the amalgamation into the main culture. The majority of Jews upheld the belief that the *ebreo errante* (wandering Jew) had found his homeland in *Ital'Yah.*

Italian Judaism lies outside the distinction made between Ashkenazim and Sephardim: Italian Jews see themselves as the crucible of locally shaped tradition, concerned as they are with a synthesis of Sephardic-Cabbalistic and Ashke-nazi-Talmudic Judaism. Among the thinkers who shaped this synthesis are: Samuel David Luzzatto (1810–1865) (Amos Luzzatto, a former president of the Union of the Jewish Communities in Italy, belongs to the same family), and Elia Benamozegh (1823–1900). Luzzatto based his work on the joint pillars of Jewish ethics and a philologically grounded biblical exegesis; among other achieve-ments, he compiled one of the first grammars of Talmudic Aramaic. Benam-ozegh represents the cabbalistic-mystical and philosophical tradition of Judaism.[1] Despite their differing interpretations of Judaism, they both supported a univer-sal and nonhistorical understanding of Jewish monotheism. Interestingly, they both stood outside the distinction between *rabbinità* and *laicità*.[2] This universal-istic concept of Judaism, which may well be called a "Roman" heritage, remains at the core of the Italian Jewish tradition.

During the twenty years of fascism in Italy, Jews had nothing to fear. About 10 percent of the Fascist Party (P.N.F.) membership was Jewish. That changed when Mussolini introduced the *leggi razziali* (racial laws) in the autumn of 1938. In order to comply with the Nazi legislation, Fascist Italy began to implement a comprehensive racial system that prohibited miscegenation between Jews and "Aryans" and expelled Jewish students and teachers from the school system. Jews no longer felt at home in what they had always believed to be their country. However, the vast majority of the Italian population never subscribed to this change in mentality. Italy had not become anti-Semitic. During World War II Italian occupying troops in southern France and Croatia actually protected Jews pursued by the SS. The situation in Italy changed dramatically under the Ger-man occupation, from October 1943 onward. The SS started roundups and de-portations of Italian Jews, which lasted until the end of the war. The Germans were joined in these actions by the militia of Mussolini's reconstituted Fascist Republic of Salò. More than eight thousand Jews were deported and sent to the death camps (Fargion 1991). The exact scope and nature of Italian anti-Semitism is still being debated (Zimmerman 2005).

Within the last fifty years, the most complex literary expression of the unity of *italianità* and *ebraicità* has been articulated by Giorgio Bassani in his *Romanzo di Ferrara* (Ferrara Novel, 1973). Although the book describes the time of the persecution after the *leggi razziali* in 1938 and the process of social disintegration that followed, it creates under the name of "Ferrara" a utopia of cultural coher-ence which stands for the belief in the possibility of an aesthetic Italian Jewish self-representation. It certainly is a utopia, and the author meant it to be thought of as such. Bassani, who completed his work in the late seventies, has remained without a successor. In a way even Primo Levi never tried to create a symbolic space as intensely Jewish-Italian as Bassani did by unifying all his narrative works under the name of *Romanzo di Ferrara*. The name of this town, where Bassani was born and lived into young adulthood, stands for both a personal and general history as well as for individual imagination and collective memory.

In Italy, as everywhere else in Europe, the Holocaust had a major impact on Jewish self-understanding and self-awareness. The literary reflection of the catastrophe can be found primarily in autobiographical form. Almost all the works that have appeared within the last twenty years make the Holocaust their point of departure. The autobiographical genre thus provides a convenient starting point for a survey of Italian Jewish writing. This chapter will reveal how this literature has increasingly employed fictional narrative forms to distance itself from strictly documentary forms of writing.

Although Primo Levi rejected the fictional description of the Holocaust in literature (Bruck 1974b, 3), fictionalized forms of Holocaust memoirs have become a popular genre of literary self-examination. How deeply discussion of the Holocaust has penetrated the general consciousness even in Italy is attested to by the fact that in the year 2000 a "giornata della memoria" (day of remembrance) was instituted by law and its date set as January 27, the day of the liberation of the Auschwitz concentration camp. Even on the part of Italian Jews there was criticism revolving around the question of how that date specifically targeted an Italian memorial. Conversely, the fact that since 1999 in Italy there has been a "giornata della cultura ebraica" (day of Jewish culture) has naturally led to an upsurge of literary activity. Also, the ubiquity of Holocaust discourse in the media in the past decade has made Jewish themes fashionable. Jewish topics have attracted an increasingly large readership. Alessandro Piperno's novel *Con le peggiori intenzioni* (With the Worst Intentions, 2005), which traces an Italian Jewish family from the sixties to the present, sold some 120,000 copies within the first few months of its publication.

Among the published autobiographical accounts of survival, that of Elisa Springer (1997) is particularly impressive. She was born in Vienna in 1918 to an old Hungarian Jewish merchant family. Acceding to the entreaties of her son, who had converted to Catholicism, she wrote from the vantage point of a seventy-eight-year-old recalling her life in Vienna, her flight through Yugoslavia to Italy, her time in hiding, her deportation, and her experiences in Auschwitz, Bergen-Belsen, and Raghun (a Buchenwald satellite camp). Her father had been murdered in Buchenwald as early as 1938. Her book belongs among the testimonies of women who survived, to which the well-known works of Liana Millù (1986), Giuliana Tedeschi (1988, 1995) and Lilia Beccaria Rolfi (1978, 1996)—a partisan—also belong.

Interest in the period between 1938 and 1945 is also attested by the fact that a "concorso per diari inediti" (competition of unpublished diaries) has been organized by the Unione delle Communità Ebraiche (Union of Jewish Communities). Much of the material that was consequently published is of interest only to the respective families (L. di Segni 2001; Tagliacozzo 1998).[3] In addition, many older texts have been reprinted since they reflect the trend combining personal memories and representative experiences.[4]

Among the autobiographies that appeared between 1990 and 2001, three illustrate the growing interest in documenting events occurring between 1938 and 1945. In his memoirs, published in 1990, Franco Levi, a physicist born in Modena in 1919, records his family's flight first to the Apennines and then to Switzerland. Thanks to his precise evocations of situations and people, as well as the poetic power of his descriptions, this work is of literary merit. Sion Segre Amar, who was born in 1910, is the author of several autobiographical texts describing the Jewish-Piedmontese milieu of the twenties and thirties. Exactly sixty years following his arrest in 1934, he wrote an account of his work in the resistance group Giustizia e Libertà (Justice and Freedom)[5] and of his friendship with Vittorio Foa. Finally, Enzo Tayar's autobiography (2001) is primarily of interest sociologically. He concentrates on his experiences as a Florentine Jew throughout the years of persecution. His subsequent life is given only scant attention, although after the war he became one of Italy's most important financial magnates.[6]

Marina Jarre (1987) and Rosetta Loy (2002) offer intriguing perspectives "from the outside" on the era of persecution. Jarre's is a most intimate memoir which she nevertheless called a *Romanzo*. Focusing on her childhood in Riga and her youth in the Aosta valley, she describes a young Jewish girl whose father was a Latvian Jew and whose mother was an Italian from the mountains in the north of Italy. In 1935 she returned as a ten-year-old with her mother to the valley of her homeland in order to be brought up as a Protestant. Her memoir also addresses her search for the hidden origins of her father.

Rosetta Loy describes how, coming from a solid middle-class Roman Catholic background, she nevertheless experienced the persecution endured by her Jewish neighbors. Combined with these childhood recollections is a sociological analysis of the behavior of the middle class in Rome at that time and harsh criticism of the anti-Semitic propaganda of the Catholic Church. Her writing continues to be motivated by a feeling of guilt. In one of her earlier books (1995) she had already provided a sarcastic description of the indifference with which *l'alta borghesia* (the upper middle class) had reacted to the *leggi razziali*.

In general, Jews born before the war who grew up in an emancipated Jewish milieu refer to their Jewishness differently from their offspring, who were born after the war. The latter are less likely to publish memoirs, partly because they are still too young, partly because their lives thus far are of less documentary interest. They normally grew up in families that didn't follow any religious rules. Thus, they have to rediscover their Jewishness, which they often do in novelistic rather than autobiographical form. The accounts of those who—within the last two decades, and at the ends of their lives—have recorded their experiences show how conscious they are of their Jewish origin even if they have detached themselves from the religious foundations of Judaism.

   This can be illustrated in the autobiographies of three Italian Jewish authors who left their mark on the Italy of the second half of the twentieth century: the memoirs of natural scientist Rita Levi-Montalcini (1987), winner of the 1987 Nobel Prize in physiology; the autobiography of politician Vittorio Foa (1991), and that by literary scholar Cesare Segre (C. Segre 1999). Each depicts a childhood shaped by the author's Jewish origins and then sketches a broad panorama of personal and public activity. These authors present themselves as Italians and do not impose their Jewish background on the portrait of their public persona.[7]

   The memoirs of Anita Salmoni (2000) and of Giuliana Segre Giorgi (1999) fall within the same category. Persecution forced both women to emigrate. Both escaped to South America. Both remained involved in politics, Salmoni turning specifically to cultural politics and Segre Giorgi becoming involved in conflicts among competing leftist parties. Throughout their experiences of exile and return, both women consider Italy the ultimate reference point. Interestingly, they do not create a Jewish framework to narrate their lives and do not discuss Palestine as a potential place of settlement to escape persecution: Italy remains the place where they feel they belong.

   There are, however, a handful of memoirists who reflect quite clearly their identity as Jews. Guido Fubini (1991) wrote the story of his life to give testimony rather than to indulge in rhetoric. The opening chapter spells out the ethical notion of service to others and striving for social justice as a way to personal freedom. As a lawyer, Fubini's involvement in the drafting of the judicial statutes of the Italian Jewish communities (1974) was decisive. He was on the editorial board of *Kheila,* the magazine of the Jewish community of Turin, and always took an active part in the life of that community. Interweaving personal memories and historical accounts, Fubini's memoir is meant to promote an enlightened, cosmopolitan understanding of Jewish culture in Italy.

   Vittorio Segre and Aldo Zargani have both written memoirs that rank high among the literary masterpieces of the last two decades. Segre writes about the first twenty-two years of his life (1922–44). The first four chapters of his book *Storia di un ebreo fortunato* (The Tale of a Happy Jew, 1985) provide an excellent overview of Italian Jewish life as it was lived by a well-to-do family since the Risorgimento. His grandparents were landlords who owned several villages. The farmers recognized them as *padroni* (masters) without any reference to their not being Catholic. On the other hand, the family's integration within the hierarchy of the surrounding Catholic society had already led to the conversion of some of its members. Segre first recalls his early childhood and then describes his arrival in Palestine at the age of sixteen, his failure to integrate into the kibbutz, and his subsequent return to Italy as an English soldier. Calling Israel a part of the Diaspora, he acknowledges how critical he is with respect to the idea of Zionism. However, his return to Italy does not lead him to embrace his "motherland." Moreover, his family's conflict-ridden relationship to their Jewish heritage remains a source of his own personal struggle. As a reaction to his decision to go to Palestine, his mother had converted to Christianity. His father had been a *commandante* in the Fascist Milice. Statistically speaking, many more Jews had joined the P.N.F. than other Italians. They had been in favor of Mussolini's so-called revolution. As Giorgio Bassani relates in his late novel *L'airone* (The Heron, 1986), they voted for Mussolini out of fear of communism, which may have been true for Segre's family as well. In fact, Segre presents the vicissitudes of his family's experiences and reconstructs the paths taken by three generations of his family from myriad perspectives, including a picture of himself as a weak hero.

Zargani, who was born eleven years later (1933), chose a narrower time frame in his memoir *Per violino solo* (For Solo Violin, 1995) to depict the final two years of the war. He tells the story of his survival: fleeing with his parents; then, separated from them, in hiding with his brother in a boarding school run by Salesian Friars; and, finally, reunited with his parents, who were living in the mountains of the Piedmont, where they were hidden by partisans and peasants. In contrast to Segre, however, Zargani integrates the story of his whole life into these recollections. He dedicates his book to his grandson. His daughter, though born of his union with his Christian wife, raised her own son in the Jewish tradition and was supported by the grandfather, who wants to see his grandson circumcised. Zargani pursues the idea of keeping the chain of generations intact, insisting that although the will to survive must never be relinquished, one also depends on others for survival. At the end Zargani addresses his grandson directly, admitting that it took him fifty years to win his struggle against the trauma of persecution. The very act of narrating the story of his life has helped him overcome it. He insists that, in the end, he has enjoyed life and wants to convey his feeling of gratitude.[8] Zargani sees in the power of humor a quasi-aesthetic mode of Jewish self-representation which allows him to mediate between the different experiences he has gained during his life. In 1997 Zargani continued his autobiographical project by turning it into a quest for his Jewish identity. He shares with his readers the story of his unrequited love for a girl of Hungarian Jewish origin with whom he had worked in a socialist youth group.

Lia Levi (1994) is another writer who presents a vivid account of her Jewish childhood lived in the shadow of persecution. Together with her mother and younger sister, Levi was hidden in a monastery and was thus protected by the church. Coming from a family fully integrated into Rome's Jewish community, in her account Levi foregrounds the family's Jewishness and ends her account with the liberation of Rome and her preparation for her bat mitzvah.

Levi has become a prominent member of the Roman Jewish community, serving for more than thirty years on the editorial board of its journal *La Rassegna Mensile di Israel* (Monthly Chronicle of Israel). She is also the author of several novels and books for children that advocate religious tolerance.

Aside from autobiographical forms, family histories represent another popular genre of contemporary Italian Jewish literature.[9] Following a long-standing tradition, some of these genealogical accounts are written only for family members and thus lack any literary ambition.[10] Those intended for a larger audience have been published, such as the works of Guido Artom (1994), Paolo Levi (1984), Miro Silvera (1993), and Aldo Rosselli (1983). Guido Artom's chronicle begins with the Napoleonic liberation (the ghettos were abolished, with their gates publically burned in the piazza) and traces the decline of the family's fortune as a result of the return to power of the house of Savoy. Artom also describes his ancestor, Isacco Artom, who was Cavour's secretary and later became the first Jewish senator of the kingdom.

Paolo Levi sketches the panorama of a Jewish family (partly drawn from his own imagination) whose fate he follows from the early nineteenth century to the present day in order to show the dissolution of family ties and the decline and fall of the traditions of the Italian Jewish bourgeoisie. Silvera, who was born in 1942 in Aleppo and has lived in Italy since 1947, uses novelistic techniques to present the history of his Syrian family. Proud of his family's Sephardic Portuguese origins, he presents family portraits against a backdrop depicting the history of the Jewish people at large, ranging from the Jerusalem of antiquity to the time of Sabbatai Zevi. With Aldo Rosselli we return to the tragic history of the twentieth century. He is the son of Nello Rosselli, one of the founders of Giustizia e Libertà, who was murdered in France on the orders of Italian Fascists. (His mother committed suicide.) Educated in New York City—a period of his life which he has described in a separate narrative (1995)—Aldo Rosselli is intent to analyze the psychological difficulties with which he has been grappling.[11]

Historical novels represent another genre favored by contemporary Italian Jewish authors. Here one can differentiate between works that project a certain Jewish self-awareness onto a distant historical setting and those which rely on archival material presented in fictional form. To begin with the latter group, in his novel *Un uomo che forse si chiamava Schulz* (A Man Probably Named Schulz, 1998) Pisa-based writer Ugo Riccarelli, who was born in 1954, reconstructed the life of Bruno Schulz, the best-known Polish Jewish writer of the Holocaust. Similarly, in *Charlotte: La morte e la fanciulla* (Charlotte: Death and the Maiden, 1998) Bruno Pedretti, a Milan-based journalist who was born in 1953, recounts the life of the Berlin painter Charlotte Salomon, who was murdered in Auschwitz.

In 2001 Antonella Sbuelz Carignani, who was born in Udine in 1961, published her novel *Il nome nudo* (The Naked Name), which she calls "un Romanzo di ambientazione storico" (a novel in a historical setting). Giulia, the protagonist, is writing a dissertation on the Venetian resistance movement and becomes intrigued by the diary of her sister Elena, her senior by some eighteen years, which was written in 1944–45. At the end of the novel we learn that Giulia is Elena's daughter and that her father was a German officer who was killed on the eastern front after he, together with Elena, had brought many Jews to safety.

In 2000 Marco Bosonetto, who was born in 1970, published his second novel, *Nonno Rosenstein nega tutto* (Grandfather Rosenstein Denies Everything), in which he disentangles the mystery surrounding the protagonist's grandfather, who is said to be the author of a book denying the Holocaust. Surprisingly, the grandfather turns out to be a Holocaust survivor who was manipulated by rightists and had to repress his past experience in order to ward off suicide.

In her novel *Le ombre della notte* (The Shadows of the Night, 2000) Maria Concetta Calabrese, a historian at the University of Catania, has her protagonist, fifteen-year-old Sara, living in Sicily in 1942. Sara can survive only by converting to Catholicism. And yet, even after her marriage to an aristocrat, Erminia (as she now calls herself) is not accepted by society. Suffering from an identity crisis, she finally finds her true self.

In 1988 Edgarda Ferri, a journalist based in Rome, was awarded a literary prize for her *Il perdono e la memoria* (Pardon and Memory), which features the stories of family members whose close relatives were either murdered during the Holocaust or were killed by acts of political assassination or terrorism. More recently Ferri has recounted the adventurous life of a woman who, fleeing the Spanish Inquisition, was persecuted all the way to Palestine (2000). Ferri's works provide fodder for the media's exploitation of Jewish destinies through sensationalist narratives.[12] The same is true for the latest literary "scandal" over Alessandro Piperno's *Con le peggiori intenzioni* (With the Worst Intentions, 2005). In this semiautobiographical novel the author comments ironically on his family's endeavor to become integrated into the wealthy Catholic milieu.

In 1998 Daniela Frassinetti Tedeschi, who was born in 1965 in Rome, published *Sefarad,* a novel dedicated to her children. In this adventure story she invents the biography of a certain Gabriele Lopez, a goldsmith in the *Judería* of a Spanish town in the Middle Ages who has to defend himself and his family against a local aristocrat eager to appropriate the worldly possesions of the Jews.

Literary critic Angela Bianchini, a student of the prominent émigré Leo Spitzer, has written several novels. In *Un amore sconveniente* (An Unbecoming Love, 1999) she describes the tensions within a wealthy Piedmontese Jewish family during the pre- and postwar years. Edoardo Ascoli has fallen in love with Flaminia, the mistress of his cousin Ottavio Ascoli. Edoardo and Fla-

minia marry but are separated because of racial laws. While Flaminia's family
affiliates itself with the Fascists, Edoardo undertakes a forced odyssey through
Europe. After the war, they meet again. She has become very poor and he tries
to help her. The book is a fine example of the psychological subtlety required
to present the conflicts inherent in the Italian Jewish experience.[13]

Another group of writers who would seem to be unique to the Italian Jewish literary scene confront their *italianità* with experiences undergone while
living in the United States. Generally speaking, these authors (Lecco 1979,
1986, 1991a, 1991b, 1998; Rosselli 1995; Kramar 2001) have not been in close
contact with the American Jewish world. Rather, they lived the antithesis of
the "old" and "new" worlds, trying either to relativize the importance of their
Italian origin or to insist upon it.

The enormous range in stylistic forms and narrative attitudes to be found in
contemporary Jewish writing in Italy can be illustrated by comparing the works
of Giacoma Limentani, Clara Sereni, and Stefano Jesurum. The educator Limentani, who was born in 1937 and resides in Rome, has been working primarily
with Jewish women who are interested in exploring the roots of Judaism. In her
publications she thematically focuses on the Jewish tradition of women's rights.
She has worked extensively on biblical exegesis in the Midrashic tradition of storytelling (1979, 1980, 1987, 1988) and has also published a rather enigmatic autobiographical sketch (1992) as well as an appraisal of the Hasidic narrative
(1996).

Clara Sereni, at one time one of Limentani's "students," is certainly among
the most impressive representatives of contemporary Italian Jewish literature.
Her mother was a non-Jewish Russian. Her father came from an upper-middle-
class Roman Jewish family and was one of the leading Communists during the
resistance and after the war. She is herself politically active and has served as dep-
uty mayor of Perugia. Among her many publications are three autobiographical
volumes, all of which are notable for the originality of their formal structure.
The departure point of her first book, *Casalinghitudine* (published in 1987 and
translated into English as *Keeping House: A Novel in Recipes*) are recipes for various
culinary dishes which are imbued with autobiographical associations and reflect
cultural differences and personal preferences. In her second book, *Il Gioco dei
regni* (The Game of the Kings, 1993), Sereni assembles archival materials relating to her paternal and maternal ancestors. Only at the end of the book does the
reader learn where the author herself is positioned, conveying a sense of the author's own struggle to resolve the enigma of her origin. Sereni's latest publication
(2002) covers more recent history and describes the author's struggle in trying to
come to terms with an extraordinarily complex identity.

Journalist Stefano Jesurum, an editor on the staff of the newspaper *Corriere
della Sera,* has so far written two novels, one autobiographical, the other fictional.

In the first, *Raccontalo ai tuoi figli* (Tell Your Children About It, 1994), he transforms himself into the *avvocato* Tullio Ascoli, who, like the author, lives in Venice with his daughter, who is called Giuditta in the novel. Tullio wants to be identified as a Jew yet also suffers from being identified as such. Although a large segment of his Venetian family had been deported, the political activities of his youth were not motivated by his Jewishness. He even married a gentile. However, he now chooses to send his daughter to a Jewish school. He wants her to have regular contact with his mother, to learn about the family history, and to be consciously Jewish herself. In fact, the terrorist attacks against Jewish institutions have brought him back to his origins. Although he continues to be politically minded, his attention is now centered on the conflict between Israel and Palestine.

Jesurum's second novel, *Soltanto per amore* (Only for Love, 1996), features the Italian bourgeois milieu as a backdrop for the protagonist's quest to come to terms with his Jewishness. Roberto Friedenthal has married Mitzi, a wealthy Catholic woman whose parents insisted on a church wedding. Having reached his midlife crisis, the protagonist now orients himself toward his own origins, seeing his own problems mirrored in those of his two children. Like his colleagues Carignani and Bosonetto, Jesurum employs generic narrative techniques to present problems to which literature can hardly do justice.

Contemporary Italian Jewish literature also includes the works of authors who are not Italian by birth and thus possess a special perspective on Jewish life within the Italian nation. Edith Bruck and Giorgio Pressburger both found refuge in Italy and eventually chose the Italian language as their vehicle of expression. Edith Bruck was born in Hungary in 1932. She debuted as a writer with an account of the first eighteen years of her life. Her book *Chi ti ama così* (Who Loves You Like This, 1974a) presents an intriguing account of her attitude toward language and writing. Only since 1958 has she been able to write in a language other than her mother tongue. In fact, she had written the manuscript first in Hungarian, eventually lost it, and rewrote it in that language. Only afterward did she herself translate it into Italian. Bruck's account of her childhood and youth—she survived Auschwitz, Landsberg, Dachau, and Bergen-Belsen—ends with her divorce in Israel and her return to Europe in 1950. In succeeding works Bruck has described the fate of the survivor (1993, 1995, 1999). Bruck has become one of the most important representatives of *scrittura femminile* in contemporary Italian Jewish literature (1988, 1990, 1997, 2002). She has occasionally followed rather contrived psychological narratives. For instance, in *Il silenzio degli amanti* (The Silence of the Lovers, 1997) she tries to convert a homosexual—who for a long time has helped his best friend meet his mistress in secret—into the loving husband of the latter. In *L'amore assoluto* (Absolute Love, 2002) she tackles one of the most ambitious and difficult themes in all of literature.

Giorgio Pressburger, one of the most interesting figures in contemporary Italian Jewish literature, also hails from Hungary, where he was born in 1937. In 1956, together with his twin brother, Nicola, he fled to Milan, where he underwent training as an actor and film producer. The brothers collaborated on several books until Nicola's death in 1985. Their *Storie dell'Ottavo Distretto* (Stories of the Eighth District, 1986) depict life in the Jewish quarter of Budapest during the middle of the twentieth century. It is a gloomy portrait of Budapest Jews suffering under fascism and communism. What finally emerges, however, is a tribute to these resilient individuals, living in the harshest of conditions. In *Denti e spie* (Teeth and Spies, 1994) Pressburger tells the story of his own life, playfully inventing names and describing the book as "un Romanzo di odontoiatria" (a novel of odontology). The book begins with a diary of "my father," who, while imprisoned in a concentration camp, receives his son's milk tooth and notes under the heading for December 4, 1944: "I swallowed the tooth of my son." The following thirty-two tragicomic chapters—alluding to the number of teeth—recount Pressburger's life in an aesthetically original fashion and draw on the great traditions of Jewish storytelling. Since August 1998 Pressburger has represented Italy culturally in Budapest as director of the Istituto italiano della cultura. It is tempting to regard this fact symbolically and consider it as proof of some sort of coherence in being Italian Jewish: born in Hungary and transplanted to Italy, the Jewish intellectual becomes responsible for the cultural link between two European countries.

Nowhere else in Europe has Jewish life existed in such a continuous state as it did—and does—in Italy even during times of fierce repression. However, compared to other European countries, Italy can look back on two millennia of relatively peaceful coexistence of Jews and non-Jews. This may explain the spirit of universality to be found in the works previously analyzed. To call oneself "a Roman Jew" of the twenty-first century implies an awareness of the tensions between particularism and universalism, as well as the realization that these contradictions need not be fully resolved in order to ensure the continued existence of a minority culture in a modern nation-state which, in itself, can only be part of the answer to the problem. To conclude, albeit somewhat hyperbolically, the future of European Judaism can be found in its origins in Italy.

NOTES

1. See the seminal work by Alessandro Guetta (1988), who, like Benamozegh, comes from Livorno.

2. Apart from literature, Italian Jewish identity has manifested itself in three spheres: scientific research; academic historiography; and, outside academia, *letteratura saggistica,* that

is, the general theoretical discourse on Jewish identity. Broad-ranging research devoted to the *cultura ebraica* is pursued not only by Jews and is supported by the Italian state. As to the *letteratura saggistica* written by Jewish intellectuals, one can differentiate between three lines of discourse: religious (Luzzatto 1997 and 1999; R. di Segni 1981 and 1985; Toaff 1987); journalistic, concerned with problems of the present (Jesurum 1987; Loewenthal 1995, 1996; Calimani 1985, 1995; Fiorentino 1989, 1992, 1997); and philosophical, concerned with cultural history (Bidussa 1989, 2002; Chamla 1996; Meghnagi 1985, 1989, 1997; Tenenbaum 1993, 1996; Levi della Torre 1994, 1995, 2000).

3. Mario Tagliacozzo died in 1979. His book is noteworthy both as document of contemporary history and literature.

4. See, for example, the recollections of Davide Jona and Anna Foa, the sister of Vittorio Foa (1997) and of Ursula Hirschmann (1993). Jona wrote his account while living in the United States (where he died in 1971), wishing to inform his children about his life in Italy and the persecution he endured. Following his death, his wife, Anna Foa, extended these recollections through 1945. Hirschmann, who was born in 1913 in Berlin, offers autobiographical notes written partly in German and partly in Italian. A member of the Socialist-Democratic youth movement, Hirschmann fled from Berlin first to Paris and later to Trieste, where she married the anti-fascist intellectual Eugenio Colorni, whom she followed into exile. After his death, she married Altiero Spinelli. Both her husbands were politically active in European unification. She herself founded the organization Femmes de l'Europe in Brussels in 1975. Hirschmann died in 1991.

5. Probably the most important group of intellectuals who fought against the fascist regime, it was founded in Turin mainly by Jews.

6. Descriptions of a particular local Jewish milieu, conditions encountered in the prewar era, and the impact of persecution are the constitutive elements of most of the autobiographies published in recent decades. Indeed, using local conditions as a springboard is fully in keeping with Italian Jewish culture. Texts considered on this basis would take us to Bologna (Sacerdoti 1983), Trieste (Voghera 1989), Gorizia (Vivaldi 2000), Mantua (Bassani 1989), Asti (R. de Benedetti 1989), Rome (A. de Benedetti 1984; L. Levi 1994; Pacifici 1993; Portaleone 2001; A. Segre 1979, 1986), Milan (Cases 2000), and Turin (C. Segre 1999; V. Segre 1985; A. S. Segre 1983, 1987; V. Foa 1991; Fubini 1991, 1996).

7. Anna Foa related to me that her father had little understanding of her interest in the bat mitzvah and told her that she did not come from a Jewish family.

8. "I owe fifty years of my life—on the whole not at all to be thrown away—to some good people, almost all of them funny, and I wrote this book to honor them" (226).

9. Family history, of course, is also the subejct of historical and sociological research. See, for example, the work by Alexander Stille (1991) and Alberto Cavaglion (1988, 1993, 1998).

10. The library of the Centro di cultura ebraico in Rome (Trastevere) contains several such privately printed works.

11. In a theoretical context, Freudian theory has been intensely discussed in connection with Italian Judaism. See, for example Meghnagi 1985, 1989, 1997.

12. The Holocaust has also become the object of highly problematic narratives. Take, for example, Giorgio Chiesura's novel *Devozione* (Devotion, 1990). Chiesura was born in 1921 in Venice, served as an officer in the war, refused service in September 1943, and was interned for two years in a German work camp. In the novel he portrays a Jew, the sole survivor of his family, who, while in Auschwitz in the infamous Sonderkommando, must extract the gold teeth of those who have been murdered. Upon his return, the protagonist lives alone since he breaks out in a rash as soon as he touches anyone. A girl from the village helps him with the house-

work. He starts to take photographs, snapping her in every imaginable situation. She abandons him, after which he hangs himself. In 2001 Chiesura published *Villa dei cani* (House of Dogs). Here he gives no hint that this book is a revision of the earlier novel. The author eliminated chapters in which the protagonist quotes and comments at length from the literary work of Primo Levi. (The latter's widow had raised bitter objections to Chiesura's earlier novel.)

In 1979 Francesco Burdin, who was born in Trieste in 1916, published his novel *Antropomorfo* (Anthropomorph). The hero is a deaf boy who has neither arms nor legs and is mentally deficient. In October 1943 the boy's own father hands him over to an SS officer. The Jewish child is carried off to Auschwitz. There he is saved by an officer, cared for, fed, and sexually abused.

13. Fausto Coen (1992), Amar Sion Segre (1984), and Bruno Tacconi (1980, 1985, 1987) have also been productive in this genre.

Translated by Beverley Placzek

WORKS CITED

Artom, Guido. 1994. *I giorni del mondo.* 2nd ed. Brescia: Morcelliana.
Bassani, Giorgio. *Il Romanza di Ferrara.* Milan: Mondadori, 1973.
Bassani, Italo. 1989. *Tanzbah: Ricordi di un ragazzo ebreo.* Mantua: Istituto Provinciale per la storia del movimento di liberazione del mantovano.
Benedetti, Rodolfo de. 1989. *Nato ad Asti: Vita di un imprenditore.* Benova: Marietti.
Bianchini, Angela. 1999. *Un amore sconveniente: Romanzo.* Milan: Frassinelli.
Bidussa, David. 1989. *Ebrei moderni: Identità e stereotipi culturali.* Turin: Bollati.
———. 2002. *La crisi di Israele: Note su politica e ideologia.* Milan: Franco Angeli.
Bosonetto, Marco. 1998. *Il sottolineatore solitario.* Turin: Einaudi.
———. 2000. *Nonno Rosenstein nega tutto: Romanzo.* Milan: Baldini e Castoldi.
Bruck, Edith. 1974a. *Chi ti ama così.* Venice: Marsilio.
———. 1974b. *Due stanze vuote.* Venice: Marsilio.
———. 1980. *In difesa del padre.* Milan: Guanda.
———. 1988. *Lettera alla madre.* Milan: Garzanti.
———. 1990. *Monologo.* Milan: Garzanti.
———. 1993. *Nuda proprietà.* Venice: Marsilio.
———. 1995. *L'attrice.* Venice: Marsilio.
———. 1997. *Il silenzio degli amanti.* Venice: Marsilio.
———. 1998. *Itinerario: Poesie scelte.* Rome: Quasar.
———. 1999. *Signora Auschwitz: Il dono della parola.* Venice: Marsilio.
———. 2002. *L'amore assoluto.* Venice: Marsilio
Burdin, Francesco. 1979. *L'antropomorfo.* Venice: Marsilio.
Calabrese, Maria Concetta. 2000. *Le ombre della notte.* Messina: Armando Siciliano.
Calimani, Riccardo. 1985. *Storia del ghetto di Venezia.* Milan: Rusconi.
———. 1995. *Ebrei e cattolici: Le colpe.* 2nd ed. Padua: Nord-Est.
Cases, Cesare. 2000. *Confessioni di un ottuagenario.* Rome: Donzelli.
Cavaglion, Alberto. 1988. *Felice Momigliano (1866–1924): Una biografia.* Naples: Istituto Italiano Studi Storici di Napoli.
———. 1993. *La moralità armata: Studi su Emanuele Artom, 1915–1944.* Milan: Franco Angeli.
———. 1998. *Per via invisibile.* Bologna: Il Mulino.
Chamla, Mino. 1996. *Spinoza e il concetto della tradizione ebraica.* Milan: Angeli.

Chiari, M., and L. de Simone. 1984. *La tortura della speranza: Testo narrativo-Sceneggiatura-Spettacolo.* Ed. M. Maymone Siniscalchi. Foggia: Bastogi.

Chiesura, Giorgio. 1990. *Devozione.* Milan: Mondadori.

———. 2001. *Villa dei cani: Romanzo.* Venice: Marsilio.

Coen, Fausto. 1992. *Quel che vide il Màt Cùssi.* Genoa: Marietti.

Ducci, Teo. 1997. *Bibliografia della deportazione nei campi nazisti.* Milan: Mursia.

———. 2000. *Un tallèt ad Auschwitz: 10.2.1944–5.5.1945.* Florence: La Giuntina.

Fargion, Liliana Picciotto. 1991. *Il Libro della Memoria: Gli Ebrei deportati dall'Italia, 1943–1945.* Milan: Mursia.

de Felice, Renzo. 1961–93. *Storia degli ebrei italiani sotto il fascismo.* Turin: Einaudi.

———. 2001. *The Jews in Fascist Italy: A History.* Trans. Robert L. Miller. New York: Enigma.

Ferri, Edgarda. 1988. *Il perdono e la memoria.* Milan: Rizzoli.

———. 2000. *L'Ebreo Errante: Donna Grazia Nasi dalla Spagna dell'Inquisizione alla Terra Promessa.* Milan: Mondadori.

Fiorentino, Luca. 1989. *L'ebreo senza qualità ovvero identità e mizwoth.* Genoa: Marietti.

———. 1992. *Guida all'Italia ebraica.* 2nd ed. Genoa: Marietti.

———. 1997. *Il ghetto racconta Roma.* Rome: Ed. Associati.

Foa, Anna. 1999. *Ebrei in Europa: Dalla Peste Nera all'emancipazione XIV–XIX secolo.* Rome: Laterza.

Foa, Vittorio. 1991. *Il cavallo e la torre: Riflessioni su una vita.* Turin: Einaudi.

Frassinetti Tedeschi, Daniela. 1998. *Sefarad.* Milan: Ed. Proedi s.r.l.

Fubini, Guido. 1974. *La condizione giuridica dell'ebraismo italiano: Dal periodo napoleonico alla reppublica.* Florence: La Nuova Italia.

———. 1991. *L'ultimo treno per Cuneo: Pagine autobiografiche, 1943–1945.* Turin: A Meynier.

———. 1996. *Lungo viaggio attraverso il pregiudizio.* Turin: Rosenberg e Sellier.

Guetta, Alessandro. 1998. *Philosophie et cabbale: essai sur la pensée d'Élie Benamozegh.* Paris: L'Harmattan.

Hirschmann, Ursula. 1993. *Noi senza patria.* Bologna: Il Mulino.

Hughs, H. Stuart. 1983. *Prisoners of Hope: The Silver Age of the Italian Jews, 1924–1974.* Cambridge, Mass.: Harvard University Press.

Jarre, Marina. 1987. *I Padri lontani.* Turin: Einaudi.

Jesurum, Stefano. 1987. *Essere ebrei in Italia nella testimonianza di ventuno protagonisti.* Milan: Longanesi.

———. 1994. *Raccontalo ai tuoi figli.* Milan: Baldini e Castoldi.

———. 1996. *Soltanto per amore.* Milan: Baldini e Castoldi.

Jona, Davide, and Anna Foa. 1997. *Noi due.* Trans. Benigno Ramella. Bologna: Il Mulino.

Kramar, Silvia. 2001. *La musica della vita: Storia di una famiglia di ebrei italiani.* Milan: Mondadori.

Lecco, Alberto. 1977. *L'incontro di Wiener Neustadt. Romanzo.* Milan: Mondadori.

———. 1979. *Un don Chisciotte in America.* Milan: Mondadori.

———. 1981. *L'ebreo: Romanzo.* Reggio Emila: Città Armoniosa.

———. 1982. *I racconti di New York.* Turin: SEI.

———. 1985. *La città grida.* Rome: Lucarini.

———. 1986. *Ester dei miracoli.* Genoa: Marietti.

———. 1989. *Il cantore muto: Sono stati gli ebrei liberi di raccontare se stessi?* Milan: Spirali e Vel s.r.l.

———. 1991a. *La casa dei due fanali: Cronaca di una passione.* Milan: Spirali e Vel s.r.l.

————. 1991b. *L'uomo del libro*. Reggio Emilia: Città Armoniosa.

————. 1994. *La morte di Dostoevskij ovvero La Morte della Tragedia. Quel giorno di decembre di sette anni fa. Menippea in un prologo, dodici quadri, un epilogo e una postfazione ragionata*. Milan: Spirali e Vel s.r.l.

————. 1998. *I buffoni*. Milan: Spirali e Vel s.r.l.

Levi, Franco. 1990. *I giorni dell'erba amara*. Genoa: Marietti.

Levi, Lia. 1994. *Una bambina e basta*. Rome: Edizioni e/o.

Levi, Paolo. 1984. *Il filo della memoria*. Milan: Rizzoli.

Levi Della Torre, Stefano. 1994. *Mosaico: Attualità e inattualità degli ebrei*. Turin: Rosenberg e Sellier.

————. 1995. *Essere fuori luogo: Il dilemma ebraico tra diaspora e ritorno*. Rome: Donzelli.

————. 2000. *Errare e perseverare: Amgibuità di un giubileo*. Rome: Donzelli.

Levi-Montalcini, Rita. 1987. *Elogio dell'imperfezione*. Milan. Garzanti.

Limentani, Giacoma. 1979. *Il grande seduto*. Milan: Adelphi.

————. 1980. *Il vizio del faraone e altre leggende ebraiche*. Turin: Stampatori.

————. 1987. *Il narrastorie di Breslav: Sacra rappresentazione in due tempi*. Tusculum.

————. 1988. *L'ombra allo specchio*. Milan: La Tartaruga.

————. 1992. *Dentro la D*. Genoa: Marietti.

————. 1996. *Il Midrash: Come i maestri ebrei leggevano e vivevano la Bibbia*. Milan: Paoline.

Loewenthal, Elena. 1995. *Figli di Sara e Abramo*. Milan: Frassinelli.

————. 1996. *Gli ebrei questi sconosciuti*. Milan: Baldini e Castoldi.

Loy, Rosetta. 1995. *Cioccolata da Hanselmann*. Milan: Rizzoli.

————. 2002. *La parola "ebreo"*. Turin: Einaudi.

Luzzatti, Segre. 1976. *Nuove poesie*. Padua: Rebellato.

Luzzatto, Amos. 1989. *Bibliotheca italo-ebraica, 1974–1985*. Milan: F. Angeli.

————. 1992. "Il pensiero ebraico in Italia fra integrazione culturale e forme originali di espressione." In *La cultura ebraica nell'editoria italiana, 1955–1990. Repertorio bibliographico*. A cura del Centro di cultura ebraica della communità ebraica di Roma, ed. Bice Migliau, 149–56. Rome: Instituto poligrafico e Zecca dello Stato.

————.1997. *Una lettura ebraica del cantico dei cantici*. Florence: La Giuntina.

————. 1999. *Leggere il Midrash: Le interpretazioni ebraiche della Bibbia*. Brescia: Marcelliana.

Meghnagi, David. 1985. *Modelli freudiani della critica e teoria psicanalitica*. Rome: Bulzoni.

————. 1989. *Ebraismo e antiebraismo: Immagine e pregiudizio*. Venice: Marsilio.

————. 1997. *Il padre e la legge: Freud e l'ebraismo*. Venice: Marsilio.

Millù, Liana. 1986. *Il fumo di Birkenau*. 5th ed. Florence: La Giuntina.

Ovadia, Moni. 1998. *Speriamo che tenga: Viaggio di un saltimbanco sospeso fra cielo e terra*. Milan: Mondadori.

Pacifici, Emanuele. 1993. *Non ti voltare: Autobiografia di un ebreo*. Florence: La Giuntina.

Pedretti, Bruno. 1998. *Charlotte: La morte e la fanciulla*. Florence: La Giuntina.

Piperno, Alessandro. 2005. *Con le peggiori intenzioni*. Milan: Mondadori.

Portaleone, Bruno. 2001. *Pru Urvù. Crescete e moltiplicatevi. Giudaico Romenesco*. Florence: La Giuntina.

Pressburger, Giorgio. 1994. *Denti e spie*. Milan: Rizzoli.

————. 1996. *I due gemelli*. Milan: Rizzoli.

————. 1989. *La legge degli spazi bianchi*. Genoa: Marietti.

————. 2000. *Di vento e di fuoco*. Turin: Einaudi.

Pressburger, Giorgio, and Nicola Pressburger. 1986. *Storie dell'Ottavo Distretto*. Genoa: Marietti. 2nd ed., 2001. Turin: Einaudi.

————. 1988. *L'elefante verde.* Genoa: Marietti.

————. 1994. *Denti e spie.* Milan: Rizzoli.

Reberschak, Sandra. 2001. *Domani dove andiamo.* Florence.

Riccarelli, Ugo. 1998. *Un uomo che forse si chiamava Schulz: Romanzo.* Casale Monferrato: Piemme.

Rolfi, Lilia Beccaria. 1978. *Le donne di Ravensbrück.* Turin: Einaudi.

————. 1996. *L'esile filo della memoria.* Turin: Einaudi.

Romeno, Giorgio. 1979. *Ebrei nella letteratura.* Rome: Carucci.

Rosenberg, Isaac. 1987. *Poesie.* Ed. M. C. Rizzardi. Milan: Guerini e Associati.

Rosselli, Aldo. 1983. *La famiglia Rosselli: Una tragedia italiana.* Milan: Bompiani.

————. 1995. *La mia America e la tua.* Rome: Theoria.

Sacerdoti, Giancarlo. 1983. *Ricordi di un ebreo bolognese: Illusioni e delusioni, 1929–1945.* Rome: Bonacci.

Salmoni, Anita Ceridalli. 2000. *Tu ritorneresti in Italia?* Turin: Rosenberg e Sellier.

Sbuelz Carignani, Antonella. 2001. *Il nome nudo.* Faenza: Mobydick.

Schweitzer, Frederick M. 2002. "Why Was Italy So Impervious to Anti-Semitism (to 1938)?" In *The Most Ancient of Minorities: The Jews of Italy,* ed. Stanislao G. Pugliese, 259–75. Westport, Conn.: Greenwood.

Segni, Lydia Terracina di. 2001. *Memorie, 1943–1944.* Milan: Proedi Editore s.r.l.

Segni, Riccardo di. 1981. *Le unghie di Adamo.* Naples: Guida Editore.

————. 1985. *Il vangelo del Ghetto.* Rome: Newton Compton.

Segre, Amar Sion. 1983. *Cento storie d'amore impossibile.* Milan: Garzanti.

————. 1984. *Il frammento sepolto.* Milan: Garzanti.

————. 1987. *Il mio ghetto.* Milan: Garzani.

————. 1994. *Lettera al duce: Dal carcer tetro alla mazzetta.* Florence: La Giuntina.

Segre, Augusto. 1979. *Memorie di vita ebraica: Casale Monferrato—Roma—Gerusalemme, 1918–1960.* "Prefazione di Renzo De Felice." Rome: Bonacci.

————. 1986. *Racconti di vita ebraica: Casale Monferrato—Roma—Gerusalemme, 1876–1985.* Rome: Carucci.

Segre, Cesare. 1999. *Per curiosità: Una specie di autobiografia.* Turin: Einaudi.

Segre, (Dan) Vittorio. 1985. *Storia di un ebreo fortunato.* Milan: Bompiani.

Segre Giorgi, Giuliana. 1999. *Piccolo memoriale antifascista.* Ed. Alberto Cavaglion. Florence: La Nuova Italia.

Sereni, Clara. 1987. *Casalinghitudine.* Turin: Einaudi.

————. 1989. *Manicomio primavera.* Florence: Giunti.

————. 1993. *Il Gioco dei regni.* Florence: Giunti.

————. 1998. *Taccuino di un'ultimista.* Milan: Feltrenelli.

————. 2002. *Passami il sale.* Milan: Rizzoli.

Silvera, Miro. 1993. *L'ebreo narrante.* Milan: Frassinelli.

Springer, Elisa. 1997. *Il silenzio dei vivi: All'ombra di Auschwitz, un racconto di morte e di resurrezione.* Venice: Marsilio.

Stille, Alexander. 1991. *Uno su mille: Cinque famiglie ebraiche durante il fascismo.* Milan: Mondadori.

————. 2005. "The Double Bind of Italian Jews: Acceptance and Assimilation." In *Jews in Italy under Fascist and Nazi Rule, 1922–1945,* ed. Joshua D. Zimmerman, 19–35. Cambridge: Cambridge University Press.

Tacconi, Bruno. 1980. *Masada.* Milan: Mondadori.

————. 1985. *Ramsete e il sogno di Kadesh.* Milan: Mondadori.

———. 1987. *Il medico di Gerusalemme.* Milan: Mondadori.

Tagliacozzo, Mario. 1998. *Metà della vita: Ricordi della campagna razziale, 1938–1944.* Milan: Baldini e Castoldi.

Tayar, Enzo. 2001. *1943 i giorni della pioggia.* Florence: Polistampa.

Tedeschi, Giuliana. 1988. *C'è un punto della terra . . . Una donna nel lager di Birkenau.* Florence: La Giuntina.

———. 1995. *Memoria di donne e bambini nei lager nazisti.* Turin: Silvio Zamorani.

Tenenbaum, Katja. 1993. *Filosofia e ebraismo da Spinoza a Levinas.* Florence: La Giuntina.

———. 1996. *I volti della raggione: L'illuminismo in questione.* Rome: Lithos.

Toaff, Elio. 1987. *Perfidi giudei, fratelli maggiori.* Milan: Mondadori.

Vita-Finzi, Paolo. 1989. *Giorni lontani: Appunti e ricordi.* Bologna: Il Mulino.

Vivaldi, Mariella. 2000. *La porta della salvezza.* Venice: Marsilio.

Voghera, Giorgio. 1989. *Anni di Trieste.* Gorizia: Goriziana.

Zargani, Aldo. 1995. *Per violino solo.* Bologna: Il Mulino.

———. 1997. *Certe promesse d'amore.* Bologna: Il Mulino.

Zimmerman, Joshua D., ed. 2005. *Jews in Italy under Fascist and Nazi Rule, 1922–1945.* Cambridge: Cambridge University Press.

TEXTS AVAILABLE IN ENGLISH

Bassani, Giorgio. 1982. *"Rolls Royce" and Other Poems.* Trans. Francesca Valente et al. Toronto: Aya.

———. 1986. *The Heron.* Trans. William Weaver. San Diego: Harcourt Brace Jovanovich.

———. 1992. *Behind the Door.* Trans. William Weaver. London: Quartet Books.

———. 2005. *The Garden of the Finzi-Continis.* Trans. William Weaver. New York: Everyman's Library.

Bianchini, Angela. 2000. *The Edge of Europe.* Trans. Angela M. Jeannet and David Castronuovo. Lincoln: University of Nebraska Press.

———. 2002. *The Girl in Black.* Trans. Giuliana Sanguinetti Katz and Anne Urbancic. Welland, Ont., Can.: Canadian Society for Italian Studies.

Calimani, Riccardo. 1987. *The Ghetto of Venice.* Trans. Katherine Silberblatt Wolfthal. New York: M. Evans.

Fiorentino, Luca, and Annie Sacerdoti. 1993. *Italy Jewish Travel Guide.* Trans. Richard F. De Lossa. Brooklyn, N.Y.: Israelowitz.

Levi, Carlo. 1951. *The Watch.* New York: Farrar, Straus & Yoring.

———. 1962. *The Linden Trees.* Trans. Joseph M. Bernstein. New York: Knopf.

———. 2006. *Christ Stopped at Eboli: The Story of a Year.* Trans. Frances Frenaye. New York: Farrar, Straus and Giroux.

Levi, Primo. 1995. *The Reawakening.* Trans. Stuart Woolf. New York: Simon and Schuster.

———. 1996a. *If This Is a Man.* Trans. Stuart Woolf. London: Vintage.

———. 1996b. *The Periodic Table.* Trans. Raymond Rosenthal. New York: Knopf.

———. 1996c. *Survival in Auschwitz: The Nazi Assault on Humanity.* Trans. Stuart Woolf. New York: Touchstone.

———. 2005a. *The Black Hole of Auschwitz.* Trans. Sharon Wood. Cambridge: Blackwell/ Malden, Mass: Polity.

———. 2005b. *If Not Now, When.* Trans. William Weaver. New York: Summit.

Loy, Rosetta. 1991. *The Dust Roads of Monferrato.* Trans. William Weaver. New York: Knopf.

———. 2000. *First Words: A Childhood in Fascist Italy.* Trans. Gregory Conti. New York: Metropolitan Books / Henry Holt.

———. 2003. *Hot Chocolate at Hanselmann's.* Trans. Gregory Conti. Lincoln: University of Nebraska Press.

———. 2006. *The Water Door.* Trans. Gregory Conti. New York: Other Press.

Millù, Liana. 1991. *Smoke over Birkenau.* Trans. Lynne Sharon Schwartz. Philadelphia, Pa.: Jewish Publication Society.

Pressburger, Giorgio. 1992. *The Law of White Spaces.* Trans. Piers Spence. London: Granta/ Harmondsworth, U.K.: Penguin.

———. 1999. *Teeth and Spies.* Trans. Shaun Whiteside. London: Granta.

———. 2000. *Snow and Guilt.* Trans. Shaun Whiteside. London: Granta.

Pressburger, Giorgio, and Nicola Pressburger. 1990. *Homage to the Eighth District: Tales from Budapest.* Trans. Gerald Moore. Columbia, La.: Readers International.

Segre, (Dan) Vittorio. 1987. *Memoirs of a Fortunate Jew: An Italian Story.* Trans. Vittorio (Dan) Segre. Bethesda, Md.: Adler and Adler.

———. 2005. *Memoirs of a Failed Diplomat.* London: Halban.

Sereni, Clara. 2005a. "Jews," trans. David Ward. In *Voices of the Diaspora: Jewish Women Writing in Contemporary Europe,* ed. Thomas Nolden and Frances Malino, 39–56. Evanston, Ill.: Northwestern University Press.

———. 2005b. *Keeping House: A Novel in Recipes.* Trans. Giovanna Miceli Jeffries and Susan Briziarelli. Albany: State University of New York Press.

Zargani, Aldo. 2002. *For Solo Violin: A Jewish Childhood in Fascist Italy.* Trans. Marina Harss. Philadelphia, Pa.: Dry.

EIGHT

~

PÉTER VARGA WITH THOMAS NOLDEN

Writing along Borders: Contemporary Jewish Writing in Hungary

Hungary lies on the border between West and East European Jewry. The religious, linguistic, and literary vestiges of this divide are still visible today and continue to inform Hungarian Jewish literature as a border phenomenon.

To be sure, this literature does more than merely straddle, in a most unique way, the fault line separating two different geographical—and cultural—spheres of European Judaism. Hungarian Jewish literature also negotiates the complexities of the past and present of Hungarian Jewry, whose unique course Susan Rubin Suleiman and Éva Forgács summarize as follows:

> For generations, despite the rising tide of ever more virulent anti-Semitism, a large number of Hungarian Jews, including the majority of Jewish writers and intellectuals, put their faith in the promises of liberalism and assimilation. After two thirds of Hungary's Jews were murdered in the Holocaust—with the cooperation of the Hungarian government and police—Hungary still stood out as the Eastern European country where the greatest proportion of surviving Jews decided to stay after the war instead of emigrating. Today, Hungary has the largest Jewish population in eastern Europe (approximately one hundred thousand, most of them living in Budapest). (2003, xi)

Many attempts have been made to define the Hungarian Jewish experience and its corresponding self-image (Braham and Vago 1985; Köbányai 1999; Ranki 1999). Hungarian Jewish literature was the focus of an international symposium held in Budapest in 1996.[1] The symposium marked a scholarly and cultural watershed. Until then Jewish contributions to the cultural scene in Hungary had been forgotten, ignored, or even actively suppressed—and not just by official decree but in most cases by Jews themselves. Prior to this very recent interest in Jewish identity in Hungary and its expression in the arts, hardly any attention was paid to Hungarian Jews' self-perception and self-expression during the second half of the last century. The entire area of inquiry was surrounded by taboos and suppressed by a false sense of shame. This now appears to have changed with the arrival of a new, contemporary form of Hungarian Jewish identity based on Jewish tradition and historical experience. The components of this identity—both old and new—reflect the long and markedly heterogeneous history of Hungarian Jews.

There have been various characterizations of Hungarian Jewish literature in the course of its history. At the beginning of the twentieth century Zsigmond Móricz, writing about the Jewish soul in Hungarian literature, described a "world of Jewish spirituality, perception, and mentality." He predicted that "the time will come when the powerful spirituality embodied by the Jews will be able to develop its potential in unrestricted honesty" (1959, 334). Aladár Komlós, one of the foremost scholars in this area, counts "every writer of Jewish origin" as part of Hungarian Jewish literature (1941, 8). In three lectures entitled "Jewish Problems in Hungarian Literature," András Komor perceived in 1935 an "authentic Jewish environment and authentic Jewish spirit" in the works of Tamás Kóbor, while branding Sándor Bródy and József Kiss "rootless" because they "lacked the courage to be truly Jewish." Komor emphasizes that "the Jewish writer should not wish to appear not to be Jewish" (1935, 29; Török 1999). He asserts that there is only one possible solution to the rootlessness of some Jewish writers, namely, to return to their roots. But this is very difficult when "János Arany is closer to us than Moses Maimonides."[2] Finally, Miklós Radnóti, one of the greatest Hungarian poets of the twentieth century, wrote in his diary for May 17, 1942: "I've never denied being Jewish. . . . I still belong to the Jewish faith. . . . Being a Jew is a problem in my life because the circumstances have made it so. . . . I don't think of myself as a Jew. . . . I'm a Hungarian poet. . . . I don't believe there's such a thing as a 'Jewish writer' nor 'Jewish literature'" (quoted in Szegedy-Maszák 1999). The critic Tamás Ungvári maintains that the "young, assimilated Jews who wrote for József Kiss's journal *Hét* at the close of the 19th century were determined to play a part in the development of Hungarian literature. While rejecting any sort of pact with conservative, aristocratic forces, they still clung to the aspect of assimilation that granted Jews membership in the Hungarian nation despite their origins" (1999, 55–56).

Such challenges, encountered in the process of constructing a modern Jewish identity at the beginning of the twentieth century, reappear periodically in Hungarian intellectual life and are always linked to the so-called Jewish question. While this chapter does not intend to rehearse these earlier debates at length, it will attempt to present the contemporary standpoints that are their legacy—both within and outside the Jewish community. In his remarks on the situation of the Jewish writer, the young Jewish author and critic Gábor T. Szántó (who was born in 1966) reflects upon the precarious situation in which Hungarian Jewish authors find themselves as a consequence of the specific circumstances in which Jewish writing is read:

> A Jewish writer must overcome his inhibitions, free himself from the notion that in everything he writes or says, as well as in his public appearances, he represents all Jews, or that what he writes will be measured against some general perception of Jews. He absolutely must not weigh or select his words according to this principle, nor direct his thoughts along this path. He must write in the first-person singular, abandoning not his Jewishness but the external restraint of a superego that imposes self-censorship. . . .
>
> He has a double trust: as an individual Jew he must remain faithful to the ideals of a disappearing community; as a writer he must remain faithful to reality. He must refuse to take even one step away from his Jewishness, while at the same time not giving in an inch in his commitment to speak the truth. Then he will make a virtue of necessity. The paradox of his existence, the source of his abiding dilemma as a writer, will be elevated to the status of a reluctant *ars poetica*. (1999, 269)

From the beginning, there have been both assimilative and dissimilative tendencies in the relation between Jews and Hungarian language and culture. For Szántó the only possible solution is "to be simultaneously inside and outside, to respect and practice the tradition, to follow it as long as it does not restrict one's freedom of thought and expression, . . . to remain part of the community but free oneself of all prejudice, inhibition, and convention and to describe the individual and the community as they are" (265).

These two tendencies appear most powerfully in representative works of postwar and contemporary Hungarian Jewish literature. In general, one can say that from the end of the World War II to the eighties authors were concerned with the loss of home and family and were preoccupied by the search for a new identity in the post-Holocaust world. Younger authors born after the war, however, prefer to address the themes of return to their parents' traditions and to search for a new homeland, whether in Hungary, abroad, or—in most cases—in Israel. Within these two general tendencies of Hungarian Jewish literature one finds a surprising multitude of voices (Várnai 1999).

Of special interest are what could be called "traditional" Jewish works, such as István Gábor Benedek's novella collection *A Komlósi Tóra* (The Torah Scroll of Tótkomlós), Charles Fenyvesi's *When the World Was Whole,* the writings of András Mezei (who, aside from Imre Kertész, engages, as it were, in a dialogue with the German Jewish philosopher T. W. Adorno), the novels of G. György Kardos, as well as the works of Péter Nádas (Sanders 1999).

Nádas was born in 1942 in Budapest, the son of a high-ranking party official. His monumental novel *Emlékiratok könyve* (Book of Memories, 1986) exemplifies how a Jewish "concentrate or distillation" can inform a literary work. As the critic Iván Sanders states, it does so not as some abstract, figurative metacommunication but rather in a very concrete yet subtle way (1999, 368). Even if Nádas's narrative is intentionally ambiguous and his distinctions blurred or stylized, his microrealistic descriptions and characters possess sociological authenticity: there is the orthodox Communist family, living the life of the bourgeoisie in Budapest, typical members of the political elite of that era; and there are those who have risen out of the proletariat. The novel sets the life of an assimilated Jewish family against a huge tableau of Hungarian society during the infamous fifties. The large number of characters includes many Jews, among them the protagonists Thea Sandstuhl and Hédi Szán, who are portrayed as complex figures navigating the meandering ideological and ethnic fault lines of a problematic society.

Nádas's novel *Egy családregény vége* (The End of a Family Story, 1977) is conceived in a similarly complex way. It has a double plot in which the stories of two families mirror each other as frame and inner narrative. The short novel is framed by the story of a lower-middle-class Jewish family persecuted by the Communists in the fifties. The fate of the family, especially its absent father, who has been jailed by the regime, is narrated from the point of view of his ten-year-old offspring as the child grows up. It is presented not as the story of a typical Jewish family but rather that of a dissident one. Only in the inner narrative does the novel take on an explicitly Jewish character, where a parable is presented in which the grandfather shares the story of two Jewish brothers, Ruben and Juda, in fifteenth-century Spain. This at first seems to have nothing to do with the story of the Hungarian family. Gradually the epic of Juda's family merges into the history of the present-day family, the fairy-tale past becoming an all too real and hopeless present: "That's the story of our family. Since the destruction of Jerusalem it has traversed six of the infinite number of circles. How will it do with the seventh? That I don't know" (1998, 183).

The family story ends with the grandfather's death, with government officials removing the child from the empty house and placing it in an orphanage.

This disappearance into an anonymous institution is a clear reference to the danger of deracination and dissolution in the surrounding culture. Nádas's narrative voice, however, never addresses this problem head-on, although the theme of deracination is a subliminal thread running throughout the entire work. Thus, through his characters Nádas subtly illustrates the Hungarian Jewish search for identity. His explicit intention, however, is to portray typical central Europeans. Hungarian authors have always been masters at obscuring the Jewishness of their characters. Thus, in a deeper sense Nádas's characters simultaneously suffer not only a Jewish fate but a complicated and many-layered crisis of human identity in general, a tragedy whose cause cannot be identified solely with their Jewishness.

In his novellas Pál Bárdos (who was born 1936) similarly addresses the identity crisis of Jews trying to find their way in the postwar world. His story "Bemutatkozó látogatás" (A Visit to Meet the Parents, 1984) features a middle-class Christian family whose Jewish origins are revealed during a visit by their young daughter Klara's fiancé. For decades they had kept their origins a secret even from their own daughter. When the young man, Dr. Imre Tóth, begins to talk about the past and rail against the Jews, the room becomes quiet. The long silence is finally broken by Klara: "You idiot! . . . Why the hell did I bring you here?" The first person in the room to reply to the young man's anti-Semitic remarks is Klara's grandmother: "Listen, Herr Doktor, let's agree that for years to come you'll still be trying to figure out how and why what happened happened. But here in this room, you will not speak ill of the Jews, not while I'm still alive, at any rate. We are an upstanding Christian, Hungarian family. In this house, nobody speaks ill of the Jews, do you understand me, Herr Doktor?" (39). The old lady doesn't say that they are Jews themselves, preferring to hide behind the apparently safe pretense that they are well-bred Christian Hungarians. Only an angry outburst from Klara reveals the truth: "Oh, shut up, Grandma! You've said too much already. I spent ten years reviling the Jews, me and my big mouth, even though I'd never laid eyes on a Jew. Or at least I thought I hadn't. Then one day I noticed the six digits from Auschwitz on my mother's arm. . . . For ten years you never said a word about it. How could you have kept silent, can you tell me that? I was living a lie because of you, a filthy lie" (40).

For the younger generation, the existential realization of falsehood and concealment of one's origins, the suppression of Jewish identity, is a traumatic experience. For Klara the primary problem is not coming to terms with being a Jew herself but rather the fact that for decades merely mentioning this was taboo in her family. The motif of the lie connects the problematic relation of one's Jewish identity to a broader complex of ethnic implications. Whether or not lying is a legitimate means of coming to terms with the traumatic family past, Bárdos intends the young woman's reaction to indicate that the genera-

tion of the eighties and nineties is no longer willing to live a lie even if the revelation of the truth, as in Bárdos's story, may lead to the end of a relationship.

The theme of Hungarian Jews' loss of identity and homeland appears in
Bárdos's earlier work as well. In the novel *Különös ismertetőjele a félelem* (Distinguishing Characteristic: Fear, 1967), based on Bárdos's own and others' lives, the
main character, Imre Vági, bursts into tears after being accused of collaborating
with the Nazis:

> And what about me? What have they done to me? As a child I cried when they
> told me that Lajos Kossuth was already dead and I couldn't fight side by side
> with him for Hungary's freedom. . . . Then suddenly I was a stinking Jew and
> told to my face that I wasn't a Hungarian. Not a Hungarian, but a Jew, a stink-
> ing Jew, a yid, a kike. Can you believe it? My father, my grandfather, my great-
> grandfather, the bones of I don't know how many of my ancestors are buried in
> this earth. Even in my dreams I only speak Hungarian. How can I look people
> in the face if that's all over? Who am I if I'm not a Hungarian? I'm nobody and
> nothing. . . . Where is my place in Hungary? (129–30)

In any event, Bárdos postulates that the suffering in the concentration camps
has created a common destiny for all Jews, whether rich or poor, religious or secular. In the novel a hardworking character named Little Leipnik accuses Vági of
scheming his way out of this common destiny by collaborating with the enemy:
"They are rich people and you're just a poor Jew. Maybe you don't go to synagogue and haven't always kept kosher—that's between you and the Almighty. . . . But withdrawing from our common destiny, sorry, but that's really
low-down. . . . A little Jew like you can't run away from his duty" (63–64).

In *Az első évtized* (The First Decade, 1986), another autobiographical novel,
Bárdos describes survivors of the concentration camps returning to the homeland that was taken from them:

> This was our greatest loss, the loss of our homeland. . . . That was the deepest
> wound, when we were driven from our home, deprived of our sense of belonging.
> I wish I could put it simply, but how can I explain it? What becomes of a glass of
> water when the glass that surrounds the water, gives it structure and form, disin-
> tegrates? Without a homeland, our atoms were scattered into the coldness of the
> universe. It's true, we're human beings of necessity and Hungarians only by acci-
> dent. But this accident is the only existence possible for us. What am I if I'm not
> a Hungarian? (281)

The theme of loss of identity and homeland thus seems to be a specifically
Jewish phenomenon within the literature of the Holocaust. As such, it is part
of the Hungarian *Vergangenheitsbewältigung,* a specifically Hungarian way of
coping with the past.

In his novel *Rámpa* (The Ramp, 1984), György Somlyó (who was born in 1920) describes in a peculiarly analytical voice how Jews were rescued by the legendary Raoul Wallenberg. The narrator focuses on the few hours Jews stand on the loading platforms by the boxcars while awaiting deportation. Each one must have his pass checked and then is either driven into the boxcars or led to a guarded building. Memories of their entire lives rise to the surface while they weigh their chances of survival.

No analysis of Hungarian Jewish literature can ignore the accomplishments of Imre Kertész (born in 1929), who received the Nobel Prize in literature in 2002. Kertész's central concern is the possibility of individual freedom in an age in which the individual is increasingly subjected to societal pressure. His work constantly circles back to his formative childhood experience, namely, his deportation to Auschwitz, which he regards as an experience of universal significance in the history of mankind.

Kertész's famous transformation of Adorno's dictum—"After Auschwitz, you can only write poems about Auschwitz"—clearly refers to the central concern of his works, a resolve which he has upheld. Among the myriad literary forms writers have used to address the Holocaust, his work stands out by virtue of its unique approach. Regarding the necessity of addressing the burden of the Holocaust, he has this to say: "The survivor must learn how to think about what he has experienced, independent of whether or not this thinking corresponds to his actual experiences." He emphasizes that "the only possible path to liberation leads through memory." Even when his topic seems at first glance to be something entirely different, the author himself has declared that he is basically always writing about Auschwitz. In his works Auschwitz undergoes a mythic and aesthetic transformation into something of universal relevance: "Everyone asks me about Auschwitz, when I really need to talk about the austere joys of writing—by comparison, Auschwitz is a foreign and unapproachable transcendence" (1997, 60). Nevertheless, Kertész has stated his impatience with representations which "drive the Holocaust out of the realm of human experience" (2001, 270). In his Nobel lecture he insisted that the Holocaust is the expression of something genuinely human and thus a part of our culture: "I never believed that it [Auschwitz] was the latest chapter in the history of Jewish suffering, which followed logically from their earlier trials and tribulations. I never saw it as a one-time aberration, a large-scale pogrom, a precondition for the creation of Israel. What I discovered in Auschwitz is the human condition, the end point of a great adventure, where the European traveler arrived after his two-thousand-year-old moral and cultural history" (2002).

In discussing his difference of opinion with Adorno, Kertész admits that speaking about Auschwitz is one of the most difficult things: "There is an unspeakably difficult contradiction: we can only really imagine the Holocaust—

that unfathomably complex reality—with the help of the aesthetic imagination. But imagining the Holocaust is a priori such a gigantic undertaking, that it is bound to overtax the powers of the person struggling to do it. Since it really happened, it is difficult to imagine it at all" (1997, 60). The contradictions inherent in these words mean that in Kertész's poetics the theme of Auschwitz is treated not as an event that is over and done with but rather a mythological question. It cannot be discussed with the aid of historiography and documentary literature since it demands a new literary language. The subject matter itself becomes the fabric of the text. Kertész insists that Auschwitz as a phenomenon of the "unwritten world" is accessible only with the help of the "aesthetic imagination," which places an enormous burden on the writer and his fiction (1975). The pressure of this burden, the need to resist the impulse to objectify, finally leads Kertész to abandon the first-person narrator, a dissolution of the subject, an abdication of intentionality when speaking about Auschwitz. In his novel *Sorstalanság* (Fatelessness, 1975) the narrator cedes to Auschwitz itself the right to speak. Speaking becomes permitting Auschwitz to speak, and thus the role of the subject in creating meaning is eliminated as a narrative construct. The role of memory and the process of recollection are thus centrally important in Kertész's oeuvre. The reflections of the first-person narrator on the narrated "I" and the inclusion of the reflective "you" of the reader undermines traditional narration. This construction points both to problems of identity (who is speaking?) and historiography as well as to the relationship between Auschwitz and the narratives it generates.

The relationship between the concepts "Hungarian" and "Jewish" has come under renewed scrutiny since Kertész's award (Vasvári and Tötösy de Zepetnek 2005). Miklós Szabolcsi, for example, maintains that Kertész's work has "given clear expression to something 'decisively Jewish,' if you will, the 'deep Judaism' we have been seeking in Hungarian literature," and that it is still possible to speak of a "deeply Jewish" literature (1999, 16). Despite the importance of Kertész in Hungarian Jewish literature, the idea that Holocaust literature is representative of Jewish literature is increasingly being contested. According to Gábor T. Szántó:

> With very few exceptions, whoever asserts this today betrays a lack of consciousness, the haunted self-image, flight—independent of the reality of persecution—and rejects the possibility of living together. Of course, the long shadow of the Shoah falls across the indispensable works of Imre Kertész, Ágnes Gergely, Magda Székely, and András Mezei. Of course, the fate of the Jews and Jewish thought in the wake of the Holocaust is the subject of works by Pál Bárdos, György Dalos, György Konrád, and Mihály Kornis. Still, this one-sidedness is insulting. (Szántó 1999, 257)

"Deeply Jewish" or "insultingly one-sided"—these are the poles between which Kertész's work is discussed. They also determine how Jewish authors view their own production. At the beginning of the twentieth century Hungarian Jewish authors positively fled from their Jewishness. Another barrier to the development of an authentic Jewish literature was the fact that there was no large group of Yiddish speakers in Hungary, whose secularization would have created the sort of broad Jewish readership which arose in other East European countries at the end of the nineteenth century. According to Szántó, "Communal spirit disappeared along with the disappearance of strict religious life. The Jewish minority increasingly assimilated into Hungarian life and only continued to practice its tradition in a fragmented and superficial way. The outward forms gradually became devoid of content. Jews were increasingly neither the subject nor the audience of Hungarian Jewish literature" (1999, 254).

The primary concerns of the first generation of postwar Jewish writers involved coming to terms with what had happened and the loss—or, later, the conscious suppression—of Jewish identity. Szántó, however, notes that younger authors born after 1945 have begun to search for that lost identity:

> The past seemed stronger than anything else. It separated [our fathers] from the new generation. The young didn't want to acknowledge a past in which Jews were not national heroes or warriors but rather a helpless mass that could be stuffed into boxcars and gassed. . . . With us it was exactly the opposite. I struggled relentlessly to reclaim my past, which was also my father's past. He didn't have to keep it a shame-faced secret like so many others. He just needed a chance, a slight push, to be able to start talking about it. (2002, 467)

After a period of enthusiastic optimism in the nineties, Hungarian Jewish literature now finds itself in a kind of no-man's-land. To move through the latter means, on the one hand, isolation and loneliness. On the other hand, in light of the meanderings and dead ends of twentieth-century history, it also suggests the possibility of trying out and communicating autonomous Jewish ways of life in the twenty-first century. The biggest challenge to the discovery of new means of literary expression is the fact that the continuity of genuine Jewish life in Hungary has not ceased to be endangered. As Szántó writes:

> What could have become a theme has not. What little remained of a middle European existence for the Jews who survived did not find its way into works of literature. There are hardly any traces of this disappearing world of the last fifty years. . . . It would still be possible for those enterprising and dedicated enough to delve into this world and absorb something of it before it disappears for good after the turn of the millennium. What will come then can serve the rebirth of the community and will surely carry the past unconsciously within itself, but it will no longer have any organic connection to it. Because of this lost connection, the continuity of Hungarian Jewish life will disappear in the coming decades. (1999, 257–58)

Szántó demands of a Hungarian Jewish author more than just a rehashing of themes from Jewish experience: "To be a Hungarian Jewish writer, to create such a literature, remains a task for the future. But the mission is not just to direct one's writing toward this theme but also to be part of the creation of a new face for this cultural enclave, representing it within the intellectual life of Hungary and integrating it into the world of Judaism. This mission gives Hungarian Jewish writers direction and responsibility. It does not restrict their freedom of expression nor their credibility but rather draws attention to them" (252).

In recent years young Hungarian Jewish writers have increasingly viewed assimilation as a loss of value and identity. They insist on both the preservation of Jewish tradition and culture and a new Hungarian Jewish social contract based on tradition and modernity, particularism and universality. Their demand also implies a desire for a new self-image more attuned to their country and to Europe as a whole, but at the same time marked by the consciousness of the Diaspora. This new sense of shared values and self-confidence strives to transcend the common fate forced upon them by political anti-Semitism and the Holocaust. Even if Hungarian Jews have experienced a loss of shared spiritual and religious values, they will continue to remain an identifiable group. A decade ago a group of authors founded the literary and cultural journal *Szombat* (Sabbath) in an attempt to combat this loss. In their works they consciously strive to thematize Jewish thought and experience, while also casting a critical and ironic eye on themselves, their fathers and grandfathers, and the broader cultural context. For these younger writers it is self-evident that there is a Jewish world order, an independently Jewish way of thinking, as well as Jewish interests that need to be expressed in secular form. This group includes: philosopher György Tatár (who was born 1947); poet Géza Röhrig (1967), who, for example, has produced a series of fictional Hasidic stories; and the prolific author and playwright Mihály Kornis (1949), who in his much-anthologized essay "Danube Blues" pays homage to the victims of Hungarian anti-Semitism.

It is more difficult to classify György Dalos (who was born in 1943), whose works only began appearing in Hungarian again at the end of the nineties. After he received a suspended sentence in 1968 for "conspiracy against the state," his works could appear in Hungary for the next nineteen years only as samizdat. From 1987 to 1995 he moved between Vienna and Budapest. In 1995 he went on to Berlin, where he served as director of the Haus Ungarn (Hungary House) until 1999.

Dalos's poems and short stories are primarily concerned with ordinary people living in a political atmosphere of uncertainty and fear. This is also the case in his 1982 utopian novel *Ezerkilencszáznyolcvanöt* (1985: A Historical Report, 1983).[3] His caricatural and often sarcastic works treat dictatorship from the point of view of the man in the street. Not until the nineties did themes from Hungarian Jewish experience begin to appear explicitly in his works.

His short novel *A körülmetélés* (The Circumcision, 1990) describes the life of Robi Singer, a Jewish boy growing up in postwar Hungary and struggling with his Jewish identity. At thirteen he is supposed to undergo the circumcision which could not be carried out during the chaotic conditions of the war. He resides in a Jewish orphanage but may only remain there if he gets circumcised. However, at the decisive moment he rejects the entire ritual. This, however, does not solve his identity crisis, for it is not just his Judaism but also his relation to his neurotic mother and the problems of puberty that cloud his perception of the world. His grandmother, an archetypal strong Jewish woman, fills the role of the missing pater familias. She sends the boy out into the world with the following piece of advice: "If anybody asks about your origin, or which congregation you belong to, just tell them, 'I'm a Hungarian Jewish Communist.' You can't go wrong with that" (2001, 45). Robi has to agree with his grandmother: he is a Hungarian, for he was born and lives in Hungary; he is a Jew since nobody's ever doubted that he was; and, finally, he is also a Communist since his grandmother joined the party as soon as she returned from the camp out of pure gratitude to the Russians, who liberated her. She pays her yearly membership dues and regularly attends the meetings of the local party group. Robi's decision against circumcision, however, means that he must transfer to a state school, where a Jewish boy from the petit bourgeoisie is classified as "Other." From then on Robi's life is characterized by a constant tug-of-war among his various identities—the typical biography of many Hungarian Jews.

Like Dalos, György Konrád (who was born in 1933) and István Eörsi (1931) also belong to the older generation. While they have earned a European reputation as Hungarian authors, they have spent or continue to spend much of their professional life as writers outside Hungary. (They are comparable, in this respect, to Budapest-born Ephraim Kishon, who left Hungary for Israel at the end of the war.) In many of his essays Konrád recounts the situation of the Jews in postwar Hungary: "Many friends of mine left after November 1956 because they believed only two extremes were possible in Hungarian politics: either Stalinist/post-Stalinist repression or the return of the right, which would open a path for spontaneous anti-Semitism" (1999, 71). In *Kerti mulatság* (A Feast in the Garden, 1989) and *Kőóra* (Stonedial, 1995), the first two parts of his semiautobiographical trilogy, he surveys the history of pre- and postwar Hungary and recounts the story of his family's struggle with Nazi persecution and communism from a postmodern narrative perspective.

János Kőbányai and Gábor T. Szántó undoubtedly figure prominently among the Hungarian Jewish writers of our time, along with Péter Kántor, Zsuzsa Forgács, György Spiró, László Márton, György Száraz, Gábor Schein, and the late poet Balázs Simon. Köbányai's exodus novel *Légy áldott* (God Bless You, 1998) is written in spare, lean prose. It follows the life of a woman who survives the war as a *Vorführjude* (model Jew), in an elite Austrian concentration camp. After being liberated she immigrates to Israel with a group of children. Although her brother and parents have also survived the war, the family gradually disintegrates as a result of postwar circumstances. The woman's elder brother becomes an officer in the Hagana, Israel's military force. Her mother gets divorced and remarries several times in Israel. Her father, abandoned by his family, dies in a Jewish retirement home in the Hungarian provinces. Although the heroine creates a new existence for herself as a nurse, her private life proves a failure. As a result of being abused in the concentration camp, she is unable to bear children. After having been exposed to the sufferings of twentieth-century Jews, she finally finds happiness. She marries a Tunisian Jewish widower with four children. Köbányai's novel is a testament to the many Hungarian Jews who began a new life in Israel. Köbányai has also published sociological studies of Jewish life in and outside of Hungary such as *Magyar siratófal* (Hungarian Wailing Wall, 1990).

In several senses the theme of absence is central to Gábor T. Szántó's tale *A tizedik ember* (The Tenth Person, 1995). The surviving congregation of a synagogue in Pest constantly lacks the tenth man needed for a minyan. For years they have been trying to fool God by smuggling old women into the prayer hall so the men can pray. When the narrator returns from faraway America to the city of his birth in order to attend his grandmother's funeral, he pays a visit to the synagogue. The man who serves as sexton and cantor begs him to return that evening and be the tenth man:

> "We'll be waiting for you!" the cantor says in farewell, putting his hand on my shoulder. "I'll be there!" I loudly reply, although I know that my train leaves in the afternoon. I just can't tell the old man. I can't steal the hope that will animate him until evening. I don't have the right to disappoint him by telling him the truth. When the handful of men gathers this evening, they'll still believe there will be ten of them, because Mr. Klein has promised to bring a guest to complete the quorum. I just can't rob him—them—of this hope. (30)

In this tale the motif of the incomplete minyan symbolizes the lack of the most important prerequisite for Jewish life in Hungary. Here is a tiny congregation of aging Jews, in a rundown synagogue in the middle of a metropolis, with no prospect of renewal.

Szántó's large-scale novel *Keleti pályaudvar, végállomás* (East Train Station, End of the Line, 2002) addresses the controversial course of Hungarian history. In the novel the famous East Train Station in Budapest is a symbolic place of memory where victim and perpetrator meet and where past and present overlap. Robert Friedmann, the first-person narrator, tells the story of his father,

Benjámin Friedmann, who was sentenced to five years in prison in 1949 as part of a show trial against the former interior minister László Rajk. The Communist regime used the trial against Rajk as a pretext for settling accounts with the Zionist movement, inventing the charge that Hungarian Zionists had worked for Rajk. In his expansive narrative Szántó describes how, only a few days after Friedmann's arrest, his interrogator György Benedek, himself a Jew, is arrested as well. Benedek has shown himself to be untrustworthy and is also sentenced as a traitor—a typical story of the fifties, with Jewish participants on both sides. Friedmann, who is persecuted by both the Nazis and the Communists—primarily because of his birth and secondarily because of his politics—is a testament to the many Hungarian Jews who suffered doubly because of their loyalty to Hungary. Conversely, the novel also portrays Jews who hope to be recompensed for their suffering from a Communist dictatorship; they, too, pay dearly for such hopes. In a frame story the narrator relates an astonishing meeting between himself and the wife of Benedek, his father's torturer, more than fifty years after the event: "I could hardly stand to listen to what she told me. With a swimming head, numbed, I thought of my mother and my sister, the years stolen from my father's life, of everything they had suffered under the Nazis, the loss of their parents; then, after the war, having to live in this cursed country under the cursed Communists. Were these simply errors? mistakes? They were sins" (485). The narrator's closing words typify the attitude of Hungarian Jews at the beginning of the twenty-first century. They turn to their own history and often return to the religion of their fathers and grandfathers, all the while maintaining a certain reserve toward Hungarian society. These are also the initial motifs pointing toward the future of Hungarian Jewish literature: "I wrote this book as if paying off a debt. It was above all a debt to myself, to my feelings of inadequacy and my burning curiosity. A wandering Jew returns to write his own story. Whether it gets read or not doesn't matter; he can only be at home in his own story" (485).

Hungarian Jewish literature has positioned itself to speak to a wider audience in Hungary and elsewhere by contributing to the dismantling of prejudices and to mutual understanding between Jews and gentiles. The international reputation of most of the authors discussed here bodes well for an authentic articulation of new, contemporary forms of Jewish identity.

When Imre Kertész was awarded the Nobel Prize in 2003, Hungarian society was again forced to confront its own Jewish heritage, and Hungarian Jews found themselves challenged to reexamine their relationship to Judaism. As Eva Reichmann has suggested (1999), contemporary Jewish authors in Hungary must decide whether they will address this relationship as Hungarians, Europeans, or Jews; as members of all three categories; or as complete outsiders free of all affiliations.

NOTES

1. The title was "The Border and What It Encloses." The proceedings were published in German as *Angezogen und abgestoßen* (Attracted and Repelled). See Lichtmann 1999.

2. János Arany (1817–1882) was the most famous Hungarian national poet of the nineteenth century.

3. The novel was first published in Germany in a German translation in 1982.

Translated by David Dollenmayer

WORKS CITED

Bárdos, Pál. 1967. *Különös ismertetöjele a félelem.* Budapest: Szépirodalmi Kiadó.

———. 1984. "Bemutatkozó látogatás." In his *Tükör elött,* 28–41. Budapest: Szépirodalmi Kiadó.

———. 1986. *Az elsö évtized.* Budapest: Szépirodalmi Kiadó.

Braham, Randolph L., ed. 1986. *The Tragedy of Hungarian Jewry: Essays, Documents, Depositions.* Boulder, Colo., and New York: Social Science Monographs and Institute for Holocaust Studies of the City University of New York.

Braham, Randolph L., and Bela Vago, eds. 1985. *The Holocaust in Hungary: Forty Years Later.* Boulder, Colo., and New York: Social Science Monographs and Institute for Holocaust Studies of the City University of New York.

Dalos, György. 1983. *1985: A Historical Report (Hongkong 2036) from the Hungarian of ***.* Trans. Stuart Hood and Estella Schmid. London: Pluto.

———. 1990. *A körülmetélés.* Budapest: Magvetö Kiadó.

———. 2001. *The Circumcision.* Trans. Judith Sollosy. Rose Bay, N.S.W.: Brandl and Schlesinger.

Kertész, Imre. 1975. *Sorstalanság.* Budapest: Szépirodalmi Kiadó.

———. 1997. *Valaki más: A változás krónikája.* Budapest: Magvetö Kiadó.

———. 2001. "Who Owns Auschwitz?" *Yale Journal of Criticism* 14 (1): 267–72.

———. 2002. Nobel Lecture. http://nobelprize.org/literature/laureates/2002/kertesz-lecture -e.html

———. 2004. *Fatelessness.* Trans. Tim Wilkinson. New York: Vintage.

Köbányai, János. 1998. *Légy áldott.* Budapest: Múlt és Jövö Kiadó.

———. 1990. *Magyar siratófal.* Budapest: Szépirodalmi Kiadó.

———. 1999. "Paradigmen ungarisch-jüdischer Geistesgeschichte im Leben von fünf Generationen." In *Angezogen und abgestoßen: Juden in der ungarischen Literatur,* ed. T. Lichtmann, 299–329. Frankfurt am Main: Peter Lang.

Komlós, Aladár, 1941. "Zsidó írók—zsidó közösség." In *Múlt és Jövö* 31 (7).

Komor, Andras. 1935. "Jewish Problems in Hungarian Literature." Lecture. OSZK Manuscript Collection. Fasc. 29. Budapest: Országos Széchenyi Könyvtär.

Konrád, György. 1989. *Kerti mulatság.* Budapest: Magvetö Kiadó.

———. 1995. *Kööra.* Budapest: Pesti Szalom.

———. 1999. *The Invisible Voice: Meditations on Jewish Themes.* Trans. Peter Reich. San Diego, Calif.: Harcourt.

Lichtmann, Tamás, ed. 1999. *Angezogen und abgestoßen: Juden in der ungarischen Literatur.* Frankfurt am Main: Peter Lang.

Móricz, Zsigmond. 1959. *Irodalomról és művészetrő* II. Budapest: Akadémiai Kiadó.

Nádas, Péter. 1977. *Egy családregény vége.* Budapest: Regény.

————. 1986. *Emlékiratok könyve.* Budapest: Szépirodalmi Kiadó.

————. 1997. *A Book of Memories: A Novel.* Trans. Ivan Sanders with Imre Goldstein. New York: Farrar, Straus and Giroux.

————. 1998. *The End of a Family Story.* Trans. Imre Goldstein. New York: Farrar, Straus and Giroux.

Ranki, Vera. 1999. *The Politics of Inclusion and Exclusion: Jews and Nationalism in Hungary.* New York: Holmes and Meier.

Reichmann, Eva. 1999. "Autoren unter Anklage? Bemerkungen zur Erforschung der ungarisch-jüdischen Literaturgeschichte." In *Angezogen und abgestoßen: Juden in der ungarischen Literatur,* ed. Tamás Lichtmann, 233–50. Frankfurt am Main: Peter Lang.

Sanders, Iván. 1999. "Metakommunikation für Fortgeschrittene: Jüdische Lesarten zum Buch der Erinnerung von Péter Nádas." In *Angezogen und abgestoßen: Juden in der ungarischen Literatur,* ed. Tamás Lichtmann, 365–79. Frankfurt am Main: Peter Lang.

Somlyó, György. 1984. *Rámpa.* Budapest: Szépirodalmi Kiadó.

Suleiman, Susan Rubin, and Éva Forgács, eds. 2003. *Contemporary Jewish Writing in Hungary: An Anthology.* Lincoln: University of Nebraska Press.

Szabolcsi, Miklós. 1999. "Einleitende Gedanken." In *Angezogen und abgestoßen: Juden in der ungarischen Literatur,* ed. Tamás Lichtmann, 13–21. Frankfurt am Main: Peter Lang.

Szántó, Gábor T. 1995. *A tizedik ember.* Budapest: Belvárosi Könyvkiadó.

————. 1999. "(Ungarisch-)Jüdischer Schriftsteller zu sein: Beschreibung einer Paradoxie." In *Angezogen und abgestoßen: Juden in der ungarischen Literatur,* ed. Tamás Lichtmann, 251–75. Frankfurt am Main: Peter Lang.

————. 2002. *Keleti pályaudvar, végállomás.* Budapest: Magvető.

Szegedy-Maszák, Mihály. 1999. "Miklós Radnóti und die Literatur des Holocaust." In *Angezogen und abgestoßen: Juden in der ungarischen Literatur,* ed. Tamás Lichtmann, 209–32. Frankfurt am Main: Peter Lang.

Török Petra. 1999. "Wendepunkte der jüdischen Literaturinterpretation in der ungarisch-jüdischen Presse von 1880 bis 1944." In *Angezogen und abgestoßen: Juden in der ungarischen Literatur,* ed. Tamás Lichtmann, 131–58. Frankfurt am Main: Peter Lang.

Ungvári, Tamás. 1999. "Assimilationsstrategien." In *Angezogen und abgestoßen: Juden in der ungarischen Literatur,* ed. Tamás Lichtmann, 49–69. Frankfurt am Main: Peter Lang.

Várnai, Pál. 1999. "Reflexionen eines in der Diaspora Lebenden unter dem Vorwand einer Definition zur ungarisch-jüdischer Literatur." In *Angezogen und abgestoßen: Juden in der ungarischen Literatur,* ed. Tamás Lichtmann, 177–93. Frankfurt am Main: Peter Lang.

Vasvári, Louise O., and Steven Tötösy de Zepetnek, eds. 2005. *Imre Kertész and Holocaust Literature.* West Lafayette, Ind.: Purdue University Press.

TEXTS AVAILABLE IN ENGLISH

Benedek, István G., and Judy Aniot. 1991. *Hungary, Democracy Reborn.* Budapest: Ministry of Foreign Affairs of the Republic of Hungary.

Dalos, György. 1983. *1985: A Historical Report (Hongkong 2036) from the Hungarian of ***.* Trans. Stuart Hood and Estella Schmid. London: Pluto.

————. 1999. *The Guest from the Future: Anna Akhmatova and Isaiah Berlin.* Trans. Antony Wood. New York: Farrar, Straus and Giroux.

————. 2001. *The Circumcision.* Trans. Judith Sollosy. Rose Bay, N.S.W.: Brandl and Schlesinger.

Gergely, Ágnes. 1997. *Requiem for a Sunbird: Forty Poems.* Budapest: Maecenas.

————. 2003. "Poems," trans. Nathaniel Tarn. In *Contemporary Jewish Writing in Hungary*, ed. Susan R. Suleiman and Éva Forgács, 199–200. Lincoln: University of Nebraska Press.

Kardos, György. 1975. *Avraham's Good Week*. Garden City, N.Y.: Doubleday.

Kertész, Imre. 2004a. *Fatelessness: A Novel*. Trans. Tim Wilkinson. New York: Vintage International.

————. 2004b. *Kaddish for an Unborn Child*. Trans. Tim Wilkinson. New York: Vintage.

————. 2004c. *Liquidation*. Trans. Tim Wilkinson. New York: Knopf.

Köbányai, János. 1999. *The Haggadah of the Apopcalypse: Imre Ámos and His Times*. Budapest: Múlt és Jövo.

Konrád, György. 1984. *Antipolitics: An Essay*. Trans. Richard E. Allen. London: Quartet.

————. 1992. *A Feast in the Garden*. Trans. Imre Goldstein. New York: Harcourt Brace Jovanovich.

————. 1995. *The Melancholy of Rebirth: Essays from Post-Communist Central Europe, 1989–1994*. Trans. Michael Henry Heim. San Diego, Calif.: Harcourt Brace.

————. 2000a. *The Invisible Voice: Meditations on Jewish Themes*. Trans. Peter Reich. San Diego, Calif.: Harcourt Brace.

————. 2000b. *Stonedial*. Trans. Ivan Sanders. New York: Harcourt.

Mezei, András, and Thomas Land. 1995. *Testimony: Voices of the Holocaust*. London: Alpha World Features / Budapest: City Press.

Nádas, Péter. 1997. *A Book of Memories: A Novel*. Trans. Ivan Sanders with Imre Goldstein. New York: Farrar, Straus and Giroux.

————. 1998. *The End of a Family Story: A Novel*. Trans. Imre Goldstein. New York: Farrar, Straus and Giroux.

Suleiman, Susan Rubin, and Éva Forgács, eds. 2003. *Contemporary Jewish Writing in Hungary: An Anthology*. Lincoln: University of Nebraska Press.

NINE

~

MONIKA ADAMCZYK-GARBOWSKA

Making Up for Lost Time: Contemporary Jewish Writing in Poland

Until World War II Poland was the main center of Jewish literary creativity in Polish, Yiddish, and Hebrew. After the war survivors tried to rebuild—at least on a small scale—the Polish Jewish community. Despite various political and economic obstacles, cultural life continued, albeit more subdued (Adamczyk-Garbowska 1999). Yiddish books and works in Polish on Jewish topics were published both by writers who had made their debut before the war and those who had come of age in the postwar years. The year 1968 saw the rise of an anti-Semitic campaign instigated by a nationalist group within the Polish Communist Party in the wake of Soviet anti-Zionism following the Six-Day War. This campaign led to what was later called the last exodus, with Poland perceived as a cemetery where no Jewish activities of any kind were possible.

Ruth Wisse's 1978 account of her trip to Poland is very telling in this respect. When she asked how many Jews lived in the country, she received the following answer: "Officially, five or ten thousand, though no one actually lives as a Jew anymore in Poland" (1978, 64). To which Wisse comments: "Inquire at the many bookstores of Warsaw or Cracow for any volume on the Jews of Poland, either of the past or present, in any region of the north or south, in any aspect of ethnography or economics, and even the dullest student of language will quickly learn the words for 'there are none,' *nie ma,* and 'nothing,' *nic.* A trip to Poland in search of a Jewish presence is a journey of the mind alone" (64).

The situation has changed quite radically since that time. More and more people are trying to live Jewish lives, and bookstores all over the country have Judaica sections. Yet how many books in the latter category are written by contemporary Polish Jewish authors? Before returning to this question, I feel some introductory remarks are in order. The historical background is very important since what one observes in the present can be characterized as a pattern of reversal and repetition of the past.

Polish Jewish writers became part of the Polish literature discourse in the second half of the nineteenth century. Although some introduced Jewish motifs, most ignored their own ethnic heritage in order to become "Polish writers." In the years between the wars, however, some authors began to define themselves as Polish Jewish writers in the sense that they would write in the Polish language without ignoring their unique experience as Jews. No Polish Jewish authors gained prominence at that time. The period may have been too brief to nurture major figures, or perhaps it was the fact that most of this writing had an ideological (e.g., Zionist) bent, which might have hindered genuine creativity. Consequently, during the interwar period in Poland several groups of writers can be distinguished who can generally be described as Jewish: Jewish writers who wrote in Polish, those who wrote in Yiddish, and those who wrote in Hebrew. (One should add that a number of authors wrote in at least two or even three languages and belonged to various literatures simultaneously.) Among those who wrote in Polish, at least three subgroups can be identified: those who openly declared their Jewishness; those who, while not denying their Jewishness, trivialized and downplayed it; and those who tried to ignore or conceal their Jewish roots.

After World War II, the situation changed once again. Most of the Jewish writers who had survived the Shoah left for Israel, western Europe, or a country in the Americas. Nonetheless, until 1968 some Yiddish writing continued in Poland. In the restricted landscape of Polish Jewish literature, a number of authors who before the war had tried to avoid Jewish topics now consciously focused upon them. For instance, Julian Stryjkowski, the best-known Polish Jewish writer, insisted that it was the Shoah that compelled him to write. At the same time, many authors continued to conceal their Jewish backgrounds and remained silent about the experience of the Jewish people unless specific events challenged them to break this silence.

We will never know what would have emerged from the culturally and linguistically rich Polish Jewish literary world if the Shoah had not happened. It is possible that the development of Polish Jewish literature would have been similar to the postwar shifts in American literature, where mature writers only emerged in the forties and fifties despite the fact that Jewish topics had appeared much earlier. If a similar process had occurred in Poland—where linguistic "Polonization" would have probably continued at a rapid pace, and Yiddish culture and schools with Yiddish as the main language would have given way to Jewish schools conducted in the Polish language—the topics in Polish Jewish literature would most likely have been similar to those in American Jewish fiction. It is likely that such issues as identity, assimilation, anti-Semitism, and self-hatred would have been addressed according to some specifically Polish variations. The tragic events of the Shoah halted such an evolution and gave a different turn to the writings of Polish Jews (Polonsky and Adamczyk-Garbowska 2001).

As a result of the complex political situation after World War II and its accompanying censorship, Jewish themes emerged in cyclical waves of suppression and disclosure in works by Polish Jewish writers. It is not surprising, therefore, that most works were published in times of relative freedom, that is, right after the war and before the onset of Stalinism in 1946–47, and again after 1956, during the political thaw initiated by Władysław Gomułka's regime.

After 1968 the situation became even more complicated. Censorship laws forbade the publication of almost all books on Jewish topics, regardless of whether they were written by non-Jewish or Jewish authors. Around that time a dissident movement developed which—since its members were not allowed to have their works published officially in Poland—relied on outlets in the form of domestic underground publications or émigré publishers in London, Paris, or Berlin. Although this process was not characteristic of Polish Jewish writing in particular, it was typical of Polish literature in general. Thus, one may speak of Polish literature's "binary circulation" (*podwójny obieg*), that is, of official books and journals, which were accepted by censors and published by state-run publishing houses, and of unofficial ones, beyond the reach of censorship and published by underground (*samizdat*) presses either within the country or by Polish émigré presses abroad. Another phenomenon typical of that period dictated that some works that were originally conceived in Polish—such as those by Ida Fink in Israel or Janina Bauman in Great Britain—first appeared in English and only later were printed in their original Polish versions. There are still some works—such as the Shoah stories by Sarah Nomberg Przytyk, which, paradoxically, are now considered part of American Shoah literature—that have not had Polish editions despite the fact that they were originally written in Polish and planned for publication in Poland.

The publishing scene in the eighties was characterized by relaxed censorship, especially during the Solidarity period (August 1980–December 13, 1981), as well as after 1983, when martial law imposed on December 13, 1981, was finally lifted. A striking feature of that period was the fact that Jewish writers received most of their support from liberal Catholic journals or publishers. For example, a number of Julian Stryjkowski's works were published by the Dominican Order publishing house in Poznań.

In the late seventies and eighties the second generation of Polish Jewish writers—those who were children during the Shoah and came of age in the late fifties or early sixties—had an important impact on the growing interest in Jewish themes. Some of them, such as Henryk Grynberg and Hanna Krall, are still quite active. Krall's book-length interview with Marek Edelman entitled *Zdążyć przed Panem Bogiem* (which first appeared in English as *Shielding the Flame: An Intimate Conversation with Dr. Marek Edelman, the Last Surviving Leader of the Warsaw Ghetto Uprising* and subsequently as *To Outwit God*) marked a breakthrough in her career as a journalist and was one of the first books on Jewish topics published in the late seventies following a tedious struggle with censors. In the eighties a number of Grynberg's and Krall's books could not be published officially (e.g., Krall's *Sublokatorka,* called *The Subtenant* in English, which appeared in Paris in 1985 and was reprinted by an underground press for circulation within Poland) and only became widely available after 1989.

Although by the mid-eighties Jewish topics had already become fashionable, the abolition of censorship in 1989 led to a second wave of titles on Jewish topics, including both new pieces and reprints of older editions. To meet the growing interest, even books published before World War I were occasionally reprinted. This set the stage for the appearance of what could be called modern Marranos, who openly addressed the Shoah as the governing framework of their experience as Polish Jews. The best-known example is that of respected critic and literary scholar Michał Głowiński. Though Głowiński had never talked about his Jewish background before, in 1997 he published *Czarne sezony* (Black Seasons), an autobiographical book in which he relates his Warsaw ghetto experience and his hidden existence in a cloister in the Lublin region. Maria Szelestowska's *Lubię żyć* (I Enjoy Being Alive, 2000) offers another example of that kind. In her case, however, the Marrano remains in disguise since the author's real name was not revealed.

Books written much earlier that had been banned or forgotten are currently being reissued, among them Władysław Szpilman's memoir *The Pianist,* which was originally published in Poland in 1946 under the title *Śmierć miasta* (The Death of the City). The Polish edition published in 2000 was in reaction to the success the book had enjoyed in Germany and to its film adaptation by Roman Polanski. Another example includes the stories by Leo Lipski, who, like Ida Fink and a number of other Polish Jewish writers, settled in Israel after the war, where he continued to write in Polish.

There are also several writers who, prior to going public, pursued careers outside the world of literature. The best known examples include: Wilhelm Dichter, a retired scientist based in Massachusetts (he left Poland in 1968), author of *Koń Pana Boga* (God's Horse, 1996) and *Szkoła bezbożników* (The School of Heretics, 1999); and Roma Ligocka, a graphic artist and stage designer who spent the last thirty years of her life in Germany. She is the author of *Dziewczynka w czerwonym płaszczyku* (A Girl in a Red Coat, 2001), *Kobieta w podróży* (A Traveling Woman, 2002), and the more recently published *Tylko ja sama* (Only Me Alone, 2004). Characteristic of these two authors is the fact that their first books concern the Shoah experience, whereas their subsequent books concentrate on later periods—although the shadow of the war still hovers above them. It would appear that only after the cathartic experience of writing about the Shoah were they able to deal with other topics.

Ligocka's case is particularly complicated. Writing from the point of view of a female Polish Jewish immigrant residing in Germany, she considers the pain derived from living in the very country responsible for the Final Solution as a prerequisite for her own writing. Dichter's case is also complex since he touches upon the controversial issue of Jewish involvement in the Communist apparatus in postwar Poland.

In 2002 the most prestigious Polish literary prize was awarded to Joanna Olczak-Ronikier for her family saga *W ogrodzie pamięci* (In Memory's Garden, 2002). As a descendant of the Cracow-based Horowitz and Mortkowicz families, she felt her ancestors' aim was to assimilate to Polish culture (the Mortkowiczs were well-known publishers before the war) as well as other cultures, including French and American. Although also fully assimilated, she makes it her prerogative to trace her Jewish roots. She admits that it was a long process that eventually led her to write the book. The first step was a need to clear out her apartment following her mother's death:

> There wasn't much of value, but from every drawer of the ash-wood chest and the writing desk came an endless stream of letters, postcards, wedding announcements, children's drawings, photographs and newspaper cuttings about the family. . . . I bought two large wicker baskets and packed it all into them without sorting or even looking at any of it. My home had died all over again, and I couldn't afford to be sentimental about a lot of old scraps of paper.
>
> For years the baskets were a faithful companion through my nomadic life, every once in a while changing address along with me. They were always in the way being a nuisance and taking up space, and I never so much as took a peep at them. I didn't feel like the rightful heiress to this particular legacy, consisting as it did of other people's affections, regrets and nostalgia. After my mother's death my encounters with my relatives became rarer and rarer. Whenever we did meet, it was said that someone should write the history of our family, but nothing ever came of it. (2004, 305)

Olczak-Ronikier claims to have experienced some metaphysical encounters while working on the family saga, as if the dead were sending their messages to her. For instance, in 1998 she profited from the presence in Cracow of Paul Chaim Eisenberg, the chief rabbi of Austria, to question him about her great-great-grandfather, Lazar Horowitz, who 170 years earlier had been the chief rabbi of the Jewish community in Vienna. She hoped Rabbi Eisenberg would give her some tips regarding searching for her ancestor's traces. To her surprise, she discovered that Lazar Horowitz was very well known to the present rabbi, who had even hung Horowitz's portrait on the wall behind his desk and was able to supply her with relevant information about his predecessor's life.

In Memory's Garden was not Olczak-Ronikier's first book, having previously published three books about artistic life in Cracow. Now, however, she seems to have found the primary theme that she intends to pursue in the future. She does not identify herself as a Jewish writer per se and prefers to dedicate her most recent work to the Polish intelligentsia of Jewish descent, who opted for Polishness and loved and served Poland faithfully without always being rewarded for that devotion (Pawłowski 2002).

Olczak-Ronikier, Głowiński, Ligocka, and Dichter were children during the war. There is, however, also a group of younger Jewish authors (born in the forties and fifties) who published works in Polish in the nineties but now mostly live abroad. They include Viola Wein and Eli Barbur in Israel, Roman Gren in France, and Ewa Kuryluk and Anna Frajlich in the United States. For obvious reasons, the Shoah is not their main topic. They focus instead on identity in a new environment, be it Israel, North America, or western Europe. In 1996 Wein's and Gren's books won awards from the Fundacja Kultury (Cultural Foundation) through its special program aimed at promoting new writers. Another prizewinner was Dichter's *Koń Pana Boga*. What these three authors have in common is that despite leaving Poland in 1968 and living in Israel, France, and the United States, respectively, they have retained Polish as their preferred language of expression.

Gren's *Krajobraz z dzieckiem* (A Landscape with a Child, 1996) is told from the point of view of a child narrator whose Communist parents occupy high positions in the party. Gren describes the absurd situation they created for the young boy by concealing their Jewish roots. For instance, they tell him that the Israeli oranges they receive from their relatives in boxes stamped "Yaffa" come from Egypt. Everything Jewish constitutes a taboo at home and it is not clear why. Perhaps they want to protect the child against anti-Semitism or are concerned about the father's career. The mystery is gradually revealed, however, thanks to old photographs bearing exotic-sounding names, like Awram or Ben Hirsz, as well as by playmates at a summer camp who want the narrator to show them his "dinky." All these events lead to the climactic announcement by the narrator's father that they will be leaving the country.

Wein's stories depict a Polish Jewish family settling down in Israel following the 1968 exodus from Poland. Previously well off and socially prominent, they experience degradation in their new environment. The mother, Mrs. Sztajn, is gradually wasting away, the only thing keeping her alive being her determination to help her children achieve some stability. Her efforts, however, prove futile and she dies leaving her daughter and son far from attaining financial and emotional stability. In the mother's eyes Israel is not a real homeland and dream country where one can discover one's Jewish roots but a hot, loud, and rather unfriendly territory full of threatening situations and ongoing wars.

In her book *Goldi* (2004) Ewa Kuryluk, a graphic artist and author of both fiction and essays, explores her own experience as the daughter of a Shoah survivor, among other topics. She recalls growing up in the shadow of the traumatic past that contributed to her mother's mental illness. During the Nazi occupation Kuryluk's Jewish mother was hidden by her non-Jewish father but never recovered from the deep trauma, which affected the entire family.

Poet Piotr Matywiecki is a member of the third generation of Jewish authors who, like his fellow poets Aleksander Rozenfeld and Gwido Zlatkes, constantly oscillate between their Polish and Jewish identities. Rozenfeld settled in Israel for a few years but decided to return to Poland in 1989, while Zlatkes (who only realized he was partly Jewish in the eighties while attending classes with Artur Sandauer at Warsaw University) immigrated to the United States to pursue Jewish studies. Matywiecki's *Kamień graniczny* (The Border Stone) received tremendous attention when it was published in 1994. An unusual work, it consists of short chapters containing quotations from letters and journals from the Warsaw ghetto, which are commented upon by the author. Despite its documentary character, the book is more a record of the awareness of the Shoah than of the Shoah itself. Matywiecki's relationship to ghetto experience is indirect. He was conceived within the Warsaw ghetto and was born on the "Aryan side" after the liquidation of the Jewish quarter, not long before his father's death in the Warsaw uprising of August 1944. As one critic has stated with reference to his name (Piotr is Polish for Peter, which is derived from the Latin *petrus,* stone), as a posthumous child of the ghetto, he himself is "the living border stone" (Mikołejko 1994, 9).

A fourth generation of Jewish writers in Poland is still in the making and may include the children of intellectuals who, like Konstanty Gebert or Stanisław Krajewski, were involved in the Jewish revival in Poland. After all, there are numerous reasons why Poland may continue to see older Jewish authors making delayed debuts as writers, witness established writers turn to the experience of their people in Poland, and welcome young authors staking out their identity as Jews writing in Polish. Present-day Polish society is showing a strong interest in minorities and regional traditions. Jewish topics are still considered fashionable, and there are people who have only recently discovered their Jewish roots, including the so-called children of the Shoah and their off-spring. This trend might bear fruit in the form of notable works written, for example, with the epic force that fuels the works of Olczak-Ronikier, or with the restraint and bated breath characteristic of Głowiński's style. It may also encourage popular writing for profit. Previously popular literature on the Shoah practically did not exist in Poland. Given the recent appearance of Polish revisionist attempts to downplay the scope of the Shoah,[1] one presumes the latter might become a marketable "product."

With progressive globalization, even the linguistic criterion assumes a different meaning. The internet journal *Manila Times* featured a portrait of the Polish journalist Agata Tuszyńska, who tended to focus on sensational elements in the lives of the assimilated Polish writer Irena Krzywicka or Isaac Bashevis Singer, to mention just two examples. In her latest book, however, Tuszyńska focuses on her recently discovered identity as the daughter of a Shoah survivor. In her book on Singer, which was first published in 1994, Tuszyńska still wrote from the position of a non-Jewish Polish woman fascinated by the work of the Yiddish master. Her memoir *Rodzinna historia lęku* (A Family History of Fear, 2005), written in Polish, was supposed to appear first in English. What is new and striking—aside from the strategy of launching an English-language edition simultaneously with the original edition—is a marketing strategy that announces the book's publication well in advance and relies on a publicity agent to create a public media event. This is a radical departure from past practice, when numerous authors in eastern Europe kept their works in the closet while waiting for a suitable moment to get them published.

The case of Agata Tuszyńska, who resides in Poland, has to be understood in the transnational context of Polish Jewish writers who, living and writing outside their native Poland, document in their works their complicated attitude toward their native tongue. One wonders whether Jerzy Kosinski or Eva Hoffman would have become writers had they remained in Poland and, if so, whether they would have become mainstream Polish authors or stressed their Jewish identity. It is worth noting that their works appear to be born of the experience of displacement—consciously chosen, in the case of Kosinski, and imposed by her parents, in the case of Hoffman—to which their new audiences turn with great interest. Similar observations could be made about Louis Begley in the United States, Irene Karafilly in Canada, and Theo Richmond or Clive Sinclair in Britain. In *Diaspora Blues* (1987) Sinclair actually tries to imagine where he would be now if his family had not immigrated to Britain.

During a visit to Cracow after many years of absence, Eva Hoffman tries to imagine what her life would have been like had she stayed in Poland. Perhaps she would have become a pianist, gotten involved in student politics, and been forced to emigrate after the anti-Semitic purges that followed the student riots in 1968:

> Where would I have gone? Israel, America, West Germany, Sweden? Here, the speculations become more attenuated, for I don't know the person who would have made that decision: I don't know how her daily life felt until then, how successful or frustrated she was, how adventurous or timid. I don't know the quality of her sensations, or what her yearnings were, or how she satisfied them. I don't know the accidents that left little scars on her skin, or the accretions of sorrow and pleasure on her soul. No, one can't create a real out of a conditional history; in the light of the simple declarative statement of actual existence, "would have been" or "as if" loses its ontological status. In a way, it doesn't count, though without it, we would have no imagination; we would be truly prisoners of ourselves. But the shadow that this conjectural history casts over my real one is not a shadow of regret but of the knowledge—to which we all must reconcile ourselves—that one is given only one life, even though so many others might have been. (1989, 240–41)

The authors who left Poland and those who remained both face a dilemma. The vicissitudes of Polish Jewry become fully visible when one juxtaposes works by Hoffman, Ligocka, and Olczak-Ronikier—three Jewish women raised in Cracow whose lives went in very different directions—with works by Grynberg, Głowiński, and Dichter—three Jewish men, born in the thirties, who shared equally traumatic childhoods, which they revisited in fictionalized memoirs written at various stages of their adult lives.

Literary criticism has accepted the challenge of defining what constitutes a "Polish Jewish author" in light of the major differences characterizing the experiences and aesthetic articulations of the authors discussed in this chapter. In her introduction to *Defining the Indefinable: What Is Jewish Literature?* Hana Wirth-Nesher examines various perspectives and enumerates the problems critics have encountered in attempting to provide a definition. She maintains that identifying Jewish literature as literature written by Jews would be a reductive approach. Similarly, the critic Itamar Even-Zohar had suggested that "only a nationalistic approach, or a racist anti-Semitic one, or ignorance . . . would adopt the term 'Jewish literature' on the basis of origin of writers" (quoted in Wirth-Nesher 1994, 3). After all, there are some prominent Polish writers who, like Tadeusz Różewicz or Gustaw Herling-Grudziński, almost never mention their Jewish descent and do not identify themselves as Jewish.

Polish literary critics have also responded to the need for clarification. As early as 1982 Artur Sandauer published his study *O sytuacji pisarza polskiego żydowskiego pochodzenia w XX wieku* (On the Situation of the Polish Jewish Writer in the Twentieth Century), which he provocatively subtitled *Rzecz którą nie ja powinienem był napisać* (A Study Someone Else Should Have Written). Sandauer regards literary self-definition as the determining factor. For him Polish Jewish writers are those who raise the question of their origin in their works either explicitly or indirectly and in whose writings Jewish topics appear either at the very beginning of their creative activity or at a later stage, suppressed permanently or occasionally for various reasons. Eugenia Prokop-Janiec, conversely, has established two main criteria for defining Polish Jewish interwar literature: thematic, requiring that the texts written in the Polish language ought to concern Jewish subjects; and biographical, according to which authors would define themselves nationally and culturally as Jewish and disclose their ties to Jewish culture (1992). More recently she has observed this fairly "permanent" form of self-definition often giving way to notions of dual identity (2002). This trend awaits amplification and modification with regard to Jewish expatriates living and writing abroad. Roma Ligocka, to cite a concrete example, conceived her first work in Germany with the help of a German editor.

Following Prokop-Janiec's distinction, in our English-language anthology of postwar Polish Jewish literature (2001) Antony Polonsky and I applied rather strict criteria, which made obvious sense for the older generation of writers, where one can even talk about a "Jewish school" in Polish literature (Błoński 1986). However, given more recent trends, ultimately it will become necessary to eschew the desire to group authors collectively and to focus instead on the uniqueness of each individual author, who may choose not to deal with Jewish topics consistently and exclusively but rather to address such notions only in certain phases of their careers.

Jewish writers, representing only a very small segment of Poland's literary scene, nevertheless attract a great deal of publicity and are met with an intense interest, especially among the more educated members of the reading public. And yet this interest has also created a highly problematic perception within the national press, according to which Jewish authors are being favored over non-Jewish Polish writers. Being a Jewish author in Poland has not yet become a neutral matter, which may also account for the fact that Polish Jewish literature has yet to address some of the most troubling events signaling Poland's complex attitude toward its Jewish population. Among them, certainly, is the pogrom in Kielce (July 1946), but also the events of March 1968. Only recently was the pogrom in Jedwabne (July 1941) and its contemporary reception discussed by Anna Bikont in her book *My z Jedwabnego* (Us from Jedwabne, 2004), in which she interweaves historical and sociological data with her personal reflections and experiences concerning her own Jewish identity.

It is interesting that despite the many public discussions held in the media, an aura of mystery and uneasiness still surrounds some of the issues concerning Jewish identity in present-day Poland. For instance, a widely discussed issue in the interwar period (especially in the thirties) concerned the apparent Jewish roots of Adam Mickiewicz, the best known and most respected Polish romantic poet. This controversy surrounding the ethnic background of the "national bard" (Mickiewicz indirectly admitted to having had a "Jewish mother") resurfaced in the Polish press in the eighties and hovered in the background of the recent discussion concerning the ethnicity of Krzysztof Kamil Baczyński, the celebrated poet of the World War II generation. Baczyński, too, was of Jewish origin, but he presented himself—and is considered by most critics—as the embodiment of the Polish patriotic poet-soldier, a hero of the Warsaw uprising of August 1944 in the neoromantic tradition. Although some of Baczyński's poetry was written at the time of the Warsaw ghetto, it is often read in the context of the Polish uprising that took place more than a year after the ghetto's final liquidation. Much as Adam Mickiewicz's famous play *Dziady* (Forefathers' Eve) has been read in the light of his alleged Jewish roots, so Baczyński's work is now being reinterpreted in view of the author's Jewish background.

During the interwar period the Polish Jewish press provided an outlet for the emergence of Polish Jewish literature. With the appearance of *Midrasz,* a lively monthly journal connected with the Lauder Foundation, one notes the reappearance of the Polish Jewish press, albeit on a smaller scale. *Midrasz* is the main sponsor of Warsaw's annual Jewish Book Fair. Paradoxically, once again the greatest support has been given to Polish Jewish writers by the liberal Catholic press. For example, the Cracow-based weekly *Tygodnik Powszechny* published large sections of Głowiński's and Olczak-Ronikier's works before they appeared in book form. Olczak-Ronikier's books were published by the prestigious Catholic publishing house Znak. Both of Dichter's books also appeared under their auspices, as did Szpilman's work *The Pianist.*

The topics most frequently discussed by Polish Jewish authors during the interwar period included: the problem of having two motherlands, Poland and Eretz Israel; Zionist ideology; the relationship to the Jewish tradition; the depiction of shtetl life; and transformations within the Jewish family due to acculturation and secularization. Today the main topics include: the Shoah experience; displacement (as a result of the postwar anti-Semitic atmosphere or political repression); and the struggle to define one's identity. In the past the readership consisted primarily of linguistically assimilated Jews, whereas today's audience is primarily composed of non-Jewish readers eager to learn about Jewish history and tradition after years of silence. Some observers see the current interest in Jewish topics as a manifestation of Polish feelings of guilt, whereas others view it as a sign of curiosity or fascination with the "exotic." Ironically, as Sandauer has pointed out, the selfsame Jews who prior to the war were ridiculed and stigmatized because of their appearance, customs, and accent are now regarded as curious reminders of the lost world of the shtetl or the Bible (1982, 84). In the case of most contemporary Polish Jewish fiction, however, the question of Jewish tradition is relegated to the background, the main motif being that of mixed identity. The authors, knowing almost as little about their tradition as their potential readers, now set out to discover it. A story by Hanna Krall depicts a visit to the United States by a group of middle-aged women—children of the Shoah—who were all raised in Christian families: "The women from Poland stayed in a student dormitory at the Jewish Theological Seminary. There were kosher refrigerators there, one for dairy products, one for meat. The hosts were extremely polite, only they were upset that the guests kept putting their *treyf* food into their refrigerators. 'If you don't know what is *treyf,* just ask us,' they repeated in despair (2001, 310). The readers learn that "the women from Poland" do not know how to recite the prayer while lighting the Sabbath candles or how to pray in a synagogue. While seeking to fill "the Jewish void of their real mothers," they are also attached to the "mothers who were not their mothers" (311). Similar sentiments are expressed in the poem "Both Your Mothers," by the Polish non-Jewish poet Jerzy Ficowski, which he dedicated to his wife, Bieta, a child of the Shoah:

> Under a futile Torah
> under an imprisoned star
> your mother gave birth to you . . .
>
> Later you slept in a bundle
> carried out of the ghetto . . .
>
> And at once a chance
> someone hastily
> bustled about your sleep
>
> and then stayed for a long always
> and washed you of orphanhood
> and swaddled you in love
> and become [*sic*] the answer
> to your first word
>
> That was how
> both your mothers taught you
> not to be surprised at all
> when you say
> *I am*
> (1993, 40–41)

This poem has inspired Romuald Jakub Weksler-Waszkinel, a philosopher at the Catholic University in Lublin, who learned about his Jewish roots when he was thirty-five and had been a practicing Catholic priest for over ten years. Following the shock of this revelation, he became deeply involved in a Christian-

Jewish dialogue. In a documentary film entitled *Wpisany w gwiazdę Dawida* (The Cross Inscribed in the Star of David) Weksler-Waszkinel recites Ficowski's poem to underscore his dual affection for the Jewish mother who gave birth to him and the Christian one who raised him.

Given the small-scale Jewish revival currently taking place in Poland—and an increasing number of people, like Weksler-Waszkinel, who are discovering the "secret" that they were adopted by Christians during the war, or that they are children of Jewish parents who chose to conceal their identity[2]—one can expect some additional manifestations of these phenomena in literature. In time future writers will perhaps attempt to describe what it means to be Jewish in Poland today. The Shoah will undoubtedly remain an important theme, as indeed it is in the works of Jewish writers in Europe and the United States, but current issues of Jewish life in Catholic Poland may very well move into the foreground.

It is difficult to predict what topics Polish Jewish literature will offer in the future, or what the prospects are for its future development. This will also depend on the political and economic situation of the country. Some Poles who immigrated to the West during the Communist years are returning to Poland, as are their children. There might even be some Polish Jews willing to return. Jewish immigrants from other countries, especially from Poland's eastern neighbors, may settle in Poland now that it is part of the European Union. At the same time, however, some young Polish Jews are still leaving the country, often following the advice of their parents, who encourage them to find surroundings more conducive to building Jewish lives. While some Jews in Poland are eager to speak of their long-suppressed or newly discovered identities, others continue to remain silent and invisible (Kowalski 2002). It is still quite common for Polish Jews mentioned in the Polish media or in documentaries made in Poland by foreigners to remain anonymous or to insist that the films should not be distributed in Poland.

Aleksander Hertz, author of a pioneering study (originally published in Paris in 1961) on the role of Jews in Polish culture, proposed that Polish literature in the past may have been richer if Jewish authors had brought a more specifically Jewish dimension to it. However, for a variety of personal as well as artistic reasons Polish Jewish authors had more or less consciously chosen not to speak of their roots before the war (1988, 230). Seeing things from a different perspective, Artur Sandauer pointed out that in Poland complete acculturation was never a possibility since the Jewish experience could not be ignored due to an exaggerated self-consciousness, on the one hand, and pressure from outside, on the other. According to him, artists with Jewish roots could not remain indifferent to their origins and were left with the choice of either denying these roots or emphasizing them. The first option would lead to a "non-authentic and faded personality," while the second would result in self-hatred and "self-demonization" (96–97).

Present-day Poland presents Jews with a completely altered yet strangely familiar environment in which some writers have succeeded in transforming what Sandauer calls the "burden of Jewishness" into a creative and even liberating force, while others continue to experience it as an obstacle.

NOTES

1. Holocaust denial in Communist Poland assumed a shape different from that found in the West. Official propaganda presented victims as "Polish citizens," with no distinction made between the fate of Jews and others. However, censorship blocked publications that denied the existence of gas chambers. Conversely, the number of victims was inflated. In a country where the Nazis established most of their labor and death camps, there were too many witnesses who knew what had happened to permit wholesale denial. With the abolition of censorship, several extremist publications surfaced which downplayed the persecution of the Jews or suggested that they were responsible for their own fate or even served as Nazi allies.

2. The documentary entitled *Secret* focuses on this particular phenomenon.

WORKS CITED

Adamczyk-Garbowska, Monika. 1999. "Is There a Place for Yiddish in Poland's Jewish Revival?" In *Yiddish in the Contemporary World: Papers of the First Mendel Friedman International Conference on Yiddish,* ed. Gennady Estraikh and Mikhail Krutikov, 57–72. Oxford: Legenda.

Bikont, Anna. 2004. *My z Jedwabnego.* Warsaw: Prószyński i S-ka.

Błoński, Jan. 1986. "Is There a Jewish School in Polish Literature?" *Polin* 1: 196–211.

Dichter, Wilhelm. 1996. *Koń Pana Boga.* Cracow: Znak.

———. 1999. *Szkoła bezbożników.* Cracow: Znak.

Dickson, Gunna. 2002. "Translations Push Sales of Popular Literature." *Manila Times* (http://www. manilatimes.net), May 22.

Ficowski, Jerzy. 1993. "Both Your Mothers," trans. Keith Bosley. In *Odczytanie popiołów / A Reading of Ashes* (bilingual ed.), 41. Warsaw: Browarna.

Głowiński, Michał. 1997. *Czarne sezony.* Cracow: Wydawnictwo Literackie.

Gren, Roman. 1996. *Krajobraz z dzieckiem.* Warsaw: OPEN.

Hertz, Alexander. 1988. *The Jews in Polish Culture.* Trans. Richard Lourie. Evanston, Ill.: Northwestern University Press.

Hoffman, Eva. 1989. *Lost in Translation: A Life in a New Language.* New York: Dutton.

Kowalski, Jakub. 2002. "Alija, czyli pod górę." *Rzeczpospolita* 301 (December 28–29): A 9.

Krall, Hanna. 2001. "Briefly Now," trans. Christopher Garbowski. In *Contemporary Jewish Writing in Poland: An Anthology,* ed. Antony Polonsky and Monika Adamczyk-Garbowska, 303–11. Lincoln: University of Nebraska Press.

Kuryluk, Ewa. 2004. *Goldi.* Twój Styl.

Ligocka, Roma. 2001. *Dziewczynka w czerwonym płaszczyku.* Cracow: Znak.

———. 2002. *Kobieta w podróży.* Cracow: Wydawnictwo Literackie.

———. 2004. *Tylko ja sama.* Cracow: Wydawnictwo Literackie.

Matywiecki, Piotr. 1994. *Kamień graniczny.* Warsaw: Latona.

Mickiewicz, Adam. 1957. *Dziady.* Warsaw: Czytelnik.

Mikołejko, Zbigniew. 1994. "Kamień graniczny." *Ex Libris* (supplement to *życie Warszawy*) 55: 9.

Olczak-Ronikier, Joanna. 2002. *W ogrodzie pamięci.* Cracow: Wydawnictwo Znak.

Pawłowski, Roman. 2002. "Nike dla sagi." *Gazeta Wyborcza* 234 (October 7): 1.

Polonsky, Antony, and Monika Adamczyk-Garbowska, eds. 2001. *Contemporary Jewish Writing in Poland: An Anthology.* Lincoln: University of Nebraska Press.

Prokop-Janiec, Eugenia. 1992. *Międzywojenna literatura polsko-żydowska.* Cracow: Universitas.

———. 2002. "Jews in Polish Literature." *Polin* (14): 359–81.

Sandauer, Artur. 1982. *O sytuacji pisarza polskiego pochodzenia żydowskiego w XX wieku: Rzecz którą nie ja powinienem był napisać.* Warsaw: Czytelnik.

Sinclair, Clive. 1987. *Diaspora Blues: A View of Israel.* London: Heinemann.

Szelestowska, Maria. 2000. *Lubię żyć.* Warsaw: Czytelnik.

Szpilman, Władysław. 1946. *Śmierć miasta.* Warsaw: Spóldzielnia Wydawnicza "Wiedza".

Tuszyńska, Agata. 2005. *Rodzinna historia lęku.* Cracow: Wydawnictwo Literackie.

Wirth-Nesher, Hana. 1994. "Defining the Indefinable: What Is Jewish Literature?" In *Defining the Indefinable: What Is Jewish Literature?* ed. Hana Wirth-Nesher, 3–12. Philadelphia, Pa.: Jewish Publication Society.

Wisse, Ruth. 1978. "Poland without Jews." *Commentary* 8 (August): 64–67.

TEXTS AVAILABLE IN ENGLISH

Bauman, Janina. 1986. *Winter in the Morning: A Young Girl's Life in the Warsaw Ghetto and Beyond, 1939–1945.* New York: Free Press.

———. 1988. *Dream of Belonging: My Years in Postwar Poland.* London: Virago.

Benski, Stanislaw. 1990. *Missing Pieces.* Trans. Walter Arndt. San Diego, Calif.: Harcourt Brace Jovanovich.

Birenbaum, Halina. 1996. *Hope Is the Last to Die: A Coming of Age under Nazi Terror.* Trans. David Welsh. Armonk, N.Y.: M. E. Sharpe.

Fink, Ida. 1987. *"A Scrap of Time" and Other Stories.* Trans. Madeline Levine and Francine Prose. New York: Pantheon.

———. 1993. *The Journey.* Trans. Joanna Weschler and Francine Prose. New York: Plume.

———. 1998. *Traces: Stories.* Trans. Philip Boehm and Francine Prose. New York: Henry Holt.

Frajlich, Anna. 1991. *Between Dawn and the Wind: Selected Poetry.* Trans. Regina Grol-Prokopczyk. Austin, Tex.: Host Publications.

Glowinski, Michal. 2005. *The Black Seasons.* Trans. Marci Shore. Evanston, Ill.: Northwestern University Press.

Grynberg, Henryk. 1969. *Child of the Shadows,* including *"The Grave."* London: Vallentine and Mitchell.

———. 1997. *Children of Zion.* Trans. Jacqueline Mitchell. Evanston, Ill.: Northwestern University Press.

———. 2001. *"The Jewish War"* and *"The Victory".* Trans. Celina Wieniewska and Richard Lourie. Evanston, Ill.: Northwestern University Press.

———. 2002. *"Drohobycz, Drohobycz" and Other Stories: True Tales from the Holocaust and Life After.* Trans. Alicia Nitecki. New York: Penguin.

Hoffman, Eva. 1989. *Lost in Translation: A Life in a New Language.* New York: Dutton.

———. 1993. *Exit into History: A Journey through the New Eastern Europe.* New York: Viking.

————. 1997. *Shtetl: The Life and Death of a Small Town and the World of Polish Jews.* Boston: Houghton Mifflin.

————. 2001. *The Secret: A Fable for Our Time.* London: Secker and Warburg.

Kosinski, Jerzy. 1972. *Being There.* New York: Bantam.

————. 1973. *To Hold a Pen.* Washington, D.C.: n.p.

————. 1979. *Passion Play.* New York: St. Martin's.

————. 1981. *The Devil Tree.* New York: St. Martin's.

————. 1983. *The Painted Bird.* New York: Modern Library.

————. 1991. *The Hermit of 69th Street: The Working Papers of Norbert Kosky.* New York: Kensington.

————. 1992. *Passing By: Selected Essays, 1962–1991.* New York: Random House.

Krajewski, Stanisław. 2005. *Poland and the Jews: Reflections of a Polish Jew.* Cracow: Austeria.

Krall, Hanna. 1986. *Shielding the Flame: An Intimate Conversation with Dr. Marek Edelman, the Last Surviving Leader of the Warsaw Ghetto Uprising.* Trans. Joanna Stasinska and Lawrence Weschler. New York: Henry Holt.

————. 1992. *"The Subtenant"* and *"To Outwit God".* Trans. Jaroslaw Anders. Evanston, Ill.: Northwestern University Press.

————. 2005. *"The Woman from Hamburg"* and *Other True Stories.* Trans. Madeline G. Levine. New York: Other Press.

Kuryluk, Ewa. 1992. *Century 21.* Normal, Ill.: Dalkey Archive.

Ligocka, Roma. 2002. *The Girl in the Red Coat.* Trans. Margot Bettauer Dembo. London: Sceptre.

Nomberg Przytyk, Sarah. 1985. *Auschwitz: True Tales from a Grotesque Land.* Trans. Roslyn Hirsch. Chapel Hill: University of North Carolina Press.

Olczak-Ronikier, Joanna. 2004. *In the Garden of Memory: A Family Memoir.* Trans. Antonia Lloyd-Jones. London: Weidenfeld and Nicolson.

Polonsky, Antony, and Monika Adamczyk-Garbowska, eds. 2001. *Contemporary Jewish Writing in Poland: An Anthology.* Lincoln: University of Nebraska Press.

Stryjkowski, Julian. 1971. *The Inn.* Trans. Celina Wieniewska. New York: Harcourt Brace Jovanovich.

Szpilman, Władysław. 1999. *The Pianist: The Extraordinary Story of One Man's Survival in Warsaw, 1939–1945.* Trans. Anthea Bell. New York: Picador U.S.A.

Tuszyńska, Agata. 1998. *Lost Landscapes: In Search of Isaac Bashevis Singer and the Jews of Poland.* Trans. Madeline G. Levine. New York: William Morrow.

Wojdowski, Bogdan. 1997. *Bread for the Departed.* Trans. Madeline G. Levine. Evanston, Ill.: Northwestern University Press.

TEN

~

RAINER GRÜBEL & VLADIMIR NOVIKOV

De-Centered Writing: Aspects of Contemporary Jewish Writing in Russia

Contemporary Russian Jewish literature can be characterized as a "de-centric" form of writing. This term—coined in opposition to Thomas Nolden's characterization of recent German Jewish literature as "concentric writing" (Nolden 1995)—is derived from the very history of Russian Jews; it refers to their geographical distribution and relates to the aesthetics of their literary production. Whereas present-day German Jewish writing, according to Nolden, describes a "concentric movement" toward the "concentrationary experience" of the Shoah, the dynamics of Russian Jewish literature do not concentrate on the most catastrophic event in modern Jewish history.[1] For Russian Jewish authors the problem of constructing a Jewish self-consciousness at Europe's periphery involves articulating and locating their own cultural position in the space between Jewish tradition and dominant Russian culture.[2] The negotiation of this de-centric positioning primarily entails a distancing from the highly centralized structure of Soviet and Russian culture.[3]

The most recent generation of Russian Jewish authors was, for the most part, born in non-Russian parts of the former Soviet Union, whereas most contemporary Russian (non-Jewish) authors come from the Russian areas. The var-

ied cultural contexts of their upbringing and education led to a considerable degree of artistic (i.e., thematic, linguistic, and stylistic) diversity, compounded by
the fact that almost no Russian Jewish author now lives and works where he or
she was born. As a result, de-centricity resists the general centralization of Russian culture. From czardom through socialism, a strong emphasis on centralization eliminated a great deal of regional—in many cases non-Russian—cultural
productivity. Destroying farming communities as well as the aristocracy and the
bourgeoisie, the Soviet regime substantiated the centrism of party and government by radically reducing the social structure until only two discernable parts
remained, namely, the governing and the governed. In doing so the Communist
Party ruined the regional cultures of peoples of non-Slavic origin, the rich oral
Russian tradition, Russian and Ukrainian peasant cultures, and the distinct cultures of the prerevolutionary Russian aristocracy and bourgeoisie. Due to a lack
of a genuine proletarian culture in Russia at the time of the Russian Revolution,
Lenin and Stalin extended the Russian petit bourgeois culture across society, en-
riched by pseudofolkloric traditions. The victims of cultural centralization included traditional Hasidism as well as the open-minded culture of Jewish intellectuals.[4] Many Jews expected that their situation under German occupation
would be better than it had been under the Soviet government. That expecta-
tion, however, proved to be tragically wrong. Between 1941 and 1944 the remnants of Jewish culture tolerated by Communist authorities were destroyed by
the German occupying forces.

Anti-Semitism is still alive in Russia,[5] which makes it a precarious endeavor to speak about Russian Jewish literature—a term canonized by Vasilii
L'vov-Rogachevskii in 1922. Any attempt to classify individual Russian authors, texts, or ways of reading as part of "Russian Jewish literature" needs to
acknowledge the false dichotomy put forth by Russian anti-Semitic national-
ists, who have been dividing Russian literature into two opposed domains.
There is "Russian literature" (*russkaia literatura*), which they imagine to be
written by so-called autochthons, or "true" Russians; and there is a "literature
in the Russian language" (*russkojazychnaia literatura*), which is supposedly written primarily by Jews.[6] To be sure, this anti-Semitic strategy has a long history. In response to it, Marina Tsvetaeva penned the celebrated lines: "In this
utmost Christian-orthodox world / The poets are Yids" (1984, 389).

Russian Jews still face difficulties in obtaining positions in government or
private institutions in present-day Russia. The origins of Russian state-sponsored
anti-Semitism can be traced back to the nineteenth century when pogroms[7] in
the southern and western parts of Russia resulted in an exodus of approximately
1.2 million Jews, mostly to the United States. Anti-Semitism became a part of
official Russian politics and policies and was only halted after the Russian Revolution for less than two decades, during which Jews were granted the same rights

as Russians living in the Soviet Union. (A number of Russians even changed their Slavic-sounding names to make them sound more Jewish.) Concealed beneath Stalin's terror campaign (1936–38) was a strong current of anti-Semitism. This may have been motivated by the fact that Trotsky—Stalin's competitor and, later, his most powerful critic—was a Jew. Russian anti-Semitism, which for pragmatic reasons was weakened during World War II, was strengthened and became government policy in 1949 under the banner of "Anti-Cosmopolitanism." Jews were considered to be cosmopolites, that is, not patriots. As a result, Stalin began to concentrate all the Jews of the Soviet Union in an area outside Europe, in the easternmost part of Siberia, called the Evreiskaja avtonomnaia oblast, or Jewish autonomous region. Since then many Russian Jews have tried to become "real" Russians by adopting Russian habits and traditions, changing their names to more Russian-sounding ones, and by marrying non-Jewish Russians. As a result of discrimination and the promise of a new homeland, many Russian Jews left the Soviet Union in the last three decades of the twentieth century. Most immigrated to Israel, while smaller numbers settled in New York, Berlin, Paris, and London. The mostly well-educated Russian-speaking community in Israel (numbering 1.5 million) and the small colonies of Russian immigrants—including Russian Jews—in the United States and central and western Europe have provided a growing audience for Jewish writers of Russian literature outside Russia.[8] In *Vera Ilyinichna* (2002), the well-known prose writer Grigory Kanovich (born in 1929 in Kaunas) tells the story of an immigrant family which feels just as foreign in Israel as it did in the Soviet Union. However, Felix Roziner (born in 1936; left Moscow for Jerusalem in 1978) shows in his family saga *Serebriania tsepochka* (The Silver Chain, 1983) how dependent Russian Jews were on Palestine/Israel (Nakhimovsky 1992, 193).

Jewish writers who have decided to remain in Russia still face censorship (Bljum 1995). Several Russian newspapers, periodicals, and publishers (*Molodaia gvardiia, Nash Sovremennik,* and *Sovetskaia Rossiia,* or the publishers Sovremennik and Sovetskaia Rossiia) continue to refuse to publish works by Jewish writers.[9] Other presses, like BSG-Press,[10] publish texts by Jewish writers without any restrictions.

Public discussion concerning the status of Jewish life and culture in Russia continues to be highly contentious, as evidenced by the debate surrounding Aleksandr Solzhenitsyn's articulation of his position in 2001. This Nobel Prize winner had summarized the cultural experience of Russians and Jews in a monograph entitled *Dvesti let vmeste, 1795–1995* (Two Hundred Years Together, 2001).[11] For instance, he argued that in the songs of the Jewish poet and singer Alexander Galich (1919–1977) the Jews were always the good guys and the Russians always the bad guys. The well-known writer Vladimir Voinovich (who never hid his Serbian and Jewish origin) responded to this claim in his *Portret na fone mifa* (A Portrayal of the Background of a Myth, 2002) by criticizing Solzhenitsyn's effort as itself anti-Semitic. He was joined by the Russian Jewish critic L. Kacis, who also recognized traces of a latent anti-Semitism in Solzhenitsyn's book (Kacis 2001).

Instead of attempting to define or differentiate Russian Jewish authors, texts, and modes of reception from non–Russian Jewish literature at large, we prefer to concentrate on the impact Russian Jewish writers have had on recent Russian culture and to discuss their work as a part of Jewish literature within the larger context of European literature. One should stress that Russian Jewish culture constitutes a unique sphere of Russian culture since it obviously relates to Jewish tradition in general and, more specifically, to the Russian Jewish tradition. To this end, we have included in our discussions Jewish authors who, although working in the Russian Jewish tradition and writing in Russian, have chosen to reside outside Russia.

Prose

THE GROWING VIEW FROM THE OUTSIDE: GRIGORII SVIRSKII

Both the "Great Purge" of 1936–38 and World War II provide essential starting points for any discussion of Russian Jewish literature since these events greatly influenced the future development of Russians, Russian Jews, and their interrelationships. Despite differing regional allegiances, the careers of poet Osip Mandelstam (Saint Petersburg) and prose writer Isaak Babel (Odessa) were both deeply integrated into Russian literature as a whole.[12] The novelist Anatolii N. Rybakov (1911–1998) alternated between a Russian and Jewish point of view, which was most clearly articulated in his novel *Tiazhelyi pesok* (Heavy Sand, 1979), which relates the story of a Jewish family in the Ukraine from 1910 until the end of World War II.[13] His peer Boris Slutskii (1919–1986) wrote the war poem "I Spoke in the Name of Russia" as well as a poetic condemnation of anti-Semitism entitled "On the Jews . . ." (which was only published in the Soviet Union in 1988). Because of the growing chauvinism of Soviet-Russian cultural politics, the Russian Jewish novelist Grigorii Svirskii (who was born in 1921) became increasingly estranged from socialist realism as well as the project of "Soviet-Russian culture." Between 1965 and 1968 he dared to criticize Soviet censorship and the official anti-Semitism of the Communist Party. After emigrating from the Soviet Union in the seventies, he published *Zalozhniki* (Hostages: The Personal Testimony of a Soviet Jew, 1974) and *Poljarnaia tragediia* (Three Stories from the Arctic Tragedy, 1976), which were soon translated into several languages. Exposing the disastrous effect of socialist realism, his *Na lobnom meste: Literatura nravst-vennogo soprotivleniia* (History of Postwar Soviet Writing: The Literature of the

Moral Opposition, 1979) served as a kind of anti-history that contrasted with the official Soviet line. While still residing in the Soviet Union, he published the no-vella *Zapoved' druzhby* (The Commandment of Friendship, 1947) plus the novels *Zdravstvui, universitet* (Hello, University, 1952) and *Leninskii prospekt* (Lenin Ave-nue, 1962), only to see his books forbidden and removed from bookshops and li-braries across the Soviet Union following his protests against Soviet dictatorship in the late sixties.

His best-known book, *Proryv* (The Push, 1983), is a montage of fact and fiction, involving historical personages as well as fictional characters. The bib-lical quotation "Neither shalt thou stand idly by the blood of thy neighbor" (Lev. 19:16) serves as the epigraph for a book whose plot opens with the death sentence of the writer Zinovy (Isaak) Romanovich Svirsky, an uncle of the au-thor. The work recounts the story of unjustly sentenced Jews who, as a result of Nikita Khrushchev's famous 1956 speech, returned to their families after having been "rehabilitated" in the Gulag (along with non-Jewish Russians). Svirskii addresses the stark differences in the way non-Jewish Russians and their Jewish compatriots were welcomed home, as well as the moral dilemma faced only by the "rehabilitated" Jewish people: either to remain victims who nevertheless conform to the Soviet system or to engage in a futile struggle for the opportunity to immigrate to Israel. The novel encompasses the entire drama of the sixties and seventies, which for many Jews resulted in emigration from the Soviet Union. Familiarizing readers with the difficulties Russian im-migrants encountered in Golda Meir's Israel (as well as in the European and American Diaspora), the book provides a kind of prehistory of all the Russian Jewish narratives that would later emerge in non-Russian-speaking countries.

THE METAPHYSICAL ETHICS OF FRIDRICH GORENSHTEIN

One of the most successful Russian Jewish writers outside Russia and Israel was Fridrich Gorenshtein (1932–2001), who immigrated to Germany in 1980, where he died. His father was murdered in 1935 by Stalin's state-sponsored terrorists, while his mother went into hiding in order to avoid persecution. Gorenshtein grew up first with relatives and then entered the dreadful world of Ukrainian children's homes. He was only able to publish the novella *Dom s bashenkoi* (The House with the Small Tower)—an account of his own experi-ence of Stalinism—in 1964 in the Soviet Union. Afterward he had to work as a ghost writer. In 1979 his second book, *Iskuplenie* (Redemption), which he had written in 1967, was first published in Israel (in *Vremia i my*) and only appeared in Russia in 1990. The book recounts the story of a sixteen-year-old boy living in extreme poverty in the Soviet Union following World War II. It articulates with brutal frankness the need for atonement and the striving for an ethical

conception of human behavior. This extreme yet honest depiction was met
with sharp criticism. (The publication of the Russian original was preceded by
a German-language edition.) His novel *Psalom* (The Psalm) was completed in
1975 and did not appear in Russia until 1991–92 (following its publication in
the West in 1984). Although Gorenshtein is again intrigued by the transformation of the ethical desire for revenge into the aesthetic principle of revelation, the tone is now less blunt. His expulsion from Soviet culture enabled Gorenshtein to consider Soviet society from the outside while still remaining
within the literary tradition of Dostoevsky and Kafka in analyzing the dark
side of humanity. The Russian critic I. V. Kondakov has even gone so far as to
conclude: "The work of Gorenshtein is the elevated creative revenge for a whole
epoch, for the totalitarian system, for the Soviet way of life, for the dense Russian anti-Semitism, for worldwide conformism, which betrayed everything
sublime and holy, and for the spiritual degradation of mankind, which happened in the twentieth century through the common efforts of the Philistines
of all nations and estates" (2000, 199).[14]

In his most expansive novel, *Mesto* (The Square, 1972), Gorenshtein utilizes
psychoanalysis in presenting the case of Gosha Cvibyshev, who suffers from an
inferiority complex and tries to analyze his behavior in terms of the ethical ambiguity between good and evil. His conclusion that there is no simple opposition
between good and bad people, between white knights and criminals, is a rejec-
tion of the totalitarian scheme of ethics, as well as the simple dual model of perpetrators and victims in post-totalitarian analyses. As the writer and critic Boris
Hazanov has shown, Gorenshtein simultaneously adopts both a Russocentric
view and one from the outside looking in—a narrative stance we have termed
"de-centered." I. V. Kondakov sees Gorenshtein in the dual position of "at the
same time belonging to Russia and being deeply estranged from it" (2000, 200),
as is Dan-Antichrist, the central character in *The Psalm*. Alluding to the opposition between the Hebrew Bible and the Christian New Testament, Dan-Antichrist is sent to earth by God in order to carry out the Lord's curse against mankind: to devastate the earth's human population through hunger and war,
adultery, all sorts of diseases, and paradoxically to save the world from complete
extermination by employing the very same plagues.

In the ensuing years Gorenshtein published works totaling more than three
thousand pages. In most of his prose he records the fate of Soviet Jews as the victims of Russian anti-Semitism. Gorenshtein continues to remain almost unknown in his native Russia, this despite the publication of three volumes of his
collected prose in Russia in the nineties. The title of his last book, *Shampanskoe s
zhelch'iu* (Champagne with Gall, 1998 [written in 1990]), points up his dishar-
monious relationship to Russian culture and to his new homeland. According to
Kondakov, Gorenshtein, who considers Germany "a country with a crippled

psyche" that exists "in a spiritual blind alley," situates himself "in the triangle of Russia, Germany and Judaism" (2000, 200). In his view, focusing on Germany and the country's struggle to assume responsibility for the Holocaust is an exemplary step toward understanding mankind in general. Interestingly, aside from Anatolii Rybakov, Vasily Grossman, and Alexander Galich, Gorenshtein is among the few Russian Jewish authors to discuss the Holocaust. Given this thematic choice, he positions his own writing in a de-centric relationship to the rest of Russian Jewish writing.

ALEXANDR MELIKHOV'S INTERMEDIATE POINT OF VIEW

The phenomenon of the Russian Jew is a recurring theme in the novels of Alexandr (Mejlahs) Melikhov (born in 1947), including *Izgnanie iz Edema* (Expulsion from Eden, 1994), *Ispoved' evreia* (The Confession of a Jew, 1994), and *Roman s prostatitom* (Novel with Prostatitis, 1997).

None of Melikhov's novels develops a traditional plot. Taken together, they constitute a chronicle of the experiences of a typical Soviet "intellectual" during the second half of the twentieth century. The central character in these novels is the so-called *polukrovka* (half-blood, i.e., half-Jew and half-Russian). The de-centric dynamics of the text is physiologically encoded in the protagonist's body, thus matching racist stereotypes. In *The Confession of a Jew* the hero bears the Jewish-sounding name Leva Kacenelenbogen (cat's elbow), whereas in the succeeding novels he is more closely modeled on the author himself: a young mathematician who lives and works in Saint Petersburg and eventually becomes a writer. Like the author, the protagonist has a Jewish father and a Russian mother. His life and his conscience are always straddling a problematic borderline: "To be a Jew is not a nationality but a social role. The role of a stranger" (14). Describing his childhood in Kazakhstan—where his father had been deported along with his family—Melikhov creates an ironic image of the Soviet paradise: "Eden, that is a world where all the people are on their own, and the strangers do not pretend to have equal rights in taste and opinion" (34). Survival for a Jew, then, means conforming to the common opinion and becoming a Soviet man. Assuming a position that is meant to decenter him historically from modern Russia, Melikhov states: "My homeland is not Russia but the Soviet Union, that is, Soviet Russia, the typical picture of my childhood, from which my heart is shrinking, and for a long time sweet tears have not come to my eyes" (240).

Melikhov's generation seems to operate according to the formula "Russian plus Jewish equals Soviet." Melikhov suggests that there are two general yet complementary Jewish characteristics. The first he calls *evrejskaja splochennost* (Jewish cohesion), a quality that saves a person from disintegration. Paradoxically counterbalancing this psychologically defined feature is the second, *evreiskaja otverzhennost'* (Jewish outcastness), which pushes the Jew toward sociological disintegration. It is the latter, Melikhov claims, which motivates Jews to be active and creative. Considered together, both features also account for the de-centric movement of the literature involved: just as the Jewish affiliation differentiates Jews from Russians, so the Jewish protagonist becomes identified as the "outcast."

In criticizing both Russians and Jews, Melikhov looks at human nature and history from a daring perspective. The protagonist of his first novel gains a wider view of life in the world by visiting western Europe and Israel. Comparing life there with that in Russia, he develops the idea of a "normal life" that Russia and its people (including non-Jewish Russians, Jews, and others) should be striving for. However, no matter how much one may sympathize with such a plea to Russians to behave "normally," the construction of such a problematic notion of normality inevitably tends once again to isolate the Jews from Russia's other citizens.

THE ETHNIC STANCE OF DINA RUBINA

Dina Rubina (born in 1953) is the most famous female Russian writer in Israel; her point of view has been increasingly shaped by her geographical and cultural position outside of Russia. (She was born in Tashkent, Uzbekistan.) The majority of her readers live in Israel, the United States, France, England, and Germany, and her prose has been translated into more than thirty languages. She started to write and publish her works in the Soviet Union in 1973, but in 1990 she immigrated to Israel, where she continues to write in Russian. Following perestroika, she was allowed to visit Russia and to publish her works there. Presently employed by the Jewish Cultural Agency in Moscow, she exemplifies the close connection between Russian Jewish culture in Russia and in Israel.

While the protagonist of Melikhov's novel *Ljubov' k otecheskim grobam* (Love with Fatherly Graves, 2001) had painted a highly critical portrait of Russian Jews settling in Israel, Rubina displays neither disappointment over life in her new homeland nor nostalgia for Russia. On the contrary, she proudly embraces her "historical homeland" and the knowledge of ancient Judaic traditions and the Bible that she has gained while living there. In the essay "A ne zdes' vy ne mozhete ne chodit" (And It Is Not Here That You Cannot Do Anything but Walk), she describes her meeting with a former compatriot who does not even understand the Jewish calendar, which she has to explain to him: "This means, I said courteously, that we remember ourselves for five thousand seven hundred and fifty three years, whereas you [remember] yourself only for one thousand nine hundred and ninety three years . . . And this is not you [i.e., the Russians] but Europe, and again not without our participation" (2001, 408). What is articulated here is an affiliation with European culture that appears to be stronger than that of the average ethnic Russian. Moreover, in Rubina's view Christianity was not founded "bez nashego uchastiia" (without our participation), that is, without a profound contribution by the Jews. This notion shows how much Russian Jews still feel obliged to demonstrate the value of their own culture to their non-Jewish compatriots.

Rubina utilizes both realistic detail and striking irony to describe the life led by Russian Jews in Israel. In her novel *Vot idet Messia* (*Here Comes the Messiah!* 1996) Rubina features Jewish characters who, like Zjama, work for the Russian media. This professional group forms a model of Russia rife with contradictions and engaged in perpetual discussions within the intelligentsia. Here we find the grotesque character Ron Katz, an erudite Jew who knows thirty-two languages and whose articles have "now an anti-Semitic, now a Russophobic character" (2000, 41).

The epigraph to the novel is a quotation from one of Maimonides' *Thirteen Principles of Faith*: "I believe with perfect faith in the coming of the Messiah, and, though he tarry, I will wait daily for his coming" (2000, 3). However, the arrival of the Messiah is announced by an ugly, mad vagabond who travels from Tel Aviv to Jerusalem as a fare dodger, causes trouble, and begs for money. The novel's title and epigraph evoke the deep pessimism characteristic of the book as a whole, in which the idea of suicide is featured prominently. A hiatus sets the Russian-born immigrants apart from their new compatriots, whom they perceive as "aborigines," uneducated "Levantines," or thoughtless exploiters. Their contempt for the Palestinians is even deeper, as is revealed by an act of spontaneous collective revenge by Israeli settlers when a Jew is hurt by a Palestinian.

Nevertheless, Rubina remains within the tradition of optimistic Jewish humor of Sholem Aleichem and the Soviet satirists Ilya Ilf and Evgeny Petrov, exemplified by *Dvenadcat' stul'ev* (Twelve Chairs) and *Zolotoj telenok* (The Little Golden Calf). Despite its many comic episodes and characters, the novel ends tragically when a young Israeli soldier tries to save Zjama from a female Arab terrorist, who is about to stab her to death with a knife, but accidentally kills her. This soldier appears to be the son of "znamenitoi pisatel'nicy N." (the famous female writer N.), who is observing the incident and is obviously functions as the alter ego of the female author.

Rubina's narratives cast Israel as an experimental space: "The genre in which the life of this country and its people unfolds is absolutely congruent with the genre in which I write" (2001, 401). This symbolic identification of literature and life attests to the aesthetic heterogeneity and tragicomic character of the narrative, and seems to reconcile the narrator with her de-centric stance.

NATIONAL AND CULTURAL SELF-IDENTIFICATION
IN SERGEI KALEDIN'S PROSE

The texts of Sergei Kaledin (born in 1949) present yet another type of national and cultural self-identification. Kaledin sees himself as a mainstream Russian writer working in the classic tradition of Russian literature. His novel *Smiren-*

noe kladbishche (The Humble Cemetery, 1987 [available 1991]), which describes the ordinary life of a cemetery in Moscow, derives its title from a line in Pushkin's verse novel *Yevgeny Onegin*. Interestingly, it also refers to an early poem of the Russian Jewish poet Joseph Brodsky about the Jewish graveyard of Leningrad (1992, 21). This double reference indicates that Kaledin is indebted both to the canon of Russian literature and to Russian Jewish writing.

Kaledin's novel *Tachana Merkazit* (1994) has an experimental plot. A simple Russian fellow named Petr Ivanovich Vasin travels to Israel in order to visit his nephew. Here everything seems strange to this typical hero of Russian "Derevenskaia proza" (country prose). He gradually realizes that most of the prejudices he had entertained prior to leaving for Israel do not correspond to reality. Petr Ivanovich has something in common with Ivan Denisovich, the hero of Solzhenitsyn's famous story, as well as with heroes of the Russian writers Vassily Belov and Victor Astafiev. At the end of the novel he and his nephew perishe in the *Beit,* victims of a bomb explosion set off by a young female Arab terrorist who vanishes without a trace.

Subsequently Kaledin reveals to the reader that his neighbor (his real name is Vladimir Ivanovich Verkula) is still alive and never traveled to Israel (although Kaledin himself had visited his son in Israel). The narrative is thus based on the projection of the writer's own experiences onto his fictional hero, who finds his prototype in Russia. The plot is invented in order to "demythologize the silly idea of a quasi-inborn Russian anti-Semitism" and to express the "feeling of mankind as a common body" (1994, 9). This de-centric projection is set against the construction of a mythical common body representing mankind which consequently functions as an almost religious attempt to limit the centrifugal power of differentiation.

STYLISTIC AND VERBAL EX-CENTRICITY IN THE PROSE OF ASAR EPPEL

The prose writer Asar Eppel (born in 1935) is primarily concerned with the problems faced by young people living in the forties and fifties in a Moscow suburb. Babel's Odessa stories and the Hebrew Bible both provide models for narratives conceived and told in the Jewish tradition. Eppel relates the stories of his lower-class protagonists in a tone reminiscent of the style of the Hebrew Bible. In his novel *Shampin'on moei zhizni* (The Mushroom of My Life, 2001) he demonstrates that pleasure is indeed derived from base sources.[15] In highly self-referential manner, the narrative, ironically labeled a "riskovannoi knizhkoi" (a risky little book), defines itself as a "champignon de ma vie" (123).[16]

The story "Na trave dvora" (The Grassy Street, 1996) features an encounter between a Russian army pilot from Moscow and a Jewish American pilot who, coming from the Bronx in New York City, speaks Russian mixed with

English words and flavored with a Jewish accent. Decentralization, here used in Bakhtin's sense of the term, is reflected in the variety of Russian spoken by representatives of two enemy countries.

SOCIAL DE-CENTERING IN THE PROSE OF LJUDMILA ULITSKAYA

In the work of Ljudmila Ulitskaya (born in 1943, during her mother's evacuation to the Urals), de-centric settings provide details that prove important for the narrative, in which mentally deficient figures or poor old women often assume major roles. The ethical questions raised in Ulitskaya's texts are often played out against settings that, neither explicitly Christian nor Jewish, are always depicted as religious and loving. When Ulitskaya writes about her Jewish childhood, she alludes to the repression of Jews (in the course of the so-called Cosmopolitanism campaign and the persecution of Jewish doctors) in Russia. In the story "March 1953" she subtly frames the experience of a young Jewish girl during the Stalin era, who has been singled out for her ethnic background, as a Purim story of female Jewish resistance. Although the parents of the heroine of Ulitskaya's famous story "Sonechka" (1992) come from a "little Jewish shtetl in Belorussia," their offspring eventually live in Israel, Paris, or New York (working at the United Nations). Not unlike the paintings of Sonechka's husband, these Russian-born Jews will be "dispersed all over the world" (71).

The quotidian life of Russian Jews, played out against Russia's political turmoil as well as the world at large, are Ulitskaya's main themes. Her novel *Veselye pochorony* (translated into English as *Funeral Party,* 1998) depicts the lot of a handful of immigrants to the United States who, critical of the so-called American way of life, prefer to remain outsiders. Few of Ulitskaya's protagonists are religious, and only a handful are Orthodox Jews. Most of them are atheists or Eastern Orthodox Christians. In *The Funeral Party* there is a comic scene where members of different religions call their spiritual leaders (including a rabbi) to join a dying painter, who himself was an atheist all his life.

Ulitskaya often favors contexts drawn from non-Jewish Russian culture. In the story "Narod izbrannyi" (The Chosen People, 1995), which was written in the 1980s, she transfers this epithet traditionally reserved for the Jewish people to the poor and disabled members of the Russian populace at large. The young hero Katja tells the disabled, sick, and destitute orphan Zinaida that they are indeed chosen people since they have been created by God so that other people can appreciate how well life has treated them. The predicament of the Jewish people has been stripped of its particularity and applied to the fate of the outcast in general.

IRONIC, HYPERBOLIC ANTI-SEMITISM
IN THE WORKS OF DMITRY BYKOV

Ulitskaya's statement "I am a Jew and a Russian writer" pertains to many Russian Jewish authors. For a writer like Dmitry Bykov (born in 1967) such a claim would need to be modified drastically. Bykov is known as a poet, prose writer, critic, political journalist, and contributor to television programs. His novel *Opravdanie* (The Justification, 2000) revisits the years of Stalin's terror, while *Orfografiia* (Orthography, 2003) describes the period following the Russian Revolutions. Both novels feature a large number of Jews, who are acknowledged by the author as a "razrushitel'nuiu silu" (destroying power) in Russia's history. It is worth mentioning that Bykov is considered *polukrovkaí* (half-blood) in Russia since only his father was Jewish. In his essayistic prose Bykov often talks with great sympathy about the nineteenth-century philosopher Vasilii Rozanov, who in his later work became an ardent anti-Semite.

DE-CENTERING THE NARRATIVE HORIZON
IN EFRAIM SEVELA'S WORKS

Efraim Sevela (born in 1928) is a major film director and a prolific author of satirical novels. Together with twenty-three other Russian Jews, in 1971 he occupied the Supreme Soviet to demand the legalization of emigration for Soviet Jews. In his novel *Monia Tsatskes* (The Standard-Bearer, 2001a) he depicts the problematic position of Jewish soldiers serving in the Red Army during World War II. The novel *Pochemu net raja na zemlje* (The Hunt for the Tongue, 1981) recounts the tale of two Russian Jewish soldiers who, at odds with their superior officer, need to find a way to avoid being retaliated against. With the help of a Lithuanian Jew who survived the German persecution of Jews by pretending to be a German, they capture a German officer who knows about upcoming German attacks. In a Schwejk-like manner, they try to barter this knowledge for better treatment by their superior, whom they had put on the spot with their frankness. The story is told both from the point of view of the Lithuanian Jew as well as of the Russian Jews, a device not commonly encountered in Russian war prose.

Sevela's adolescent novel *Why There Is No Heaven on Earth* (1982), which was never published in Russian, presents the account of a Russian Jew who remembers a friendship torn apart by the Nazi invasion in Russia. The novel opens with a brief history of recent Jewish life in Russia:

> After the Revolution the Jews in Russia were in fashion and no one was ashamed of having a Jewish name. The word *Jew* had almost the same ring as *revolutionary*. Because practically all the Jews were on the side of the Revolution in the Civil War and many gave their lives for the workers' and peasants' government.

I was born much later. . . . But when the government of the workers and peasants had taken firm hold in Russia, interest in the Jews waned, people began to
be ashamed of having Jewish names, and on orders from the leader of the Soviet
Union, Joseph Stalin, Jews began to be abused even worse than they had been
by the Tsarist anti-Semites before the Revolution. (5)

Poetry

The impact of Jewish poets on Russian literature of the twentieth century is
considerable. Besides Boris Pasternak (1890–1960), who never emphasized his
Jewish ancestry, Ilya Selvinskii (1899–1968) should be mentioned. According
to Efim Etkind, early in his career he incorporated references to Jewish diction
and intonation in his poetry.[17] Nikolai Gumilyov and Anna Akhmatova, along
with Osip Mandelshtam, developed the art of Russian acmeism.[18] The last
Russian poet who belongs to this tradition is Joseph Brodsky.

THE NEO-AVANT-GARDISM OF JOSEPH BRODSKY

The de-centric dynamics of Russian Jewish poetry concerns its relationship to
the traditions of form and language and to the position of the lyrical voice. Joseph Brodsky (Iosif Brodskii), who has greatly influenced the development of
Russian poetry since the early eighties (he was awarded the Nobel Prize in
1988), places his own work within the wake of Russian acmeists. Established
around 1912, this group of authors strove to write less abstractly than the Russian symbolists and avoided the utopian concepts and images found in the poetry of the Russian futurists (e.g., Vladimir Mayakovsky); the latter tradition
was subsequently followed by Soviet poets like Yevgeny Yevtushenko and Andrei Voznesenskii. Though Brodsky did not emphasize any Jewish elements in
his poetry—*Evreiskoe kladbishche okolo Leningrada* (The Jewish Graveyard Near
Leningrad, 1958) is a famous exception—his work is often discussed (most
forcefully by Russian nationalist writers) within an explicitly Jewish context.
Brodsky's decision to write in English rather than in Russian (mostly in his essays) is often seen as a symptom of his Jewish cultural background and can be
read as a rebuff to the old stereotype of Russian as a superior language.

It is remarkable that a man of letters like critic Vladimir Solovyov (born
in 1942), who lives in the United States, emphasized Brodsky's ethnicity in his
book *Tri evreia* (Three Jews, 1993). The book's cover contains photographs of
Brodsky, Aleksandr Kushner, and Solovyov himself. Although he is a writer of
minor literary standing in Russia or the United States, Solovyov's book documents a general interest in the discussion of Jewish identity as an important
feature of contemporary Russian-language poetry.

THE POETRY OF BORIS KUSHNER

At least three of the Jewish poets who, in the late fifties and sixties, belonged to the circle of Anna Akhmatova conceived of themselves as "Russian poets": Alexandr Kushner (born in 1936), Yevgeny Rein (born in 1935), and Anatoly Naiman (born in 1936). Eschewing the epithets "Soviet" and "Jewish," they initially saw themselves working within the tradition of "great poetry." Interestingly, all three poets placed themselves within the Christian culture. The most Orthodox was Naiman; the least religious was the "aesthete" Kushner. Their estrangement from Judaism was typical of poets at this time; they were in the company of Semyon Lipkin (1911–2003), Inna Lisnyanskaya (born in 1929), Naum Korzhavin (born in 1925), Jury Kublanovsky (born in 1947), and Tatyana Bek (1949–2005). Russian poets of Jewish descent thus played an important role in the reorientation that took place from the sixties through the eighties. This period was marked by a turning away from "Soviet" aesthetics toward the so-called Silver Age of symbolism and acmeism, both of which rejected Soviet atheism in favor of Christian ethics as part of a religious renaissance.

Among contemporary poets, Boris Kushner (born in 1941; no relation to Aleksandr Kushner), who lives in the United States, stands out in terms of his ties to the Jewish religion. A professor of mathematics, he is an observant Jew who published several volumes of poetry in the nineties. When asked how he identified himself ethnically and/or nationally, he replied: "You called me a Russian poet. I am not sure whether I am a poet . . . but 'Russian' I cannot call myself at all. I use the Russian language since it is the only one which, by the chance of my birth, is at my disposal. . . . However, I feel the contact to my people spiritually and with great strength: I am a Jew—everywhere, always, every moment" (Shalit 2002, 51). Kushner's poem "Vykrestu" ("To the Baptized") is addressed specifically to the Jews who converted to Christianity:

> By all his life repudiating the Fathers,
> Forgetting mother at the ringing of the birches' ecstasy,
> He did not start to weep, and at the end of ends,
> As Peter wept, having betrayed just three times. (2000, 181)

The poet loves his former homeland—Russia—and is willing to pray for it; he will pray, however, to the "Jewish God." The de-centric structure of the text becomes manifest in the distance between the "you" and the apostrophe of God:

> Russia—
> Scorched from memory.—
> Although I blew out the candle,—
> I ask you,

God of Israel,
May Russia survive. (43)

THE MEMOIR LITERATURE OF SEMEN LIPKIN

One of the most prominent memoir writers to speak to Jewish and Russian
Jewish matters is the dissident Semen Izrailevich Lipkin. In *Zapiski zhil'ca*
(Notes of a Tenant, 1991) and *Dekada* (Decade, 1999 [written in 1981]), he
traces the spiritual and religious transformation of a character modeled on
himself. His attitude toward Judaism is also articulated in his biography
Zhizn' i sud'ba Vasiliia Grossmana (Stalingrad of Vasily Grossman, 1986). As a
de-centered observer of Russian culture and Soviet politics, Lipkin is sensitive
to the colonial attitude of Russians toward non-Russians living in the former
Soviet Union and in Russia, as well as to understanding the origin of the slave
mentality displayed by the suppressed. Lipkin is critical of the idea of nationality based on the principle of blood and instead champions a community
founded on a shared culture. Coming from Odessa, he partakes of the aloof attitude of the narrator in Babel's stories, which is reflected in his poem "Tech-
nik-intendant" (The Technical Quartermaster, 1963). His well-known poem
"Moisei" (Moses, 1967), while traditional in form, is provocative in its content,
with the poet identifying the fire of the gas flames in the concentration camps
with the apocalyptic view of the Mosaic God:

> On the concentration . . . path
> Along all German and Soviet
> And Polish and other ways
> Along all passions, along all deaths,
> I went. And terrible and spiritual
> God revealed himself to me
> As glowing flame of gas chambers
> In the bush, which cannot be scorched. (2003, 158–59)

This vision of God questions the possibility of ending the extermination of
human beings and yet represents a form of revelation, thus articulating Lipkin's tragic view on world history.

Critic Mikhail Krutikov has summarized his reading of contemporary Jewish writing in Russia as follows: "Current Russian fiction is not rich in distinctly
Jewish characters. Jewish 'markers' appear frequently in works of Mark Khari-
tonov, Sergei Gandlevsky, Anatoly Naiman, and other leading Russian writers of
Jewish or partly Jewish origin, but the Jewish theme is never more than a minor
one in their writing." In post-Soviet perceptions of Jewishness, Krutikov continues, "Jewishness has become a mere fact of life and no longer alerts the reader" the

way it used to in Soviet times (2003, 271–72). Jewishness nevertheless remains a powerful force with which contemporary Russian Jewish writers have been grappling in a variety of creative ways and which many readers have yet to appreciate.

NOTES

1. For a discussion of the Shoah in relation to the Soviet Union, see Gitelman 1998.

2. Shimon Markish considers Russian Jewish literature a kind of regional literature alongside Siberian-Russian literature or literature on the Don. See Markish 1996, 2005.

3. Markish (1996, 2005) convincingly relates the appearance and development of Jewish literature written in Russian "to the ideas of the Haskalah" and parallels it with the development of Jewish literature in German in Prussia and Austria. Among the common features shared by Russian Jewish, German Jewish, and American Jewish literature, he singles out: (1) free choice of national-cultural attribution, (2) rootedness in Jewish civilization, (3) social representativeness, and (4) a dual allegiance to Russian and European civilization (Markish 1994, 525–26). Markus Wolf, however, misses in this list of distinguishing characteristics "immanent features of the text" (1995, 283).

4. A good example of this culture is provided by the Saint Petersburg salon of Nikolai Maksimovich Minskii (1856–1937) and Liudmila Nikolaevna Vil'kina (1873–1920) during the first decade of the twentieth century.

5. See Igor' R. Shafarevich's pamphlet "Russophobia" in Gibian 1991, 6.

6. In other cases they distinguish between *rossijskaia literatura* and *russkaia literatura*. See Markish 1990.

7. The term "pogrom" is of Russian origin and originally meant "bloodshed."

8. In contrast to the period between World War II and perestroika and parallel to that between World Wars I and II (Markish 2005, 8), Russian Jewish literature has blossomed in central and western Europe during the last two decades.

9. Other journals have changed their attitude toward Jews. Thus, the monthly *Znamia* (The Banner) has not published any anti-Semitic works since the period of perestroika. The newspaper *Den'* (The Day) was forbidden to publish in El'cyn-times and was replaced by *Zavtra* (Tomorrow).

10. A Russian translation of Isaac Bashevis Singer's *Liublinskii shtukar'* (The Magician of Lublin) appeared in 2002 in the series *Inostranka* (The Foreign) of this publisher.

11. It is worth noting that the Soviet KGB fabricated rumors suggesting that Solzhenitsyn himself was Jewish; on this point see Rancour-Laferriere 1989. The second volume of Solzhenitsyn's book, covering the last decennia up to 1987, was published in Moscow in 2003.

12. Alice Stone-Nakhimovsky points to Isaak Babel as an example of a dual (Jewish and Russian) identity claimed by a number of Russian Jewish writers.

13. The novel was turned into a twelve-part TV miniseries.

14. This conclusion misses the important sociological and cultural differentiations by emphasizing the global dimension Gorenshtein attributes to his diagnosis.

15. This idea had already been put forward by Anna Akhmatova, in whose poem "Mne ni k chemu ordicheskie rati . . ." one reads: "Oh, if the reader only knew out of what dirt poetry is made!" (1990, 197).

16. "Shampin'on moei zhizni" is also the title of Eppel's second volume of stories.

17. Etkind (1985) has noticed a "poetical import" and, most of all, the introduction of intonation into Russian literature of the twenties through Jewish poetry.

18. Russian acmeism was a movement in Russian literature that began in the second decade of the twentieth century. Unlike symbolism, which stressed the abstract, ideal dimension of the poetic word, acmeism emphasized its concreteness.

WORKS CITED

Akhmatova, Anna. 1990. *Sochineniia v dvuch tomakh.* Moscow: Khudozhestvennaia literatura.

Bitov, Andrei. 1996. *Pushkinskii dom.* Vol. 2: *Imperiia v chetyrech izmereniiach.* Kharkov: Liter-
aturno-chudozhestvennoe izdatel'stvo.

Bljum, A. 1995. "Evreiskaia tema glazami sovetskogo cenzora. (Po sekretnym dokumentam
Glavlita epochi Bol'shogo terrora)." In *Evrei v Rossii: Istoriia i kul'tura.* Vol. 3: *Trudy po iu-
daike,* ed. D. A. El'iashevich, 186–96. St. Petersburg: Petersburgskii evreiskii universitet.

Branover, Herman, ed. 2000. *Rossiiskaia evreiskaia enciklopediia.* 3 vols. Moscow: Russian
Academy of Natural Sciences / Israel-Russian Encyclopedia Center EPOS.

Brodskii, Iosif. 1992. "Evreiskoe kladbishche okolo Leningrada." In *Sochineniia,* vol. 1, 21. St.
Petersburg: Molodaia gvardiia.

Bykov, Dmitrii. 2000. *Opravdanie.* Moscow: Vagrius.

———. 2003. *Orfografiia.* Moscow: Vagrius.

Dering-Smirnov, Ioanna R., and Igor' Smirnov. 1982. *Ocherki po istoricheskoi tipologii kul'tury . . .* →
realizm → postsimvolizm (avangard) → . . . (NRL-Almanach). Salzburg: Institut für Slawistik.

Dreizin, Felix. 1990. *The Russian Soul and the Jew: Essays in Literary Ethnocriticism.* Lanham,
Md.: University Press of America.

Eichenbaum, Boris. 1929. *Moi vremennik.* Leningrad: Izdatel'stvo pisatelei v Leningrade.

Eppel, Asar. 1996. "Na trave dvora." *Shampin'on moei zhizni.* Moscow: Gesharim.

———. 2001. *Shampin'on moei zhizni.* Moscow: Symposium.

Etkind, Efim. 1985. "O poeticheskom «importe» i, v chastnosti, o evreiskoi intonacii v russkoi poezii dvadcatyx godov." *Cahiers du monde russe et soviétique* 27: 193–218.

Friedberg, Maurice. 1978. "Jewish Themes in Soviet Russian Literature." In *The Jews in Soviet
Russia Since 1917,* 3rd ed., ed. Lionel Kochan, 197–217. London: Oxford University Press.

Garrard, John Gordon, and Carol Garrard. 1996. *The Bones of Berdichev: The Life and Fate of
Vasily Grossman.* New York: Simon and Schuster.

Geizer, Matvei. 2001. *Russko-evreiskaia literatura 20go veka.* Moscow: MGPPU.

Gershenzon, Michail. 1923. *Sud'by evreiskogo naroda.* St. Petersburg: Epocha.

Gibian, George. 1991. "The Quest for Russian National Identity in Soviet Culture Today." In
The Search for Self-Definition in Russian Literature, ed. Ewa M. Thompson, 1–21. Amsterdam: Benjamins.

Gitelman, Zvi. 2001. *A Century of Ambivalence: The Jews of Russia and the Soviet Union, 1881 to
the Present.* 2nd ed. Bloomington: Indiana University Press.

———, ed. 1998. *Bitter Legacy: Confronting the Holocaust in the U.S.S.R.* Bloomington: Indiana
University Press.

Gitelman, Zvi, Musya Glants, and Marshall I. Goldman, eds. 2003. *Jewish Life after the U.S.S.R.*
Bloomington: Indiana University Press.

Goes, Gudrun. 1998. "Fridrich Gorenshtejn: 'Psalom'—jüdische versus sowjetische Geschichte?" *Zeitschrift für Slawistik* 43 (2): 227–45.

Gorenshtein, Fridrich. 1964. *Dom s bashen'koi. Junost'* 10.

———. 1984. *Ulica krasnych zor'.* Moscow: Al'manach "Chistye prudy."

———. 1990. *Iskuplenie. Junost'* 11–12.

———. 1991–92. *Psalom. Oktiabr'* 10–12 (1991) and 1–2 (1992).

———. 1991–93. *Izbrannoe.* Moscow: Slovo.

———. 1998. *Shampanskoe s zhelch'iu. Aprel'* 2.

Grönke, Kadia. 2001. "Rollenmasken und Identifikation in der Musik Dmitrii Schostakowitschs." In *Dmitrij Schostakowitsch und das jüdische musikalische Erbe,* ed. Ernst Kuhn, Andreas Wehrmeyer, and Günter Wolter. Berlin: Kuhn.

Grübel, Rainer. 2000. "Ein literarischer Messias aus Odessa: Isaak Babels Kontrafakturen des Chassidismus und der odessitische Kontext jüdisch-russischer Kultur." In *Jüdische Autoren Ostmitteleuropas im 20. Jahrhundert,* ed. H.-H. Hahn and J. Stüben, 429–81. Frankfurt am Main: Peter Lang.

———. 2001. "Judenfreund—Judenfeind: Eine problematische ästhetische Imagologie mit aporetischem Sprung aus der Theorie in die Praxis." In *Materialien zu Pavel Florenskii,* ed. Michael Hagemeister and Torsten Metelka, 7–58. Berlin: KONTEXTverlag.

Ingold, Felix Philipp. 1981. *Dostoevskii und das Judentum.* Frankfurt: Insel-Verlag.

Ivanov, Viacheslav Vs. 1979. "Rozhdenie mastera: O proze Fridricha Gorenshteina." *Vremia i my,* 42.

Kacis, Leonid. 1997. ". . . Palestinskie otroki s krov'iu chernoi. . . ." *Novoe literaturnoe obozrenie* 28: 134–49.

———. 2001. "Evreiskaia enciklopediia—organ antisemitskoi mysli?" *Nezavisimaia gazeta: Ex libris* 25 (July 12).

Kagan, Judit. 1993. "O evreiskoi teme i bibleiskix motivax u Mariny Cvetaevoi." *De Visu* 3: 55–61.

Kaledin, Sergei. 1991. *Smirennoe kladbishche.* Moscow: Sovetskii pisatel'.

———. 1994. *Tachana Merkazit.* Moscow: Vagrius.

———. 2001. *Zapiski groboiskopatelia.* Moscow: Vagrius.

Kanovich, Grigory. 2002. "Vera Il'inichna. Povest'." *Ierusalimskii zhurnal* 13.

Karsavin, L. P. 1928. "Rossiia i evrei." *Versty* 3: 65–86.

Kolganova, Ada, ed. 1994. *Menora: Evreiskie motivy v russkoi poezii.* Moscow: Gesharim.

Kondakov, I. V. 2000. "Gorenshtein." In *Russkie pisateli 20 veka: Biograficheskii slovar',* ed. Galina Romanova, 199–201. Moscow: Bol'shaia Rossiiskaia enciklopediia.

Kosta, Peter, Holt Meyer, und Natascha Drubek-Meyer, eds. 1999. *Juden und Judentum in Literatur und Film des slavischen Sprachraums: Die geniale Epoche.* Jewish Studies, 5. Wiesbaden: Harrassowitz.

Krutikov, Mikhail. 2003. "Constructing Jewish Identity in Contemporary Russian Fiction." In *Jewish Life after the U.S.S.R.,* ed. Zvi Gitelman et al., 252–74. Bloomington: Indiana University Press.

Kushner, Boris. 2000. *Bessonnica solnca.* Baltimore, Md.: Via Press.

Lipkin, Semen. 1990a. *Dekada.* Moscow: Knizhnaia palata.

———. 1990b. *Zhizn' i sud'ba Vasiliia Grossmana.* Moscow: Kniga.

———. 2003. *Semen. Vol'a.* Moscow: OGI.

L'vov-Rogachevskii, Vasilii. 1922. *Russko-evreiskaia literatura.* Moscow: GIZ.

———. 1979. *A History of Russian-Jewish Literature.* Trans. A. Levin. Ann Arbor, Mich.: Ardis.

Markish, Simon. 1982. "O russko-evreiskoi literature (predvaritel'nye zamechaniia)." In *Festschrift für Fairy von Lilienfeld zum 65. Geburtstag,* ed. A Rexheuser and K.-H. Ruffmann, 317–37. Erlangen: Universität Erlangen-Nürnberg.

———. 1985. "À propos de l'histoire et de la méthodologie de l'étude de la littérature juive d'éxpression russe." *Cahiers du monde russe et soviétique* 26 (2): 139–52.

————. 1990. "O russkoiazychii i russkoiazychnyx." *Literaturnaia gazeta.* October 12: 2–3.

————. 1994. "Russko-evreiskaia literatura." In *Kratkaia evreiskaia enciklopediia 7,* ed. Itzhak (Nadel') Oren, Naftali Prat, and Ahituv Avner, 525–52. Jerusalem: Keter.

————. 1997. *Russko-evreiskaia literatura: Sbornik statei,* ed. G. S. Knabe. Moscow: RGGU.

————. 2005. "Russian Jewish Literature after the Second World War and before *Perestroika.*" www.ceu.hu/jewishstudies/pdf/01_markish (November 4).

Melikhov, Aleksandr. 1994. *Ispoved' evreia.* St. Petersburg: Novyi Gelikon.

————. 1997. *Roman s prostatitom.* St. Petersburg: Limbus.

————. 2001. "Liubov' k otecheskim grobam. Roman." *Novyi Mir* 9: 11–71; 10: 24–80.

Nakhimovsky, Alice Stone. 1992. *Russian-Jewish Literature and Identity: Jabotinsky, Babel, Grossman, Galich, Roziner, Markish.* Baltimore, Md.: Johns Hopkins University Press.

Nikolaev, P. A., ed. 2000. *Russkie pisateli 20 veka: Biograficheskii slovar'.* Moscow: Bolshaia Rossiiskaia enciklopediia.

Nolden, Thomas. 1995. *Junge jüdische Literatur: Konzentrisches Schreiben in der Gegenwart.* Würzburg: Könighausen und Neumann.

Prochanov, Aleksandr. 2001. "Duma vzmachnula toporom russofobii." *Zavtra* 21, 23, May (quoted in *Novyi mir* 9: 233).

————. 2002. *Gospodin Geksogen.* Moscow: Ad Marginem.

Rancour-Laferriere, Daniel. 1989. "Solzhenitsyn and the Jews: A Psychoanalytic View." In *Russian Literature and Psychoanalysis,* ed. Daniel Rancoeur-Laferriere, 143–73. Amsterdam: Benjamins.

Roziner, Felix. 1983. *Serebriania tsepochka.* Tel Aviv: Biblioteka Aliia.

Rubina, Dina. 1996. *Vot idet Messia!* Moscow: Izd-vo Ostozh'e.

————. 1999. "A ne zdes' vy ne mozhete ne chodit'." In *Vot idet Messiia!* Moscow: Izd, Dom "Pogkova".

————. 2000. *Here Comes the Messiah!* Trans. Daniel M. Jaffe. Brookline, Mass.: Zephyr.

Rybakov, Anatolii. 1979. *Tiazhelyi pesok.* Moscow: Sovetskii pisatel'.

Sevela, Efraim. 1981. *Pochemu net raja na zemlje.* Jerusalem: Stav.

————. 1982. *Why There Is No Heaven on Earth.* Trans. Richard Lourie. New York: Harper and Row.

————. 2001a. *Monia Tsatskes—znamenosec.* St. Petersburg: Kristall.

————. 2001b. "Zagadochnaia slavianskaia dusha." In his *Popugai, govoriashchii na idish,* 96–121. St. Petersburg: Kristall.

Shalit, Shulamit. 2002. "K tvoim kamniam, Sion (O Borise Kushnere, poete i cheloveke)." *Vestnik* 15.

Slonim, Marc. 1944. "Pisateli-evrei v sovetskoi literature." In *Evreiskii mir: Sbornik II.* New York: Suiuz russkix evreev v N'iu-Jorke.

Solovyov, Vladimir. 1993. "Tri evreia." *Taina Izrailia.* St. Petersburg: Sofiia.

Solzhenitsyn, Aleksandr. 2001. *Dvesti let vmeste, 1795–1995.* Vol. 1. Moscow: Russkij put'.

————. 2003. *Dvesti let vmeste, 1795–1995.* Vol. 2. Moscow: Russkij Put'.

Sluckii, Boris. 1988. "Pro evreev." In *Stichi raznyx let,* 121. Moscow: Sovetskii pisatel'.

Svirskii, Grigorii. 1947. *Zapoved' druzhby.* Leningrad: Voennoe izdatel'stvo.

————. 1952. *Zdravstvui, universitet. Oktiabr':* 1–2.

————. 1962. *Leninskii prospekt.* Moscow: Sovetskii pisatel'.

————. 1974. *Zalozhniki.* Paris: YMCA-Press.

————. 1976. *Poliarnaia tragediia.* Frankfurt am Main: Posev.

————. 1979. *Na lobnom meste: Literatura nravstvennogo soprotivleniia.* London: Overseas Publishers.

———. 1981. *A History of Post-War Soviet Writing: The Literature of Moral Opposition.* Ann Arbor, Mich.: Ardis.

———. 1983. *Proryv.* Ann Arbor, Mich.: Ermitazh.

Taina Izrailia: Evreiskii vopros v russkoi religioznoi mysli 19go—pervoi poloviny 20go veka (sostavitel': V. F. Boikov). 1993. St. Petersburg: Sofiia.

Tsvetaeva, Marina. 1980. "Evreiam." In *Stichotvoreniia i poemy v piati tomach,* vol. 1, 259. New York: Russica.

———. 1984. *Sochineniia v dvukh tomakh 1.* Moscow: Chudozhestvennaia literatura.

Ulitskaya, Ljudmila. 1992. "Sonechka." *Novyi Mir,* 7.

———. 1995. "The Chosen People." In *Lives in Transit: A Collection of Recent Women's Writing,* ed. Helena Goscilo, 84–92. Dana Point, Calif.: Ardis.

———. 1998. *Veselye pochorony.* Moscow: Vagrius.

———. 2005. *"Sonechka": A Novella and Stories.* Trans. Arch Trait. New York: Schocken.

Voinovich, Vladimir. 2002. *Portret na fone mifa.* Moscow: Eksmo.

Vysockii, Vladimir. 1999. *Sochineniia v dvuch tomach I.* Ekaterinburg: U-Faktoriia.

Wolf, Markus. 1995. "Sprache *Russisch*—Autor und Sujet *Jüdisch:* Über die Methodologie für eine 'russisch-jüdische Literatur.'" *Wiener Slawischer Almanach,* 275–90.

Yevtushenko, Evgenii. 1989. *Grazhdane, poslushaite menia: Stichotvoreniia i poemy.* Moscow: Chudozhestvennaia literatura.

Zolotonosov, Mikhail, and V. E. Kel'ner. 1993. "Skazanie o pogrome: Kishinev, 1903 g.: Povestvovanie o dokumentach." *Druzhba narodov* 5: 186–210.

TEXTS AVAILABLE IN ENGLISH

Brodsky, Joseph. 1995. *On Grief and Reason: Essays.* New York: Farrar, Straus and Giroux.

———. 1998. *To Urania.* New York: Farrar, Straus and Giroux.

———. 1999. *Discovery.* New York: Farrar, Straus and Giroux.

———. 2000. *Collected Poems in English.* New York: Farrar, Straus and Giroux.

———. 2001. *Nativity Poems.* Trans. Melissa Green et al. New York: Farrar, Straus and Giroux.

Eppel, Asar. 1998. *The Grassy Street.* Trans. Joanne Turnbull. Moscow: Glas.

Gorenshtein, Fridrich. 1991. *Traveling Companions.* San Diego, Calif.: Harcourt Brace Jovanovich.

Grossman, Vasilii S. 1972. *Forever Flowing.* Trans. Thomas P. Whitney. New York: Harper and Row.

———. 1986. *Life and Fate: A Novel.* Trans. Robert Chandler. New York: Harper and Row.

———. 2005. *A Writer at War: Vasily Grossman with the Red Army, 1941–1945.* Trans. Antony Beevor and Luba Vinogradova. London: Harvill.

Grossman, Vasilii S., and Ilya Ehrenburg. 2002. *The Complete Black Book of Russian Jewry.* Trans. David Patterson. New Brunswick, N.J.: Transaction.

Kaldein, Sergei. 1990. *The Humble Cemetery* and *Gleb Bogdyshev Goes Moonlighting.* London: Collins/Harvill.

Markish, Simon. 1986. *Erasmus and the Jews.* Chicago: University of Chicago Press.

Roziner, Felix. 1991. *A Certain Finkelmeyer.* Trans. Michael Henry Heim. New York: Norton.

Rubina, Dina. 2000. *Here Comes the Messiah!* Trans. Daniel M. Jaffe. Brookline, Mass.: Zephyr.

Rybakov, N. Anatolii. 1956. *The Bronze Bird.* Moscow: n.p.

Sevela, Efraim. 1976. *Truth Is for Strangers: A Novel About a Soviet Poet.* Garden City, N.Y.: Doubleday.

———. 1977. *Farewell, Israel!* Trans. Edmund Browne. South Bend, Ind.: Gateway Editions.

————. 1982a. *Viking.* New York: Black Sea Book Store.

————. 1982b. *Why There Is No Heaven on Earth.* Trans. Richard Lourie. New York: Harper and Row.

————. 1983. *The Standard-Bearer.* South Bend, Ind.: Icarus.

————. 1989. *We Were Not Like Other People.* Trans. Antonia W. Bouis. New York: Harper and Row.

————. 2002. *I Love New York.* St. Petersburg: Kristall.

Svirskii, Grigorii. 1974. *Legends from Invalid Street.* Trans. Anthony Kahn. London: Robson.

————. 1975. *Three Stories from the Arctic Tragedy.* N.p.: n.p.

————. 1976. *Hostages: The Personal Testimony of a Soviet Jew.* New York: Knopf.

Ulitskaya, Liudmila. 2002a. *The Funeral Party.* Trans. Cathy Porter. New York: Schocken.

————. 2002b. *Medea and Her Children.* Trans. Arch Tait. New York: Schocken.

————. 2005. *"Sonechka": A Novella and Stories.* Trans. Arch Trait. New York: Schocken.

Voinovich, Vladimir. 1977a. *The Life and Extraordinary Adventures of Private Ivan Chonkin.* Trans. Richard Lourie. New York: Farrar, Straus and Giroux.

————. 1977b. *The Ivankiad: Or, The Tale of the Writer Voinovich's Installation in His New Apartment.* Trans. David Lapeza. New York: Farrar, Straus and Giroux.

————. 1979. *In Plain Russian: Stories.* Trans. Richard Lourie. New York: Farrar, Straus and Giroux.

————. 1987. *Moscow 2042.* Trans. Richard Lourie. San Diego, Calif.: Harcourt Brace Jovanovich.

————. 1989. *The Fur Hat.* Trans. Susan Brownsberger. San Diego, Calif.: Harcourt Brace Jovanovich.

————. 1995. *Pretender to the Throne: The Further Adventures of Private Ivan Chonkin.* Trans. Richard Lourie. Evanston, Ill.: Northwestern University Press.

Contributors

The Editors

VIVIAN LISKA is professor of German literature and director of the Institute of Jewish Studies at the University of Antwerp, Belgium. She co-edited (with Astradur Eysteinsson) the volume on *Modernism* in the ICLA series *History of the European Literatures*. Her books include: *Die Nacht der Hymnen: Paul Celans Gedichte, 1938–1944* (The Night of the Hymns: Paul Celan's Poems, 1938–1944, 1993); *Die Dichterin und das schelmische Erhabene: Else Lasker-Schülers "Die Nächte Tino von Bagdads"* (The Poetess and the Trickster's Sublime: The Nights of Tino von Bagdad, 1997); and *Die Moderne—Ein Weib': Am Beispiel von Romanen Ricarda Huchs und Annette Kolbs* (Modernism—A Woman, 2000). She has written numerous articles on Nietzsche, Benjamin, Arendt, Adorno, Blanchot, modern German literature, contemporary Jewish literature, and literary theory. She is currently working on a book examining the tension between collective identity and the modernist self in German Jewish literature of the twentieth century.

THOMAS NOLDEN (Ph.D., Yale University) has taught comparative literature at the Freie Universität Berlin, German literature at the University of California, Berkeley, and was visiting professor at M.I.T. He currently directs the comparative literature program at Wellesley College, Mass., where he is professor of German. He has published widely in the field of contemporary Jewish life and literature in Europe and is the author of several books, including *Junge jüdische Literatur: Konzentrisches Schreiben in der Gegenwart* (Young Jewish Literature: Concentric Writing by Contemporary Authors, 1995) and *In Lieu of Memory: Contemporary Jewish Writing in France* (2006). He is also co-editor of *Voices of the Diaspora: Jewish Women Writing in Contemporary Europe* (2005).

The Authors

MONIKA ADAMCZYK-GARBOWSKA is professor of American and Comparative Literature and head of the Center for Jewish Studies at Maria Curie-

Sklodowska University in Lublin, Poland. She is a translator (English and Yiddish) and has been a visiting scholar at the YIVO Institute for Jewish Research, Columbia University, and Brandeis University. Her major publications include books on Isaac Bashevis Singer's Poland and on Jewish literature as a multilingual phenomenon. She has co-edited (with Antony Polonsky) the anthology *Contemporary Jewish Writing in Poland.*

STEPHAN BRAESE is professor of German and Comparative Literature at the Technische Universität Berlin. He has been a fellow at the Franz Rosenzweig Research Center at The Hebrew University, Jerusalem, and at the Center for Advanced Judaic Studies in Philadelphia, Pennsylvania. He is the author of a book on Jewish authors in postwar Germany and one on satire and National Socialism–Fascism. He also has edited several volumes on German literature and the Holocaust.

BRYAN CHEYETTE holds the chair in Modern Literature at the University of Reading. His books include *Constructions of "the Jew" in English Literature and Society: Racial Representations, 1875–1945;* and *Muriel Spark.* He is the editor of *Between "Race" and Culture: Representations of "the Jew" in English and American Literature; Contemporary Jewish Writing in Britain and Ireland: An Anthology;* and (with Laura Marcus) *Modernity, Culture and "the Jew."*

EVA EKSELIUS is a journalist and literary critic at the daily newspaper *Dagens Nyheter* in Stockholm. She holds a doctorate in comparative literature from the University of Stockholm and is the author of many articles and several books.

RAINER GRÜBEL has taught at the University of Utrecht and the University of Leiden, the Netherlands, and is professor of Slavic literature at the University of Oldenburg, Germany. His publications include editions of the works of Michail Bakhtin and books on Russian constructivism, Russian modernism, and Vasilij Rozanovs.

ELRUD IBSCH is professor emerita of Comparative Literature at the Vrije Universiteit, Amsterdam. With Douwe Fokkema she has published *Theories of Literature in the Twentieth Century, Modernist Conjectures,* and *Knowledge and Commitment.* She is the author of *Die Shoah erzählt: Zeugnis und Experiment in der Literatur.*

CHRISTOPH MIETHING is the founder of Romania Judaica (Center for the Study of Jewish Culture in Romance-Language Countries) at the University of Münster, Germany, where he is professor of Romance Literatures. He is the author of several books and the editor of a series on Jewish culture in France and Italy.

VLADIMIR NOVIKOV is professor at Moscow State University and a founding member of the Academy of Contemporary Russian Literature. His publications include books on parody, the Russian Jewish writers V. Kaverin and Y. Tynianov, and a biography of V. Vysotsky.

PÉTER VARGA teaches at the Eötvös Loránd University in Budapest, Hungary, and is the author and editor of several books, including one on the influence of Moses Mendelssohn on the East European Jewish Enlightenment.

Index

www.ingramcontent.com/pod-product-compliance
Ingram Content Group UK Ltd.
Pitfield, Milton Keynes, MK11 3LW, UK
UKHW022150090225
454837UK00003B/108